FROM REVOLUTIONARIES TO CITIZENS

PAUL B. MILLER

FROM REVOLUTIONARIES TO CITIZENS

Antimilitarism in France, 1870–1914

DUKE UNIVERSITY PRESS

Durham and London

2002

© 2002 DUKE UNIVERSITY PRESS
All rights reserved
Printed in the United States of America
on acid-free paper ∞
Typeset in Minion by Keystone Typesetting, Inc.
Library of Congress Cataloging-in-Publication
Data appear on the last printed page
of this book.

For my parents,

Leonard and Phyllis Miller

IF EVERYONE WOULD ONLY
FIGHT FOR HIS OWN CONVICTIONS,
THERE WOULD BE NO WARS.

Prince Andrei to Pierre, in

War and Peace, by Leo Tolstoy

CONTENTS

ACKNOWLEDGMENTS xi

INTRODUCTION:
"The Revolution That's Coming" 1

1. ORIGINS OF WAR:
The Roots of Antimilitarism
in the Third Republic 12

2. ANTIMILITARIST ARMIES:
Structures and Strategies 37

3. ENEMIES AND ALLIES 65

4. ANTIMILITARIST MILITANTS:
The Question of Commitment 92

5. GLORY TO THE 17TH! 116

6. ANTIMILITARIST WARS I:
The Battle Within 145

7. ANTIMILITARIST WARS II:
The Battle Without 173

EPILOGUE: *En Avant!* 201

NOTES 213

BIBLIOGRAPHY 249

INDEX 267

ACKNOWLEDGMENTS

This manuscript lay essentially dormant from spring 1995, when I submitted it as a Ph.D. thesis, to summer 1999, when I finally had the time and, truth be told, income to worry about it. Thus my first words of thanks deserve to go to my new employer and academic life savior, Western Maryland College. While all the faculty, administration, and especially my history colleagues have been tolerant of my frantic efforts to finish this book during my first years of teaching, I especially want to mention President Joan Develin Coley and Professor Ted Evergates, whose initial support helped me to realize my dream of publishing, and Professor Donna Evergates, who never let me feel guilty when the publisher's deadlines conflicted with departmental ones.

At Yale my advisers John Merriman and Paul Kennedy made graduate school a delight in more ways than just intellectual ones. I am overjoyed to now call them friends, foremost, but also colleagues. Other professors whose knowledge and kindness helped usher this book from hell to hardcover include David Bell, Michael Burns, Roger Chickering, Sir Michael Howard, Douglas Porch, Len Smith, Jay Winter, and my Duke readers—Paul Jankowski and the anonymous reviewer. My grad school buddy, Talbot Imlay, has put up with so many questions from me over the years that I feel guilty being able to offer only my thanks to him.

In France Professors Jean-Jacques Becker, Rémy Cazals, Jacques Julliard, and Christophe Prochasson, whom I am sure have long forgotten me by now, were gracious with their ideas and, most important for a novice American researcher, encouragement. L'Institut CGT d'Histoire Sociale was gracious with its photos. Thanks, too, to the numerous archivists and librarians from Kew to Carcassonne who survived my time constraints and accented

French to get me the goods. Teo Ruiz and Rachel Fuchs helped make several of these contacts possible, and memorable.

At Duke, my editor Valerie Millholland's patience with the revisions and her unflagging support for my efforts calmed my anxieties and made me feel fortunate to be publishing with such a professional press. My day-to-day crises were ably handled by Valerie's assistant Miriam Angress. Back in Maryland, Margaret Griffin never flinched when I asked her to photocopy or paginate the manuscript, yet again; nor Wallace Newsome when I asked him to reprint it.

On the financial end, generous research support came from a Georges Lurcy Fellowship, the MacArthur Foundation, and a WMC faculty development grant.

Sources of moral support were even more forthcoming. My undergraduate mentor and close friend Charles Dellheim has suffered it all, and then some, and I thank him for always sticking close by. In Europe, Karin, Jürgen, and Julian Findeisen gave and continue to give me a home away from home that has made my time abroad, and my life in general, much more meaningful. Karin additionally helped me translate some German documents, while Jürgen helped me dig them up. Hilari Allred, John Eglin, Aunt Gloria, David Herrmann, Stéphanie Laithier, Jan Mahoney, James Najarian, Jay Schwartz, and Danno and Ange were more important to me—whether they read the manuscript or not—than they will ever realize. Mom, Dad, Ellie, Bill, and Tyler kept me going in ways that, come to think of it, they probably realize all too well.

INTRODUCTION

"The Revolution That's Coming"

Toward the end of a series of articles on revolutionary syndicalism that appeared in 1906 in the conservative Paris daily *L'Écho de Paris*, journalist Gaston Dru wrote in exasperation:

> I stop myself, for it would take me a book to give the history of antimilitarism since 1902, to study the formation of groups like the Ligue internationale pour la défense du soldat, the Ligue antimilitariste internationale . . . to analyze the issues of *La Voix du Peuple, Le Conscrit* . . . to recapitulate the outcome of this agitation: the incidents in the Brest and Toulon arsenals, where soldiers sang the "Internationale" . . . Poitiers, where artillery men revolted . . . Auxerre, where thirteen soldiers deserted in less than a year. I stop myself, for it is impossible to describe the storm of insanity that, for two years now, has swept away the reason of the country.[1]

The "storm of insanity" that Dru felt demanded a book-length account to comprehend fully is the subject of this work. Yet rather than stopping in 1906 when the storm was near its height, this study will examine French antimilitarism from the establishment of the Third Republic during the Franco-Prussian War of 1870–1871 to the outbreak of World War I in 1914. Further, it will not be limited to syndicalists (trade unionists) but will range from anarchism to socialism in an effort to encompass the different antimilitarist ideologies and strategies that existed in this period.

One objective of this book, then, is to produce a long-overdue narrative of the antimilitarist propaganda and activities of the French Left prior to the First World War. Yet it is bound to be tricky to write such a history when the most devastating and, some have argued recently, "unnecessary" military conflagration the world had ever seen comes at the end of it.[2] The obvious problem is that one tends to be blinded by the outcome—the yielding of the antimilitarists before the forces pressing for war—and thereby lose all sense of the processes that allowed the Left to accept the war. In other words, although scholars have variously sought to explain why antimilitarists "failed" to move a single man to resist war in August 1914, they themselves have failed to look closely at the steps that led the Left to do nothing in the first place.

How was it that the French Left, which succeeded in creating the most antimilitarist culture and society in pre-World War I Europe, came to accept and, in many instances, support war in 1914? By posing the central question thus, this study shifts the emphasis from the weaknesses of the Left to its undeniable strength as a force for popular resistance to unjust militarism, and as a threat, in the eyes of the public powers, to a successful mobilization. This does not mean that I have ignored the dominant explanations for the lack of a coherent leftist response to the war, such as the waning of revolutionary syndicalism from 1909 to 1914 and its inability to formulate a definitive plan for what to do in the case of war. On the contrary, these and other causes for "capitulation," including governmental repression and ideological and strategical disunity, are explored through much new research from local police and Interior Ministry archives.

Yet alongside the general account of the rising and declining fortunes of the Left, this work examines the changing language and meaning of the antimilitarist propaganda. It is concerned, in short, with how the experience of protest shaped the identity of Frenchness. In this regard I refer more generally to French citizenship than to republicanism, although after the Dreyfus Affair republicanism is increasingly part of it. As Philip Nord has shown, various aspects of republican culture, including national holidays, public monuments, newspapers, and membership in assorted leagues, gave strength to democratic public life in the nineteenth century and gave shape to "a particular kind of citizen: a conscientious human being who revered the *philosophes* and the revolutionaries of 1789, who valued liberty, laicity, and the riches afforded by literacy and a vital associational life." There is no need for Nord to study anarchists, trade unionists, or even socialists because their modus operandi, in theory, was to reject this "bourgeois" national model of civil society in favor of an international, socialist one. But as he shows so well, the staying power of the Third Republic was in large measure a result of its ability to attract citizens into its fold.[3]

The literature on citizenship in the broader sense has been growing rapidly in France, the world's second-leading immigrant nation. Although Charlotte Wells has argued that many legal categories and even emotional ties associated with French citizenship predate 1789, the Revolution still stands out as the shining moment when the idea of "citizen" was linked to the advent of democracy. More specifically, civic equality, coupled with political rights and empowerment for the Third Estate, created a national identity that was, and still is, based on political and ideological factors rather than ethnic and "racial" ones.[4]

Yet these new rights entailed new responsibilities in the shared national community, and the greatest of them in the revolutionary era was defending the *patrie* from her enemies. Thus with *liberté, égalité, fraternité* was also born—at Valmy in 1792—the *nation armée* (nation in arms), transforming war from an affair of the privileged into an obligation of the citizen-patriot. When in 1889 landmark legislation was passed extending French citizenship to second-generation immigrants, supporters hearkened back to this notion that those born and living in France should not be exempt from her principal national duty—military service.[5] Two decades later, the socialist leader Jean Jaurès would propose the creation of a national militia of "all valid citizens" as the best, indeed only, means to defend the *patrie* from foreign aggression.[6] Jaurès and fellow antimilitarists of varying colors exercised their legal rights as citizens in a republic to protest what they understandably perceived as grave injustices committed against the working classes on the part of the government and "its" military. By looking at how they expressed themselves, we can begin to make sense of the process by which these antimilitarist citizens came to identify their cause with that of the often vilified *patrie;* a process that was consummated, not commenced, when war broke out in 1914.

◆ ◆ ◆

Since I began to specialize in nineteenth-century European history as a graduate student, one of the questions that has most intrigued me pertains to how such an ideologically variegated period ended in a war that met with near universal acceptance, if not outright enthusiasm, from virtually all social and political strata. At no other time in history has the organization of nationalist and militarist groups stood in such contrast to the size and sway of international socialism and pacifism, and never as in the decades before 1914 has there been at once so much anticipation about war and agitation against it. Books such as Bertha von Suttner's *Die Waffen Nieder!* (*Lay Down Your Arms*, 1889), Ivan (Jean de) Bloch's *La Guerre future* (*The Future of War*, 1898), and Norman Angell's *The Great Illusion* (1910), to name just the most well known, warned in strident tones against the senseless destructiveness, economic irrationality, and even unfeasibility of modern war. By contrast, social imperialists such as Benjamin Kidd and the hardened militarist General Friedrich von Bernhardi used twisted Darwinistic language to argue that war and international rivalries were natural processes that ensured the necessary hegemony of stronger societies, or "races." "War," Bernhardi wrote in *Deutschland und der nächste Krieg* (*Germany and the Next War*, 1911), is "not merely a necessary element in the lives of nations, but an indispensable factor of culture, in which a true civilized nation finds the highest expression of truth and vitality."[7] In France, the popular novelist Maurice Barrès preached "blood and soil" nationalism, while the poet/political writer Charles Péguy and his young Parisian followers turned to philosophical ideals of spiritual renewal and moral regeneration to locate in war the ultimate liberation from bourgeois decadence.

These are, of course, the extreme examples, but the important point is that war was much touted and even more talked about by European leaders and intellectuals in this period. This was due in part to the fact that by the turn of the century Europe had passed through the unusually long span of thirty years since its last major military conflict, while in the interim a tradition of left-wing antimilitarism and middle-class pacifism had taken hold of a significant portion of society. In the case of the Left, antimilitarism fit directly into its campaign against bourgeois capitalism. War violated the very ideals of socialist internationalism and working-class solidarity, and with the use of troops to suppress strikes antiarmy attitudes became a defining element of socialist, syndicalist, and anarchist ideology. Likewise, the middle-class peace societies formed in the wake of the Napoleonic wars continued to expand through 1914. In relative isolation from the labor movement, these groups sought to prevent war through arbitration and governmental pressure for disarmament, establishing an international network and Europe's first interparliamentary union.

The upshot of all of this is that European leaders simply did not expect the near universal popular acceptance of war in August 1914. It may only have been an urban minority that welcomed the war enthusiastically, but the most striking fact was that the opposition was infinitely smaller. The German Social Democratic Party far outnumbered Heinrich Class's Pan-German League, but that did not stop the largest party in the Reichstag—which had won 34.8 percent of the vote in 1912 campaigning against "dear bread for militarism"—from approving the credits so crucial for financing the military campaign.[8] Similarly, the powerful French Socialist Party, which under the leadership of Jean Jaurès had made the struggle against militarism one of its most constant themes, triumphed in the April 1914 election and was on the verge of repealing the new three-year military service law when the war intervened. In the end, the party supported the Republic in the name of national defense. The socialist leaders Jules Guesde and Marcel Sembat even joined the "bourgeois" government on August 26, 1914.[9]

The case of France in this period is unquestionably the most important in Europe because of the nation's combination of republican government, military tradition, and revolutionary political culture. While the German, Russian, and Austro-Hungarian empires simply outlawed or exiled the kind of antimilitarist propaganda and groups I examine here, Britain's longer experience with democracy and placating its discontented classes ensured the Left a more moderate voice. Moreover, the Liberal Party, which traditionally begrudged excessive military spending, won three successive elections beginning in 1906. And because Britain did not have conscription, the army never became the focus of animosity that it did in France, where revolts against requisitioning in the countryside were as old as the Old Regime. Antimilitarism had strong support in Italy, but the country possessed neither the geopolitical importance nor military might to make it a suitable barometer of the prewar *mentalité*. Italian leftists, like those in the rest of Europe and to some extent in the United States, took their cues on antimilitarism from its epicenter in the land of the belle époque.

We cannot underrate France's importance in gauging European antimilitarism generally, yet neither can we understate the complexity of her leftist political culture with its anarchist, syndicalist, and socialist elements. While moderate socialists relied on international forums, army reforms, and governmental influence to diminish the chance of war, a sizable faction within the party led by Gustave Hervé openly preached antipatriotism and exhorted workers to revolt at the onset of mobilization. In the syndicalist movement, where Hervé had many supporters and which had come under the sway of anarchists, antimilitarism, to the dismay of government officials, often overshadowed its economic mandate. Finally, several antimilitarist groups, which usually were constituted on anarchist initiative and strived for national and international followings, came and went in the conflict-ridden first decade of the twentieth century.

In an effort to gauge the reaction of the public powers to the antimilitarist activity in France, historian Jean-Jacques Becker has studied the infamous Carnet B, the government's list of leftist revolutionaries it planned to arrest at the first declaration of mobilization. That in August 1914 authorities decided not to act on the Carnet B is puzzling, particularly since Becker's study conclusively establishes that the government believed antimilitarism to pose a real national danger. The Carnet B, Becker argues persuasively, was a serious means of state control, not a "fanciful document." Moreover, antimilitarism was not "a marginal current animated by a few dreamers and low lifes," but lay "at the heart of the political thought of the workers' movement." So why did authorities not arrest the marked men when war broke out? Here is where, for our purposes, Becker's study falls short. Conceding that his work was not meant as a comprehensive examination of prewar antimilitarism, because such an undertaking would have required him to consult "infinitely more important sources than those we have used here," Becker suggests only that the strength of antimilitarism was proportional to that of the Confédération Générale du Travail (CGT), the umbrella organization of French syndicalism. When the CGT, and in particular its revolutionary wing, began to weaken from governmental repression and lack of support, so too did antimilitarism.[10]

This is straightforward reasoning, yet it evidently did not satisfy Becker because at the end of his book he suggests another, perhaps equally important, factor: the circumstances surrounding the war itself. Becker thus devoted his next and most important work to a vast study of French public opinion on the eve of World War I. In *1914: Comment les Français sont entrés dans la guerre* (*1914: How the French Went into the War,* 1977), he gives more evidence for the decline of syndicalist antimilitarism and the lack of coherence among socialists with regard to what to do in the case of war. By the time war came, Becker argues, it had become evident to working-class leaders that their propaganda had not permeated the population sufficiently, and their hopes of coordinating an antiwar strategy such as a general strike with Germany would not be realized. Moreover, the war had descended on Europe more quickly than anyone had anticipated, and although there was not the sudden, romanticized conversion to overt patriotism in the face of the German attack, there did develop a strong, almost universal, sense of resignation and resolution in the face of the reality: "Equipped with an inapplicable strategy [the CGT's general strike] and another [strategy] that circumstances had rendered ineffective [socialist pressure on governments], working-class militants were reduced to powerlessness."[11]

Other historians who have examined why the largest and loudest antimilitarist "movement" in Europe suddenly became subdued and silent in August 1914 have similarly stressed the internal problems of the Left, the CGT in particular. In 1918 the syndicalist leader Georges Dumoulin argued that he and his colleagues supported the war for fear of governmental repression: "Fear is neither syndicalist, nor socialist, nor any 'ist.' It is human. At the CGT we were afraid of the war, we were afraid of repression, simply because we are men."[12] A decade later, Roger Picard asserted that the CGT's sense of isolation as the sole antimilitarist power in Europe drove it to accept the international situation.[13] Virtually all studies of the French Left that have appeared since highlight what Georges Lefranc in 1967 called the "crisis of revolutionary syndicalism,"[14] as well as the gradual decline in power and influence of the trade unions generally and the lack of a uniform, working-class strategy for how to react to war.[15] After studying the CGT's attitude toward war from 1900 to 1914, historian Jacques Julliard concluded that what happened in August 1914 was no surprise. Rather than a betrayal of its ideals, the CGT's acceptance of war confirmed many of its leaders' suspicions about the real chances for collective action.[16]

This idea of "failure," a term Julliard did not hesitate to use, has persisted in more recent works as well. In *Revolutionary Syndicalism and French Labor* (1971), Peter Stearns went so far as to call revolutionary syndicalism "a cause without rebels."[17] In his broad-based study *Objecteurs, insoumis, déserteurs* (*Objectors, Insubordinates, Deserters*, 1983), Michel Auvray concluded that the acceptance of war by the Left, what he overstates as "this sudden warlike feverishness," attests to "the bankruptcy of International socialism and the failure of the workers' movement."[18] Writing on the international labor movement, Susan Milner has argued that a large gap existed between theory and practice with regard to the CGT's antimilitarist strategy. In the end, she could give no more weight to the antiwar rhetoric than just that: more talk than action.[19]

Although these works might help us understand why the Left did not respond to the war, they barely scratch the surface when it comes to interpreting the Left's overwhelming acceptance of it. The main reason for this is that they do justice neither to the extent to which antimilitarism permeated working-class political culture nor to how its presence there was felt. When Becker wrote that "the circumstances of the outbreak of World War I were such that all prior opposition movements dispersed themselves like wisps of smoke," he also added, "there is no smoke without fire."[20] The fire of antimilitarism is this book's main theme. Its major premise is that only by examining the motives and meanings of the Left with regard to antimilitarism can we truly understand how the Left could accept a war it had spent over a decade trying to prevent.

This study is thus rooted in the notion that antimilitarism was a vital aspect of leftist social and political culture from the turn of the century to the outbreak of World War I. As we have just seen, however, most works—with the exceptions of Becker's books and Milorad Drachkovitch's comparative study of French and German socialists' attitudes toward war—relegate it to a bit part in their overall story.[21] And although the topic does slide easily under the more general categories of socialism, syndicalism, and anarchism, in the early 1900s *l'antimilitarisme* freely traversed and, frequently, sought to transcend them. The endless police reports, journal articles, monographs, trial records, and propaganda that constitute the sources for this book bear this out well.

Antimilitarism will refer here to that which it approximately meant to French security forces a century ago: the ideology and activities of socialists, syndicalists, and anarchists aimed at reducing the civil power of the military and, ultimately, preventing international war. This is necessarily a broad definition encompassing the programs of very different groups that fall into the French Left. In order to distinguish their varying perspectives, one may subdivide "antimilitarism" to include the following types of discourse: anticapitalism, antiarmy, antiwar, and antipatriotism. As we shall see, these codes for antimilitarism actually represented different conceptualizations of morality by the various groups under examination. Yet the definitional typologies are not meant to correspond to any specific group at any specific time; they merely indicate the nuanced and often overlapping formulations of antimilitarist propaganda in this period. Although this may not seem obvious in light of the glaring ideological and strategical differences between a parliamentary socialist such as Jaurès and a revolutionary, antipatriotic syndicalist such as Georges Yvetot, at bottom these men came out of a similar working-class tradition and had the same general objective. As the anarchist Miguel Almereyda explained it: "As antimilitarists we have different political ideas, but we always come together on antimilitarist terrain. Some are bourgeois antimilitarists, others are Christian antimilitarists. There are also libertarian, anarchist, communist, and syndicalist antimilitarists.

But we can all work together to fight for a common goal: the suppression of war."[22]

Although Almereyda's formulation serves this study well, it did not, in practice, include all the groups in Europe that were working to abolish war. Thus another means by which we must define antimilitarism is to contrast it with that other, often neglected nineteenth-century movement: pacifism. Just as one can delineate antimilitarism by its association with the Left, the term *pacifisme* specified the middle-class peace societies that clamored for disarmament and arbitration within the existing, bourgeois capitalist society. This may seem confusing because the antimilitarism of Jaurès's moderate socialist faction has been labeled "pacifist" by no less an expert than Becker. To be sure, many informal ties and much ideological overlap existed between socialist and pacifist leaders such as Jaurès and Frédéric Passy, the founder of the Ligue Internationale et Permanente de la Paix. As Roger Chickering has shown, Jaurès's well-known humanism, his conceptualization of international politics, and his acceptance of the reality of the nation brought him closer to the bourgeois pacifists than to the militant Hervéists in his own party. Moreover, Jaurès's advocacy of arbitration and disarmament came to dominate the party after it unified in 1905, and many socialists belonged to peace societies such as the Ligue Internationale and the Association de la Paix par le Droit. Jaurès's paper *L'Humanité* even had a membership with the International Peace Bureau. In contrast to Germany, Chickering concludes, French pacifists were generally more successful in cooperating with the labor movement.[23]

Yet if the two sides could at times bridge their differences, the terminological distinction holds. Between pacifists and antimilitarists the norm was considerable, even rancorous, debate, and Passy himself felt that class divisions were irrelevant to peace activism. The pacifists' main adversaries were revolutionary syndicalists and socialists, especially the antipatriotic forces of Gustave Hervé, whose calls for military sabotage undermined national defense. "Pacifists are not antimilitarists," declared French peace movement leaders Passy, Charles Richet, Émile Arnaud, Gaston Moch, and Théodore Ruyssen. And the German pacifist Alfred Fried warned: "Antimilitarism is not only dangerous for governments and states but also for pacifism. Antimilitarists do not merely pursue the same aim as us by different means . . . they only reject the symptoms; we attack the causes of militarism."[24]

Predictably, leftist revolutionaries did not always hold their rivals in great esteem either. The difference between antimilitarists and Passy's Ligue de la Paix, *L'Action* contended, was that "the Ligue de la Paix addresses itself to the government and calls for 'general disarmament.' In complete contrast, we address ourselves to the governed and urge them to join our plea for the 'suppression of the entire armed forces.' "[25] The socialist journal *Le Conscrit* asserted more haughtily: "The peace societies parade their pacifist airs in vain; their little sentimental flutes will never overpower the sound of the tempest, and the crashes of the class struggles."[26] The pamphlet *Pacifisme et antimilitarisme* accused the former of being no more than "a purely hypocritical, inconsequential movement, not going to the source of evil that it is necessary to destroy, and thus powerless and, let's be frank, ridiculous and inept." The "source of the evil," of course, was the prevailing social order, which in turn was bolstered by the army. Antimilitarism, because it aimed to upset this order by striking the army first, was also, according to this argument, the only antiwar ideology that could possibly succeed.[27]

◆ ◆ ◆

My study of antimilitarism in France begins and ends with war. Yet although the Franco-Prussian War and the First World War were more than four decades apart, the first chapter of this work will advance quickly from the shaky establishment of the Third Republic in 1870–1871 to the height of the Dreyfus Affair at the end of the century. It was in the 1890s that police and government officials undertook their diligent campaign of monitoring antimilitarist meetings, clipping journal articles, making arrests for provoking servicemen to disobedience and indiscipline, collecting the innumerable *affiches* (posters), flyers, and brochures that circulated in French cities large and small, and filing lengthy reports on *l'antimilitarisme*. Chapter 1 will examine the factors behind this revitalization of antimilitarism after the defeat at Sedan.

Chapter 2 begins my study of antimilitarist organization, propaganda, and what it all meant to the various groups of the French Left. It introduces the main factions, their journals, and the ideologies and strategies of their leaders. The chapter also shows how the anticapitalist/bourgeois rhetoric of the Left set it apart from, although not completely outside of, the *patrie*, encouraging socialists, syndicalists, and anarchists alike to see themselves as the true representatives of the nation, a nation of workers.

The third chapter shifts the focus to the official repression of the revolutionary Left. It attempts to understand how government and military authorities perceived the antimilitarists and, in turn, how they viewed themselves, especially in relation to the analogous activities of their German counterparts. Chapter 4 questions the extent to which the antimilitarist typologies defined above can actually be used to predict behavior. In other words, how successful were antimilitarists in shaping the attitudes and actions of French workers? This question is applied to the military in chapter 5, which seeks to understand the role played by antimilitarist propaganda in the breakdown in discipline and the lowering of army prestige after the Dreyfus Affair. The sixth chapter examines the factors that allowed (or did not allow) the diverse groups of the Left to formulate and execute unified responses to specific abuses of military and governmental power. Finally, chapter 7 takes up the question of change and constancy in antimilitarism in light of the renewed militancy of the government, the "nationalist revival," and the growing sense of the imminence of war. In all of these chapters I have strived less to reaffirm the sources of weakness in the antimilitarist Left than to emphasize its important place in French social and political culture; a place that, I argue, had more in common with the defense of French interests than with any revolutionary aspiration to topple them.

1. ORIGINS OF WAR

The Roots of Antimilitarism in the Third Republic

From the beginning of the French Third Republic in September 1870, antimilitarists were an embattled group. The complete capitulation of the imperial armies in the Franco-Prussian War, the "rape" of Alsace-Lorraine, and the near destruction of the revolutionary working classes in the suppression of the Commune were events hardly conducive to a popular upsurge of antimilitarist activity. If France harbored any victors in 1870–71, they were nationalists who, regardless of political affiliation, were dedicated to rebuilding the army's strength and prestige and to restoring the eclipsed grandeur of France. For those who had worked to undermine military power during the Second Empire, the events surrounding the establishment of the Republic were, ironically, a resounding defeat.[1]

History, moreover, conspired to ensure antimilitarists a long struggle to regain ascendancy. The Napoleonic era at the beginning of the century had created an indelible link between the greatness of France and the glory of her army, and many still cherished the heroic stories passed down by relatives. In *The Debacle*, Émile Zola's novel of the Franco-Prussian War, the soldier Maurice Levasseur grows up on the "Homeric narratives of battle" his grandfather endlessly retold to hallow his years in the *grande armée*. The quickness and completeness of the defeat two generations later was incompatible with this historical image of France; an image built largely around her army.[2]

Yet in contrast with the downfall of Napoleon III and the foundation of the Third Republic, Waterloo had been a propitious event for aspiring antimilitarists. European civilians had had enough of two decades of warfare; the spread of liberal doctrines from the French Revolution created a favorable climate for prevailing antiwar sentiments; and France, after a quarter century of revolution and war, remained highly unstable both politically and militarily.[3] From Burgundy to Brittany and Picardy to Provence, war had invaded virtually every French home. Approximately one-fourth of eligible males were mobilized, and like the "Conscript from Languedoc" in the popular 1810 song, many went reluctantly, not expecting to return alive to their towns and villages.[4] Historians estimate that almost a million men—a quarter of those born in the appropriate age cohort—never did.[5] If there ever were a time in European history that popular opinion was on the side of peace, this was it. "It is indeed from the end of the Napoleonic Wars," writes military historian Michael Howard, "that one can date the beginning of what was to become known as the 'Peace Movement.'"[6]

By the term "peace movement" Howard is, of course, referring to the liberal, middle-class variety defined earlier. In the first half of the nineteenth century, before Marx's crystallization of socialist theory and the mass unionization of workers, organized objections to war derived primarily from issues such as free trade and Christian morality. Consequently, most antiwar exponents came from the commercial middle classes and religious groups such as the Society of Friends, or Quakers. One year after Waterloo, the first peace society—the Society for the Promotion of Permanent and Universal Peace—was founded in London.[7] In 1821, reform-minded aristocrats and bourgeoisie, many of whom were Protestant, created the Société de la Morale Chrétienne in Paris. Although not exclusively a peace organization, it aimed "to diminish the causes of intestine discords and foreign wars by opposing party hatred and the prejudices of an extravagant and blind patriotism." By 1844, the Saint-Simonienne Eugénie Niboyet had launched *La Paix des Deux Mondes*, the first newspaper on the continent expressly devoted to peace issues.[8]

In August 1849 European pacifism reached a high point when the Third International Peace Congress met in Paris. Sandwiched between the 1848 revolutions and the counterrevolutionary current that was sweeping toward France from central Europe, the congress profited from the volatile political climate to bring together Alexis de Tocqueville, Victor Hugo, the archbishop of Paris, and the grand rabbi of France. This distinguished group, along with respected business and political leaders, made the congress a huge success, "a rich source of peace movement lore and legend in future decades." By midcentury, European pacifism was confident, growing, and well-supported.[9]

Although much work remains to be done on the pacifist movement, what is important here is how the development of antimilitarism was influenced by this early pacifist current and abetted by the same political and social factors, and yet took a very different attitude and, ultimately, direction. When French authorities permitted pacifists to meet in 1849, one of the conditions was that they avoid talking about current political issues. Yet as the delegates quickly learned, this was nearly impossible in light of their purpose. How does one discuss peace without making reference to contemporary topics, such as the decline of the Ottoman Empire, that could (and did) lead to war?

Throughout the nineteenth century, pacifists organized congresses, published journals such as Charles Lemonnier's *Les États-Unis d'Europe*, rallied to limit weapons spending, denounced military atrocities in such places as China and South Africa, and, basically, flourished. By 1914 there were 190 peace societies in Europe publishing twenty-three journals in ten different languages.[10] In France in 1909, even the traditionally nationalist Catholics had a Ligue des Catholiques pour la Paix, with several hundred members and international ties.[11] Yet the conservative approach to contemporary issues imposed on pacifists in 1849 still guided their outlook. Pacifists were, for all intents and purposes, mainstream. Right up until August 1914 they remained intensely optimistic that one day European leaders would realize the futility of war and heed the call of *Lay Down Your Arms!*, the best-selling pacifist novel of the period.[12]

As pacifists attracted notice with their theoretical and philosophical ideas about the value of peace and the senselessness of war, antimilitarists did so by attacking the source of conflict itself. From the fall of Napoleon I to Napoleon III, a liberal and later socialist current of antimilitarism sought to discredit military careers and devalue the army's role in French social and political culture. De Tocqueville was outspoken in his disgust with "military tyranny," and Benjamin Constant accused the army of demeaning a noble and just people to something barely distinguishable from barbarians. The nation, he predicted, "will set itself backwards in the midst of [military] victories."[13]

Napoleon's victories did not come cheaply, and the reality of defeat pointed out many of the failures of organizing social and political life around a strong army. Before long, the same conditions that gave rise to a peace movement had fostered an antimilitarist current. The two antiwar efforts remained closely related until the later decades of the century and the surge of leftist antimilitarism that constitutes the main subject of this book. But in the mid-nineteenth century, a definite shift took place when, as one scholar put it, "behind war, one began to see the army."[14]

The establishment of the Second Empire by means of military force and election fraud was not immediately auspicious for antimilitarists, but the resentment it bred boosted their cause considerably. When Louis-Napoleon Bonaparte's coup of December 2, 1851, turned the Second Republic into an authoritarian regime in all but name, his enemies on the Left, both in Paris and the provinces, did not submit easily—almost seventy thousand took up arms.[15] The government handily defeated the rebels, but the brutal suppression and often exile of the *démoc-socs* ("democratic-socialists") encouraged the kind of dissent that manifests itself in more insidious ways: by the 1860s antimilitarism was gaining ground.

The change perhaps signaled itself foremost with the reappearance of debates over national militias versus professional armies, debates that had been fixtures of the Restoration and Second Republic with regard to the national guard. Now the "problem of permanent armies" was discussed at the First International congress of 1866 and again in 1868. In 1869, the republican politician Léon Gambetta advanced the Belleville program to eliminate professional armies as a "cause of ruin for the nation's finances and business [and a] source of hatred between peoples and of distrust at home."[16] By the outbreak of the war with Prussia, antimilitarists had achieved a certain presence and power in French political life.

That war and the events that followed, however, soon turned these antimilitarist insiders into outsiders and even exiles of their own political culture. When Paris refused the harsh terms of surrender agreed to by Adolphe Thiers's "Goverment of National Defense," a coalition of revolutionary socialists and trade unionists led the resistance that in March 1871 became the famous Paris Commune. Nearly half of the Commune's leaders had previously been involved in a labor organization; nearly all looked to the revolutionary wars of the 1790s for inspiration.[17] Indeed little had changed since then in terms of the Left's intense patriotism. And although it is true that many saw the Commune as an opportunity to bring about important, even revolutionary, reform, the point is that its origins lay in resistance to the dishonorable peace made by the newly elected government.[18] Now socialist as well as republican, it was still the Left that took up arms to defend the *patrie,* while the Right appeased her enemies. In the difficult years that followed the bloody suppression of the Commune and the disorganization of the workers' movement, the task of reviving national prestige went hand-in-hand with the need for a strong military. Cries for *revanche*—revenge—were to drown out those of *à bas la guerre*—down with war![19]

Driven into hiding by the events surrounding the Franco-Prussian War, what were the ideological roots and political, social, and economic causes of the reemergence of antimilitarism by the century's end? The Republic played its part through liberalization and amnesty in the 1880s, enabling workers' organizations to begin reconstituting themselves. When in 1886 a patriotic wave swept the nation in favor of a coup d'état by the popular war minister General Boulanger, the army's singular threat to the Republic became apparent to all parties and political groups, as France narrowly escaped military rule. But what returned antimilitarist ideas to the fore were changes to the military itself. With a Right-Left consensus that rebuilding the army was crucial to the national recovery, the National Assembly wasted little time in passing a military service law (1872) that mandated universal male conscription for five years. Republican in principle, the law was not entirely free of loopholes through which wealthy young men planning careers in the liberal professions could leave after a year's service.[20] But this unfairness, which was smoothed out over the years and eliminated altogether with the three-year law of 1889, does not overshadow the impact of 1872: for the first time since the heady days of the Revolution, military service was shared by all classes—"the army took its place in the familiar panorama of French life."[21]

For antimilitarists the law's effect was neither immediate nor absolute, for the Dreyfus Affair would show just how difficult it was to tarnish the army in the midst of its crucial recovery. Yet there can be no doubt that the honor ascribed to military life that surged after the war received its first challenge in the late 1880s, just as General Boulanger's star began to fade. Universal conscription had opened doors to a new and intriguing world for thousands of educated and cultivated young Frenchmen. What many of them found behind these doors, however, quickly turned their naïve idealism and unbiased admiration for the military into fear, loathing, and even disrespect. It was the stuff of novels, and it is not surprising that the first "phase" of the antimilitarist renaissance was a literary one.

Literary Antimilitarism

The publication of Abel Hermant's *Le Cavalier Miserey* in 1887 marked the onset of a stream of scathing eyewitness accounts of military life. Hermant, a young, urbane sophisticate frustrated with the teaching profession and disillusioned by his year in the 21st Regiment of *chasseurs* (riflemen), set out "to apply an artist's vision and the methods of a *roman d'analyse* [psychological novel] to the study of the nature of the soldier."[22] The outcome is a detailed and rather disturbing description of the gradual moral and social degradation of the title character Miserey, a young conscript. Well-intentioned if not optimistic as a recruit, Miserey experiences a series of setbacks and humiliations that, while hastening his decline, constitute a devastating critique of military life. The novel's message is clear and the writing powerful: the tragedy of Miserey could be that of any soldier, as the real tragedy lies within military culture itself.

The theme of Hermant's novel—the immorality of military life and its pernicious effect on the soldier—is typical of the antimilitarist literature of the late nineteenth century. In Henri Fèvre's *Au Port d'armes* (*To Bear Arms*, 1887), the hero, also a young conscript but this time unable to contain his frustration, shoots at his commanding officer! His military career ends as a murderer executed by firing squad. Two years later, Lucien Descaves describes in his novel *Sous-offs* (*Noncommissioned Officers*, 1889) how personal, moral abasement can lead to success in the army. As the soldier Favières accrues ranks he also acquires "all the cunning of intimidation, of responsibilities eluded and shifted, and the cynicism that constitutes fraud. . . . One might say he traces the order of his promotions to the degrees of infamy to which he has descended."[23]

In *Un An de caserne* (*A Year in the Barracks*, 1901), one of the later but most representative works of the genre, Louis Lamarque recounts his experience as a sensitive and cultivated Parisian who is forced to spend a precious year living among men he openly paints as boorish and inferior. "This military service is rather distressing," he writes, "because the men one finds here are naturally bad and, what's more, they are idiotic." Ironically, the author's sole consolation is that the year gives him a heightened appreciation for life itself, particularly the charmed one of theaters and "floodlit cafés" that he led in Paris. But these thoughts are hardly compensation for this privileged youth, whose story reads like an extended lament on the ignorance of his fellow soldiers, the prison-like setting of the barracks, the disgusting and pointless work, and his growing isolation from home. "It is absurd," Lamarque haughtily submits, "to try to sustain a horse in the middle of wolves."[24]

Fortunately for this rich, pitiable bourgeois, there is an escape. Lamarque is able to buy leisure by paying another soldier to clean his boots and weapons, care for his horses, and keep his things tidy. Then for four hours every evening he retreats to a rented room in the city to "read, write, rest, be alone, finally to collect myself, to rediscover myself and to continue to live my inner life a little."[25] This is, quite obviously, not the lifestyle of the average conscript. Of all the *romans militaires* that I know of, in fact, *Un An de caserne* relies on the most pronounced element of *snobisme* to deliver its critique. Yet the author's origins and biases should not wholly overshadow the significance of the work. Lamarque, as with all the writers examined above, did not write for the masses. His privileged readers got a firsthand look at their own sensibilities through someone who was independent and insightful enough to understand them. This may not have stirred a revolt inside the barracks, but it did cause many young men to think twice about their future in the army.

What, then, was the impact of these military novels with antimilitary themes? Girardet alleges that they touched on the real failures of an outdated and uncensored military hierarchy: "The customs of the army had hardly changed since the Second Empire, the discipline there remained very crude, material life particularly hard, moral concerns practically non-existent."[26] Certainly abuses were rampant, living conditions substandard, prostitution ubiquitous, and the food horrendous, as the writers emphasized ad infinitum. What made their complaints distinctive was the sincerity and believability of the literature itself. The authors all had direct experience in the military as well as the education and sophistication to write about it. Moreover, they often did so in the naturalist, real-life style that was gaining popularity in France, particularly through the works of Émile Zola. When in 1890 Georges Darien's acclaimed *Biribi* took readers to the North African military prisons, he knew firsthand the atrocities described there.[27]

The tell-all *romans militaires* touched a raw nerve in French society. On the publication of *Le Cavalier Miserey*, the commanding officer of the 21st Regiment of *chasseurs* ordered that any copies found inside the caserne be burned on a pile of dung in the main courtyard.[28] Descaves's *Sous-offs* unleashed a storm of controversy when, by sheer coincidence, it appeared just after General Boulanger backed down on his popular bid for power. Already living in Belgian exile, the hapless general could still count on French supporters to combat Descaves's assault on the army.[29] On December 24, 1889, *Le Figaro* published the protest of fifty-one writers, "unified when art is concerned," including Émile Zola, Maurice Barrès, Edmond de Goncourt, and, most strikingly, Abel Hermant. A month later the government tried Descaves and his editors for insults to the army and affronts to public decency. It was only the start, as we shall see, of many court appearances for antimilitarists.[30]

Was Descaves a revolutionary seeking to undermine the military with his biting critique of barrack life? That this probably could not be further from the truth indicates something about the state of antimilitarism as it first emerged in the literary milieu: in the late nineteenth century, it was not an easy business to criticize the army. The *arche sainte,* as Girardet designated it, was above reproach, for the future glory of the nation depended on it.[31] That's why the writer Anatole France, who was still a staunch nationalist in the 1880s, could comment on *Le Cavalier Miserey:* "It is necessary that the writer can say everything, but he should never be permitted to say everything, in any case, in all circumstances, and to all sorts of people. . . . He is free to clarify and embellish life; but not to trouble and compromise it. He is held to touch sacred things with respect. And if there is anything that is sacred in human society, agreed upon by all, it is the army."[32] These writers, in other words, had crossed a dangerous Rubicon by revealing the army's imperfections. Certainly it had its share of deficiencies. No doubt the institution harbored some awful characters. But why harp on the matter-of-fact when the pride, joy, and hope of the nation was at stake? No, the antimilitarist writers were not revolutionaries. Rather, I would agree with Madeleine Meyer-Spiègler's assessment that "the world they describe, a mixture of sordid incidents, of dismal debaucheries, of frustrated ambitions, of sad daily tyrannies, earns them, like their more celebrated contemporaries, the reproach of wallowing in the mire, the morbid."[33] As for Descaves, who was acquitted in March 1890, it also earned him a good deal of attention: *Sous-offs* sold thirty thousand copies in its first year and was reprinted numerous times thereafter.[34]

Not everyone recognized these basic realities of the antimilitarist literature. Journalists at the socialist daily *Le Petit Sou* praised Lamarque's *Un An de caserne* as "the best of all the propaganda books."[35] The writer Octave Mirbeau waxed equally enthusiastic in the preface, calling it "more than a book, a social act."[36] There was nothing social nor propagandistic about *Un An de caserne* or, for that matter, most of the *romans militaires.* They were, plain and simple, books written by a disgruntled bourgeoisie for a like-minded elite, in which the military experience pointed up the persistence of irreconcilable class differences, not the existence of a common enemy. As we shall see, revolutionary, working-class antimilitarism, while often voicing similar complaints, took its cues from different sorts of frustrations.

Nonetheless, this literary onslaught was not without its impact, and there can be little doubt that the heedless patriotism and military spirit of the generation following the Franco-Prussian War slipped a degree as a result of it.[37] For in the unanimous and keen judgment of these writers, the reality of day-to-day military life was distinctly incongruent with the glamorized version of a "nation in arms." Hermant's character Miserey discovers this when he stumbles across a war monument near the barracks. Reading the names of the battles inscribed in the standard, it suddenly hits him "for the first time . . . that there were really battles, charges, men who were killed. No one had yet spoken to him of these things since his arrival to the regiment. He wondered if they weren't just tales. Charge? . . . The 21st!"[38] Of major importance in this respect was Zola's *The Debacle* (1892), which broke a national taboo by directly faulting and at times even taunting the army for the bungled Franco-Prussian War. The book's tremendous success, one commentator has suggested, attests to the "painful self-examination still going on in France after the most traumatic humiliation any country had so far received in modern times."[39]

Zola's novel was published twenty years after that defeat, but all twenty were needed before Frenchmen could confront it with a degree of objectivity and understanding. In the interval, a generation had grown up for which the war was not in living memory and Alsace-Lorraine not in France.[40] The more time that passed, it seemed, the easier it became to accept the defeat as fact and the new border as reality. In the decades following the war, *revanchisme* had been the mainstay of the army's impenetrable veneration. By the mid-1890s, many historians now agree, the average Frenchman had more weighty concerns than going to war for these "lost provinces."[41] One of the most irreverent yet also revealing expressions of the decline in *revanchisme* was the satirical one of Rémy de Gourmont. "Personally," he wrote in the April 1891 edition of *Le Mercure de France*, "in exchange for these forgotten lands I would give neither the little finger of my right hand: it serves to support my hand when I write; nor the little finger of my left hand: it serves to shake the ashes off my cigarette."[42]

Intellectuals and bourgeois youth were in the vanguard of ambivalence when it came to the question of *revanche,* and were among the first to voice a sentiment that would have been unthinkable a decade earlier. This is, of course, not to say that it was their doing that undid the Alsace-Lorraine myth. As mentioned above, popular opinion, especially in the provinces themselves, no longer tolerated aggressive war for the return of the provinces to France. Moreover, this change in *mentalité* can only be understood in its proper context. Toward the end of the nineteenth century the rise of socialism, coupled as it was with the resurrection of the humanitarian and pacifist ideology of the Second Empire republicans, prompted a turning away from overtures of patriotic Jacobinism and a reemphasis on the themes of internationalism and universal fraternity that had flourished in the earlier period. In sum, once the war was behind them, a new generation of ordinary Frenchmen could begin to take seriously political solutions and popular movements that addressed more pressing concerns, both for the nation and for themselves.

Working-Class Antimilitarism

With the enfeeblement of popular zeal for *revanche,* the justification for war against Germany also suffered. Moreover, French colonial policy in the 1890s called into question just who France might fight in the event of a European war. Although her greatest enemy on the continent was Germany, her primary rival overseas was Britain. In Africa, the situation came to a head in July 1898 when a small contingent of French troops arrived at Fashoda, the site of an old Egyptian outpost in the Sudan, shortly before British General Kitchener's army got there fresh from victory at Omdurman. The French backed down, but the standoff nearly resulted in war between Britain and France. It did result in better Franco-German relations, and even in the tentative first steps toward collaboration against the British.

As the international scene blurred, domestic conditions in France favored the resurgence of antimilitarism. Beginning in the 1880s, the incidence of working-class protests, most specifically strikes, began a dramatic climb that would continue until after the Second World War. From 1880 to 1884, twice as many strikes occurred as in the previous four-year period or, for that matter, any other period of French history. The flip side of the belle époque was that record numbers of workers were now taking part in an average of over a thousand strikes per year.[43]

An untried and panicky Third Republic responded to the demonstrations with increasingly stringent measures. In the scheme of French history there is nothing novel about employing the army to quell domestic unrest, and by 1851 this was already the source of bitterness: "It is less against foreign invasion that these legions exist than against domestic revolutions."[44] As for the soldiers, policing the interior could be agonizing, even demoralizing, particularly if they sympathized with the revolutionaries or strikers. In 1871, the army hardly greeted with the euphoria of a military victory over a foreign foe the "Bloody Week" of fighting and executions that destroyed the Commune.[45] One might recall too War Minister Boulanger's remark during the coal miners' strike at Decazeville in 1886, when he elicited wild applause in the Chamber of Deputies by suggesting "perhaps, at this very moment, each soldier is sharing his soup and bread ration with a miner."[46]

When the traditionally patriotic French Left suddenly found itself in direct conflict with the new "republican" bulwark of state power, it had a rude awakening to the realities of workers' rights. In 1884, the doctrinaire socialist Jules Guesde asserted that the army no longer looked toward the border, but rather "towards the workshop. It is against the working class that it is turned and that it works its wonders . . . its only goal, its unique raison d'être, is to defend the capitalist and ruling bourgeoisie."[47] Guesde pointed to the use of the army to quiet working-class uprisings at Lyon, La Ricamarie (near Saint-Etienne), and Paris as signal events that should awaken workers to their abuse at the hands of the army, guard dog of the capitalist class.[48] Consciousness did not come so quickly, but waves of strikes and the fear they generated hastened the impression that the "national" army did not serve much of the populace.

In the late nineteenth century, nothing set this more deeply into the collective conscience of the working classes than the Fourmies massacre on May Day 1891. Although demonstrations took place across France to mark the first annual celebration of international working-class solidarity, it fell to this small textile town in the Nord to provide the first martyrs. When the 145th Infantry opened fire on the crowd, killing nine people immediately (several died later) and wounding some eighty others, the relationship between the army and the working classes changed forever. Henceforth the revolutionary Left defined the military as an instrument in the hands of industrial capitalism, a deadly weapon for the exploitation of workers. Anarchists began encouraging soldiers to desert, and the socialist leader Paul Lafargue predicted a broader awakening of class consciousness: "Modern armies are no more than police forces. The Fourmies massacre will have enormous reverberations in the army. It will awaken in the soul of the soldier, himself working class, that dutiful feeling toward his class which brutal and ferocious discipline seeks to snuff out."[49]

This connection between antimilitarism and working-class solidarity had temporarily been held in check. After the Left's heroics in the Commune, the first real burst of antimilitarist activity came from the secure middle and upper classes, who resented being subjected to the same living conditions and moral standards as their social inferiors. But it was not long before the use of the army to control strikes had moved antimilitarism to the fore of socialist agendas and into the realm of the growing trade unions. Anarchists too, for whom hatred of the army was a natural part of their general desire to do away with the state, now recognized the value of focusing on the military. The antimilitarist shift leftward, then, was perfectly consistent with the overarching struggle for workers' rights in a world many perceived, and understandably so, as biased and unfair.

The Socialists

In their endless philosophizing about the proletariat future, French socialists always considered the role of the army. Long before Fourmies, socialist theory refuted and refashioned the army's position in society. Saint-Simon believed it to be a vestige of the feudal past, destined to disappear with industrialization. Similarly, in the early 1840s the socialist theoretician Constantin Pecqueur advocated transforming the soldier into a worker and, by extension, "a vile profession" into a chivalrous one.[50]

With the 1848 revolution, socialism moved from the realm of theory to that of a full-blown doctrine and movement. The short-lived Second Republic was ill-prepared to resolve the problems of the working class, but ironically the emperor Louis-Napoleon Bonaparte, who came to power by crushing his left-wing opposition, was willing to try. It was during the latter half of the Second Empire and with Bonaparte's permission that a delegation of French workers went to London to meet with their British counterparts. The outcome was the Association Internationale des Travailleurs—the First International—officially inaugurated in 1864. That same year, Napoleon III annulled a law that forbade strikes, and for the first time working-class leaders proposed putting their candidates up for election.[51] Four years later, at the First International congress in Brussels, the French socialist Charles Longuet advocated a general strike in the case of war. Back in France, the law of June 6, 1868, gave workers the right to meet, albeit with stipulations as to topic and organization. In 1871 these public meetings proved crucial to revolutionary mobilization in the Commune.[52]

The crisis of 1870–1871, following as it did this period of expansion and escalating confidence, upset the momentum of socialists but not their principles. Michel Winock has traced the continuity of socialist attitudes toward patriotism and the army through the First World War, including the critique of permanent armies. As noted, early socialist theory and the First International proposed their elimination. During the Commune, Winock emphasizes, this position persisted. Although socialists and other leftists were the first to pick up arms and continue to fight the Prussians, this did not prevent them, in the first days of the insurrection, from abolishing conscription and declaring the national guard the sole military force, with all eligible citizens enlisted. "Thus for the first time," writes Winock, "the military doctrine of the socialists was put into practice."[53]

According to this argument, if the suppression of the Commune was a setback for socialists, it only strengthened their commitment to eliminating permanent armies. The recovery of socialism in the 1880s and 1890s provides abundant evidence for this. Auguste Blanqui and his followers were ardent proponents of replacing conscription and the permanent army with a "permanently garrisoned national army." The Blanquistes created a league for this very purpose, and in 1884 they proposed legislation to carry out their ideas. Socialists at the Le Havre congress in November 1880 had made a similar proposition, and by 1891, although the movement itself was becoming factionalized, Blanquistes, Guesdistes, Broussistes, and Allemanistes all supported the suppression of permanent armies. The international congresses of 1889 and 1891 reaffirmed this position.[54]

But as Winock readily admits, criticizing armies is one thing, waging war on militarism another. It was not really until Fourmies that working-class leaders began to extend their economic arguments to the arenas of political and national policy. Capitalists were in power not merely because they owned the factories, but also, it now seemed, because they controlled the army. In the early 1890s, socialists began to assault military culture with more virulence and less vigilance than ever. They branded the caserne a "school of national demoralization," attacked military life for everything from its excessive disciplinary measures to its insufficient protection from training hazards, and lambasted the perks and unprofessionalism of officers. In a few short years, writes Winock, "the satire of the 'professional soldier' became a fertile genre throughout the socialist press." One need only leaf cursorily through *Le Parti Ouvrier* or *Le Parti Socialiste* to find article after article aimed at preparing young socialist conscripts for the realities of military life. In 1893, *La Revue Socialiste* even published Augustin Hamon's *Essai du psychologie militaire professionnel*, a pseudoscientific tract positing that hereditary factors underlie the debased behavior of officers, likening their comportment to "teratological criminals."[55]

In the early 1890s socialists presented the first concerted plan for a national army and debated the first serious proposal for what (or what not) to do in the case of war. "The army," wrote Jaurès, "is no longer what it was: the nation herself, united to defend the soil." To bring it back, socialists revived Blanqui's "nation in arms" legislation after their electoral success in 1893. That same year, Guesde, Jaurès, and Prudent-Dervillers introduced legislation that would give unranked soldiers access to justice in military tribunals. Guesde and his colleagues also proposed that the army gain the right to vote that it had lost with the military law of 1872; an idea that in the long term was designed to boost socialist candidates.[56]

Internationally, the congress of the Second International, which met in Brussels in August 1891, forced European socialists to grapple with that ultimate of antimilitarist questions—what to do in the case of war. On the surface the problem was largely theoretical, as the various parties had to ask themselves if the fight against militarism was a priori to the success of socialism, or did the struggle for socialism subsume the war on militarism. But when the Dutch socialist Domela Nieuwenhuis lit a fuse with his proposition that a general strike be declared as soon as war broke out, the question quickly moved into the realm of reality.

The debate that ensued pointed up divisions within French socialism that would persist through 1914. Although it is not the place of this chapter to examine the nuances of French socialist politics, at one extreme were the Allemanists, who favored the general strike, and at the other were Guesdists, who refused to place the struggle for peace before the struggle for socialism. What is important here is that although the proposition was defeated in favor of a less dogmatic version by Karl Liebknecht and Édouard Vaillant, French and other European socialists came face-to-face with antimilitarism at its most extreme.[57] Moreover, several socialists applauded the initiative; even Guesde's journal *L'Égalité* praised Nieuwenhuis's courage and energy and called armies "the biggest obstacle to the emancipation of the working class."[58] A police report concluded that Nieuwenhuis's opinion actually represented that of the majority of French socialists in attendance.[59] Whether the report was true or not, the debates that took place at Brussels in the late summer of 1891, notably close to Fourmies in both space and time, demonstrated how far socialists had come in acknowledging the question of antimilitarism to their broader movement.

How did the traditional Jacobin patriotism of the socialists stand up to this change in the status of the army and the tone of the debate? It is useful to return to Winock's essay here, as he helps to answer this important and inevitable question by examining socialist reactions to the Franco-Russian alliance concluded in 1894. Allemanists, Blanquists, and, more hesitantly, Guesdists chided it as "patriotic groveling," Tsarist opportunism, and undisguised belligerence. "The Russian alliance means peace like the Empire meant peace," read an editorial in *Le Socialiste*. The politicians Jaurès, Brousse, Millerand, and Viviani were more pragmatic, accusing the triple alliance (Germany, Austria-Hungary, and Italy) of forcing France to seek allies of her own. Perhaps Millerand argued the point best, reminding his fellow socialists that they are "patriots, profoundly patriots, patriots of feeling and of reason. . . . It's not a vanquished, dismembered France that can take the initiative of disarmament and deliver itself, bound hand and foot, to the appetites of its implacable enemies."[60]

While *revanchisme* is certainly prevalent here, more noteworthy is that both sides felt that they were serving the cause of lasting peace with their opposing positions on the alliance. For the socialist Left, this meant going against popular sentiment, including that of many of their own constituents, by refusing to accept an agreement with an autocratic power. For more conservative socialists such as Jaurès, the politics of peace were as much a diplomatic issue as a doctrinal one. For neither, it was now clear, could the struggle for socialism be separated from that against war.

Before the Dreyfus Affair split France along more complex lines, socialists were coming apart on the issue of how to implement antimilitarist policies. There can be little doubt that in the Socialist Party by the mid-1890s, as D. W. Brogan writes, "antimilitarism and something like dogmatic pacifism were almost universally accepted."[61] Antiwar internationalism was the ideological by-product of the conviction that capitalists made wars to increase profits, maintain power, and subjugate workers. But what to do about it? What would be the grand strategy of socialists with regard to war and militarism?

This was the question that began to trouble French socialists at the end of the nineteenth century, and would continue to plague them until the war rendered it moot. Some already felt that the Third Republic had proven itself an inhospitable environment for working-class rights and that socialists needed to accept their outsider status in the new political culture. Consequently they turned their aversion for militarism against the *patrie* itself. Antipatriotism was a rebellion from within, the guttural cry of radical leftists who sensed that their traditional patriotic impulses only satisfied the whims of capitalists, the sole true citizens in the new republican culture. "The only *patrie*, the only [one], is profit," said Guesde, who managed to confine his own antipatriotism to the economic sphere. For Alexandre Zevaès patriotism was akin to religion, because one must submit to it without questioning its basis for existence. "What does it mean to defend the *patrie*?" he wondered, "[it means] our slavery."[62]

Allemanists were the one socialist faction in this period that refuted the *patrie* altogether. In *Catéchisme du soldat* (1894), Maurice Charnay, the self-styled champion of antimilitarism in the Parti Ouvrier Socialiste Révolutionnaire, delivered one of the most vicious diatribes to emanate from socialist ranks. In the question-answer style of a religious catechism, a soldier is queried on such topics as the meaning of the *patrie*, the purpose of war, life in the caserne, and military honor. The answers are generally predictable: militarism is an "instrument of servitude" by which poor workers do the bidding of rich bourgeoisie; casernes are the equivalent of prisons, where soldiers busy themselves with shoe polishing, puppet-like exercises, and drink; wars are meaningless orgies of killing and destruction, fought solely in the interests of governments and the bourgeoisie. To be sure, the nation has to defend itself, and here too Charnay does not surprise, advocating the "general armament of the people." The twist in his logic comes at the beginning of the piece, when he insists that the whole notion of the *patrie* is "a false idea and a lie" created by the ruling classes to oppress the workers.[63]

Charnay paid for his impudence with a six-month prison sentence and a fine of one hundred francs. Authorities confiscated the brochure, and a proposition to read from it in the Chamber of Deputies was defeated, so it probably never received the exposure the author had hoped for.[64] But this radical leftist, whose ideas bordered on anarchism, had introduced a new face of socialism by taking antimilitarism to the extreme of attacking *la patrie* itself. Whether this was a viable strategy for socialists as a whole, however, remained to be seen.

Anarchists and Syndicalists

For the anarchists, who stood at the far left of the political spectrum and who were free of the ideological encumbrances of a full-fledged party, waging a campaign against militarism was much less constrained. As early as 1880 a Cercle des Sans-Patrie existed in Paris.[65] In August 1886, when Boulanger was at the height of his popularity, the "Anarchist Youth of Belleville" changed its name to "The League of Antipatriots" and began collecting money for men who agreed to dodge military recruitment. Three months after the league's formation, police reported it had no less than two thousand members in Paris and five thousand in the provinces.[66] These figures may have been overblown, but the existence of an organization with the express purpose of combating the *patrie* was real and, what's more, remarked upon: "There are therefore people who can be enemies of their *patrie*? Who really, it is true, exist? There is somewhere in France something that calls itself the 'Antipatriotic League'—that says it, and boasts about it! This monstrous thing functions; this 'league' has followers and meetings; it openly professes this abominable doctrine, and even places its ignominious posters on the walls."[67]

In the 1880s and 1890s, anarchist antimilitarist propaganda spread in Paris and the provinces. Placards urging soldiers to use their weapons against their sergeants and the bourgeoisie appeared in the Aude,[68] and in 1891 police reported on the League of Antipatriots in Roanne (Loire).[69] The journal *Le Père Peinard* first appeared in February 1889 and quickly became "probably the most effective vehicle of propaganda in the French anarchist movement." Its scathing critique of French colonialism, barrack life, military discipline, and *revanchisme*, which still was in bad taste to denounce openly,[70] produced articles such as "French Barbarism" (against colonialism in Indochina), "Filthy Profession!" (weighed the possibility of desertion), and "When Is the Conscript Strike?"[71] By late 1892, the journal had been prosecuted seven times and its managerial staff sentenced to over ten years in prison.[72] Other anarchist/antimilitarist journals that would prove durable and disreputable included Jean Grave's *Les Temps Nouveaux* and Sébastien Faure's *Le Libertaire*. Both were launched as weeklies in 1895, lasted until 1914, and reached print runs ranging from seven thousand to nine thousand copies.[73]

By late century anarchists dared to take their antimilitarism directly to its source. On the night of April 19, 1891, they gathered flyers reminding soldiers of their working-class roots and exhorting them to revolt against their military leaders ("decorated bandits," "repugnant parasites") and tossed them into the courtyard of the caserne de Lourcine in the Val-Grace quarter of Paris, the base of the 117th Regiment. A year later on May Day, a flyer reminding soldiers of Fourmies and calling for "death to the sergeants!" was pasted to the walls of the caserne des Tournelles in the 20th arrondissement. Unfortunately, this is all we know about the incident because, "in spite of the most active pursuit," police failed to catch the anarchist spotted putting up the notices.[74]

What were the ideological underpinnings of anarchist antimilitarism? In the sixty-seven-page report "L'Antimilitarisme et l'antipatriotisme en France," the section on anarchism begins: "Anarchists are, by definition and by essence, antimilitarists and antipatriots."[75] It certainly is no great shock that a group violently hostile to the organized state should also target the army, a principal source of governmental stability. The "Father of Anarchy" Pierre-Joseph Proudhon himself predicted at mid-century that the disappearance of the state and its economic infrastructure would engender the transformation of permanent armies from "instruments of oppression and subjects of mistrust" to "industrial companies" heralding the end of warfare.[76] Yet it would be wrong to dismiss anarchists as mere utopians. In *La Guerre et la paix* (*War and Peace*, 1861), Proudhon considered the issue of war and peace within the framework of human society. Political and economic stability might end wars between nations, he argued, but there still would be conflicts between people in the form of labor and industrial strife. In the end, Proudhon's thinking on war and militarism pointed anarchists in the direction of the working classes.

The parallel between anarchist and socialist (and later syndicalist) grounds for making antimilitarist propaganda central to their larger goals is clear from the language of early anarchist propaganda. In its first year, the League of Antipatriots launched posters and flyers conflating antipatriotic and antimilitarist messages with the struggle for working-class rights. On October 18, 1886, for example, the league urged workers to "stop being victims of the *Patrie*. . . . It is not about international wars that one should dream, it is [about] the Social War, this war of the exploited against the exploiters. . . . This war has no borders, it takes place in the entire world." A notice addressed "to the conscripts" (February 1887) implored them to use reason as their guide and not to let the army turn them into "unconscious executioners."[77] The Marxist conception of working-class consciousness, in other words, was adapted to the moral agenda of antimilitarists. In posters placed around the Lourcine and Tournelles casernes, anarchist rhetoric expounded on "bourgeois autocracy" and the fraternity of workers.[78] Further evidence for overlap in anarchist and socialist antimilitarism is the League of Antipatriots' creation of an Anarchist International, of sorts, on September 18, 1887.[79] Their literature even patronized socialism directly: "It is no longer the time when socialists are only utopians, crazies . . . No! We are beginning to confer with them; one worries about their numbers always growing!"[80]

In the late nineteenth century anarchists were doing more than just conferring with socialists—they were ardently striving to infiltrate their ranks. Ideologically, anarchists, who favored a social solution akin to communism, were not so far apart from radical socialists such as the Allemanists. Due to the autonomous nature of their movement, they soon recognized the advantages of moving into the socialist camp to diffuse their ideas and tap the revolutionary manpower of the working classes. A September 1886 report cautioned that the new League of Antipatriots might well be in Guesdist hands.[81] Yet a permanent alliance never materialized. The anarchists' violent methods, including random bombings and unrepentant murders, proved unpalatable even to radical socialists. Anarchists were unceremoniously expelled from the Zurich congress of the Second International in 1893. And after Auguste Vaillant threw a bomb in the Chamber of Deputies later that year and an Italian anarchist killed president of the republic Sadi Carnot in June 1894, socialist leaders refused outright to permit anarchist representatives at the 1896 International in London. Thus ended a brief albeit serious period of flirtation between the two leftist movements.[82]

This was not, however, the end of anarchist efforts to join forces with the organized working classes. Repulsed by the socialists, they increasingly turned toward the growing trade unions, or *syndicats,* and it was there that the anarchists would find a home for their antimilitarist propaganda. The law of March 21, 1884, legalized professional *syndicats* for the first time since the Commune, and their numbers and influence had grown steadily thereafter.[83] So too their independence, for despite the efforts of socialists such as Guesde who tried to bring trade unions into close association with his party, the *syndicats* chose a path that was free from political affiliations, a move that ultimately opened the door to anarchists. Syndicalist thought in particular favored direct industrial action by means of the general strike, as affirmed at the 1888 Bordeaux congress. Not an idea acceptable to most socialists, Guesde's followers walked out of the syndicalist congress in Nantes in 1894. For some fifty years, French trade unions and the Socialist Party would be independent players on a common turf.[84]

Organizationally, syndicalism was little better off than the various socialist parties in late-nineteenth-century France. Working-class unions took two main forms. There were the *syndicats,* which consisted of workers from individual factories or industries. In 1886 they coalesced into the Fédération des Syndicats et des Groupes Coopératifs, a reformist body with ties to Guesde's Parti Ouvrier Français. A year later the Bourses du Travail, another form of union, were organized separately and on a local basis. Their principal function was to unite workers of all trades and help them find jobs, but they also promoted worker education, industrial health, and solidarity during disputes.[85] These local *bourses* soon became centers to discuss workers' problems and disseminate ideas, including ideas on antimilitarism. They grew rapidly throughout France, and in 1892 they were linked into the Fédération des Bourses du Travail.[86]

Anarchists began entering the unions almost from the start, although it was some time before a clearly antimilitarist course took shape. While the first statutes of the Fédération des Bourses du Travail (voted at Saint-Etienne in February 1892) did not mention antimilitarism, the local *bourses* proved particularly amenable to anarchist decentralism and quickly came to serve as operational bases for radical activity.[87] In 1895 the anarchist Fernand Pelloutier was named secretary-general of the Fédération des Bourses. A gifted young journalist (he was twenty-eight at the time) who moved in both Radical and Guesdist circles, Pelloutier held that direct industrial action, rather than circuitous political inaction, would ensure the social revolution. In the less than six-year period that he led the Fédération des Bourses before his untimely death, Pelloutier set it on the ineluctable path of revolutionary syndicalism. It was the anarchists "in general," George Woodcock argues, who "brought with them into the Bourses du Travail their hatred of the state and their extreme anti-militarism."[88]

Anarchists also concentrated efforts on the Fédération des Syndicats. In 1892 Paris police seized a circular from anarchist exiles in London instructing their colleagues to penetrate the *syndicats* actively, and it was ultimately anarchist influence that dislodged Guesdist control by 1894. But whereas the anarchist infiltration of the Bourses du Travail solidified that organization's revolutionary course, it only exacerbated the problems of the Fédération des Syndicats. In 1895 the Fédération split on the question of whether to affiliate with the socialists, and shortly thereafter the Confédération Générale du Travail (CGT) emerged as its weakened successor. The influence of moderates in this new organization, highlighted by a failed railway strike in 1898, delayed the union of the Fédération des Bourses and CGT until 1902. In the long run, however, it ensured anarchists the upper hand in French trade unionism.[89]

As anarchists infiltrated syndicalism, their antimilitarism gradually permeated the agendas of its leaders. The process was gradual because the *syndicats* themselves had a relatively late start, and because in the early 1890s anarchist bombs were doing more to hinder than help their cause. Yet the government would inadvertently steer them on the more radical course. In July 1893, following violent demonstrations in the Latin Quarter, Interior Minister Charles Dupuy ordered the army to occupy the Paris Bourse du Travail and expel its occupants. It was a highly criticized move that, like Fourmies, made a lasting impression. For the rising Pelloutier, it proved antimilitarism to be the ethical as well as logical path: "Our duty is to instruct ourselves and the workers of Europe about the dangers of militarism; to teach people that by marching against each other they do less for the greatness of their homeland than for its exhaustion, and that they consolidate above all the power and tyranny of their masters. That is the goal and virtue of the internationalist doctrine."[90]

The early career of Émile Pouget further illustrates the roots of antimilitarism in French syndicalism. Founder of *Le Père Peinard*, Pouget was a relative unknown when in 1879 at age nineteen he took part in the formation of a textile union (not legally recognized) and drafted its first publication: a violently antimilitarist brochure. After becoming an anarchist, Pouget continued to mix his antimilitarist sympathies with his syndicalist involvement. On March 9, 1883, he was arrested for leading a rally of the Employers' Federation of Cabinet Workers. In his possession were a loaded revolver and postal receipts for packages recently sent to Amiens, Bordeaux, Marseille, Vienne, Roanne, Reims, and Troyes. A search of Pouget's room at 31 rue de Bretagne revealed, along with chemical vials and the draft of an anarchist circular, six hundred copies of the brochure *À L'armée* (*To the Army*), which had been printed in Geneva by the anarchist George Herzig. It urged soldiers to burn their barracks and kill their officers to signal the social revolution.[91]

It did not take long for police to link the brochures with the receipts and build a strong case against Pouget. On learning that Herzig had sent him twenty thousand copies of *À L'armée,* police traced the packages to Pouget's luckless contacts and forced them to stand trial with him and other leaders of the March 9 rally. As Edward Fitzgerald shows, the government adroitly used the evidence of Pouget's anarchist plottings to tie the workers' demonstration to a nationwide revolutionary/antimilitarist conspiracy, "a sinister design to overthrow the Republic." Consequently the June trial, dubbed the "Louise Michel Affair" after the female anarchist who led the protest, made headlines for a week and included evidence that Pouget's chemicals could be used to make explosives. It was all too much for the jury. Although Pouget defended himself with a spirited speech contrasting the humane justice sought by anarchists with that of the established republican order, the court sentenced him to eight years in prison.[92]

Was this the selfsame Émile Pouget destined to play a leading role in the CGT? Liberated after three years thanks to the 1886 amnesty, the anarchist exhibited no ill effects from his prison term when he rejoined his comrades. This lasted until January 1894. Then increased police surveillance, including the seizure of *Le Père Peinard,* drove Pouget into exile in England. In an effort to resurrect the journal and smuggle it into France, he changed tactics in favor of an organization that not only had the advantage of legality, but the proletarian support base to go with it: "The problem is this: 'I am an anarchist and I want to sow my ideas—on what ground will they grow best?' The factory, the bar, I have these already . . . it's something better I'm after: a spot where I'll find *prolos* who are starting to realize something about our common exploitation, and who are searching like mad for a solution—Does such a spot exist? Hell yes! And it has no rival: it's the trade union!" Pouget's strong, early identification with anarchist antimilitarism never did prevent him from representing the CGT at national and local congresses in the late 1890s; nor from being named, in 1900, to edit *La Voix du Peuple,* the organization's new weekly paper.[93]

Still, for the reasons discussed above, syndicalists were relative latecomers to organized antimilitarism. It was not until September 1897, at its ninth national corporative congress, that the CGT called for the "suppression of all work done by the military element in the casernes, be it for the upkeep and diverse services of the barrack buildings, or for anything involving dress, equipment, and harnessing."[94] Meaning, in short, that the CGT wanted a hand in regulating military labor. It was a tentative first step. A year later at Rennes, Edmond Briat, "who was then of extremely advanced opinions on syndicalist matters," advocated the active pursuit of antimilitarism. In his doctoral thesis, André May suggested that the unification of the Fédération des Bourses du Travail and the CGT came about partly as a consequence of their merging positions on radical issues such as antimilitarism. This alliance was not achieved until 1902. Once established, however, it was not long before syndicalism became the most active and controversial source of antimilitarism before the war.[95]

◆ ◆ ◆

This chapter began by posing the question of the origins of antimilitarism in late-nineteenth-century France. Is it not inevitable, then, that it should end with the Dreyfus Affair? For just as the eighteenth century seemed to climax and turn with the French Revolution, the conflicting ideologies of the nineteenth converged upon and were reshaped by the "Dreyfus Revolution," as one historian has called it.[96] This formula works particularly well for the military. If ever there were an event in French history that did more to damage the military's image, the Dreyfus Affair is it. The question of whether the Jewish army captain Alfred Dreyfus had been unjustly accused of espionage put the military's own honor on trial at the very moment that honor was regarded as sacrosanct. The Dreyfus Affair was thus the big break antimilitarists needed to bring their campaign into the open.

This is a sound interpretation that, unquestioned, pervades nearly everything written on the origins of French antimilitarism. The historian René Garmy asserts that "before 1900, antimilitarist action is not yet openly engaged."[97] An accomplished scholar of the Left agreed: "It is thus with the Dreyfus Affair that leftist anti-militarism is born or, at least, emerges considerably."[98] A more recent study of youth movements refers to the Dreyfus

Affair as "a detonator" igniting antimilitarist themes "with tenfold vigor."[99] The sentiment is even confirmed by history. At the peak of the turmoil in 1898, the German socialist Karl Kautsky exclaimed: "Just as in France, [German socialists] are against the army and against war, and if we had a Dreyfus Affair here our 2.5 million constituents would assail the officer corps and succeed."[100]

Yet the evidence presented in this chapter does not corroborate this story very well. Before Dreyfus's personal saga became a national and international affair in 1897–1898, before he was even arrested in 1894, antimilitarists were well on their way to reclaiming ground that had been lost after the Franco-Prussian War and the virtual idolatry of the army that followed. By the late 1880s, anarchists were manifesting antimilitarist propaganda on walls and buildings in Paris and the provinces, while the more domesticated bourgeoisie were doing the same, albeit less caustically, with their literature. Similarly, as socialists recovered from the Commune, earlier theories on the "nation in arms" and internationalism were revived with them. Before anyone had even heard of Alfred Dreyfus, socialist congresses were debating the all-important question of what to do in the case of war.

Further complicating the picture is the fact that the Dreyfus Affair did not neatly divide France between Left and Right, and that the working classes and their leaders were particularly distraught over which side, if any, to take in it. The main problem was ideological: Dreyfus was a bourgeois, his supporters were bourgeois; neither anarchists nor parliamentary socialists wished to jeopardize the revolution by backing their enemies, especially one who might have fired at them during a strike. Jaurès himself voiced the dominant leftist sentiment that if the sentence had befallen a man without money and connections, the privileged class would not be fighting over him. A CGT pamphlet in spring 1898 read: "We the Workers, constantly exploited, have no call to take part in this conflict between Jews and Christians! They are both the same, since they both dominate and exploit us!"[101]

Eventually, however, the pursuit of justice, even if it was on bourgeois terms and in support of a Jewish defender of the capitalist order, became too great for most working-class representatives to resist. Although Pouget and Jean Grave never committed themselves, Sébastien Faure perhaps best captured the paradox of an anarchist-Dreyfusard:

> We have declared loud and clear, and as frequently as police intolerance has permitted us, how much the *patrie*, the army, the flag, are to us all the same bloody iniquities we seek to destroy. A captain does not

interest us any more than a *patrie*, . . . but a man condemned in the most frivolous fashion by a *justice* to which we are bound, . . . but the oppressed, whatever his rank, tribe, or country, becomes our comrade in misery, our brother in suffering.[102]

Faure spoke out before Jaurès and many socialists did, inhibited as they were by electoral and other political concerns. What finally brought working-class representatives around was the moral compulsion to oppose militarism and reactionary clericalism, even if it meant defending the Republic. In September 1898 Jaurès published a collection of articles titled *Les Preuves* (*The Evidence*), hoping to convince colleagues "that if the bourgeois Republic, in opposing the military conspiracy, needed Socialist energy, it was, on the contrary, for a daring party eager for conquests and opportunity sent by destiny, an historic opening." Although some still denounced this as "domesticated middle-class socialism," the ideological compromise could not be avoided by a movement, or a man, that viewed Dreyfus's plight as the fundamental moral issue that it was. The only remaining question is whether "antimilitarism" had inadvertently forfeited its ideals—as socialist and crusading Dreyfusard Gustave Hervé would later argue, and historian Zeev Sternhell has since maintained with regard to socialism—by allying itself with the Republic and integrating the workers into the nation.[103]

Although it is still too early for us to pass judgment on this issue, it does appear that the role of the Dreyfus Affair in the rise of antimilitarism has been overrated by scholars anxious to impose neat historical explanations on the conundrums of the past. Yet I will not pursue this point further. The significance of the affair does not lie merely in what came before and after it, but in how it entered the collective consciousness of ordinary French people. We know that it barely entered at all outside of Paris, but in the capital and other urban centers the guilt or innocence of Dreyfus was no less than a moral assessment of the army.[104] And as the *arche sainte* of the *patrie*, the army reflected directly on the Republic itself. This was the dilemma of those who fought against Dreyfus, regardless of whether they believed he was guilty or not. It was also the problem faced by the Dreyfusards, who defended the officer for the same reasons that their adversaries prosecuted him: the honor and virtue of France.[105] The army, caught in this swirl of controversy, could not hope to emerge unscathed. And the antimilitarists, the anarchist Victor Méric noted, were prepared to reap the reward:

> The Dreyfus Affair, by unveiling military crimes and disgraces, by demonstrating the ignominy of the great leaders, was of unquestion-

able utility to us. It is permissible today to have only mixed admiration for the army; it is possible to state—not without some danger nevertheless—one's entire thought on military institutions, and one's disgust at the slaughters perpetrated by decorated [officers].[106]

The Dreyfus Affair, one might say, created a climate of confrontation, the feeling that there were no absolutes, no institutions that were beyond reproach or above redress. In this sense it could not have been better suited to antimilitarists, who previously were perhaps more keenly aware of the ramifications of their propaganda. The affair had other repercussions as well: the increased political successes and respectability of the socialists; the growth spurt of trade unions; the heightened role of the press as an instrument of propaganda; and, politically, the sharper delineation between a nationalist, often anti-Semitic Right bent on destroying the Republic and a more inclusive republican Left committed to parliamentary government and defending individual rights against established state powers.[107] In short, the most important outcome of these turbulent years cannot be reduced to some artificial measure of what it meant to progress. Rather, it was the moment that antimilitarists realized their cause had an acceptable social and political value that they became emboldened enough to bring it to larger audiences and into more respected milieus. As one militant syndicalist put it: "One should not forget that, since the Dreyfus Affair, antimilitarism in France has marched at the pace of giants."[108]

2. ANTIMILITARIST ARMIES

Structures and Strategies

In 1898 two matters arose that were to leave important legacies for the years 1914–1918. First was the appointment of Théophile Delcassé as French foreign minister. Delcassé had come to the Quai d'Orsay when Anglo-French relations were at an all-time low because of the Fashoda crisis. By the time he left, the Entente Cordiale (1904) had converted enmity into alliance. From the beginning to the end of his unprecedented seven-year term, through all the twists and turns of European diplomacy, Delcassé never veered from viewing Germany as the probable enemy in a future war. His admirable "prescience," as one historian put it, set French foreign policy on a course that, a decade later, still had the force of conviction and the comfort of familiarity.[1]

The second development was the publication of the six-volume *La Guerre future; aux points de vue technique, économique et politique,* by the Russian railroad magnate Ivan (or Jean de) Bloch. On the basis of meticulous research into contemporary military technology and strategy, Bloch argued that Europe's large armies and modern armaments (machine guns, long-range artillery, and so forth) had so altered war as to render it virtually unwinnable, at least without enormous casualties and total economic collapse. This frighteningly prophetic work demanded serious attention, yet most military experts remained skeptical, adopting instead the strategic doctrine of the "offensive" for what Bloch predicted would be a long, entrenched stalemate spread out over an enormous front. Although the work is likely to have encouraged Tsar Nicholas II to convene the first Hague Peace

Conference in May 1899, it failed to prevent war as much as the "offensive" would to win it in 1914.[2]

The two examples given above—Delcassé's foreign policy and the reliance on traditional military thinking to plan for a "future war"—illustrate a degree of constancy and coherence in French policy-making and strategic thought from the early 1900s on. Can we say the same for antimilitarism? Did the new century mark the onset of a consistent style of understanding and expressing antimilitarist ideology and strategy that carried it beyond the indiscriminate and disunited propaganda of the late nineteenth century?

◆ ◆ ◆

In early 1900, Charles Albert complained in *Les Temps Nouveaux* about people who continually criticized war but did nothing to prevent it. He took the Boer War, at the time taxing the British beyond expectations, as evidence that "war in our day is impossible," echoing Bloch's conclusion. Yet European nations continued to lavish huge sums on the military and conducted diplomacy as if preparing for "the future war" rather than securing future peace. That is why most antimilitarists, Jaurès included, viewed the Hague Conference as a "big hypocrisy" or "comedy."[3] Indeed a prominent historian has pronounced it "no more than a ripple in the current of international politics."[4] Yet none of this allayed Albert's concerns. What *were* antimilitarists actually doing in 1900?[5]

What appears to have been the first specifically antimilitarist organization of the period—the Groupe de Propagande Antimilitariste de Paris (GPAP)—seems to have been doing something, namely getting indicted. Founded in December 1899, the group printed at least three placards ("crimes militaires," "assassins galonnés," "justice militaire"), held conferences in Paris and the provinces, and was the subject of several inquiries before it vanished from the historical record after only two years. *Le Libertaire* reported that the GPAP sought to graft itself onto other revolutionary socialist groupings, suggesting that a purely antimilitarist stance was not serving it very well.[6]

The Ligue Antimilitariste and Ligue (Internationale) pour la Défense du Soldat faced similar predicaments. The former, created in December 1902 by the anarchists H. Beylie, Paraf-Javal, Albert Libertad, Émile Janvion, and Georges Yvetot (who had succeeded Pelloutier as secretary-general of the Fédération des Bourses du Travail), would form the seedbed for the French section of the Association Internationale Antimilitariste (AIA).[7] The latter, if one can judge from the sheer quantity of documents on it collected by Paris police, did achieve a certain success before being undermined by internal strife. According to the first official report on this independently funded society with the express purpose of defending soldiers against military abuse, the original Ligue pour la Défense du Soldat had 232 sections and twenty-five thousand members. Its founder and president, Charles Chevallier, who wrote for *L'Aurore* under the pseudonym Ch. Vallier, expressed confidence in the ligue's success in October 1902, when he boasted that the misleading name was the key to its broad appeal. In reality, Chevallier candidly asserted, the Ligue pour la Défense du Soldat was no less than an antimilitarist league, heeding a battle cry nothing short of "down with the army!"[8]

Lending weight to its cause, the word "Internationale" curiously slipped into the ligue's designation in December 1902, despite the lack of evidence for any international ties.[9] A more likely interpretation is that the name reflected a new image, one that integrated leftists of all persuasions to combat military injustice. By mid-December, ligue meetings were advertising the likes of Jean Allemane, Marcel Sembat (the socialist deputy of Paris), and Urbain Gohier, the journalist/anarchist author of the Dreyfusard tract *L'Armée contre la nation* (1898). Moreover, the ligue's early actions, in particular its direct intervention on behalf of unfairly disciplined soldiers, seemed proof that this antimilitarist group was not just about posters and pamphlets. By targeting specific instances of military abuse, such as the universally despised war councils, the ligue assured itself a degree of legitimacy that the others never attained and that anarchists could not overlook.[10]

So why did the Ligue Internationale pour la Défense du Soldat only last a year? Despite some creative propaganda that used pictorial representations to denounce military justice, the group failed to unite adherents behind its directed antimilitarist program.[11] In particular, the anarchist presence opened it to controversy. At the December 14, 1902, meeting, debate erupted after Henriette Meyer extolled the organization for taking its fight to the president of the Republic, Émile Loubet, adding that he was partisan to their cause. In angry response, Albert Libertad insisted that the army in general, rather than just the war councils, was the enemy; and that the goal was not to safeguard soldiers' rights by collaborating with republicans, but to abolish armies and, in turn, the need for soldiers altogether. For Libertad and likeminded anarchists, these half-measures were just that—partial solutions, feeble distractions from the weighty problem of bourgeois government and its military guard dog. As another anarchist put it: "We are anti-militarists by necessity, not by sentiment. We no longer want the army because it is in our way, not simply because we have a compassionate heart."[12]

Was this ruthless approach a viable new strategy for antimilitarism? The police report went on to proclaim a new era in "the antimilitarist movement"; a no-holds-barred, anarchist-led age in which attacking and even killing servicemen was acceptable. Yet this life-or-death redefinition of antimilitarism by a handful of anarchists only led to scisson and, eventually, the disintegration of the ligue. The only hope for these hard-liners, it now seemed, was to broaden their appeal with a league of their own.[13]

The Association Internationale Antimilitariste

The Association Internationale Antimilitariste des Travailleurs, or AIA, was not born on French soil. Its founder was the Dutch pastor and part-time revolutionary Domela Nieuwenhuis, and its inaugural congress took place in his hometown of Amsterdam. Nieuwenhuis himself was as readily identified as a socialist or syndicalist as an anarchist. Beginning his public career as the only socialist in the Dutch Parliament, he turned to more radical extraparliamentary forms of activism after becoming disillusioned with party politics.[14] A growing presence in anarchist circles in the early 1900s, a poster announcing his participation at a Paris meeting billed him as a delegate of the Dutch syndicalists.[15]

Nieuwenhuis came to antimilitarism by the usual route—as a champion of the working classes. His pamphlet *Le Militarisme et l'attitude des anarchistes et socialistes révolutionnaires devant la guerre* (*Militarism and the Attitude of Anarchist and Socialist Revolutionaries Toward War*) is as revealing in its hatred of the capitalist order as it is of war and militarism. Perhaps the most telling element of the work is the author's binding suspicion that the present political and economic system has essentially brainwashed people. "Militarist spirit" becomes something artificially maintained in citizens through the capitalist press, politicians, and education. And he defines the army as a "collection of persons who do not think, docile instruments with which the leaders can do what they like."[16]

I highlight these passages not because they are innovative in any ideological sense, but because of their very consistency with late-nineteenth-century anarchist and radical socialist propaganda. Nieuwenhuis's appeal here is to consciousness. He writes, in essence, don't be duped by your social betters; think before you act; you are people too! It is foremost a personal and humane message, with its reference point in the working-class struggle. In short, it is the kind of language that, in times of rampant military abuse, transcended political affiliations.

Yet if such flourishes had not sufficed for the League of Antipatriots to succeed more than a decade earlier, how did Nieuwenhuis and his supporters plan to alter the course of antimilitarist history, so to speak, with their new association? The key lay in the emphasis on "workers" and "international." In organization, ideology, and activity, the AIA was committed to becoming a kind of alternative Socialist International in which all workers—socialist, syndicalist, anarchist, or none of the above—would participate in a cause equal to, yet inclusive of, all these: that is, antimilitarism. As Yvetot wrote in the AIA bulletin: "There is no need that is more revolutionary and more urgent than antimilitarist propaganda. . . . This is why, outside of political groups, outside even of economic groups, the AIA truly has its raison d'être."[17]

This broad-based appeal was evident from the start, when delegates from seven European countries convened in Amsterdam on June 26–28, 1904. Although the anarchists dominated the congress, the twelve-member French delegation included representatives from the Paris and Roanne bourses, and there was no shortage of syndicalists, communists, and even journalists. It is difficult to know how many actually attended if the leading nation sent only twelve representatives. *L'Ennemi du Peuple* reported 4,500 at the final public meeting, and one may assume from the publicity that the world's first antimilitarist congress did not pass unnoticed.[18]

Once the excitement subsided, however, the AIA's disavowal of partisan loyalty stood out as its most revolutionary and difficult achievement. Indeed one of the first debates in Amsterdam concerned the role of *syndicats* in the new organization, particularly because the CGT had already undertaken its own exhaustive antimilitarist campaign. Additionally, a proposal that the group adopt the refusal of military service as part of its strategy set off a debate that split down familiar lines.[19] Such controversies would continue to convulse the AIA, which tended toward activist tactics. But transcending the partisan battles was the AIA's commitment to its founding principle of universal participation, which even extended to women.[20]

The AIA was similarly serious about living up to its international designation, creating national sections with direct links to a general committee in Amsterdam. The anarchists Miguel Almereyda (née Eugène Vigo) and Georges Yvetot headed the French section and thus sat on the committee. Membership cards bearing the motto "not a man, not a cent for militarism," and monthly dues (equivalent to twenty French centimes) tied each member to his or her local, national, and international committees.[21] Whenever a particular nation drew attention to itself with an antimilitarist incident, the secretary-general pledged to support it. The organizational emphasis from the start, in short, was that of a "new International," and delegates returned to their homes to spread this word.[22]

How well it worked, however, depended largely on whom one asked. An article titled "La Nouvelle Internationale" in the small leftist paper *L'Action* displayed high hopes from the beginning: "The International Antimilitarist Association of Workers! Who today knows about the existence of this organization? It is nevertheless destined to make some noise, and its actions will probably have unprecedented repercussions."[23] This article appeared shortly before the AIA's grand inaugural meeting at the Sociétés Savantes in Paris. "Barely formed, the AIA functions marvelously," announced a flyer for the meeting, which attracted between 800 and 2,000 people.[24] In its first two years, a steady stream of propaganda documents the even progress of the AIA. After just one year, police estimated there were 5,500 members in ninety-three sections in Paris and the provinces.[25] "As soon as it was formed," stated a lengthy report filed October 27, 1905, "the AIA would have met, among militants, with the most rapid success." A list of sections included most quarters of Paris, its suburbs, and the cities of Lyon, Marseille, Bordeaux, Amiens, Saint-Etienne, Bourges, Lille, Reims, Roubaix, Cherbourg, Brest, Toulon, Fourchambault, Nice, and Saint-Nazaire. In Paris the group met "at least once a week" in a rented space at the Maison commune, also home to the Université Populaire, Fédération Socialiste de la Seine, and the Ligue des Droits de l'Homme. But members were equally comfortable discussing "the course to follow and tactics to employ in the work of antimilitarist propaganda" at the local brasserie.[26]

"However," this early report insisted, "one does not have to believe, before these numbers [of sections and members] and because of the notoriety of certain members on the national Committee . . . that the importance and action of these various sections or groups are considerable. In reality, their importance and action are mediocre, for none of these groups or sections function regularly." The report drew attention to the AIA's lack of an established office, as well as to the paucity and youth of its members. This account basically built on a report filed in July that had determined the AIA's support base to be thinner than that indicated by the organization's own figures and self-image. This earlier report admitted that there were sections, notably at Chalon-sur-Saône, Marseille, Bourges, and Trélazé, "but, outside of these, the AIA has not gained any recruits." As for Paris, it alleged there were really only three sections, "or rather three skeletons of sections," including those of the 17th, 12th, and 20th arrondissements. "These so-called sections group a minority of anarchists not surpassing forty or fifty individuals. Moreover, the action of this association has completely stopped, at least for the moment, and is non-existent from the standpoint of the antimilitarist propaganda currently operating in France and even in the Army." The "really effective" propaganda, this report contended, came from socialists and anarcho-syndicalists. "The share consumed by the AIA is minuscule."[27]

Can we take these reports at face value or should we dismiss them as premature? The answer probably lies somewhere in between. Their main thrust is that the AIA's French section had some competent leaders and a well-defined organization, but a year after its founding there was reason to believe it had not attracted much support. Still, the AIA existed and, like any new group, needed time to build; especially if, right from the start, anxious officials already had their doubts.

Another gauge of the success of the AIA was its ability to attract non-anarchists. Judging from its earliest meetings, French leaders were committed to honoring the founding provision that leftists of all shades had a stake in the new International. Two well-attended meetings in October 1905 brought socialists and anarchists together, and one meeting ended with them all singing the "Internationale." Amédée Bousquet of the Paris *bourse* presided over the latter, which was attended by five hundred people and featured the socialist deputy Dr. Meslier as speaker. Gustave Hervé attended the AIA's national congress in July 1905 and spoke to a crowd of some three hundred that August.[28] These early meetings too show few signs of the radicalism that anarchists brought, for example, to the Ligue pour la Défense du Soldat. The AIA did advocate the workers' revolt in the case of war, and it admitted discussion of extreme measures such as desertion and sabotage. Yet the latter were not made doctrine.[29] From the outset, there seems to have been a conscious effort on the part of the section's founders to make the ideology of antimilitarism a self-standing and universally appealing one.

Not all parties concerned, however, were willing to accept this compromise, and the AIA had its dissenters too. Several pieces in the new journal *L'Anarchie* denounced "AIAT-ism" as a degradation of true anarchist principles: "Antimilitarism is essentially of anarchist origins. Antimilitarism can only be anarchist." André Lorulot argued that the AIA, as a socialist organization, was authoritarian by nature and would only constrain individual initiative (e.g., desertion and sabotage) and increase the likelihood of repression.[30]

Although "individualists" such as Libertad and Lorulot lambasted the AIA's pluralistic aspirations, some police reached different conclusions. Several officers give the impression that the group got off to a slow start precisely *because* its efforts to integrate socialists had failed. "The socialists stay and will stay out of the way," predicted one official, who referred to the AIA as the "Ligue Antimilitariste" in allusion to its predominantly anarchist constitution.[31] In a more thorough analysis, the reporter concluded that the AIA was no different from the earlier anarchist leagues: "It is not Malato, Gohier, Yvetot, Janvion, Almereyda, and some editors from *Libertaire* [all anarchists] who can create a movement and a new international." This was not a good prognosis for a group that had just emerged from a rousing inaugural congress. The author did suggest that if the AIA became a lightning rod for other antimilitarists, particularly during parades, strikes, and the like, it might well have to be taken seriously.[32]

The fact that these reports vacillate so much leads me to believe that socialists probably joined some sections and not others. Furthermore, as more meetings in more places came to the attention of authorities, their heightened interest alone attests to a certain achievement for the AIA in its first year. Despite continual complaints from the treasurer that "the cash box is almost always empty"; despite the self-adulatory protests of the Libertads and Lorulots; despite even police reports that downplayed the organization's claims to a growing membership, there can be little doubt about official concern for the AIA's potential.[33] Even the skeptical reporter who called its following "minuscule" felt compelled to add that "a state of mind" was animating the anarchists and revolutionary syndicalists.[34] Whether the group's nationwide membership had really shrunk to 2,000, as reported in April 1906, or the earlier figure of 5,500 was more accurate, this antimilitarist league had emerged from its first year in better shape than its predecessors.[35]

Perhaps the best evidence for this is the fact that the AIA held a national congress one year after its founding. Faithful to its goal of becoming a new International, delegates from across France gathered in Saint-Etienne on July 14 to 16, 1905. There were no breakthroughs at the congress, yet no major disruptions either. After debate on issues such as "desertion and its practical value," the section returned to the principles that had united it in the first place, in particular its commitment to insurrection (the workers' revolution) in the case of war, and the more conciliatory position that because "desertion only constitutes an individual action without practical value from the antimilitarist viewpoint, the AIA would "neither condemn nor advocate" it. These issues, which will be examined at length in subsequent chapters, are fundamental to antimilitarists. That the AIA leaders came to some agreement on them attests to a tenacious belief in the goals and principles of their organization.[36]

The most important commitment made to antimilitarism at Saint-Etienne, however, was that made to the working classes themselves. The first question on the agenda of the congress was an old one for the relatively young association: "Should the AIA be the expression of a doctrine (anarchist or socialist) or should it conserve its exclusively antimilitarist character?" The majority favored the latter: "The delegates . . . agree to conserve the exclusively antimilitarist, revolutionary character of the AIA. The Association remains therefore, as in the past, open to all antimilitarists without distinction of school, provided they cooperate, if the case arises, with the insurrectional action advocated by the Association."[37]

The anarchist/revolutionary syndicalist Georges Yvetot was in many respects an ideal representative for the AIA. A founding member of the Ligue Antimilitariste who went on to head the AIA's French section, he established his antimilitarist credentials as secretary of the Fédération des Bourses du Travail, a position he achieved with the support of socialists Jean Allemane and Paul Brousse.[38] Indeed it may be deceptive to separate syndicalist and anarchist antimilitarism, and Yvetot is a good example of why. Like so many anarchists who moved into the syndicalist milieu, he kept a foot in both camps through his antimilitarist activity. As the second-highest-ranking member in the CGT when it merged with the Fédération des Bourses, Yvetot was well established and well known when he became AIA secretary. Soon he published under AIA auspices one of several antimilitarist tracts, a pamphlet decrying military excess titled *La Vache à lait* (*The Milk Cow*). And connections between the groups were reinforced when the AIA moved its headquarters into the CGT building at 33 rue de la Grange-aux-Belles in Paris. Around 1905, police reported that, "though not having any tie with the AIA, the CGT marches with it." The links were there—in people, proximity, and overall program—but the syndicalists established antimilitarist strategies and dogmas of their own and, most importantly, had a preexisting national network in which to implement them.[39]

Georges Yvetot and French Syndicalism

In its third year of publication (1903), purposely timed with the military's annual conscription lottery, the syndicalist weekly *La Voix du Peuple* depicted on its cover two officers inspecting a group of conscripts, or *bleus*. The caption read: "What will these young men become? . . . Soldiers? . . . No! Anti-militarists!" The rest of the issue explained why this was so important to an economic organization such as the CGT. The lead article "Conscrit!" (the lead article was always addressed directly to the recruits) chided the ritual recruitment as "a useless corvée . . . that by itself symbolizes admirably all the stupidity of Militarism." It likened the experience of going to the caserne to that of an animal being led to slaughter, although the beast, at least, is ignorant of his fate. The article "L'Action syndicale et la désagrégation de l'armée" (Union Action and the Disintegration of the Army) attacked the army as the "sole impediment to the defense of our economic interests and the realization of our aspirations." Other articles included an appeal to mothers ("is it thus for the slaughterhouse that you raised your son?"); a comparison of the two schools of life—the caserne ("school of crime") and the *bourse;* and a fictional piece titled "La Dernière Révolte" (The Last Revolt), in which a young soldier faces the agonizing decision of how to respond to a workers' uprising. In this single issue, in sum, one has an abridged version of the basic arguments of French antimilitarism. What one lacks, however, is an answer to how the *bleus* would actually be made into antimilitarists, as opposed to brutal, undignified, and disciplined soldiers.[40]

One way was to get the conscripts before they left, and *La Voix du Peuple* played a crucial role in this endeavor. Ever since Pouget launched the journal in 1900, it had published a special biannual edition during the conscript recruiting period (*tirage au sort*) and subsequent fall departure (*l'appel de la classe*). Its themes were the same as those outlined above. The army was depicted as the arch defender of capital, a bastion of crime and vice (especially alcoholism and pederasty) that corrupted youth and betrayed class. The caserne was where young men went to learn how to serve the bourgeoisie, and in the process were stripped of their reasoning faculties and proletariat identities, and transformed into brutal, inhuman killers. Conscription was a "bourgeois invention, an institution of capitalist patronage."[41] If *La Voix* had an overriding message, it was to remind the twenty year olds to remain men, in the humane sense of the word, rather than becoming good soldiers to protect their social betters and, likely, be killed in a foreign war. Look at any issue from 1900 to 1914, and these are the predominant themes.

The cover of these special editions was typically a full-page drawing of soldiers being used and degraded at the hands of their superiors and/or the bourgeoisie. In a 1910 issue, an officer leads his recruits by rope past the

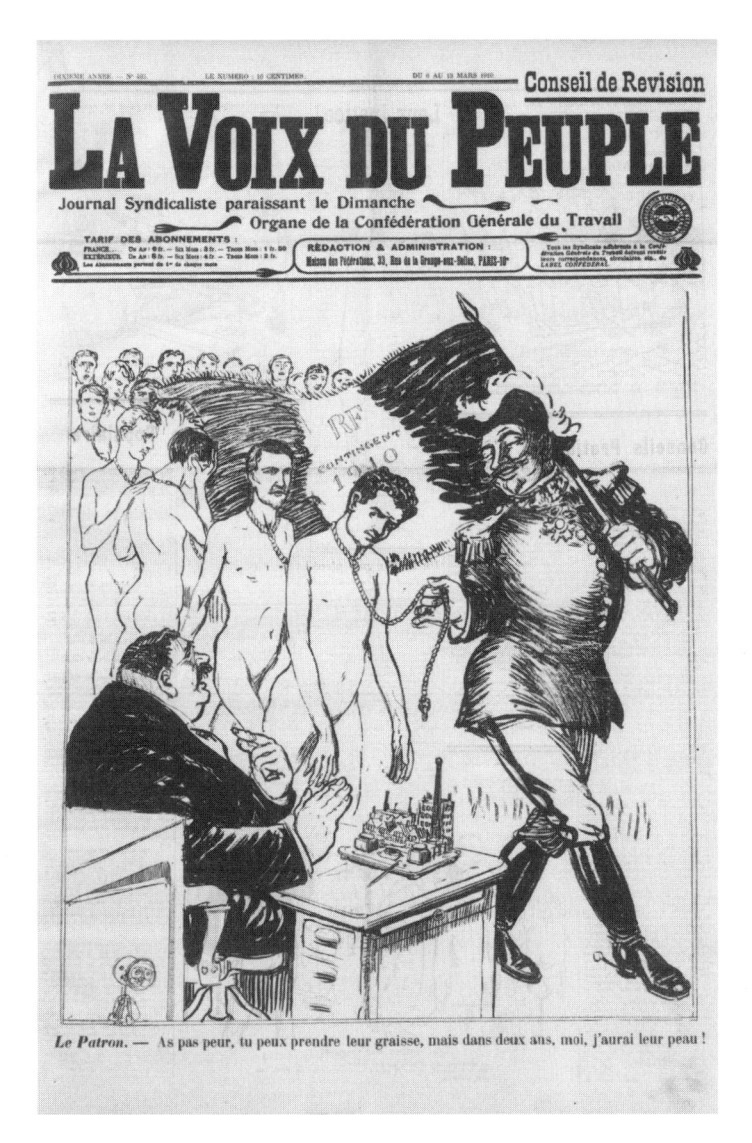

The Owner: "Have no fear, you can take their fat, but in two years I will have their skin!" From *La Voix du Peuple*, March 6–13, 1910. Reprinted with permission of L'Institut CGT d'Histoire Sociale.

desk and safe of a plump factory owner, *le patron,* who assures him: "Have no fear, you can take their fat, but in two years I will have their skin!" The caricaturist Jules Grandjouan was particularly fond of scenes depicting the army's role in social conflicts. A 1907 cover portrayed a soldier returning home after the Narbonne massacres, only to have his working-class parents spit at him. On another cover, bourgeois parents greet their soldier-murderer son as a hero. In yet another drawing, the soldier returns from firing on workers to find his own father dying from a bullet wound. Not surprisingly, these editions were frequently indicted. But while hazarding confrontation with authorities was the main obstacle to reaching workers outside the caserne, getting the antimilitarist message into the garrison was trickier yet.[42]

This task was the basis for the celebrated Sou du Soldat (soldier's penny): to link soldiers with their comrades in the workshops and remind them of their syndicalist roots. As far back as 1897 the General Strike Commission had recommended a supplementary fee, "the proceeds of which would be spread among comrade-soldiers."[43] Although nothing ever came of this, three years later the eighth national congress of the Fédération des Bourses voted unanimously to establish connections between young workers in the military and the local Bourses du Travail. Taking its name from a successful fund that the Catholic Church ran for religious purposes, the Sou du Soldat ensconced itself in the sphere of labor.[44]

On the surface the Sou du Soldat appeared both innocent and essential—the expression of a legitimate fear that, once exposed to disciplined military life, the soldier would be lost to the working-class, revolutionary cause: "We all know that, as soon as one of ours becomes a soldier, he breaks all ties with his previous comrades and, absorbed by the useless as much as absurd military exercises, unlearns his profession, loses the taste for work, and, what is even sadder, forgets too often that he is a man and that, his three years of service completed, he will cease being the armed defender of capital and become once again, until the grave, the eternal exploited." This may not have been the antimilitarists' answer to a call to arms, but in its earliest form the Sou du Soldat was nothing short of an appeal for consciousness; an appeal, that is, to *all* workers, including those "left outside of the syndicalist movement."[45]

How and how well did it work? The success of the Sou du Soldat depended largely on the generosity of workers. It simply asked them to make a small donation (one sou at least) to a fund for their colleagues under arms.[46] And there is no evidence that workers were tight-fisted or that the local *bourses* resisted. The Sou du Soldat seems to have expanded modestly after

Top: Soldier returns home to his parents from Narbonne; *bottom:* "Oh! Jackass! You fired on the People!" From *La Voix du Peuple*, October 1907. Reprinted with permission of L'Institut CGT d'Histoire Sociale.

Soldier returns home to his parents from Raon l'Etape. From *La Voix du Peuple*, February 1908. Reprinted with permission of L'Institut CGT d'Histoire Sociale.

its creation. The Fédération des Métiers was one of the first on board, declaring in September 1901 that the Sou du Soldat was needed "to attract soldiers to the CGT by fair means or foul." The Employers' Federation of Coppersmiths from Lyon and Roubaix-Tourcoing supported this impulse, and according to a comprehensive report from December 1912, several *bourses* and *syndicats* also created funds. As with the Employers' Federation of Precision Instrument Workers, this meant that they regularly sent a small sum, usually accompanied by a letter of support, to their coworkers in the caserne. The Union Syndicale du Bronze went further, advocating the creation of a "resistance fund to support insubordinates" in France and abroad. The congress of the Fédération des Bourses du Travail held a year later (1901) did the same, certain confirmation of the need that antimilitarists attached to the Sou du Soldat.[47]

It was at this early juncture that Georges Yvetot, "the most fiery of the anti-militarists running the CGT," became involved. In 1902 he sent five hundred circulars to each Bourse du Travail (fifty thousand in all) with a cover letter entreating local leaders to distribute them to soldiers by whatever means possible.[48] The circular itself towed a familiar line, reminding soldiers that "above all you are men" and can find "truly sincere and fraternal affection" at the *bourse*. He criticized military life insofar as its typical escapes were to "thought-destroying libations."[49]

But this outwardly tame (although numerically teeming) circular did not escape the attention of the war minister, General André. In April 1902 he sent a "confidential" letter to the military governor of Paris requesting that "all propaganda be carefully excluded from the caserne, and that measures be taken to prohibit access to all documents or analogous printed matter that, in some form or another, would claim to exercise on the soldier an action independent of or not controlled by military authorities."[50] Its bureaucratic language aside, the letter created quite a stir. The journals *L'Aurore, La Lanterne, Le Petit Sou,* and *La Voix du Peuple* mocked "le brave général André," who kept leftist propaganda outside the caserne in order to keep the slaughter machines running.[51] "But it is in vain that governments strive to separate soldiers from the rest of the nation by the highest wall of China."[52] Yvetot himself countered the general in a bold, open letter: "You know better than us, M. André, that the caserne is the school of Crime and Vice, since you are a professional."[53]

The debate that ensued and, for the forces of the Left, succeeded in the Chamber of Deputies, painted André's desire to prevent the *bourses* from contacting soldiers as a double standard. The Catholic Church, after all, had been doing it for years. This was the position adopted by the socialist deputy M. Dejeante, who viewed the Catholic circles as "the most ardent of all the Republic's enemies" due to their traditionally right-wing views. At the height of an anticlerical debate that would lead in two years to the separation of church and state, it was a persuasive argument. Yet Dejeante went further, extending the double standard from a question of moral equivalence to one of social justice. It was the bourgeoisie, he insisted, who ranted against the Republic and threatened its institutions, while the workers and peasants served three full years in the military. What constitutes "antimilitarism" if it did not undermine their commitment to defend the *patrie?* Dejeante's closing is one of the most emphatic statements I found on what citizenship might mean to those who felt most at odds with their own government: "We are antimilitarists first because [we are] workers; we are antimilitarists because [we are] socialists; we are antimilitarists because [we are] republicans; and finally because we are French."[54]

This stirring defense of syndicalism, delivered by a socialist in the name of basic civil rights, came none too soon, as the CGT was poised to enter a new, more radical phase in its nascent antimilitarist campaign. The threat of the Sou du Soldat's suspension was a jolt that called for more coordinated action. After debating a proposition from the Union des Syndicats de la Seine to institute a central Sou du Soldat Fund (as opposed to leaving it to the initiatives of local *bourses*), delegates to the tenth congress of the Bourses du Travail (in Algiers on September 15–18, 1902) decided instead to draft an antimilitarist brochure that they could distribute to the conscripts. Yvetot got the job of writing the *Nouveau manuel du soldat* (*New Soldier's Manual*) and the anarchist-cum-syndicalist took full advantage of his task.[55]

What Yvetot did single-handedly with the *Nouveau manuel* was to raise the antimilitarist tenets of the CGT to a higher, more seditious level, without alienating the organization from its national identity and values. In the first section of the three-part brochure, he attacks "this magic word *la Patrie*. For it is one of the words that have most made human blood run. How many dupes this word has made! How many victims!" How too, he marvels, is the word fixed into our conscience and culture from an early age. Yvetot blames teachers, parents, even history texts for cultivating brutal instincts and glorifying war at the expense of nobler, universal ideals such as love for humanity and learning.[56]

Yet rather than do away with patriotism, Yvetot decides to teach young workers its true and purest form. Here he makes the important distinction between love of one's country, of which he approves, and love of the *patrie*, of which he emphatically does not. The closest thing we get to a definition of *patrie* is that it is akin to a religion—twice he calls it a "stupid religion"—that exists only to keep workers' material life miserable and soldiers enslaved. Its essence is that of a ruse or empty promise that ensures that class differences and military ideals remain in place. As Becker points out, this definition is not simply a reiteration of Marx's "the worker has no *patrie*," or the notion that under capitalism the bourgeoisie alone define and profit from the country.[57] The word "bourgeois" does not even appear in the first section of the *manuel*. Rather, Yvetot's insistence that the nation's producers love their country derives from his belief that the *patrie* exists wherever one finds "the peasant who labors, the worker who manufactures, the inventor, the savant, the artist who creates material well being," and the revolutionary who resists social injustice. "The *patrie* is ourselves or it is nothing at all."[58]

Yvetot's abiding attention to patriotism, we learn, is because militarism is its "most awful consequence." Defining it as the overblown cult of the army ("this invincible force against us"), he treats militarism as a form of servitude. Contrary to popular celebrations of military life, the caserne serves no end but to transform men into "passive brutes," unthinking "machines to obey . . . the most idiotic, the most contradictory, the most immoral, the most crude orders." Isolated from the real world in a "sanctuary" of their own, officers form "a veritable caste of brutes," obstructing the progress of civilization while "the bestial force is carefully maintained, idealized and many-colored, gilded and decorated" (a reference to military dress and honors). Nothing but "moral cowardice, the habit of surrendering oneself, and trembling," can result from this "apprenticeship of brutality and vulgarity" that constitutes the military regime.[59]

So what can be done? After dismissing the Hague conference and the creation of a citizen's militia as so many liberal, bourgeois schemes, Yvetot settles on two solutions—education and consciousness—that amount to one program: self-reliance. In a section of the *manuel* titled "Counsel to the Conscripts" he advises: "If you think you cannot stand the humiliations, the insults, the imbecilities, the punishments, and all the depravities that await you at the caserne: Desert!" Yet he does not dissuade men who, for whatever reason, decide to go to the regiment. Instead Yvetot encourages them to "try your best to remain a man. Overcome your disgusts. . . . Out of the school of crime make a school of revolt." The crucial point here is that whatever the ultimate, *individual* choice, the CGT would support it. The *manuel*'s chief message was thus a contingent one, accepting the duties of citizenship up to the point of respecting personal moral responsibility.[60]

When the French government passed a law on March 21, 1884, that permitted the re-formation of workers' unions, it never envisioned a *Nouveau manuel du soldat*. But less than twenty years after the first legal *syndicat* came into existence, 20,000 first-run copies of a brochure that critiqued patriotism, accepted desertion, and defamed the army were being run off the presses of the Fédération des Bourses du Travail. Nine editions of 10,000 copies and five of 15,000 soon followed, quickly reaching an impressive 185,000 copies in print. The author, a ranking member of the CGT, was acquitted in December 1903 for provocations to desertion and disobedience, ensuring "an inexhaustible mine of citations for anyone who wanted to illustrate the antimilitarism of the CGT."[61] Many did, and the *manuel* remained an epicenter of accusation right up to the war.

By 1905, few doubted that the CGT had overstepped the "strictly determined role" assigned to it in 1884.[62] In congress after congress, poster after poster, and article after article, antimilitarism was the "order of the day," the headline story right alongside the organization's circumscribed economic tasks. In the midst of the first Moroccan crisis, the Bourse du Travail of Bourges, "Mecca of the pacifist combat," put the following question to its counterparts: "At the declaration of war, will you respond by the revolutionary general strike? . . . We are counting on a unanimous, affirmative response." A year later, the Amiens congress (October 8–15, 1906) affirmed, albeit grudgingly, Yvetot's resolution that "the antimilitarist and antipatriotic propaganda should become still more intense and audacious." The tenor would escalate with congresses in Marseille (1908) and Toulouse (1910), and in response to further threats of war. But it was essentially from 1900 to 1906 that French syndicalism made antimilitarism an integral part of its overall program for greater social justice.[63]

Gustave Hervé and the Socialists

For French socialists, who did not unify into a single political party until 1905, the formation of a coherent antimilitarist ideology and strategy posed different problems. Socialists had long defined themselves as antimilitarists because of their internationalism, and war inevitably meant two workers on either end of a bayonet. They thus favored coordinated, working-class action, both nationally and internationally, to ensure peace. Because they also all agreed that permanent armies were the most serious menace to peace, socialists uniformly advocated the armament of the people, or *contre-armée*, be it a citizens' militia or the armed insurrection.[64]

Apart from these points of accord, deep ideological rifts between French socialists hindered their progress on many issues, including antimilitarism. One of the most important fractures occurred in 1899, when the socialist deputy Alexandre Millerand accepted a post in Waldeck-Rousseau's ministry. At issue was whether a socialist could serve in a capitalist government and still be loyal to his party's founding principles. Guesdists and Allemanists thought not and argued adamantly. Their defeat was a powerful blow from which they never fully recovered.

At the end of the century socialists seemed also to be losing influence over the left-wing radicals and Radical-Socialists on their immediate right in the Chamber of Deputies. In November 1899 Alexandre Zevaes, the democratic socialist and historian of 1848, introduced legislation to prohibit the use of troops to suppress strikes. Once firm champions of labor's right to strike, only nineteen Radical-Socialists voted for the measure. Thus while the Millerand crisis alienated the far Left, antimilitarism and antipatriotism on the far Left was prompting the disaffection of former allies on the Right (not to mention the disfavor of moderate socialists in between). In addition, the growing radicalism of the CGT, in particular its rejection of parliamentary politics, pushed socialists in both directions. So, although antimilitarism was well entrenched doctrinally, implementing policies without sacrificing popularity did not seem to be getting easier.[65]

One action socialists did agree on was the need to form antimilitarists from an early age. In the same year that the Fédération des Bourses established the Sou du Soldat, the Paris congress of the Second International resolved "that the socialist parties apply themselves everywhere to educate and organize youth in view of the struggle against militarism, and that they accomplish this task with greatest energy."[66] Although nothing on the order of a Sou du Soldat was implemented, numerous sections of socialist youth (Jeunesses Socialistes) began transforming themselves into antimilitarist cells. Directly affected by the annual recruitment, these youth brought a degree of idealism and zeal to antimilitarism that made it, in the words of Yolande Cohen, their "preferential form of political action."[67]

As locally organized outlets for agitation, the youth sections brought the most radical antimilitarist themes to larger and more remote areas. A propaganda barrage by six sections in the Saône-et-Loire, for example, helped prevent soldiers from using their arms against striking miners in Creusot and Montceau-les-Mines in July 1900. In recognition of this successfully managed outcome, the socialist youth created their own journal, *Le Drapeau Rouge*—sure proof of the seriousness and permanence of their cause.[68]

Two other socialist/antimilitarist journals founded at the turn of the century were *Le Conscrit* and *Le Pioupiou de l'Yonne* ("The Tommy Atkins of the Yonne").[69] *Le Conscrit,* a Guesdist-Blanquist tract, functioned much like the special editions of *La Voix du Peuple,* imploring recruits to "reflect!," maintain self-respect, and not lose touch with their proletarian identity in the midst of the bourgeois stronghold. In keeping with this message, the journal condemned individual acts, such as desertion, on the grounds that they did not advance socialism, and railed against militarism as another abuse of the bourgeois-dominated *patrie:* "Understand, now, that national Defense is merely a word, a pretext by which the ruling classes use you, soldier, against yourself, peasant; against yourself, employee; against yourself, worker." By 1905, when *Le Conscrit* began aiming for a wider audience, this appeal was reaching one hundred thousand subscribers—socialist, syndicalist, and anarchist alike.[70]

Le Pioupiou de l'Yonne achieved neither the circulation nor the universality of *Le Conscrit,* although its notoriety would be far greater. Perhaps the journal's most interesting feature was its decentralized origins and inauspicious beginnings. The department of the Yonne, lying slightly more than seventy miles southeast of Paris, had a tradition of radical, Allemanist socialism traceable to 1848 and the Left's survival after 1851.[71] Given this history, it is surprising that the first issue of *Le Pioupiou,* which appeared in 1900 as a supplement for the local *Travailleur Socialiste,* stuck to traditional antimilitarist themes. Yet from 1901 to 1905, the journal's staff were tried on four separate occasions for provoking soldiers to disobedience. These were not the first antimilitarist trials in the period and none led to a conviction, but they captivated a wide audience and increased sales markedly. The local *Le Pioupiou,* and in particular its fiery writer Gustave Hervé, would almost single-handedly radicalize antimilitarism in France.[72]

"Seldom has a minor historical figure stirred up so much passion among his countrymen as has the subject of this study." Thus begins the author of one of the few full-length treatments of Gustave Hervé.[73] This "minor historical figure" arrived at Sens in 1899 to teach history at the *lycée,* quickly established himself as the leading revolutionary socialist in the region, and went on to become one of the most prominent journalists of his day, a "star" of the Socialist Party and a long-standing member (1905–1911) of its Permanent Administrative Committee. Hervé even lent his name to a faction within the Section Française de l'Internationale Ouvrière (SFIO)—the Hervéists.[74]

From birth to death, Hervé's life was shaped by war. Born in 1871 during the Franco-Prussian War, he died shortly before the end of the Second World War, just weeks after Paris was liberated. In between, World War I would serve as a catalyst for his ideas and a turning point for his life. Even at home the shadow of war seemed to follow Hervé. His father had been a serviceman in the navy at Brest; his grandfather made emblems and flags for the officers stationed there. Ironically, these were the very kinds of symbols the native Breton would earn a national reputation for loathing.[75]

With the death of his father when he was ten, Hervé, the oldest of four siblings, assumed a position of responsibility in his modest family. Fortunately for his overburdened peasant mother, he possessed both the intelligence and devotion necessary for the task. A brilliant if sometimes rebellious student, Hervé took his diploma at age eighteen, gaining admission to the prestigious Lycée Henri-IV in Paris. Yet family concerns forced him to leave school and seek work, and over the next several years Hervé supervised several *lycées* in Brittany. The work was not much, but he could support his family and, "with the pigheaded perseverance of a Breton," find time to prepare for the *agrégation* in history, which he obtained in 1897. Hervé first taught in Rodez, where his ardent Dreyfusard sympathies clashed with the conservative politics of his colleagues and led him to transfer to the Norman town of Alençon (Orne). This move was just the beginning of a long career of public scrutiny.[76]

When Hervé arrived in Sens in 1899 after exchanging posts with another professor, he immediately threw himself into its revolutionary socialist milieu. Although he joined Jaurès's Parti Socialiste Français, Hervé became affiliated with the Allemanist journal *Le Travailleur Socialiste de l'Yonne* almost on arrival. By November 1900 he had published his first controversial article, a parody of a mass to be given by the local archbishop during the annual conscript recruitment. Into the mouth of the archbishop, Hervé inserted the heresies of the antimilitarist: "In truth, I tell you that the profession of the soldier, the profession of a murderer of men, is incompatible with the nature of Christianity." During the heated debate that ensued in *Le Travailleur* and *Le Croix de l'Yonne,* Hervé had the distinct advantage of anonymity. In previous months he had taken to signing his articles "Un Sans-Patrie," a direct affront to anti-Dreyfusards who maliciously applied the term to their enemies.[77]

It was not long before the archbishop came to suspect Hervé as his adversary, but the circumstances that exposed the Sans-Patrie also helped to legitimize him. In early 1901, as Hervé's offenses toward the military and exchanges with the archbishop continued to pour forth from the *Le Tra-*

vailleur and *Le Pioupiou*, War Minister André, via the minister of public education, ordered the college of Sens to question their recent addition to the history department. Hervé refused to be interrogated, was immediately suspended, and only caved in when the government moved to indict the director, printer, and an editor at *Le Pioupiou* for an article in which Hervé had, among other things, ridiculed military parades as "puppet exercises."[78] In a letter to the public prosecutor of Auxerre (capital of the Yonne), he revealed himself as the Sans-Patrie and requested to be tried with the others. By now Hervé's name had spread to Paris, and Aristide Briand, editor of *La Lanterne* and a future interior, justice, and foreign minister, agreed to represent him.[79] Before he could do so, however, the Sans-Patrie would again live up to his name.[80]

Indeed before the trial even got underway, Hervé captivated the French public with an article more audacious than the one that had earned him the indictment in the first place. The ominous occasion was the anniversary of Napoleon's victory at Wagram, which Hervé learned was to be fêted by the regiment at Auxerre. In an article innocuously titled "The Anniversary of Wagram," the Sans-Patrie waxed indignant that this "folly of murder," completely foreign to the spirit of 1792, could actually be cause for celebration. The history professor cited Marbot's *Mémoires* and Thiers's *Histoire* on the carnage that followed the battle, then suggested a "truly worthy and symbolic" way to commemorate it:

> As long as there are barracks for the edification and moralization of the soldiers of our democracy, then in order to dishonor militarism and war of conquest in their eyes, I would like all the filth and all the horse dung of the barracks to be gathered in the main courtyard of the quarters and, solemnly in the presence of all the troops in their best uniform, at the sound of military music, the colonel, wearing his large plume, to arrive there and plant the flag of the regiment.[81]

Hervé probably never anticipated the fury unleashed by this passage; a fury he would never fully live down yet always maintain was based on a misunderstanding. For anyone who read the entire article, Hervé wrote two weeks later, it was clear that the flag he dragged through the dung heap was not "the national flag of the Republic, the flag of Valmy," but rather "the flag of a crowned ruffian [Napoleon], the flag of Wagram, the flag symbolizing militarism and wars of conquest." Hervé defended himself in numerous articles over many years, but the Sans-Patrie was now also the "man of the dung heap," a label that would dog him for the rest of his life.[82]

The press was out in force and the crowd at the Auxerre courthouse was controlled by armed police when the November 1901 trial at the Court of Assizes opened. Inside, the day belonged to Hervé, who responded to the judge's questions with exclamations of "Long live universal peace! Down with war! Rather than fire on your brothers during a strike, raise your rifle butts in the air!" In his defense, fellow Breton Briand spoke of Hervé as a friend with whose ideas he was in complete sympathy, as "a man in whom the spirit of this French Revolution is carried on." So powerful was his argument that the jury, after acquitting all the accused, congratulated the staff of *Le Travailleur* and contributed their jurors' compensation to the next issue of *Le Pioupiou*.[83] "Victory" could not convey the significance of the moment for Hervé, who lost his teaching post but gained a national reputation. Charles Péguy would devote an entire issue of *Cahiers de la Quinzaine* to the Sans-Patrie, who used the widely read intellectual journal to contemplate his jobless future.[84] In a sense, however, his role had just been determined.

Over the next several years Hervé became, in the words of one historian, a "traveling salesman of socialism," spreading his antimilitarism into the countryside and writing for *Le Pioupiou, Le Travailleur Socialiste*, and, up to May 1903, *L'Action*.[85] His distaste for parliamentary politics prompted him to refuse several bids for a seat in the Chamber of Deputies, but it was essentially in this period that he prepared for the political entanglements ahead. For now Hervé studied law and became more active in Jaurès's party. In March 1902 this brought him to the fourth congress of the Parti Socialiste Français at Tours. There he reined in his extremist impulses, calling for the renunciation of colonial wars and wars of revenge, the resolution of conflicts by arbitration, and vowing that socialists "would participate in the defense of the Republic in case of aggression from any country."[86] Compared to his articles, these were curiously conservative positions. One may discern a bit of the politician in the early career of the Sans-Patrie.

Yet ultimately Hervé's public persona would be shaped more by controversy than by compromise. When he wrote a history text in 1903 for "all those who are convinced of the need to react energetically against the militarist and nationalist poisoning of the people by history texts," the only energetic reaction it garnered came in the form of the traditionally republican French school system. The debate that ensued in the Chamber of Deputies and led to the book's being banned pending modifications also divided socialists and distanced Jaurès and Briand from their colleague.[87]

Once the party had been unified, Hervé, despite sitting on the "unity" commission in 1904–1905, probably did more to disunite the Parti Socialiste

Unifié than anyone else. Before the elation had even worn off, he brought dissension into the ranks during a large public meeting at Tivoli Vauxhall in Paris, when he berated his fellow socialists for their patriotic and reformist tendencies and called for a reservist strike in the case of war, without regard as to whether France was the attacker or the attacked. Criticized harshly by Jaurès and Viviani for reviving a dead issue (recall here Nieuwenhuis's repudiation at Brussels in 1891) and for giving the young party a bad image, Hervé refused to moderate his outbursts.[88] At the Limoges party congress (1906), in *Le Pioupiou* and in his new journal *La Guerre Sociale,* and in his book *Leur Patrie (Their Country,* 1906), he urged French socialists back to their revolutionary "Blanquist" roots, while adding yet another memorable aphorism to his public aura: *Plutôt l'insurrection que la guerre*—rather the insurrection than war!

"Hervéism" essentially derived from its namesake's frustration with the Socialist Party for devolving into a bastion of politics and parliamentarism. Just as he had been an unbending critic of "Millerandism," Hervé saw antimilitarism as a means to regenerate a "revolutionary" socialist movement and free it of bourgeois political corruption. This involved two main tenets: the rejection of "their" patriotism, and a commitment to the working-class insurrection in the case of war. In *Leur patrie,* Hervé gave the best exposition to date of his antimilitarism and its relevance to the survival of French socialism.

The principal argument of *Leur patrie* is that patriotism and socialism are incompatible. Hervé did not dispute the existence of *patries* outside the imaginations of the privileged classes, but like Yvetot's *Nouveau manuel du soldat* and Paul Lafargue's *Le Patriotisme de la bourgeoisie,* he essentially saw them as being in the wrong hands.[89] Moreover, although Hervé admitted *patries* were as real "as the rain of Limoges," he protested the notion that there were fundamental differences *between* them that made them worth dying for.[90] In the chapter titled "Almost All *Patries* Are Alike," Hervé argues that but for a few uncivilized exceptions such as the Ottoman Empire and Russia, all European countries are essentially the same. What is ubiquitous, what is the source of his pronouncement that he would be equally at home in Germany, Italy, England, or America, is social inequality: "this shameful exploitation of a nation by a privileged class."[91]

In language similar to Yvetot's, Hervé explains how it is that patriotism has indoctrinated the people and enabled the ruling classes to maintain power. He likens it to a religion and refers to the "cult of the flag." Chapters on "the patriotic lesson in the family" and "patriotic lies" systematically refute such "classic definitions" of *patrie* as "the land of my ancestors" and "the land where they speak our language." The church, theater, literature, and the press are accused of promulgating the illusion that France is of a superior mettle. Thus it is through "poisoning that begins in the cradle that [the bourgeoisie] succeed in impressing upon those poor wretches who possess nothing, and for whom the *patrie* is a step-mother, that they should go die for her joyously." Turning the traditional mother/family image of the *patrie* into a more distant and stereotypically evil stepmother, Hervé, like Yvetot, was not denying that the working classes were part of the nation, only that, in its present, exploitative form, they could feel little kinship, loyalty, or even love toward her.[92]

The antipatriotism of Gustave Hervé, like the issue resulting from the "flag in the dung heap" article, was less radical than it appeared. In large part, his expression of antipatriotism was a directed effort to steer socialism onto a path of decisiveness and action. In *Leur patrie* and elsewhere, Hervé condemned his colleagues for becoming "too soft," too focused on fundraising and vote winning, and increasingly out of touch with *l'esprit révolutionnaire*.[93] The net result, he feared, was a party without principles: "Powerless to reconcile patriotism and internationalism, the military obligation of socialists towards their *patrie* with their revolutionary duty, the international Socialist party . . . has preferred to avoid the problem."[94]

Hervé, by contrast, had worked out his own plan for war, starting with sabotage of the mobilization by reservists and followed by desertion of socialists in the military and open, working-class insurrection while the army was at the front. The drawbacks and merits of this plan can be discussed later. The point is that Hervé's call for socialist revolution at the outbreak of war was a strategy he wanted the entire party to implement, not merely scoff at as anarchist extremism on the socialist fringe. Anything less was a betrayal of what he and, he believed, the socialist movement had always stood for: "To declare that social Revolution is not feasible in the case of war, which is to say at the only moment it has a chance to succeed, is to say that one is opposed to all social Revolution, that one is purely reformist, [and] that one regards the ballot box as the only means of realizing socialism."[95]

At the end of *Leur patrie* Hervé took account of the spread of antimilitarism since the beginning of the century. He lauded *Le Conscrit* for its penetration of working-class districts and "flatly anti-patriotic" ethos;[96] praised Yvetot's *Nouveau manuel du soldat* and insisted that censorship had only facilitated its diffusion; and did not forget to thank the war minister for the free publicity he had given *Le Pioupiou*. Four trials in three years had, to

Hervé's mind, helped increase circulation from a first run of five thousand to the current printing of twenty thousand, making his journal the driving force behind the Yonne's antimilitarism.[97] Yet when it came to actual readiness for war, the Sans-Patrie was less optimistic: "We will moan, we will curse the government, we will shake fists at it . . . but we will march."[98]

◆ ◆ ◆

From mid-April to July 1900, Le Libertaire ran a series on antimilitarism that concluded with the article "Contre le sabre" (Against the Saber). Because this piece could add little to the litany of examples of military excess that had occupied the previous months, it reserved its criticisms for the antimilitarists themselves:

> Apart from a few isolated individuals who fight on their own account, there is nothing, no serious group, no means of action. . . . Why is there not an antimilitarist group concerned with this propaganda? Why not create an antimilitarist library, where each week we could have interesting discussions . . . where we could become involved in the education of future soldiers? Above all, why do we not have our own journal, a purely antimilitarist journal . . . leading an active campaign against the saber, ruthlessly denouncing the crimes and horrors that our admirable army conceals. . . . It is absolutely essential that the comrades organize themselves, group themselves, so that the antimilitarist propaganda can bear fruit.[99]

It should be clear from this chapter that in the first years of the new century antimilitarism overcame many of the organizational problems bemoaned in this article. Anarchists, many from Le Libertaire itself, had succeeded in forming a "group," the AIA, that placed antimilitarism above economic and political concerns and, it was hoped, would end the internecine squabbling that confined anarchists to the outskirts of working-class politics. Syndicalists had entered the fray with an "antimilitarist library" in the guise of the local bourses and their links to the caserne through the Sou du Soldat. And in December 1906 Hervé added to the growing list of antimilitarist publications with the weekly La Guerre Sociale, destined to become the most important journal of its kind in the prewar years. Starting with an estimable circulation of 15,000, the journal's provocative style carried it to 55,000 by 1910, with eventual highs of 60,000 to 70,000—enough to appear in a prewar café scene in François Truffaut's 1961 film classic Jules and Jim. By comparison, Jaurès's L'Humanité, a daily, was printing 72,000 copies, while La Voix du Peuple, Les

Temps Nouveaux, Le Libertaire, and *L'Anarchie* combined for just 31,500.[100] Finally, it was in this period that antimilitarism got impetus from the upper echelons—Hervé and Yvetot built their reputations as committed antimilitarists operating from important posts in respected leftist milieus.

Although antimilitarism would never achieve the structure of a genuine movement, by 1906 it clearly had the semblance of one: dedicated leaders, reasonable strategies, and, within the framework of working-class issues, its own ideological justifications for action. According to a survey taken by Hubert Lagardelle in 1905, it also had the backing of most syndicalist leaders. Lagardelle interviewed forty-one syndicalists on their feelings about the *patrie*. For our purposes, the most interesting question was the third: Does working-class internationalism mix with antimilitarism and antipatriotism? Almost unanimously syndicalist leaders asserted, as did R. Lenoir, secretary of the Fédération des Syndicats d'Ouvriers Mouleurs (casters), that "working-class internationalism would be but a fiction, if it did not have antimilitarism as a corollary."[101]

Another interesting outcome of the survey was that several respondents declared their solidarity with Hervé, particularly in their answer to the question: What do you think of the general military strike? Most respondents favored "this marvelous idea of combat," as J. Cazaux of the Comité Fédéral de la Fédération des Travailleurs de l'Alimentation wrote. Some, such as Léon Torton of the Rouen Bourse du Travail, even expressed support for Hervé's general strike in the case of war. These positions probably should not come as a surprise. If revolutionary syndicalism held the Sorelian general strike as unassailable doctrine, then Hervé's strategy was not as radical as it appeared. At least on the surface there were important ideological and strategical commonalities between syndicalists and Hervéists, just as there were with AIA anarchists. This study has not yet examined the more moderate currents of antimilitarism within the socialist and syndicalist milieus. Nor has it treated independent positions on questions such as desertion and sabotage. But the individuals and groups that made the most noise and did the most to bring antimilitarism to the forefront of working-class politics tended to agree on the strategy of a general strike or insurrection in the case of war, and the ideology of antipatriotism as long as the Republic did not feel like their *patrie*.[102]

◆ ◆ ◆

France came perilously close to war in 1905. German Emperor Wilhelm II's state visit to Morocco, the last contested territory in North Africa, set off a diplomatic crisis that brought down Delcassé and created a tense standoff in Europe. Charles Péguy bought boots and thick woolen socks in anticipation of mobilization.[103] And the CGT launched the poster *guerre à la guerre!* (war on war!), proclaiming the proletariat's refusal, in France *and* Germany, to go to war.[104]

What would have happened if France *had* gone to war against Germany in 1905? According to D. W. Brogan, it probably would have been "deeply unpopular and certainly disastrous."[105] The Dreyfus Affair, the church-state controversy, and the two-year service law (1905) had taken a heavy toll on army morale and divided the nation against herself.[106] On the other hand, there were the diplomatic achievements of the past years, notably the detachment of Italy from the Triple Alliance in 1902 (eliminating the strategic problem of having to fight in both Savoy and Lorraine) and the Entente Cordiale with Britain in 1904. The Coup de Tanger, ironically enough, did an additional service to France of strengthening confidence in her British ally and confirming her likely German enemy.[107]

Could antimilitarist leaders have engineered an effective resistance to war in 1905? Although they too had made impressive strides since the beginning of the century, there is no evidence of any coherent plan for the outbreak of war. The AIA was new and untested, the socialists had only just united, and the CGT, which had probably come the furthest the fastest in terms of propaganda, had done nothing in the way of instructing local *bourses* on how to respond to a mobilization. Writing in the midst of the Algeciras conference to resolve the Moroccan crisis, Hervé complained about this very lack of preparation: "We make speeches, again speeches, always speeches. And if war broke out tomorrow, we would be distraught, we would not know what to do."[108]

3. ENEMIES AND ALLIES

On the morning of October 7, 1905, Parisians awoke to find their city deluged with antimilitarist *affiches* bearing the stamp of the AIA and the signatures of thirty-one members of its "national committee." Like much of the antimilitarist propaganda that preceded it, these particular *affiches* appeared on the eve of the annual departure of conscripts for the caserne. As with earlier propaganda too, they appealed to the young men in language that turned the conventional mother/family image of the *patrie* on its head, imploring them to embrace their true family of workers rather than the illegitimate one of the bourgeoisie: "Workers, you must commit yourselves above all to the working class. The bourgeois *patrie* that claims years of servitude from you and that demands, if necessary, the sacrifice of your life, has been nothing but a step-mother for you. You owe her neither devotion nor obedience."[1]

By now such direct, unabashed language would have been familiar to readers of *Le Conscrit* or *Le Pioupiou,* and probably merited no more than a report from local police. What followed, however, was considerably more audacious than the propaganda that typically issued from these presses:

> When you are commanded to fire your guns at your destitute brothers [during a strike]—like what happened at Chalon, Martinique, and Limoges—workers, soldiers of tomorrow, you will not hesitate; you will obey. You will shoot, but not at your Comrades. You will fire on the decorated ruffian who dares to give you such orders.

When you are sent to the border to defend the capitalist safe box against workers as exploited as you yourselves are; you will not march. All war is criminal. When mobilization is ordered, you will respond with an immediate strike and insurrection.[2]

With threats such as these, police wasted little time tearing down the *affiche rouge,* as it became known, and in the process caught several people in the act of putting it up. Émile Coulais of the café waiters union, for one, was seized as he pasted the *affiche* to a fence protecting the building site of the Paris Métro on the boulevard Magenta.[3] Judicial action came no less swiftly. The commissaires aux délégations judiciaires Martin and Berthelot ordered an immediate search of the offices of *Le Libertaire* and the AIA presses, where they confiscated three hundred *affiches* (many believed some ten thousand had been sent to the provinces). Twenty-eight signers of "the squalid lampoon," as the nationalist *L'Éclair* called it, were indicted for "provocation to murder and disobedience addressed to military servicemen." A hearing took place the following week, and by year's end twenty-six of the signers had been sentenced to between six months and four years of prison. Hervé and Yvetot received the harshest penalties, with four and three years respectively. The reaction of police and judicial officials, in sum, was quick, coordinated, unexpectedly severe, and impressively effective.[4]

This chapter is an examination of the ways in which enemies of antimilitarism—government, military authorities, and the conservative press—viewed and responded to the propaganda. It is a question that necessarily courses through the entire period addressed in this study, but became particularly acute around 1905. The improved organization of the Left, a marked increase in strikes, and the threat of war over Morocco heightened worries about antimilitarism as a serious threat to both internal and external security.[5] Further, the revolution in Russia that year, and the 1907 revolts in the Midi, indicated the capacity of revolutionary ideas to infiltrate both the working classes and military castes.

One determinant for perceptions of the Left was how antimilitarists actually interpreted and portrayed themselves. Thus an underlying theme here pertains to the ways in which leftist leaders construed their own position and achievements within the larger borderless movement they sought to construct. The signers of the *affiche rouge* clearly saw themselves as victims of a state system that did not hesitate to maintain order at the cost of workers' lives. Understandably resentful over this injustice, they simply reversed the morality of the state by calling on worker-soldiers to fire back at their commanding officers. Yet not everyone accepted this logic. Many, such as Jean Jaurès, preferred the morality of nonviolence (that is, urging the soldiers not to fire at all) to that of an eye-for-an-eye. How might the antimilitarist Left overcome these differences to present authorities with what appeared to be a unified, monolithic force that had to be stopped before the outbreak of war? The following pages are largely devoted to perceptions of antimilitarism, and how these perceptions shaped the ideas and actions of leftist enemies and allies alike.

As we have already seen, the *affiche rouge* affair was not the first governmental crackdown on antimilitarist propaganda. What made this particular *affiche* worthy of such a heavy-handed reaction? Under the press law of 1881, which was modified on July 28, 1894, as the infamous anti-anarchist *lois scélérates* (villainous laws), authorities saw clear evidence of anarchist intrigue in an *affiche* that incited soldiers to disobey their officers.[6] Moreover, it was the product of an organization—the AIA—with the sole stated purpose to promote and coordinate antimilitarist activity throughout the nation. Besides the thirty-one names on the *affiche,* there were listed all the sections in Paris, its *banlieue,* and numerous French cities, towns, and bourgs that adhered to the AIA and, in theory, supported its antimilitarism.[7]

Yet in order to make sense of the mindset that led to the convictions, it is necessary to delve into the trial itself. How did the antimilitarists present their arguments? How did the prosecution understand its position? What did the press have to say? This trial essentially represented a clash of world views; not merely socialist versus capitalist, but one that portrayed itself as the defender of human decency and civil rights versus the characteristically cold pragmatism of national security interests and power politics.

In the case of the defendants, one of the most salient features of the affair was the apparent depth of their support. As early as October 13 *L'Aurore* published a protest from the Socialist Party against the application of the *lois scélérates* to *affiche rouge* signers.[8] During the trial, the socialist deputy Dejeante, who three years earlier had defended the Sou du Soldat, argued that the prosecution was more politically motivated than driven by any realistic assessment of antimilitarist strength. Another deputy called the accusation an infringement on the basic right of individual opinion.[9]

Even that most moderate of forces in the Socialist Party, Jean Jaurès, defended the signers despite the fact that the language of the *affiche* was blatantly contrary to his own humanitarian principles. For Jaurès the defendants deserved support and even praise because they had dared to confront a crucial, undiminished issue: the use of troops to suppress strikes. As the socialist leader stated repeatedly, he could never advocate that soldiers turn their guns on their commanding officers. Instead he favored their refusal to obey the immoral order altogether. Could judicial authorities possibly try soldiers who *avoided* bloodshed, be it of striking workers *or* of officers? For Jaurès the only sensible place to draw the line was at murder itself, which is how he was able to set aside his glaring ideological differences with the defendants and to speak on their behalf: "If the *affiche* was wrong to place governmental responsibilities on the heads of individual officers, it has the merit of putting the question before society."[10]

This position was difficult to argue with. Between 1900 and 1902 state expenditures to control strikes had soared from 528,000 to 1,542,635 francs, and since late 1904 the number of strikes had been rising.[11] As recently as April 1905 soldiers of the 78th Infantry fired on a crowd of porcelain workers in Limoges, without having actually received an order to do so. One worker died and several were wounded in a scene that socialists there likened to Fourmies.[12] The AIA responded with a series of propaganda labels that read: "The last victory of the French Army: LIMOGES!"[13]

Sadly, it was not to be the last on the domestic front. In September 1905 government troops clashed with workers at Longwy; and conflict with miners in the Nord followed shortly. And when in 1906 the CGT intensified its campaign for the eight-hour day and began organizing civil servants, tensions with the government escalated: a worker died in Nantes in March 1907; in June the 139th Infantry killed five demonstrators in Narbonne, among them a young woman; two workers died at Raon-l'Étape (Meurthe et Moselle) in July; and six were killed at Draveil and Villeneuve-Saint-Georges the following year.[14]

Into this quagmire of labor unrest stepped Georges Clemenceau, first as minister of the interior in March 1906, then as prime minister (and his own interior minister) from October of that year. In neither capacity would he be known for sympathy toward popular protests. On May Day 1906, the date set for a nationwide demonstration for the eight-hour day, Clemenceau turned Paris into an armed camp, arresting CGT leaders Victor Griffuelhes and Pierre Monatte in advance to ensure that there would be no major disturbances. Designated "France's premier cop" for his zealous repression of strikes, Clemenceau summed up his attitude toward the CGT in response to a socialist-led attack against his cabinet's systematic pursuit of the *syndicats*: "I am the adversary, I would even say the enemy of the Confédération Générale du Travail as long as the association propagates doctrines of anarchy and antipatriotism."[15]

In his statement before the Court of Assizes during the *affiche rouge* trial, Urbain Gohier argued that what the judiciary interpreted as "provocation to murder" was for antimilitarists an "exhortation to legitimate defense."[16] Persistent military intervention in strikes demanded such an exhortation, or moral outcry. In fact as all the accused recognized, it was sometimes necessary to go to extremes to realize important changes and achieve fundamental rights. By late 1905 the violent repression of strikes had a long, tragic history in France, with no end in sight. It had become a collective grievance for working-class leaders, permitting them to cast ideological differences aside in favor of effective and immediate action.

In a speech so long-winded that the court assessor actually dozed off, Hervé capitalized on this conciliatory climate (as well as the immunity provided to him by the tribunal) to expound his ideas on patriotism and war,[17] ideas he insisted "form a solid body of doctrine that has, behind it, to support it, men who have lots of pluck and are not merely a handful . . . they are the opinion of *syndicats* who count in the thousands."[18] As evidence Hervé pointed to the previous day's procession of syndicalist leaders who, like Henriot of the Matchstick Makers Federation, testified that his workers, "in case of a European conflict, would try to incite a general soldiers' strike."[19] Nor did he hesitate to expound his antipatriotic ideas in front of a national audience: "We are strangers to your *patries,* and to everything that concerns them. . . . If we have to risk our skin, which like you is the only one we have, we will not risk it to defend your *patries* for you, but to establish the socialist *patrie* that already resides in our heads."[20] Broadening the specter of antimilitarism, Hervé painted socialists as the best rampart against Germany because of their humanitarian internationalism: "The kaiser is not afraid of your guns, but of the guns of the German Social Democrats, comrades who . . . make exactly the same propaganda we do."[21] Although he did not cite sources, it was intimidation rather than verification Hervé was after, as he admonished the jury: "Fear that a war does not come, one day soon perhaps, to cut down, in the flower of youth, the loved ones who are most dear to you. Fear that the mother of your son does not have to say to you one day: 'Poor wretch! There were men who, at the peril of their liberty, had found a means to prevent governments from unleashing war, from massacring my son, and it is you, miserable wretch, who threw them in prison!' "[22]

Hervé never believed, or at least he pretended not to believe, that the jury would break with its past record of forbearance and throw the "man of the dung heap" into prison. The irony is that his dogged confidence only encouraged jurors to prove him wrong. The show of unity and commitment antimilitarists made at the trial had, in a real sense, secured their fate. It did not, however, injure their spirit. As soon as the verdict was read, several of the condemned reiterated their devotion to the *affiche* and sarcastically thanked the court for unwittingly boosting their cause. In one of the most dramatic scenes of the week, Félicie Numietska, the only female signer and one of the acquitted, rose to denounce her "preferential treatment."[23]

If antimilitarists strove to show that a few years of jail for their most visible members would hardly damage the iceberg of support that reached down into the working classes, the prosecution showed itself unwilling to underestimate them. Attorney General Seligman contended that the AIA, thanks to the liberal political culture of France, was a powerful organization with the capacity to endanger the nation in the event of war. The fact that it had only taken root in countries that, in his opinion, were not likely to affect the outcome of a war with Germany anyway (England, Belgium, Switzerland, Spain), was hardly reassuring for the attorney general.[24] Thus he argued that if authorities chose to treat the *affiche* merely as a "crime of opinion" rather than the "provocation to murder and disobedience" that it was, they would be doing an injustice not only to the political freedoms of France, but to the fate of the *patrie*.[25] An article in the relatively moderate *Le Temps* captured these sentiments perfectly:

> If this delegation of *sans-patries* had left the Court of Assizes unscathed and head high, the Hervéist propaganda could henceforth have spread without hindrances and worries. Hervéism, with the stamp of the jury, would have become a political opinion like any other, perfectly legitimate and defensible. It would have been a veritable disaster, a moral capitulation the consequences of which would have been fatal for national security . . . a dreadful mourning for all good Frenchmen and for all the friends of France.[26]

I begin this chapter with the *affiche rouge* affair because it is typically interpreted as a crucial turning point for antimilitarism: the "decapitation" of the AIA as heralding its decline.[27] An October 1907 report concluded that after the sentences the AIA "was deprived of its leaders. The groups it had formed in the provinces were too exclusively libertarian, and thus not disciplined enough to continue the work of its founders."[28] Although the government amnestied the signers only six months into their sentences, the blow to the AIA had been irreversible, and by 1908 the French section had dissolved into the more narrowly defined anarchist group, the Fédération Révolutionnaire.[29]

Although the AIA's later breakup is undeniable, the cause and effect scenario described above was never so clear to antimilitarist leaders *or* to their adversaries. The importance of the *affiche rouge* affair was that it put a national, even international spotlight on French antimilitarism. An article in *Les Temps Nouveaux*, although predisposed toward the accused, best understood that the five days in court had

> really been five days of antimilitarist propaganda. The firm and energetic attitude of the accused impressed everyone and has really been a force, even for the most reactionary journals, to recognize that they have something to reckon with in such men, so self-important and convinced of their ideas. None of them weakened. It is good to have the truth from them, that they have, one after another, affirmed their hatred, common to all exploited people, of war and vile militarism.[30]

All major journals, both on the Right and on the Left, covered the trial.[31] The German and British embassies began to file reports on "the antimilitarist question," so to speak, in France. And as these reports and articles show well, the trial had been a showcase for Hervé.

Hervéism

In a dispatch to British Foreign Secretary Sir Edward Grey, Paris Ambassador Sir Francis Bertie endorsed a report from the military attaché referring to the *affiche rouge* affair as "the trial of M. Gustave Hervé and his twenty-seven associates."[32] Not only had Hervé's defense been the high point of the week, but, as Maurice Rotstein points out, the moral language of the *affiche* could have come right out of *Leur patrie*. The fact that Hervé received the harshest sentence, and even that the Paris bar revoked his (probationary) membership, only reinforced his position as France's leading antimilitarist.[33]

Hervé wasted little time in prison either. He planned *La Guerre Sociale* with Eugène Merle and Miguel Almereyda and proved his ideological commitment by rejecting an offer to run for the Chamber of Deputies (if he had been elected, his release would have been hastened). Once amnestied, Hervé was soon back in form. During a Fête des Conscrits in September 1906, he caused an uproar by trying to speak over the patriotic crowd (they recognized him immediately), and had to be detained for questioning by the police commissioner.[34] By the time of the Socialist Party's third congress at Limoges in November, Hervé was prevailing on his colleagues to confront the question of how to respond to war.

And confront it they did. Hervé's motion at Limoges was fervently attacked and praised, but hardly dismissed. It consisted of the following: If war should break out, do not go to the caserne ("into the lion's jaws"), but stay at home, incite a reservist strike, and "when the army is occupied at the front, rise and foment an insurrection."[35] "[A] position simple and clear, too simple perhaps," comments Becker.[36] Most delegates who opposed the motion agreed. Hervé's main rivals, older socialists such as Gérault-Richard and René Viviani, took the Sans-Patrie to task for assuming that an insurrection in France would prompt a parallel uprising in Germany. Few were willing to wait for war to learn otherwise. As Jaurès argued, this barefaced reliance on the SPD, despite its being the largest Marxist party in Europe, risked adding a foreign oppressor—the Germans—to the preexisting capitalist one.[37]

More forthright in his criticism of Hervé was Jules Guesde, a doctrinaire Marxist who was unwilling to wait for war in order to launch a revolution: "You preoccupy yourselves with what the proletariat will have to do in times of war; preoccupy yourself from now on with what it should do in times of peace!" At the party congress at Nancy (August 11–14, 1907), he made his priorities clear: "And I add that when you have made one socialist, it is worth more than making twenty antimilitarists à la Hervé . . . who only think not to put a bullet in their own skin for the defense of a nation that they have not had the courage to conquer." The dispute between Guesde and Hervé was really less about militarism than a particular conception of socialism, as Guesde insisted at Limoges: "I am as antimilitarist as you are. But it is only out of socialism that has developed, expanded, and become all powerful that we will bring militarism to an end. Everything that strays from true socialist propaganda strays from this goal." His own motion reflected this caution by relying on specific measures—reduction of military service, refusal of credits for war, the navy, and the colonies, and the substitution of a people's army for the professional one—to make socialism the means to antimilitarism, rather than vice versa.[38]

At Limoges, and ten months later in Nancy, the motions of Hervé and Guesde failed decisively. Jaurès's and Vaillant's imprecise although not ambivalent proposition to prevent war "by all means," including parliamentary intervention, public agitation, popular demonstrations, and, if necessary, a general strike and insurrection, won 153 votes at Limoges and 188 at Nancy to Hervé's 31 and 41 and Guesde's 98 and 123, respectively. In the end it appeared to be a massive defeat, even humiliation, for the Sans-Patrie. At its worst, he had to endure his colleagues' derisive laughter when, in a debate with Jaurès, he hurled, "Listen to me, Jaurès!" in response to which the socialist leader stood up, saluted, and said: "Speak, corporal!" Yet others have argued, and I agree, that all was far from lost for Hervé. Only if one forgets that it was he who was responsible for the vote in the first place does it really look like a major setback. As Becker reminds us, Hervé had "built around himself a group that counted."[39] What other socialist leader had been willing to go to jail for his convictions? With an international congress planned for Stuttgart a week after Nancy, it was Hervé more than anyone else in the party who had positioned himself as the lead delegate when it came to discussing what to do in the case of war.

It is both ironic and telling that Jaurès, whose proposition defeated Hervé's and who criticized the Sans-Patrie severely, was also the person most responsible for allowing the debate to proceed. Although he haughtily qualified Hervé's proposition as "nothing more obscure than the motion of Yonne peasants," he tolerated his colleague far better than did other influential party members such as Guesde.[40] As was the case during the *affiche rouge* trial, Jaurès supported Hervé's right to an opinion, always taking seriously the party's adherence to the principle of proportional representation. This was significant. As one of France's preeminent figures, Jaurès could be criticized but not ignored. That is why Charles Péguy, who turned against the Sans-Patrie after the *affiche rouge* affair, attacked Jaurès with nearly as much virulence as he had Hervé. In *Notre Jeunesse,* Péguy moaned about "this incredible perpetual capitulation of Jaurès before Hervé, this groveling, this indefatigable obsequiousness. . . . Without Jaurès, Hervé was nothing. By Jaurès, with Jaurès he became authorized, he became authentic, he became (like) a member, and secretly to many near him the most feared [member], of the government of the Republic."[41]

Péguy, who was well on his way to the Right by this time, may have exaggerated his critique of *le jauressisme,* but the decision to consider Hervé's ideas within the formal context of party congresses led to what certainly was the most significant source of friction in the French socialist movement. Even before the *affiche rouge* trial, the German embassy in Paris observed that Hervé's antimilitarist faction had "driven a wedge into the Socialist Party," and depicted Jaurès as "walking on eggshells in the Parliament and press."[42] The historian L. O. Frossard has argued that "the incendiary campaigns of Hervéism caused the most serious damage to the party." In 1906, a group of former *possibilistes* derided Hervé's theories as "monstrous, exceedingly anti-socialist, and harmful to party interests."[43] Guesde once warned that Hervéism was "more than a deviation, an insurmountable obstacle to the extension of the socialist movement; capable of setting back the hour of the social revolution."[44] As late as 1913, the socialist leader Albert Thomas would look back and realize that "the Socialist Party remained for everyone the party of disarmament, the party of insurrection and of treason."[45] It was, in some important ways, the party of Hervé.

When Hervé left jail in the summer of 1906, it was an ominous time for the French Left and for republicanism in general. Just days earlier, the High Court of Appeals had absolved Dreyfus of his conviction at the Rennes court-martial, and fully reinstated him in the army. With this final act of a long, drawn-out tragedy, one of the most divisive episodes in French history officially ended. It came, however, at a steep price. The Dreyfus Affair had forced the army to accept its complicity in the intrigues that convicted Dreyfus; and it had made the Republic, yet again, painfully aware of its shortcomings. Hervé profited from both of these consequences. Nothing about the Sans-Patrie would have led anyone to believe he was prepared to mend his ways. He remained, as ever, a menace to the army and an enemy of the "bourgeois capitalist state." Yet three and a half years before his sentence would have expired, the Third Republic gave Hervé another chance. Once he was out of jail, even the Paris bar returned the probationary status it had stripped from him during the trial. Why was he suddenly released when so many considered Hervé to be a danger to national defense in the event of war; when his last trial had been such a *scandale;* when he gave the Socialist Party a bad name and threatened it with schism? There is probably no adequate answer to this question other than the idealistic one being offered here. As with Dreyfus, Hervé helped keep the Republic honest by forcing it to uphold those traditional *libertés* at the cornerstone of democratic, civil society. Hervé would continue to flourish, in other words, as long as the system permitted him to. The *affiche rouge* merely clarified where those limits might lie.

Repression: The AIA and the CGT

Just as the *affiche rouge* convictions boosted the stature and confidence of Hervé, it also spawned a general upsurge in antimilitarist propaganda. A forty-one-page dossier listing major antimilitarist incidents from 1900 to 1909 indicates a significant rise around 1905–1906.[46] Without the benefit of statistics, the German military attaché in Paris reported on February 22, 1906: "The antimilitarists are always stepping more boldly forth in their agitation. Almost every day the newspapers announce posters that had to be removed by the police."[47]

One of the most conspicuous of these posters was launched by the vindictive Félicie Numietska and the remnants of the AIA (some three hundred in Paris according to one source[48]) to protest the sentencing of their comrades. Conceived in the same terms as the *affiche rouge* but endorsed by over two thousand names, this "appel aux soldats" presented authorities with a formidable problem: How could they prosecute so many people? On April 6 Numietska and about a hundred followers marched on the Palais de Justice to demand that, for the sake of fairness, they prosecute each signer.[49] As will be discussed in the next chapter, authorities investigated many of the names, although the incident caused them much embarrassment: How could they single out individual leaders when the rest were equally guilty? Above all, how could the government avoid turning this *affiche* into the same sort of publicity stunt its predecessor had been? The dilemma, in sum, was where to draw the line for the repression of potentially subversive propaganda. The *affiche rouge* had set a precedent.

Authorities faced a similar predicament in Lyon, Limoges, Toulon, Bordeaux, Lorient, Brest, and Auxerre, where protest *affiches* issued from local *syndicats* and socialist groups. To prove its solidarity with the convicts, the Fédération de la Chapellerie (hat industry) gathered five thousand signatures in eastern France.[50] The Fédération de l'Alimentation (food trade union) collected money to support the families of the accused and continued to pay Amedée Bousquet's wife the one-hundred-franc salary her now imprisoned husband normally drew as secretary-general.[51] In Cherbourg, the Solidarity Group for the Freedom of Opinion was formed in response to the verdict.[52] "Almost the entire working class has been outraged by the Paris decision," observed one official.[53]

The irony of this outward support for the accused was that it did little to broaden the AIA's support, and it likely encouraged governmental repression. In other words, although ordinary people across France defended the signers' right to profess their ideas on the army's unjust role in strikes, this did not necessarily make them hardened AIA antimilitarists, even if it did make the group appear more suspect. This helps explain, for example, the AIA's failure to organize a counterdemonstration for Bastille Day (July 14) 1906 because several potential leaders, including Jean Allemane and Marcel Sembat, simply feared arrest too much.[54] By September, with the accused out of jail, the AIA's acting head Numietska still faced having to reconfigure the national committee (which according to this report had never even existed).[55] Several proposals to reconstitute the AIA—from Hervé's journal *La Guerre Sociale*, which sought total direction, to creating an intermediate group between *Libertaire* anarchists and the CGT—were already on the table by late 1906.[56]

On the decline as an organization, but spurred by the effect of its moral crusade on a wider, working-class public, the AIA continued to support antimilitarist propaganda just as the government continued to repress it, although the indicted were typically acquitted or amnestied. In November 1906, in time for the fall departure of conscripts, the anarchist Victor "Luc" Méric published *Lettre à un conscrit* (*Letter to a Conscript*), eloquently recalling the antimilitarist themes of Yvetot's *Nouveau manuel du soldat* (although it ambiguously urged conscripts to "choose your victims" if ordered to shoot at strikers). The *manuel* itself had been acquitted, yet officials in Saint-Etienne (where the *Lettre à un conscrit* was first distributed) pursued the *Lettre* with alacrity. They investigated the alleged AIA printers (at 45 rue de Saintonge in Paris), filed a long report on Méric, and indicted an accomplice for distributing the brochure. In the process, police found no printer, only a kind of red herring for the AIA's image.[57]

The government's stepped-up repression became a cycle as seemingly endless as the Left's propaganda. Despite reports in 1907 from police and subprefects in the Dordogne that attested to the absence of antimilitarist groups there, when a dozen placards were found on the sidewalk in front of a post office in Bergerac, "rigorous surveillance" was ordered to trace their source.[58] In response to rumors that an antimilitarist group at the Gare St. Lazare in Paris was pushing soldiers to desert, the general commandant of the 20ème Corps d'Armée, Bailloud, notified the war minister, and before long the interior ministry was instructing the police prefect to exercise "close surveillance" in and around the station.[59] Even a small handbill that stated "the soldier is a man disguised in costume who practices collective murder," which did not appear to be associated with any one group, led to four arrests.[60] Based on the sheer number of documented antimilitarist incidents, it seems that public officials could have been more discerning. In an October 1907 report on the Bourses du Travail, the section "Antimilitarist Incidents since the 1st of May 1907" listed the nature, date, and place of only the "most important" of these; the section ran for seven pages.[61]

In April 1907 the AIA section in Paris's 10th arrondissement joined with the Union des Syndicats de la Seine in an *affiche* urging soldiers to disobey orders to intervene in strikes. Listing twenty-one adherents including the secretary of the union, Alexandre Aulagnier, the *affiche* said nothing about shooting at officers. In a sense it acted merely as a recruiting tool for antimilitarism: "You who are oppressed at the caserne, and who will be [oppressed] tomorrow at the factory, profit from the circumstances to enter the ranks of the rebels, and join us in the fight against the parasites and the rogues." The final line of the *affiche,* its most extreme, stated: "Comrades, no hesitation, rifle butts in the air and break ranks!" Yet despite this mild language relative to the *affiche rouge,* authorities indicted twelve of its signers. "They preached indiscipline. They will think about it in prison," read the matter-of-fact headline in the widely circulating newspaper *Le Matin.*[62]

A moving plea by defense attorney Jacques Bonzon before the Court of Assizes of the Seine saved the signers from this fate. Bonzon marshaled evidence from French history in arguing that the Joan of Arcs, Dantons, and Zolas who were persecuted in their own time are revered today as true patriots. "Everywhere the magistrates condemn the man they will glorify tomorrow," he declared in a tone reminiscent of Hervé's speech in the same courtroom a year and a half earlier. "It is not out of adherence to an idea that it is necessary to respect it," Bonzon continued, "it is by the eternal incertitude of what the future holds in store for disapproval and reprobation at the verdict returned against this idea." His peroration stressed that it was just this open, democratic future—a republican ideal that was perhaps closer to the antipatriotic motives of the revolutionary Left than it realized—that antimilitarists ultimately sought: "We want a France where one can say anything, where one can discuss everything. We have demeaned the Clergy. . . . We dare to combat the Magistrature. We can say to the army that it is our guardian and not our master, that it exists to defend us and not to oppress us, that even its existence is subject to criticism. . . . Let's build a France that is enlarged by feelings, fraternal by mutual tolerance." This time the jury acquitted all twelve defendants.[63]

This verdict followed directly on the heels of the vine growers' protests in the Midi region, where soldiers killed and wounded striking workers in Narbonne and where one regiment mutinied to avoid further conflict. Although the questions that these events spawned are better suited to my discussion in chapter 5, their implications could not have been far from the jurors' minds. Indeed in comparing this verdict with that more famous one less than two years earlier, one of the defendants explained that it was "essential because blood had run at Narbonne. The jury acquitted because it understood that the antimilitarists wanted to prevent blood from running." This may have been simple logic, but it was not unreasonable. Antimilitarists, as the *affiche rouge* trial had shown, were at their most persuasive when protesting the use of troops to suppress strikes, an issue viewed universally as an immoral affront to their basic rights as French citizens. Because this particular *affiche* said nothing about war, the court would have been hard pressed to do anything less than acquit. Yet in another sense the outcome was misleading. The signer quoted above also proclaimed the trial—as had the accused in the *affiche rouge* affair—a sure indication of the recrudescence of antimilitarism. Whether this would prove an exaggeration or not, most noteworthy was that a prosecution had occurred at all against this relatively tame *affiche,* and that the signers had fended off prison with genuine appeals to a certain French identity.[64]

◆ ◆ ◆

Governmental repression of syndicalist antimilitarism seems to have been no more discerning than it was toward the AIA, but the broader economic mandate of the CGT made its repercussions more problematic. In February 1906 CGT Secretary-General Victor Griffuelhes, who had refrained from signing the *affiche rouge,* found himself facing the High Court of the Seine (along with Pouget and other prominent syndicalists) for that month's issue of *La Voix du Peuple.* Particularly offensive had been the cover drawing by Grandjouan titled *Le Marché à la viande* (the meat market), in which officers inspect soldiers, nude and with the words "good to kill" tattooed on their shoulders, as if inspecting animals for slaughter.[65] Two years later, Deputy Pugliesi-Conti would denounce the antipatriotism of the CGT, calling "purely and simply" for its dissolution. It was neither the first time, nor would it be the last, that the Chamber of Deputies debated the CGT's very right to exist.[66]

The prosecutions against the CGT were not without effect. The trials of Griffuelhes and his colleagues interfered directly with May Day preparations, and Alphonse Merrheim, secretary of the Copper Federation, once regretted that the antimilitarist campaign was smothering that of the eight-hour day. A March 1906 report warned that CGT leaders might have to relax their antimilitarist propaganda, at least until they could make room for important economic issues.[67] Another insisted that the *bourses* had already become "more prudent" since the *affiche rouge* trial. On the part of the CGT, suspicion was rife that the government's crackdown on antimilitarism was actually part of a larger scheme to derail syndicalism. Antimilitarist doctrine may have been well-entrenched in the CGT, but as long as its leaders were on trial and its responsibilities to the working classes held in check, it quickly could become more of a liability than an asset.[68]

For the legally sanctioned Bourses du Travail, the risks were more direct. As early as September 3, 1905, the Municipal Council of Algiers voted to close

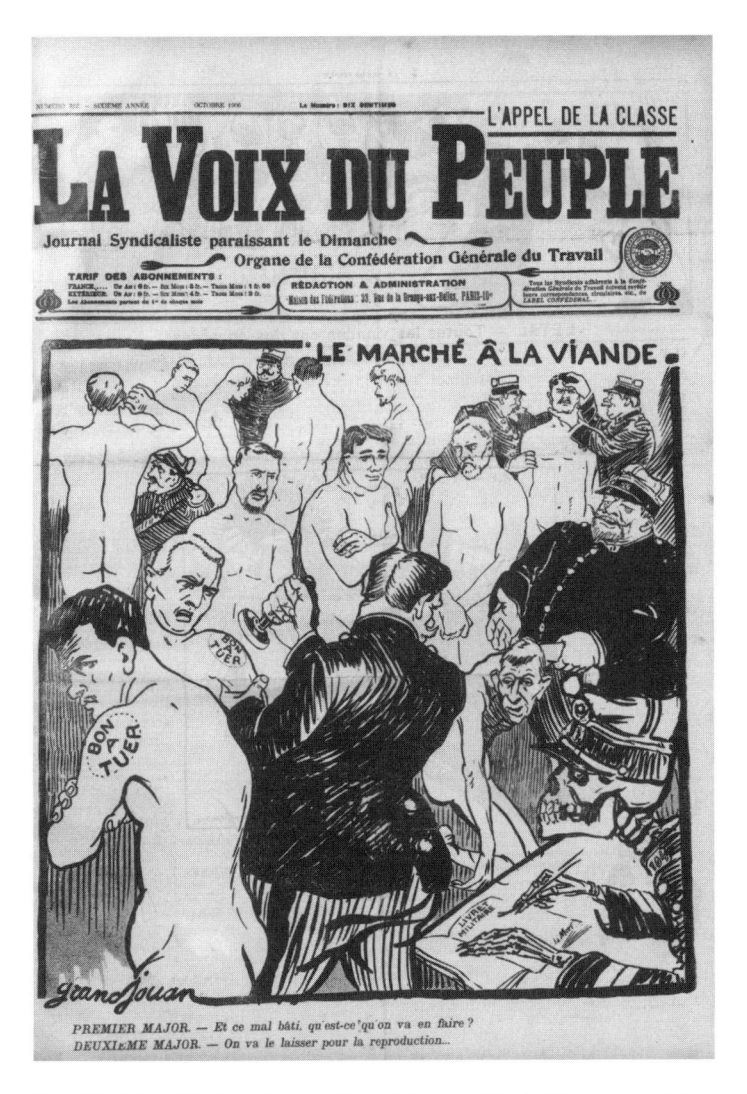

Top: The Meat Market; *bottom:* First Adjutant: "And this scrawny thing, what are we going to do with him?" Second Adjutant: "We'll save him for breeding." From *La Voix du Peuple*, October 1906. Reprinted with permission of the L'Institut CGT d'Histoire Sociale.

its *bourse* after authorities discovered antimilitarist placards there. The same happened in Marseille, Tunis, and Lyon (1905), and in Caen, Oran, and Nancy (1906). In 1905 officials evicted the CGT and *La Voix du Peuple* from the Paris Bourse du Travail. In early October of that year, the AIA section in Cherbourg was prohibited from using the *bourse* for its headquarters. There were, of course, exceptions. The Radical-Socialist municipality of Lorient (Morbihan) subsidized its *bourse* with the very intention of encouraging antimilitarist propaganda.[69]

This sort of collusion between local Bourses du Travail and socialist municipal governments had caused problems before for police chiefs and prefects.[70] Now, with the fear that the trade union centers also served as outlets for antimilitarist propaganda, they faced a more dangerous and delicate matter because many were subsidized at the municipal or departmental level. We have already seen the efforts of General André in 1902 to prevent the *bourses* from bringing their propaganda into the casernes. In March 1905, the minister of the interior sent a confidential and carefully worded letter to local prefects requesting information on "the fashion in which the Bourses du Travail in your department are organized and function," including whether they were being subsidized. Although there was no direct mention of antimilitarism, it could not have been far from the minister's mind.[71]

After the events in the Midi, it would no longer be necessary to be so circumspect. The military revolts convinced authorities of a direct link between the Bourse du Travail at Agde (Hérault) and the mutiny of the 17th Infantry regiment that originated there, and it gave antimilitarists a lift similar to that which followed the *affiche rouge* convictions. Government officials now inquired into the extent of antimilitarist activity in every French city, town, and bourg that harbored a trade union center. These results will be the subject of analysis in the next chapter; what interests us here is how authorities in 1905 probed local officials for what they were doing about *bourses* that plied antimilitarism alongside their presumed economic responsibilities. In a single report, we see both how seriously the public powers regarded antimilitarism and yet how their republican sensibilities only enabled them to take guarded action against it.

The premise of this inquiry was that the Bourses du Travail served an important function in society, but the recent spate of antimilitarist activity had drawn them away from their designated tasks. Thus the government implied no sarcasm when it praised the "Professional Association of Workers [as] an instrument of material, intellectual, and moral progress," even encouraging its further development with regard to the "professional interests" and "responsibilities" of wage earners. Yet it had one not so minor scruple: "It only asks—in the general interest as in that of the organizations themselves—that those who direct them not lose sight of the double task they have to fulfill: the education of workers and the defense of their professional interests." The rest of the report addressed the fact that their advocacy of "sabotage, the general strike, and antipatriotism" was doing just that, and that the end result will be "to endanger the national existence."[72]

Because it recognized the value of the *bourses,* the government, which stressed the need to stop this agitation, preferred not to have to "resort to extreme means" in order to do so. Officials were thus heartened by the fact that several municipalities proved they did not have to wait for instructions from above to do things such as cut off subsidies, which could amount to as much as half a *bourse's* income and often paid the salaries of its leaders. This was the case in 1901 at Le Havre (350 franc municipal subsidy, 200 departmental), Laval (républicain de gauche, 350 and 200 francs), and La Rochelle (républicain de gauche, 400 and 200); in 1906 at Bourges (progressiste, 400 and 1,800), Limoges (progressiste, 1,500 and 1,000), Caen (nationalist, 600 and 200); and in 1907 at Lons-le-Saunier (radical, subsidies unlisted), Chalons-sur-Marne (radical, 500 municipal), Périgueux (radical, 126,800 and 250), Rochefort (radical, 500 and 200), Nancy (nationalist, 5,650 and 1,000), Dijon (socialist, 4,000 and 1,000), Chateauroux (radical, 1,300 and 266), Agen (1,000 for both), and Fougères (radical-socialist, 2,500 and 300). In Toulon (socialist, 9,060 and 4,000) the municipal council stopped giving a lump sum to the *bourse* and began distributing the subsidy on a union-by-union basis according to each union's membership. Because several of the most important *syndicats* were not affiliated with the *bourse,* this amounted to a total cessation of funds.[73]

In other cities authorities adopted a wait-and-see attitude toward the *bourses.* The local governments of Nice (républicain de gauche, 5,000 francs), Angoulême (républicain de gauche, 3,000), St. Brieuc (républicain de gauche, 800), Bayonne (progressiste, 500), Perpignan (radical, 3,500), Versailles (nationalist, 1,000), Melun (républicain de gauche, 3,000), and Cherbourg (radical-socialist, 3000) notified prefects that they would suppress subsidies if antimilitarist tendencies continued to grow. In Sedan (radical-socialist, 800), Clermont (radical, 1,800), and Cherbourg (radical-socialist, 3,000), officials warned the *syndicats* that they would lose funding should they become too embroiled in the propaganda. So if the government seemed to be moving cautiously even in October 1907, they did so with good reason: "The militants of the Confédération Générale du Travail or of the *bourses,* terrorized by repression in their ranks, are no longer eager to show off their antimilitarist and antipatriotic sentiments. They fear firstly for their organization, which will be deprived of municipal or departmental subsidies. And they fear for themselves, since they were paid with these subsidies and are afraid they will be replaced if imprisoned."[74]

Syndicalists faced a similar setback on the international front. In January 1906, as politicians were reeling from the Moroccan crisis, CGT Secretary-General Griffuelhes went on a secret mission to Berlin in hopes of organizing simultaneous working-class antiwar demonstrations in Paris and the German capital. The General Commission of German Unions that welcomed him, however, could do little without the consent of the Socialist Party. Yet Griffuelhes found the Social Democrats equally constrained by formality. Party Chairman August Bebel politely yet firmly dismissed him on the grounds that he did not represent the SFIO or use the International Socialist Bureau as an intermediary. In the end, as Griffuelhes well realized, his trip had been a severe disillusionment for French syndicalism.[75]

Instructively, Griffuelhes's experience was another instance of the overbearing nature of the press and police when it came to antimilitarism. The mission was supposed to be secret, but all the major journals got wind of it and publicized the failure broadly. This was no doubt demoralizing, as a report in mid-February attested. It gave the impression that, when it came to antimilitarism, syndicalists could always be put in their place. As Griffuelhes himself allegedly said: "The good soldier should avoid blows."[76]

Griffuelhes's contact with the German Left was further revealing as to the antimilitarism of France's potential enemy. Writing in *Le Mouvement Socialiste*, Robert Michels, a theorist for the German Social Democratic Party (SPD) and a revolutionary syndicalist in his own right, contended that the reliance of German working-class leaders on unwritten protocol to foil the plans of their French colleagues was really just an excuse for their own proven reluctance to engage in antimilitarism internationally. Germany, he pointed out, had never brought antimilitarist issues to the forefront of international congresses, and during the Moroccan crisis remained notably aloof from French, British, and Belgian propositions to prevent war. Michels attributed this stance to the structure of the party itself. Despite "prodigious resources of wealthy men," its fear of losing supporters had made the SPD, in his opinion, the weakest European socialist party with regard to antimilitarist propaganda.[77]

For French syndicalist leaders, the take-home lesson of Griffuelhes's mission was that the antimilitarism of their German "ally" was not comparable to that in France, as Hervé had insisted it was at the *affiche rouge* trial and at Limoges and Nancy, and as so much of the propaganda had (and still) claimed. A crucial factor for this was the intolerance the government of Wilhelmine Germany harbored toward the Left. As Michels explained it: "In France, Hervé was sentenced to four years of prison for having preached antimilitarism; we would have had forty [years] in Germany if we had said only a quarter of what he said."[78] According to another source, in every German city with a garrison, soldiers were severely punished for entering a brasserie operated or frequented by socialists.[79]

Further evidence that German antimilitarists could not equal their French counterparts owing to the stricter political system appeared in a story published in the widely read daily *Le Journal* on an attempt to circulate antimilitarist brochures inside German casernes. In February 1907, Berlin police arrested three anarchists carrying fifteen thousand copies of the *Bréviaire du soldat* (*Soldier's Bible*). To disguise the work's true nature, the cover depicted a Prussian eagle perched over a quote from a speech the emperor gave to recruits in 1892; the bottom read: "Published by the Prussian Minister of War." The real ingenuity of this publication event involved actually transporting the brochures into the country and, next, into the hands of German soldiers. First the anarchists hid the fifteen thousand copies in several pigeon cages, buried beneath the excrement of the prior occupants. Then a blind and lame person passed the cages over the German border from Holland, where they had been printed. Finally, to facilitate their movement into the casernes, boxes of soap (to improve the smell?) were wrapped in the leaves of the brochures, enabling children or local women to avoid detection and bring them to the soldiers. Yet with all this trouble, the anarchists' efforts came to naught. *Le Journal* viewed the arrests as a terrible blow to German antimilitarism, although only one of the anarchists actually turned out to be German.[80]

Although the active repression of leftist propaganda in Germany, enhanced by the recent memory of antisocialist laws (1878–1890), denied the empire the political climate for antimilitarism to flourish, the party still had Karl Liebknecht. Best known for his role in the Revolution of 1918, Liebknecht "saw in militarism the basic and ultimate weapon of capitalism against the upsurge of Social Democracy." His work *Militarism and Antimilitarism* (1907) was the most important analysis of European antimilitarism in the period. Yet Liebknecht's efforts to step up the campaign in his own party were met largely with criticism and even outright condescension. When he proposed at the 1904 Bremen congress that the party undertake extensive measures to spread antimilitarist propaganda among potential recruits, the delegates rejected him "with a certain amount of scornful laughter." A year later at Jena, with the Moroccan crisis in full swing, Liebknecht introduced a resolution calling for public meetings to inform conscripts of their rights under military law; thus they could "see for the first time how the service regulations are violated by their superiors" and develop "a repugnance for militarism." Party Chairman Bebel agreed to the part about the meetings, but balked at the idea that this was a "first step" toward increased antimilitarism in the party.[81]

Liebknecht suffered his most severe setback at the Mannheim congress in 1906, when Bebel opposed his idea for a central antimilitarist commission on grounds that it constituted an undisguised attempt to undermine his own authority. Bebel particularly resented Liebknecht's arguments comparing the weakened state of German antimilitarism to that of France and Belgium. At a time when so many political elites openly discussed the possibility of war between France and Germany, it is hard to believe that the Socialist Party chairman could say the following:

> It is incomprehensible to me how he [Liebknecht] can hold up to us the example of Belgium. A country that signifies nothing, and whose army cannot be compared to Prussian military organization. In France it's the same. There antimilitarist agitation has been carried on only in the last two years. (Liebknecht: And excellently) No! in such a one-sided and exaggerated fashion! (Lively approval) If it were done in like manner in Germany—no, thank you! I should decline.[82]

Responding to these differences between antimilitarism in France and Germany, an article in the conservative *La République Française* warned of an "antimilitarist peril" to the *patrie*. In the same year German socialists rebuffed Liebknecht's proposition at Mannheim, the AIA redoubled its agitation in response to the *affiche rouge* affair. The author might have added that the AIA did not even have an active section in Germany, and, a week later, that French syndicalists meeting in Amiens (on October 13, 1906) had voted to increase antimilitarist and antipatriotic propaganda. The differences, in any case, were palpable: "While Bebel prudently continues to shy away from certain dangerous responsibilities, Hervé, Yvetot, Almereyda, Galilée, Bousquet, and a good number of others shamelessly mount the tribunes and improvise meetings in Paris and the provinces in order to urge soldiers energetically 'to clear off' in case of war and to shoot at officers during strikes."[83]

Yet despite the overwhelming evidence for the lack of German antimilitarist initiative, Hervé and others clung to the notion that it was a mighty force, equivalent to that in France. In *Le Conscrit,* the article "Beyond the Borders" began: "One sometimes asserts that our antimilitarist propaganda is criminal because it weakens France relative to neighboring countries in which antimilitarism does not exist. [This] allegation is so insignificant that we cannot support it in good faith." The article proceeded to praise the antimilitarist cause in countries such as Switzerland, Italy, and Germany, "that famous Germany that all our professional jingoists declare ready to carve up France; [but that] reacts energetically against militarism."[84] In a 1906 debate with Abbé Desgranges at a Montluçon (Allier) amphitheater, Hervé exhorted: "Do not forget that German workers are prepared to imitate the example of the French."[85] A year later *L'Aurore* quoted the Sans-Patrie on German antimilitarism: "Oh! it works very well. I am in contact with Liebknecht, with Michels. I have succeeded in shaking Germany up in that respect."[86]

In truth and as the *L'Aurore* piece attested, less than a decade before World War I German antimilitarism was barely a shadow of that in France. French officials who recognized this thus appeared to have good reason to feel that the unbalanced situation constituted a serious threat to national integrity. Even in *Le Mouvement Socialiste,* Robert Michels warned that those

> who would abandon themselves by passing from theory to action would be vainly compromised, and antimilitarism would play into the hands of the powers that are the most reactionary and the least imbued with the modern spirit of Europe. . . . All the beautiful élan of French antimilitarism, all its sacrifices and all its grandeur will serve nothing, or very little, if there is not, in Germany, a corresponding movement. Now we all know that there is absolutely nothing there.[87]

In an address to War Minister Etienne and Minister of the Marine Thomson, Victor Camboulin was more direct, qualifying Hervé's belief that the class war and antimilitarism he had ignited in France could be transferred to Germany as "glaring of bad faith and infamy."[88] He was right, in a way, although his real purpose was to condemn antimilitarism more broadly. For those such as Camboulin who made their career in the military, antimilitarism was not a mere question of freedom of expression and social justice, but, more narrowly, one of national survival.

The Doomsayers

Lieutenant-colonel Émile Driant had written over twenty books on the military when, in 1906, he confronted the question of antimilitarism. In *Vers un nouveau Sedan* (*Toward a New Sedan*), Driant predicted that "a disastrous war" awaited France. "We would be beaten as in 1870. More completely even than in 1870," and it gave him "infinite sadness" to think how much had changed since, some twenty years earlier, he had forecast sure victory in his revanchist work *La Guerre de demain* (*The War of Tomorrow*).

Driant should have been one to know. *Vers un nouveau Sedan* first appeared as a series of articles in *L'Éclair,* which had sent him to Germany to commingle with the troops and "war union" there. That experience convinced Driant that antimilitarism had not made the same progress across the Rhine as it had in his own country. In the articles and subsequent book, he described the lowly state to which France had sunk as a result: "The antimilitarist gangrene has spread out in extraordinary proportions . . . not only amongst the people, but in the so-called enlightened classes, and in one year the repercussions of this evil in the military body have been enormous." The lieutenant-colonel further admonished that it was not enough to treat this "evil that eats away at the leadership" as mere "provocation to disobedience" perhaps with a short jail sentence attached, but rather as the real threat that it was: "If, as is my right, I have the honor to command a territorial regiment in the next conflict, before leaving for the border I would have killed without pity, if he fell into my hands, the bandit who planted the flag of France on the dung heap."[89]

Driant was not alone in sounding the alarm on antimilitarism. Numerous "doomsayers" from military hierarchies past and present viewed it with disdain and were convinced (or at least saw it in their interest to pretend they were convinced) that leftist ideas had penetrated the army to an appalling extent. Jacques Harouée, a former officer who voluntarily quit the service, wrote *La Détresse de l'armée* (*The Distress of the Army*) to explain why he left, despite being "in spirit and in heart passionately attached [to it]." All the expected reasons are there, the decline of officer morale since 1870–1871 and the Dreyfus Affair perhaps above all. But Harouée reserved special venom for the Left. In the chapter "Indiscipline" he writes: "The methodical and persevering provocations of the internationalists and the army's enemies have produced results such that, without taking them as tragic, it is nevertheless impossible not to be alarmed and worried about them." Nor did he hesitate to accuse the war minister of being rather cowardly with regard to the situation.[90]

Although Harouée only wrote in 1904, he did so with urgency: "The army is in distress, protect us against the poison of debilitating and fatal doctrines." This was no mere plea for government intervention. Written for an audience of military officers and former colleagues, it was a serious effort to set off loud and flashing warning signals about changes Harouée perceived in the army that reflected broader changes in society. "They try to do to the army what has succeeded for all social forces: disorganization by rotting." The "they," the Left, was yet another distressing symptom of the many social ills that had ravaged the state and now menaced its last true bastion of power.[91]

Conservative perceptions of antimilitarism invariably came down to this theme of a mass epidemic that had infected the social body and now threatened the pillar of that body—the French army. Galinier Osman, writing from Oran, Algeria, saw in the divisions in Europe, particularly those working to undermine her armies, a parallel to the forces of social and military degradation that brought down the Roman empire in Africa two thousand years ago. His tendentious writings, suffused with the distortions of Social Darwinism and nightmare visions of a Japanese army entering Paris, place a large part of the blame on Hervéism, or what Osman calls the "New Gospel": "Here the results of the Hervéist Gospel amount to a formidable increase in anarchy in the army." Hervé, in other words, assumes a larger-than-life role in the decline of the West.[92]

No doubt Hervé gloated over this image, and it is striking to see how many of the doomsayers aimed their arsenals directly at him. Camboulin chose a biological metaphor to illustrate Hervé's alleged social poisoning: "Hervéism in our day arrives like a shoot of weak trunks, a shoot with dense foliage, noxious to the soil that nourishes it, little destined to become a tree again. . . . [May] he never be master of our destinies!" He goes on to accuse the Sans-Patrie of falsely coopting the ideal of permanent peace: "Yes, the dream of a fraternal and definitive peace touches all hearts. Hervéism voices the pretension to prepare for it. Who goes against it? Hervéism itself."[93] In *L'Antimilitarisme?* (1906), the political publicist and Germanophobe André Chéradame opens with a cartoon that depicts Hervé ordering a civilian to shoot a soldier whose flag displays the names of victorious French battles.[94] The historian James Joll was right when he wrote that, in the eyes of the enemies of socialism, "every school was staffed by men like Hervé corrupting the native patriotism of the young."[95]

"Antimilitarism wreaks considerable havoc," wrote Camboulin shortly after the first Moroccan crisis, "it is organized: Leadership, Sections, Groups, it lacks nothing. . . . It is therefore necessary to react."[96] Although the perceptions offered here now seem like the highly superficial overreactions of an entrenched conservative elite, they carry an important message: just as military planners considered the strength and resources of France's potential foreign enemies, they were not about to overlook the supposed domestic threat posed by antimilitarists. The British General Staff acted no differently. In the confidential report *The Military Resources in France* (1905), it expressed concern that the French military revival since 1870–1871 could be compromised by the introduction of socialism into the ranks. As France's potential wartime ally, Britain had good reason to be concerned.[97]

Still, for the French government the fine line between harsh repression and cautious tolerance based on democratic political freedoms could not be transgressed solely on the basis of some posters and articles. It thus moved warily. In April 1907 the Interior Ministry instructed prefects to "indicate all antimilitarist demonstrations, including the distribution and sales of brochures and the apposition of *affiches*."[98] After the Midi revolts and the wave of propaganda that followed, Clemenceau's sense of urgency increased, as the following directive from September 1907 indicates: "I attach the utmost importance to being kept very precisely up-to-date concerning antimilitarist propaganda, and to be informed not only of the incidents to which this propaganda could give rise, but also of the means by which it exerts itself on the individuals who indulge in it." A month later, Clemenceau requested an *état nominatif* (list of names) with a description of the individuals in each department who engaged in antimilitarist propaganda.[99] It may not have been the doomsayers' answer to their feared domestic dimension of security, but it was a definite first step toward that most famous repressive measure: the Carnet B.

The Carnet B

The Carnet B did not, as is usually depicted, emerge in direct response to left-wing pacifist and antimilitarist agitation in the years immediately prior to World War I. According to Becker's authoritative study, the gendarmerie had "for a good long time" kept *carnets*, or notebooks, known as "B," in which they listed espionage suspects. In 1886, a memo approved by War

Minister General Boulanger instructed gendarmes on how to locate these spies. It said nothing about antimilitarists, and as Becker shows neither do the first two decades of extant *carnets*.[100]

Only in 1909 did the purpose of the Carnet B begin to move toward that with which we associate it today. On February 5 a letter from the prefect of the Lozère informed the general of the 16th Corps at Montpellier that the prime minister wanted to create a new category for draftees: "Frenchmen whose attitude and actions could be of a nature to disrupt the order and hinder the smooth operation of the duties of mobilization (propagandists by the deed, partisans of direct action, antimilitarists)." Of the six nationals inscribed in the Carnet B of the Vosges that year, two were signaled for their antimilitarist activities.[101]

On September 18, 1911, a secret and, unfortunately for historians, missing circular set in motion the Carnet B's further transformation from mere weapon of accusation to, in the case of war, actual apprehension. We know about the document because in response to it the Lozère prefect informed the government that he would arrest and imprison individuals on the list when so instructed (that is, during a mobilization). During the next years, the Carnet B evolved into "a complex, adaptable, even disturbing institution." Clearer instructions as to the contents of the individual notices, how to inform the minister of the interior, what to do when someone changed departments, omissions, and so forth honed the identity of listees and kept officials abreast of where they were and what they were up to. In a letter to the Vosges prefect in 1914, the minister of the interior reemphasized that "the consequences of inscription in the Carnet B can be particularly serious, since they must end in measures of arrest in the case of mobilization." Becker argues that the steps leading to this point correspond "very exactly" to the "authorities' realization of the danger posed by antimilitarism."[102]

For the purposes of this examination of the repression of antimilitarism, an important point about the Carnet B in addition to what it did is when it did it. It was not until February 1909 that government officials took the first steps to implement a plan to censor and later arrest antimilitarists. Why did they not do this in 1905 during the Moroccan crisis and the *affiche rouge* affair; or in 1907 after the Midi revolts? Have we moved too far ahead of the story? This chapter has tried to provide some important answers.

◆ ◆ ◆

From the end of 1905 to the outbreak of the Midi disturbances, French antimilitarism passed through a trying period. It experienced its first major convictions: Yvetot, Hervé, Almereyda, and other leaders served prison time or came very close to it; debate broke out among syndicalists and socialists over the place of antimilitarism in their broader political and economic agendas, especially as municipal and departmental subsidies were cut off; the French parliament deliberated the fate of the CGT, while the ruthless prime minister denounced it; hopes for an accord with the powerful German syndicalists were shattered by the realities of intransigent German Social Democracy; and the AIA began to experience serious, even debilitating, breakdowns. There can be no doubt that repression of the Left had a certain sobering effect on antimilitarists. An October 1907 report on the "present situation" took credit for the fact that "antimilitarism in France had only been able to develop with the speed we are aware of thanks to the leniency, sometimes of the Public Powers, sometimes of the various juries to which we subjected the most straightforward crimes. But with the severe sentences inflicted against the *affiche rouge* signers, there was a veritable scattering."[103]

For the government in 1907, then, this had been a sufficient, if ad hoc solution to its antimilitarist quandary. Indeed there appears to have been a certain reluctance to go too far in terms of repressive actions, hence the amnesty, acquittals, and the toleration of Hervé and the *bourses*. Even Clemenceau, that "strikebreaker" and self-professed enemy of the CGT, was capable of discouraging overreaction that could compromise political rights and, possibly, enhance the image of antimilitarists.[104] During a ceremony at Amiens in October 1907 to inaugurate a statue to the late René Goblet (Radical Party leader and four-time cabinet minister), he expressed his feelings thus:

> As long as base enmities gave themselves free rein against a diminished France, who could have anticipated that foreigners would soon be surpassed in their anti-French furor by the French? . . . Messieurs, let's not be so ridiculous as to allow ourselves to believe for one sole instant that we could seriously fear the effects of criminal propaganda, which can only excite a feeling of horror in all Frenchmen worthy of the name.[105]

The conservative press and military realists, on the other hand, were far less discreet, openly treating antimilitarism as an internal enemy that had to be stopped to wage war successfully. In contrast to what they viewed as government pandering to the Left, these reactionaries were prepared to implement more severe measures, and sooner. A September 1905 article in the popular nationalist journal *La Patrie* captured their anxieties well:

> In the middle of Paris the revolutionary *syndicats* and anarchists organize their schemes. They are preparing to inundate the department of the Seine with dishonorable placards . . . they are allowed to turn the caserne into an active, revolutionary foyer. . . . When will this scandal cease? When the government makes up its mind to force out the wretches who have installed themselves there as masters so as to carry out this abominable work.[106]

A January 1907 piece in *L'Écho de Paris*, the official organ of the Ligue de la Patrie Française with a circulation of over one hundred thousand, blamed antimilitarists for a recent spate of indiscipline in the caserne, and the "prudence of the politicians" for not taking the "energetic measures" necessary to protect French military institutions. "We have waited in vain [for such measures]. Are our political leaders finally going to open their eyes?"[107]

The government had certainly "opened its eyes" and "made up its mind" to punish antimilitarist leaders and closely monitor local groups. It regarded antimilitarism seriously, and took numerous precautions to check its expansion. But in the wake of the Dreyfus Affair and in the spirit of a young democracy, officials restrained themselves from implementing the draconian measures called for by militant nationalists and conservative journalists. Although actively opposed to antimilitarism, the Third Republic was, in a way, also its best ally. As ironic as this may seem, perhaps the most accurate commentary on how the government viewed the rise of Hervéist thinking came, even more ironically, from Hans von Flotow, the German chargé d'affaires in Paris. Conversing in government circles at the time of the *affiche rouge* affair, Flotow learned that the diffusion of antimilitarism, particularly its manifestations among reservists and general acceptance by socialists, was regarded as an "unsettling reality," openly debated by French politicians. One of those political leaders explained it thus to the German: "The conflict between democracy and military discipline, between freedom and the necessities of the state, that always existed and will always exist in a democracy, and which Hervé laid bare with a brutal hand, will, I fear, cause us many serious problems yet."[108] Probably no single perception would prove more sound.

4. ANTIMILITARIST MILITANTS

The Question of Commitment

In an April 1906 edition of *L'Anarchie,* André Lorulot confessed to his earlier, perhaps too facile, assumption that after the *affiche rouge* affair and the wave of incidents it generated, antimilitarism would secure the grassroots support necessary to turn it into an authentic, national "movement." With Hervé, Yvetot, and Almereyda in jail, the campaign required momentum from below if it were to become the viable domestic threat to security that key enemies and allies alike were already convinced it was. "If the antimilitarist propaganda comes to naught and appears to wear itself out," Lorulot predicted, "it is because there are not enough individuals to lead it."[1]

Lorulot was not alone in questioning the extent to which revolutionary antimilitarism permeated the working classes. "If [antimilitarist] thought really speaks to the masses," wrote a German military attaché shortly after the December 1905 trial, "the future alone will tell."[2] In an effort to assess that future, this chapter poses the question: How effective were antimilitarists in diffusing their ideas and shaping the attitudes and behaviors of French workers? Or as Lorulot sarcastically put it: "Apart from our imprisoned comrades, where are the militants? And the fierce syndicalists, the fiery antipatriots, the barroom revolutionaries? Where are they? In their Bourses, at the bistro? *That is the question!*"[3]

It is a question the public powers also asked, but that remains difficult to answer based on available sources. There are no records of the exact numbers of antimilitarists who, for example, supported Hervé's plan for a general strike in the case of war. The AIA does not seem to have kept any good data, and the CGT and Socialist Party would have been hard pressed to estimate how many of their members, who typically joined for economic and political reasons, also supported the antimilitarist platforms beyond their pleas for lawful respect of working-class rights. Again we are forced to rely on the estimates and evaluations of the antagonists—government, police, judicial, even military officials.

Fortunately, in the aftermath of the *affiche rouge* affair, with antimilitarist leaders in jail and the threat of the same looming over the rest, the authorities had a good chance to observe the antimilitarists. One official ventured that, despite the national outrage following the convictions, antimilitarists had "a dearth of speakers" and "such mediocrity" among those sent to the provinces that "they do not seem to me likely to lead a large current in favor of their theories." The reporter viewed their prior successes as part of a pattern where "as almost always, the majority allow themselves to be imposed upon by a minority who exploit their audacity to the fullest. It is thus that the level-headed men of the Confédération have not been able to hold their own against the impulse-driven extremists who lead this organization down a road where certainly the masses will not follow them."[4]

How, then, do we explain the 2,317 signatures on the protest *affiche* circulated shortly after the verdict on the *affiche rouge*? Was this clear evidence that antimilitarism had the numbers to wage a large-scale action on short notice; or rather just another example of the imposition of a remnant of leaders such as Numietska, Grandjouan, and the anarchist Charles Malato?[5] After the *affiche rouge* affair, authorities in Chartres were afraid to remove the poster because they were unsure of their support.[6] At issue is whether the more than two thousand signers were committed antimilitarists.

Perhaps we should first inquire whether all thirty-one signers of the *affiche rouge* knew what *they* were doing. Several reports in October and November 1905 give the impression that certain names on the *affiche*—Jean-Marie Frontier, Jules Leguery, Charles Desplanques, Raymond Dubéros, Pierre Le Blavec, and Jules-Albert Nicolet—had not been solicited, and that Almereyda and Yvetot may have taken the liberty to write in those names themselves. Although each received a one-year prison sentence, some showed surprise at the use of their name; others claimed never to have set foot in AIA headquarters. The report also raises the question of why more prominent antimilitarists such as CGT Secretary-General Victor Griffuelhes, the Treasurer Lévy, and Paul Fribourg, who sat on the AIA's national committee, did not sign the *affiche* at all.[7]

Laurent Tailhade, libertarian anarchist, collaborator on *L'Action* and *Le*

Libertaire, "convinced pacifist," and "resolutely antimilitarist" author of *Pour la paix* (*For Peace*) and *Lettre aux conscrits* (*Letter to the Conscripts*) was nonetheless incensed to find his name on the *affiche rouge*.[8] His swift response came in a letter in the October 9, 1905, edition of *L'Action,* protesting this "most unpleasant misunderstanding" on the grounds that he had not been properly informed of the *affiche*'s contents, and that it was "identical to the printed matter one receives by the dozen each morning." Tailhade added that the *affiche* went against his dogmatic abhorrence of murder, regardless of the victim. The anarchist had certainly come far since he praised Vaillant for dropping a bomb in the Chamber of Deputies (December 9, 1893) with the oft-quoted phrase: "Of what significance are the victims if the gesture is beautiful?" Perhaps tempered, as Thierry Maricourt suggests, by a recent trial and short incarceration, Tailhade no longer even wanted to affiliate himself with the AIA, or as he wrote, "the crude, the shallow outbursts of the antimilitarists."[9]

The investigation into the names on the protest *affiche* was not an easy undertaking for authorities who felt the recent sentences had already given antimilitarists too much exposure. But as Malato correctly foresaw when he proposed the *affiche,* "if they do not bring proceedings against [the new signers], how will they be able, even in a capitalist and authoritarian regime, to apply the sentence against the [original] signers?" For Malato, revenge was in the air:

> First of all, it is a question of retaliating against the verdict striking the antimilitarists. The latter have to demonstrate at once to their friends and enemies that they extend into the masses, with strong roots branched out all over; that the convicted manifesto expresses the feelings not of twenty-eight militants, but of innumerable proletarians who have grown weary of the honor of giving their blood to cement the social order that crushes them.[10]

The judicial inquiry opened shortly. Acting AIA head Numietska furnished the examining magistrate André with a list of 511 signers who resided in Paris or in the Seine region. André then assigned an investigatory commission to the criminal department in order to obtain information on the AIA, its printing facilities, connections with the CGT, and the circumstances in which it drafted the *affiche*. The commission hoped to learn whether those who signed the poster had done so willfully, or rather were misled by the antimilitarists as Tailhade claimed he had been. The AIA, in short, was being put on trial.[11]

The results of this inquiry, which lasted over a month, can never be one hundred percent infallible because they rely on individual testimony, and it proved nearly impossible to track everyone down. Of the 511 names provided by Numietska, only 242 were interrogated. Some were not even on the *affiche,* while others had given a false or incomplete address. A few simply did not obey the summons. Of the 242 who did, only 85 (approximately one-third) confessed to having signed the *affiche* with full knowledge of its cause and contents. The rest (157) used various pretexts to complain against the appropriation of their names. Most common was that they had been led to believe their signatures would be used only to protest the sentences of Hervé and his comrades. Others defended their action as an expression of the republican right to think and act freely.[12]

The inquiry also provided examples of how the AIA obtained so many signatures so fast. A typical story might go something like that of André Huch, a thirty-two-year-old turner from the burgeoning industrial town of Le Creusot (Saône et Loire):

> I did not sign the *affiche* you have shown me, and I am a victim of the abuse of my name. Here are the circumstances in which I gave my signature: In January 1906, one evening after the atelier I work at let out, some comrades were signing a paper saying it was a protest against the guilty verdict of Hervé and the others, and like them I gave my signature. I put my signature on a sheet that had no writing on it, simply signatures. It is only very recently that I learned of the terms of the *affiche* you show me, and I want to tell you that I do not approve of the ideas expressed therein. I am neither an antimilitarist nor an anarchist.

There are so many examples of such chicanery that it is hard to disallow them as evidence. The stonecutters of Ravières, who thought their signatures would be used to set up a fund for the families of the indicted, wrote *Le Journal* protesting "very energetically against the way they have used our signatures. . . . We are neither antimilitarists, nor revolutionaries, nor anarchists, and we aspire only to remain good French citizens. We have been shamefully fooled."

Others such as Arthur Collet of Nantes; Jacques Cohen, a musician in Paris; Paul Louis Collet of La Roche Pauzée (Creuse); and the doctor Eugene Alfred Currie from Senoncourt (Haute Saône) claimed not to have realized that they had signed the controversial placard until the court contacted them or they saw their name in the local newspaper. Additionally, although only 10 percent of all signers were accounted for, an article sent to the commission from Auxerre titled "The Antimilitarist Affiche: How They Obtained the Signatures of Yonne peasants," claimed that more than 1,000 of the 2,317 names came from that rebel department. It told of how AIA representatives had combed towns in search of potential recruits: "If you want war, refuse your signature! If, on the contrary, you do not want it, give us your name!" Women and children from the region were "completely distraught" on learning that they had supported aggressive provocations to desertion and insurrection.[13]

What of the one-third who admitted prior knowledge of the *affiche*'s contents? Interestingly, many insisted that they acted as antimilitarists, but not as anarchists. This is an important distinction because it was the anti-anarchist *lois scélérates* that judicial authorities applied against the signers. Also, it was widely known that anarchists and the so-called anarcho-syndicalists largely influenced and operated the AIA. Léo Cazes, a hairdresser's assistant from Toulouse, did not try to hide the fact that he had consciously signed "a new antimilitarist *affiche* exactly reproducing the preceding [one]," but did make it a point to tell the commission: "I am not an anarchist. It is not necessary to be an anarchist in order to be an antimilitarist. I am a socialist delegated to the Federal Council of the Department of the Seine for the Socialist Party, and I consider that antimilitarism, a corollary of anti-patriotism, is one of the integral parts of the socialist program."[14]

It would be easy to refute this evidence on the basis that we can never know whether these individuals had told the truth. Even the jailed signers, on learning of the protest poster, predicted that most would disavow responsibility.[15] They may have been right, yet it seems highly unlikely that so many would have independently fabricated the same story about signing a blank paper allegedly in support of their imprisoned comrades. It indeed was that, as Malato made clear when he came up with the idea, and one could even argue that all 2,317 thought the verdict was wrong. But the point is that for the AIA devout the protest had to repeat verbatim the language of the *affiche rouge*. Thus one cannot take lightly the fact that two-thirds of the "signers" tried to separate themselves from this propaganda, and untold others did the same with respect to the largely anarchist milieu from which it arose. Antimilitarism had widespread support as a vehicle for voicing working-class rights, but threats of violence and murder were further than most needed, or were willing, to go.

Although the above evidence is useful for our purposes, it may have been superfluous to contemporary observers. Before the Saint-Etienne Congress, some officials already estimated that it "will only be a veritable 'bluff,' because the composition of the AIA has completely failed."[16] Less than a year later, police described the majority of the AIA's members as "virtual" (that is, nominal), meaning that they existed only on paper: "A militant member of the AIA, belonging to a revolutionary *syndicat* or socialist group, collects the signatures of some comrades during a meeting: A section is founded." The section then convenes, names its secretary, and purchases an embossed stamp. And although attendance dwindles over the next several gatherings, the AIA continues to record the original membership.[17]

If many viewed the December 1905 convictions as the immediate cause for the AIA's decline, the consensual structural factor was the general lack of support. An April 1907 report on antimilitarism in eastern France asked how, "if the elements that made up the AIA were most indestructible," it had been "able to founder so fast": "At the conferences and meetings that focused on antimilitarism, the listeners hardly turned out, and those that came were already antimilitarists. The propaganda was thus not very efficacious; it did not touch the mass of workers, which nevertheless was the goal of the Association."[18] The prefect of the Rhône described a similar collapse among sections in and around Lyon. Only three years after the AIA's founding, all that remained was a single active group, Section Lyonnaise, the mere sixty members of which had fused with a local anarchist association.[19] Likewise the remaining twelve members of Nancy's AIA section had joined the Section Libertaire de France, taking the more neutral name Groupe d'Émancipation.[20] By mid-October 1907, Paris police reported that the only real sections left in the capital were those in the 12th and the 20th arrondissements, which had merged, and one in the 10th, which "considered it useless to intensify its antimilitarist propaganda." Each counted fifteen to twenty members.[21]

Apathy and embezzlement contributed to the AIA's faltering in France. "Despite insistent invitations in the journals, there were hardly twenty people" at an October 11, 1907, meeting. Three days earlier, efforts to re-form the section had attracted a dozen. This specific meeting had the unpleasant task of expelling the AIA treasurer-secretary for greater Paris, Coulais, on evidence that he had extorted subscription fees from the various groups (around one hundred francs), and rumors that he was in the pay of the police.[22] A similar scenario ousted one Issaly of the "very important" Levallois section. His "complicated and amusing" story is that he had provided *L'Écho de Paris* with the text of an *affiche* that had never been circulated, was justly compensated for the right to publish it, and headed for the country. Two years later he claimed to have fled because, as the *affiche*'s author, he feared government reprisals. In truth Issaly had cheated the AIA out of crucial funds (about two hundred francs), and hence, as police commissioner Foureur recognized, dealt "a harsh blow that precipitated the end of the organization."[23]

Early outward appearances often masked the reality of the AIA's decline. Nearly all the reports in 1906–1907 acknowledge the opening successes of the AIA, even as they sound its death knell. "The propaganda in France seemed to succeed at the outset," began one report before it launched into an explanation of why it had failed. "Nevertheless," Foureur writes a year and a half later, "there had been in France up to 17,000 registered members [of the AIA]; there had been more than 500 sections and, certain months, there were three and four thousand Francs of receipts. . . . But this was only a flash in the pan; a few months later, the adherents no longer paid; the sections had four to five members, or less . . . and they no longer took a collection."[24]

Somehow the flash persisted even as the pan dried up. In April 1907 the AIA launched an *affiche* calling on "oppressed" soldiers and workers to prepare for the imminent "great general strike." In September, during the annual departure of conscripts, AIA flyers extolled their familiar morality: "It is preferable to kill a French general than a foreign soldier." This was followed by an antipatriotic "manifesto" that advised conscripts: "It is better to live free in a foreign country than as a slave in the caserne." And the list goes on. Rather than elevating the moral message of its propaganda in an effort to reconstitute its ranks, the AIA chose to go down in flames. Although it would attempt a comeback in March 1908 with the anarchist Georges Durupt as secretary and with the future secretary of the Union des Syndicats de la Seine, Gaston Delpech, as treasurer, as a uniquely antimilitarist but decided anarchist-inspired organization it could never acquire a support base commensurate with the quantity and virulence of its propaganda.[25]

The above report, which reads more like funeral rites for the AIA than a serious assessment of it, did not give the "naïve enthusiasts" who wanted to reestablish the section much chance. In September 1907, even *Le Libertaire* confessed that the AIA had been a disillusioning experience, although it pretended this was not because of a lack of antimilitarists. Characteristically, it called for the formation of a new fédération antimilitariste française "that will have no excuse to be jealous of those [antimilitarist sections] existing abroad, notably in Germany."[26] None existed in Germany, and elsewhere the AIA had only been established in countries of lesser geopolitical significance. But for this association, it was the image which, more often than not, belied the reality. As the police commissioner readily confessed, it would not take a huge effort to recreate the appearance of a large, threatening antimilitarist "movement":

Two or three individuals without notoriety, fortune, or even much intelligence, are sufficient, in meeting once a week at a wine merchant, to make public opinion believe that in France there is an antimilitarist organization. This may "frighten the government and the bourgeois," but above all it will suffice to encourage gestures of revolt amongst conscripts or soldiers. Domela [Nieuwenhuis], [Pierre] Kropotkin, [Jean] Grave, Hervé know the truth . . . there is hardly anyone behind them; they make up part of the facade, and profit from their situtation to make a living from it.[27]

Where AIA leaders had gone wrong was in thinking they could go it alone, making antimilitarism into a self-standing ideology and, thereby, a "movement." Their only failure was in not recognizing antimilitarism for what it was: a highly effective moral language to assert workers' rights against the government and capitalist class; one best left to preexisting working-class groupings such as the socialists and syndicalists. When the anarchists Tissier and Grandidier tried to reestablish the French section of the AIA, the police bluntly concluded: "This recrudescence has no chance of lasting. A new organization similar to the former AIA cannot be reconstituted, and antimilitarism will only find its way back through the Jeunesses Socialistes, the Bourses du Travail, [and] journals like *L'Égalité* and *La Guerre Sociale*."[28] Another report stressed that although anarchists had failed to create special centers such as that of Malzéville (just outside of Nancy), this had not prevented the development of a regional network for the unimpeded extension of their revolutionary ideas:

Wherever syndicalist propaganda passes, antimilitarist propaganda passes. Members of the Jeunesses Socialistes come to the regiment imbued with the deleterious ideas inculcated in them at the workers' centers. Maybe there are a lot of antimilitarists in the East because conscripts from Paris are generally sent to this region, and in Paris they have had more opportunities to attend syndicalist meetings. . . . It is only in forcing the *Syndicats* and Bourses to withdraw strictly into the limits laid out by the law of 1884 that we will succeed, after several years, in wiping out all traces of antimilitarist propaganda.[29]

These reports on the decline of the AIA thus by no means heralded the end of French antimilitarism, merely the acceptance that the source of its success lay in the groups from which it originated. Antimilitarism was alive and well, even though the AIA was dead and done for.

Regions, Revolutionaries, and Reformists: The Politics of Antimilitarism

In *Les Bases du syndicalisme* (*The Foundations of Syndicalism*), Emile Pouget argued that in order to achieve the syndicalist aims of capitalist expropriation and integral communism "it is necessary to disorganize the army, which alone prevents the social revolution."[30] For revolutionary syndicalists such as Pouget, everything hinged on the army, the primary obstacle to their entire raison d'être: destruction of the democratic, bourgeois state. Writing in his series on revolutionary syndicalism for *L'Écho de Paris*, Gaston Dru warned: "There exists in the State an organization for which the openly acknowledged goal is the inversion of society and that, ready for nothing but violent action, puts itself outside the law."[31] This was the version of syndicalism that Frenchmen typically heard and read about in the early 1900s.

To what extent did this "extralegal" ideology reflect mainstream syndicalist thought in France? In order to gauge the impact of the CGT's antimilitarist campaign on the average trade unionist, it is first necessary to assess how representative the opinions of someone such as Pouget were to syndicalism as a whole. French trade unionism was far from ideologically harmonious. With its reformist and revolutionary wings constantly at loggerheads, the subversive propaganda of the revolutionaries regularly overshadowed that of their more subdued counterparts. Although reformists were content to work for piecemeal measures such as the improvement of work conditions and the use of collective contracts, revolutionaries would stop at nothing short of the total transformation of society. So whom did the working masses believe?

In the early 1900s, the revolutionaries were well positioned to exert their will. The top echelons of the CGT were dominated by ex-anarchists (Griffuelhes as general secretary; Pouget as assistant secretary and editor of *La Voix du Peuple;* Yvetot as secretary of the Fédération des Bourses; and Paul Delesalle as assistant secretary for the Bourses, secretary of the general strike committee, and writer for *Les Temps Nouveaux*) whose motions held sway at national congresses. Two years after delegates to the Amiens congress (1906) passed Yvetot's proposal to accentuate antipatriotic and antimilitarist propaganda, they accepted a resolution at Marseille that brought a general strike in the case of war closer to the realm of possibility. Formulated in response to the violent encounters between workers and soldiers at Narbonne, Raon-l'Étape, and Villeneuve-St.-Georges, the resolution deemed it necessary, "from an international point of view, to educate workers so that if war is declared between the great powers, they respond by declaring a revolutionary general strike."[32]

Jacques Julliard has pointed out that a commitment to education is not the same as a directive for action.[33] This is certainly true, and what happened in 1914 is even less blameworthy when viewed as a deficit of instruction rather than initiative. But this was 1908, and revolutionary syndicalists had triumphed again. A report said the resolution "only confirmed . . . that without the energetic intervention of the government and Parliament, the CGT's antimilitarist and antipatriotic propaganda will capture all workers' milieus and cause the nation irreparable damage."[34] The revolutionaries would score another victory two years hence, when the congress of Toulouse (October 1910) reaffirmed with a larger majority the Marseille resolution, and passed a new measure calling for the intensification of propaganda inside the caserne.

Still, the votes at Amiens and Marseille were by no means landslides. They came only after long, intense debates during which reformists tried to sidetrack the propositions of their adversaries. This point has been emphasized before, but the successes of the revolutionaries in these years owed a great deal to the undemocratic system of representation the CGT used at its congresses. Rather than issuing mandates based on *syndicat* size, as in a procedure of proportional representation, each union received a single vote. In this way small *syndicats* had as many mandates as large federations (composed of several *syndicats*) such as the Fédération du Livre (printers), which since 1884 had been led by the reformist Auguste Keufer. When one breaks down the Marseille vote according to *syndicat* size, the outcome looks quite different: *for*: 670 *syndicats* with 114,000 members; *against*: 406 *syndicats* with 127,000 members. Because out of a proletariat in 1906 of approximately 12,000,000 only 836,000 were unionized, and of these the CGT had a nominal membership of 300,000 and a paid membership of 200,000 the political theorist F. F. Ridley has reasoned that small tended to equal revolutionary. The vast majority of French workers did not belong to any *syndicat,* so it seems sensible to assume that those who helped form the smaller, less established ones usually did so out of sympathy with the vociferous, revolutionary wing.[35]

By contrast the large *syndicats* and federations, with the exceptions of the Fédération du Bâtiment (building industry), the maritime workers, and the metalworkers, were almost exclusively reformist. Keufer's Fédération du Livre, 47,000 members strong in 1913, was the bulwark of reformism in the French syndicalist movement.[36] Keufer himself, "spiritual chief of reformist syndicalism," had been the lone exception to the forty-one militants surveyed by Lagardelle in 1905, and he was an adamant opponent of antimilitarist and antipatriotic excess during his long tenure as secretary (1884–1920). But his opinions, as those of his constituents, were largely suppressed at congresses.[37]

Another factor for what Henri Dubief has called "the specter of revolutionary syndicalism" was the authoritarian selection process for delegates. In accepting the anarchist Pierre Monatte from the Bourse du Travail in Bourg-en-Bresse (capital of the Ain), for example, CGT leaders overlooked the more natural candidate, Liochon, then adjunct secretary of the printers' federation and a native of the town. Similarly, the "extremely moderate" Bourse of Chartres was represented by one Métivier, an *agent provocateur* paid (and later arrested) by Clemenceau in an effort to make the CGT look worse than it really was.[38]

The fact that less than half the *syndicats* belonging to the CGT actually sent delegates to its congresses aided Clemenceau in this respect. In 1906 only 43 percent (1,040 out of 2,399) took part; in 1912, 45 percent. Considering that the CGT overall represented less than a tenth of the proletariat, it is logical to regard the revolutionaries with suspicion. There are numerous explanations for this, the best probably being the revolutionaries' control of the national offices from which doctrine emanated. And as Ridley points out, the congresses likely attracted the extremes. Because the majority stayed home, it is unlikely that the opinions of these militant delegates accurately reflected their constituents.[39]

Although useful in forming a clearer picture of the relative power of the revolutionaries in the CGT, these statistics cannot tell us their exact numbers nor help us to calculate the true reach of their propaganda. Scholars have merely confirmed that the CGT's electoral methods invariably favored the revolutionaries during their heyday in the early 1900s. Still, appearances count, and while the CGT's antimilitarist image might have been engineered by a powerful minority, these were intelligent, highly qualified men who understood that it was often necessary to bend rules in order to advance a cause. The best evidence for this comes from the contemporaries themselves. In a 1912 study, Sylvain Humbert concluded: "It is certain that if proportional representation is introduced in the domestic constitution of the CGT, the reformist elements would incontestably take over the direction."[40] Even Pouget was not afraid to admit that "if the democratic mechanism was practiced in the worker organizations, the lack of volition on behalf of the unconscious majority and non-union member would paralyze all action. . . . Consequently, for the conscious minority there is an obligation to act, without taking account of the refractory mass."[41] For antimilitarists this duty to act meant, very likely, also to distort.

The problem when one knows and hears so much about a few leaders is that it becomes easy to lose sight of everyone else, which in this case numbered in the tens of thousands. As a sort of corrective to Lagardelle's 1905 survey, an inquiry of reformists in France proved the existence of a silent majority. Of the twenty-four queried about their attitude toward antimilitarism, only one pronounced himself a "convinced antimilitarist" and antipatriot. Most, like J.-P. Granvallet of the National Railroad Syndicat and Bourse of Epernay, called it "a political question that should be excluded from the Syndicat." Others replied that their antimilitarism only went as far as the army's intervention in strikes: "I reject with all my might the other genre of antimilitarism," stated F. Mammale of the Proofreaders-Typographers Syndicat and Bourses of Reims and Soissons. Most provocative were the remarks of L. Doizié of the Paris typographers (Fédération du Livre), who saw in the revolutionary doctrines nothing but problems for workers as a whole:

> Antimilitarism, antipatriotism, anti-this or anti-that? I think it is all essentially politics, and a *syndicat* that has told its members that it is enough for them to belong to the union and try to obtain the best conditions from employers does not have the right to impose any political or philosophical credo which risks creating tensions that lead to the division and reformation of patriotic, militarist, christian, etc. *syndicats* . . . working class against working class.[42]

Even in working-class milieus, politics bulked large. The penetration of antimilitarism was as much a factor of regional issues such as political alliances and municipal governments as it was the dedication and manipulation of revolutionaries. According to a report dated October 10, 1907, out of 139 Bourses du Travail in France, 58 made or favored antimilitarist propaganda. Even when one takes into account that 122 of them actually belonged to the CGT, this is still less than half of all *bourses*. Obviously there are as many reasons for this as there were trade-union centers, but both the report itself and a sense of French political geography can go a long way in explaining why some were more receptive to the propaganda than others.[43]

"It is not pointless," continued the report, "to mention that the great majority of Bourses du Travail that engage in antimilitarist propaganda maintain regular relations with the Socialist Party."[44] The socialist municipality of Limoges, in conjunction with the local *bourse,* for example, regularly held punches for conscripts about to be inducted into the army.[45] According to this report, 42 of the 58 antimilitarist *bourses* (72 percent) had contact with the SFIO. This is significant, because, with the decline of the AIA, militant workers who would have already belonged to the Socialist Party, *syndicats,* and *bourses* began turning to these established groupings to carry on their propaganda. In particular the Jeunesses Socialistes, which existed in most towns with party affiliates (Saint-Etienne, Montceau-les-Mines, Montluçon, Lyon, Brest, Toulon, and so forth), became a crucial means to continue the AIA's work (these cities also had active antimilitarist *bourses*). Perhaps not too ironically, the Jeunesses Socialistes maintained headquarters in the same Paris building (45 rue de Saintonge) that the AIA had occupied. As the report added, "the Socialist Party incurs a large responsibility for the present state of affairs because it favors, supports, and often forms the 'Jeunesses Socialistes.' "[46]

Yet this simplified picture neglects the array of regional factors such as labor force (predominantly artisanal, industrial, or agricultural) that influenced local receptivity to revolutionary syndicalism. In Lorient, the principal *bourse* directors worked at the arsenal and belonged to the active, revolutionary Fédération du Bâtiment, and four were listed in the Carnet B.[47] Conversely, one would not expect antimilitarist *bourses* to have flourished in Guesdist strongholds such as the Massif Central and the departments of the Nord and Dordogne, which were generally hostile toward syndicalism. Indeed in the mining region of the Nord only the Saint-Amand Bourse is cited for "rather active" antimilitarist propaganda, while the department as a whole was not found to promote revolutionary syndicalism. Similarly, the *bourse* in Périgueux (capital of the Dordogne) remained unremarkable for its revolutionary propaganda. And except for the Corrèze on the western border of the Massif Central, none of its departments (Cantal, Haute Loire, Puy-de-Dôme) showed signs of an active antimilitarist campaign with the *bourses.* By contrast, in Hervé's Yonne the *bourses* in Sens and Auxerre served as centers of revolutionary propaganda.[48]

According to these reports, the following regions had particularly active antimilitarist *bourses:* Paris and its environs; Brittany (especially Lorient, Brest, and Fougères); the Centre, including the departments of the Cher (Bourges), the Allier (Montluçon), the Indre (Issoudun and Chateauroux), the Haute Vienne (Limoges), and the Saône-et-Loire (Mâcon and Montceau-les-Mines); the Loire-Saint-Etienne region; and the Midi méditerranéen, including the Aude (Narbonne), the Gard (Nîmes), the Hérault

(Sète), and the Var (Toulon); as well as the departments of the Yonne (Auxerre and Sens), the Côte d'Or (Dijon), the Marne (Reims), the Meurthe-et-Moselle (Nancy), the Seine-Maritime (Rouen), and the Pyrénées Atlantiques (Bayonne).[49] In regions where syndicalism successfully mobilized workers—such as Saint-Étienne, where it attracted artisans by emphasizing day-to-day shop floor issues and supporting artisan-industry solidarity during strikes—antimilitarism also tended to find its way into the local Bourses du Travail.[50]

Agricultural regions such as Brittany and the vine-growing Midi méditerranéen figure prominently among the areas where antimilitarism (characteristically in the form of anticonscription) entered local *bourses*. French rural workers indeed had a long history of antimilitarist agitation, as peasant productivity typically depended on each individual laborer, and the loss of a single hand to the army could ruin a family or parish. In 1860, the mayor of Plozévet (Finistère) begged for the discharge of a peasant's son, "for if he has to return to service . . . his father will be forced to abandon his farm." More cunningly, well into the 1870s a small Bourbonnais village in the Allier regularly recorded its male births as females. Until the Third Republic's first military reform went into effect in 1873, farmers could "buy off" their sons for fifteen hundred to eighteen hundred francs. About twenty thousand farmers a year took advantage of the *substitution*, although it often meant serious financial sacrifice. For rural workers, antimilitarism, or more precisely an instinctive resentment of the army, was a natural response to the imposition of a competing power.[51]

Eugen Weber has argued that the 1890s marked a crucial mental shift during which military service went from this intrusion of the "other" to an accepted form of national responsibility for ordinary people. After the 1889 reform bill reduced service from five to three years and abolished exemptions (for students, teachers, priests, seminarians, and the oldest sons of widows or large families) and the fifteen hundred franc dispensation for one-year volunteers, military participation came to represent a shared national duty. By the late nineteenth century conscripts could even count on a better diet and standard of living in the caserne than they had back home on the farm. The army, according to Weber, served as a crucial "agency of change" to assimilate peasants and forge the national identity.[52]

Weber's "modernization" theory has been roundly attacked for its tendency to gloss over regional differences and treat rural France as if it moved toward national integration as a single unit over the narrow time frame of 1870 to 1914. The "cake of custom," whether already broken by the late eighteenth century through capitalist means of exchange, as Charles Tilly has argued, or still subject to convulsions and dislocations well into the twentieth, was never completely destroyed with respect to peasant attitudes toward the army.[53] As Weber himself acknowledges, antimilitarism in the early twentieth century played on and preyed upon these fundamental, ingrained animosities.[54]

In his study of the largely agrarian Var, Jean Masse confirms the traditional antiarmy attitudes of rural workers. He views, for example, the hostile campaign waged against the three-year military law in 1913 as more of an awakening of "latent peasant antimilitarism" than the manifestation of some newly developed ideas about military corruption. The Var prefect thus reassured the interior minister that although public concern was warranted, he understood this traditional element: "In the first place, rural property is very divided and manpower rare and costly: the parents need the labor of their children and bear with difficulty the sacrifice of a supplementary year."[55]

But the Var also had a small, important industrial sector[56] and, as the 1907 reports indicate, it was friendly terrain for antimilitarism—an "avant-garde department." To understand what happened in 1914, why antimilitarists did not carry out a single threat, is thus a more complicated matter. Fortunately two good area studies have thrown light on the extent to which the propaganda touched regions noted for their antimilitarist *bourses*. Masse's work on the Var and Roland Andréani's study of the Mediterranean Languedoc (Gard, Hérault, and Aude) are particularly useful because they were far from the contested area of Alsace-Lorraine and had large, well-organized working-class populations in both industry and agriculture.[57]

The Var was especially amenable to antimilitarism owing to its high worker density and syndicalist and anarchist networks. Toulon had had a Bourse du Travail since 1889, and the towns of Saint-Raphaël, Hyères, and La Seyne established *bourses* shortly thereafter. By 1910 the Var boasted eighty-six *syndicats* comprising 10,352 members, with another 9,410 organized peasants. Anarchism also seems to have maintained a foothold, especially in Toulon.[58] One day after an *affiche* addressed to conscripts appeared on city walls (on November 14–15, 1904), Almereyda and Francis Jourdain (AIA founding members) spoke to a crowd estimated at four hundred, after which some hundred people formed the Groupe Antimilitariste Toulonnais. In all likelihood, the new city library distributed the group's propaganda.[59]

Socialism was also important in the Var, and Tony Judt has shown that it made significant inroads not only among urban industrial workers but in rural areas as well. By 1898 socialists were the dominant political force in the department, with victorious candidates in Draguignan, Toulon, and Brignoles. Their successes, which paralleled the rise of antimilitarism, lasted through 1914, when the party won all four seats allocated to it in the Chamber of Deputies.[60] *La Guerre Sociale* counted sixty subscribers in Toulon.[61]

Antimilitarism, however, was a factor of individuals and not parties, of organizers and followers and not simply unions and disgruntled workers. In examining beneath the surface, the reality of its impact in the Var becomes apparent. According to the subprefect of Brignoles, his arrondissement, despite some socialist activity, "was never directly touched" by antimilitarist propaganda. Draguignan, the (then) capital, was "very little" affected. In Toulon, which can be further divided into Hyère, La Seyne, and Toulon proper, only one group seems to have made a consistent effort at antimilitarism—the Jeunesse Libre (formerly Jeunesse Syndicale), a mixed bag of Hervéist, anarchist, and intellectual influence whose activities authorities judged to be "rather platonic" (the distribution of *La Guerre Sociale* and *La Voix du Peuple*, for example). Some suggested that this was due to a lack of funds and the poor health of one of its leaders.[62]

Still, Jean Masse is able to give several examples of demonstrations in this period that became embarrassing scenes for the military and filled reams of police reports. The arsenal workers, who alone comprised half of the "known and confirmed" anarchists in Toulon, were particularly conspicuous (along with the anarchist paper boys). A German attaché even attributed "dangerous influence" to them.[63] Reporting for *L'Écho de Paris*, Henri de Noussane found local police in a state of confident, though cautious, alert: "The morale of our men remains excellent. . . . We have trouble just containing them. In spite of troop and gendarmerie reinforcements, the service is very difficult. If you could see this unfortunate city, you would understand how much our fears were justified when we spoke the other day. . . . I am not angry, nevertheless, to have seen my rogues at the test of the crowd.[64] Clearly, Toulon antimilitarists had the capacity to disrupt civil order, and authorities did not dare to take their outbursts lightly.

For the Var, the antimilitarists' inability to launch a protest in 1914 had as much to do with regional factors as national ones. The fact that Guesdist (as opposed to Allemanist or Hervéist) ideology was most successful in mobilizing rural people certainly played a part.[65] The primarily anarchist rather than syndicalist domination of Toulonnais antimilitarism was a likely factor as well. Most important, Masse argues, was that Varois antimilitarism "had to remain eminently superficial." The rallies and posters, even if they became violent or provoked a regiment to sing the "Internationale," ultimately spoke more to a preexisting hostility toward the army than to any real feeling about how to prevent the next war. In the Var, Masse concludes, antimilitarist propaganda served as a lightning rod for workers to manifest their frustration with the army and the way it impinged on their lives. The lightning struck hard, but it struck only intermittently and, above all, inconsistently.[66]

In the vine-growing country of Languedoc, antimilitarist propaganda tended to reach the groups facing the greatest economic difficulties. In particular, Andréani finds that the wage-earning agricultural workers who suffered most in the 1907 wine-producing crisis, as opposed to the small landowners (who were able to break even) and city workers, were the most susceptible. But in Narbonne, Sète, Montpellier, Alès, and Nîmes, antimilitarist activity rose and fell more with the fate of individual leaders such as Louis Niel (secretary-general of the Montpellier Bourse) or Louis Jeannot (Sète), than with the economic problems that culminated in 1907. A good example is the *affiche rouge,* which a local antimilitarist group posted in the declining port town of Sète on October 8, 1905. Following the lead of Paris, officials sentenced the group's secretary to six months in prison, temporarily stifling antimilitarist initiatives. Andréani's conclusions in this respect are similar to those of Masse: the working classes were ultimately more absorbed in their day-to-day problems, as well as how unions and leftist political action could help solve the local economic crisis, than they were with any grandiose projects such as antimilitarism. They turned to antipatriotism and insurrection only if they had nowhere else to turn.[67]

With respect to the Bourses du Travail and Socialist Party in Languedoc, Andréani's study supports Laura Frader's conclusion (for the Aude) that socialism and syndicalism "developed tactically, in response to local conditions, interests, and capacities for action." For example, although Frader has shown that revolutionary syndicalism was important in mobilizing rural workers, Andréani's research found no evidence of a Sou du Soldat fund in any of the local *bourses.* This is consistent with Frader's argument that "syndicalism in the Aude focused on bread-and-butter improvements for workers instead of social revolution." Even in the volatile Languedoc, which saw "some of the most dramatic conflicts between labor and capital and between vine growers and the state of the prewar years," economic issues took precedence over the CGT's antimilitarist program.[68]

The evidence for the SFIO, which was also strong in the region, similarly indicates that it followed moderate lines and did not owe its success to Hervéist thinking.[69] A meeting planned for Carcassonne on March 20, 1909, which featured Hervé as the speaker, was almost canceled when city officials failed to secure a lecture hall. In the end, only about sixty "curious" went to hear the renowned socialist.[70] By contrast, when Jaurès spoke at a congress in Narbonne in October 1907, the room, which held 3,500, was "full to the gunwales." The local journal *La Dépêche* reported that the socialist leader was welcomed with "bravos that shook the boards of the stage and reverberated in the distance as far as the street." Nor did the applause let up when Jaurès struck a strong, characteristic note of Jacobin patriotism: "We, the socialists, are two times patriots. . . . Our forefathers of '93, when they defended France against foreign countries, did not only defend their soil, but above all the new *patrie,* the new right that the counter-revolutionaries contested against them." Coming only four months after government troops killed six workers in Narbonne, this reception testifies to the contentment of most ordinary people with traditional means of protest.[71]

Perceptions and Deceptions

Prefects and police commissioners of the early twentieth century obviously did not have the hindsight of Masse and Andréani. Regardless of the unremarkable number of *bourses* specified for antimilitarist propaganda, governmental apprehensions about it were not in the least bit assuaged: "But the evil is deep. A long tolerance has allowed antimilitarism to conquer a large part of the working mass, which is accustomed to confusing Syndicalism with Antipatriotism, and it will take several years to compel the *Syndicats* and the Bourses du Travail to withdraw strictly within the limits the law has traced for them." Was such an outlook warranted? Shortly after the October 1907 report, a new survey signaled just 36 Bourses du Travail for active antimilitarist or revolutionary propaganda. But this figure was deceptive. If one tallies all the *bourses* for which the "degree of their revolutionary activity" fell between the categories of "rather active" and "very intense," then the total is 68, a definite increase from the earlier report. On the other hand, only 33 *bourses* were classified as exhibiting "little" or "no" propaganda of a revolutionary nature (the rest were ambiguously labeled "moderate" or "very moderate").[72] Furthermore, a new inquiry in October 1911 named 93 Bourses du Travail or Unions des Syndicats (out of 170) for their active antimilitarist or revolutionary propaganda.[73] Although this figure is not a tremendous increase percentage-wise (about 55 percent of the total), it cannot be taken lightly. It was in this same year that the interior ministry turned the Carnet B into a list of revolutionaries to be arrested at the start of mobilization. Based on this statistical evidence, then, it appears that the government vindicated itself when, in 1907, it anxiously concluded: "It is to be feared that, little by little, all the Bourses du Travail will be won over to this propaganda."[74]

Yet as we have just seen, these formal computations are meaningless until examined at the regional level. Just what, exactly, constituted "active revolutionary and antimilitarist propaganda" to these investigators? The reports by no means ignored the local situation, but it was usually rendered in such a superficial and quantitative fashion that the presence of *any* antimilitarist activity was enough to convince authorities of the potential for a major disruption. Thus, for example, in response to the October 1907 inquiry, the prefect of the Nord named no less than seven antimilitarist groups in this otherwise nonsyndicalist department. They turned up in the capital of Lille, as well as in Roubaix, Tourcoing, Dunkerque, and Fresnes. The Roubaix group was the largest, with thirty-one members, while that in Dunkerque had just eight. Antimilitarism certainly existed in the Nord but, realistically, what sort of a threat did such small groups pose to the mobilization for war?[75]

By 1912, five years after the October 1907 report painted the *bourses* in most Languedocian cities as active antimilitarist centers, police could identify only one antimilitarist in Béziers, twenty-four in Montpellier, nine in Sète, and a few in the smaller towns of Marsillargues, Ganges, Frontignan, Pézenas, and Montagnac, for a grand total of forty-eight in the Hérault.[76] This time the statistical evidence worked in reverse: one of the seemingly most active antimilitarist regions proved illusory a few years later.

Jean-Jacques Becker's research in Calvados provides a more thorough example of how easily authorities succumbed to distortion with regard to this data. In this "neither uniquely agricultural nor particularly industrial department," where officials signaled the *bourse* in the capital of Caen as "little active" in 1907, Becker has nonetheless unearthed a dossier of all antimilitarist acts, "large and small," that provoked administrative intervention from 1907 to 1913. Here are some examples: fifty people in the Catholic pilgrimage site of Lisieux who had fallen under antimilitarist influence (1907); seven *affiches* with sayings such as "soldier, reflect and conclude yourself" in Falaise (1909); the expulsion of a *colporteur* (peddler) of revolutionary songs from the local fairgrounds (1912). Throughout Calvados, one might conclude from this single dossier, antimilitarism had made itself felt.[77]

The irony is that without government interference, none of these groups or isolated incidents would have come to light. "In fact," Becker writes, "pushed by the continual governmental directives, by the dangers of a tense international situation, the authorities are prey to a veritable antimilitarist paranoia: the most minor incidents, the affixation of one single *affiche*, provoke a cascade of reports from commissar to sub-prefect, sub-prefect to prefect, prefect to the criminal investigation department (Sûreté)."[78] The prefect of the Haute-Vienne reached a similar conclusion with regard to the press after a crowd of antimilitarist hecklers greeted General Tournier in Limoges, often out-shouting the nationalist crowd. The events surrounding the general's arrival, he wrote, were "deformed, exaggerated, and distorted by the Parisian press . . . [which] latched onto them and dramatized them."[79] None of these examples is meant to devalue clear-cut cases of antimilitarism, only to put them into proper perspective. The army was not popular in this period, particularly because of its policing of working-class protests and the burden of universal conscription. Any move to undermine it did not necessarily indicate an unwillingness to defend France, but rather how deeply popular dissatisfaction with the moral code of the military ran; far deeper, that is, than Hervéism did.

In Pouget's short-lived journal *Révolution*, Commandant Draveil is quoted as saying that "the first cause" of antimilitarism was that it "resides organically in the mind of the worker, not only the union or socialist worker, but that of the isolated worker, he who leads, all alone, far from comfort and collective hope, the cruel combat of life." Hervé and the CGT had thus moved into "a marvelously prepared terrain," plowed over by innumerable discontented workers who had suffered at the hands of military discipline and regimental life. The irony, as Draveil himself proudly recognized, was that it took an officer to bring this to light. This obviously made him biased, but Draveil was no doubt on to something. Antimilitarism did not need a large and organized national following to have an impact, but took advantage of latent, though long-standing, resentments against the army that were shared by ordinary people, the working classes above all. A few local activists to organize rallies around the town square, to cover the walls with *affiches*, and to turn the *bourses* and left-wing journals into vehicles for the spread of their ideas, and *voilà*, the elements of a powerful, threatening "movement."[80]

Is this to say that antimilitarism was merely the hollow rumblings of a disaffected and disillusioned minority? This study hardly purports to advance such a thesis. The evidence for the inability of antimilitarist leaders to secure a firm commitment from workers in no way obviates their importance in French political culture. And although the decline of the AIA was perhaps a clear indication of the general lack of support for a coordinated, antimilitarist effort, the syndicalist movement and Socialist Party were well-supported, influential, and prepared to take up the slack. The AIA leaders themselves came from these milieus and learned to concentrate their efforts within them, which is one reason authorities took them so seriously. Another reason was that antimilitarism continued strong through 1914. As we shall see, there were many more opportunities for the government to gauge the influence of the revolutionaries on the working classes and to conclude for itself how much of a threat to mobilization they really posed. The story, in other words, is far from over. The political and diplomatic events of the years prior to World War I would reshape the actions and attitudes of the antimilitarists, just as they heightened the anxiety of the government.

Above all, it is impossible to dismiss antimilitarism as the rhetoric of a few diehards such as Yvetot and Hervé, who were important leaders in their own right and had a significant impact in France generally. Hervé provides the best example. How should we judge his influence in the Socialist Party if he was reviled by most of its leaders? Were Hervéists merely one extreme faction with little weight on the whole and destined always to wallow on the outskirts of the SFIO owing to their leader's unequivocal repulsion of parliamentary politics?

This is hard to imagine considering Hervé's overall renown and the rapid success of *La Guerre Sociale*. In mid-1906, after his release from prison, Hervé seemed to ride a wave of popular support. He defended several prominent leftists such as Yvetot and the representative of the Dock Workers Union, Marck, who had been accused of fomenting violence during a seamen's strike. He also had broadened his contacts to include anarchist and syndicalist leaders such as Almereyda, secretary of the editorial board, and Eugène Merle, manager of *La Guerre Sociale*. Pouget, Vignée d'Octon, the Greek revolutionary Amilcare Cipriani, and Frédéric Stackelberg (a rich Russian aristocrat with anarchist pretensions) now joined their own struggles against militarism to that of Hervé.[81] Jaurès and Guesde may have been wary of his antipatriotism and its disruptive potential for the party, but by 1906–1907 Hervé had branched out, no longer relying on socialist politics to spread his ideas.

By the same token, he did not depend on ideological dogma and charismatic speech delivery to publicize his ideas. Hervé was active in many of the working-class confrontations of the day, including the vine-growers' revolt in the Midi (1907) and the strikes of postal workers (1909) and railroad men (1910).[82] International politics also propelled him into action. One of Hervé's most controversial and likewise potent stands came in the articles on Morocco he wrote for *La Guerre Sociale*. Hervé was adamantly opposed to French intervention in the colony ("Moroccan brigandage"), and was even prosecuted for encouraging the Moroccan people to "knock hard on the bandits who invade you!" (December 4–10, 1907). His 1911 article "Attila in Morocco" earned him three months in prison.[83]

In France and abroad, Hervé's ideas made important gains. Outside the Yonne he won supporters in scattered enclaves of small farmers in the Jura Mountains, the south of the Rhône corridor, the Somme, the Meurthe-et-Moselle, and the Saône-et-Loire.[84] Beyond France, in the spring of 1908 Italian socialists from the northern industrial city of Turin launched *La Guerra Sociale* to spread the Sans-Patrie's ideas. A young ideologue named Benito Mussolini was one of its contributors, although the journal was short-lived due to government prosecution. Even in Germany Hervé enjoyed a certain notoriety among a minority of socialists who were dissatisfied with the conservative leanings of their party. In 1906 a German translation of *Leur patrie* appeared. In 1910 it was published in English. A syndicalist paper in the United States advertised Hervé's books and pamphlets. But it was in September 1907 that he attained the height of his national and international fame during the Socialist International congress at Stuttgart.[85]

What Hervé achieved at the first International on German soil was to force the socialists to accept a resolution that left open the possibility of an internationally organized general strike or insurrection in the case of war. It was not an easy task. Led by the intransigent Bebel, the Germans felt that the question of action in the event of war was a moot one, and they adhered to Guesde's position that the socialist revolution, *when* it came, would take care of war by itself. Hervé would have none of this simplistic hand wringing, and in his speech to the assembly he made clear his frustration with the stale bureaucracy and *embourgeoisement* of the SPD: "You are no more than a machine for voting and counting contributions. You have absolutely no revolutionary spirit. . . . You are a herd of sheep under the leadership of your kaiser Bebel." Hervé's rage made for an awkward moment at the congress, but achieved its goal: German socialists could no longer avoid the issue of antimilitarism.[86]

Although Hervé did not sit on the subcommittee that drew up the resolution on militarism and international conflicts, his spirit was certainly in it. Likewise was that of all factions, from Hervé (and Lenin-Rosa Luxemburg) to Jaurès-Vaillant to Bebel-Guesde. The declaration began with a reiteration of the Marxian notion that "wars are . . . inherent in the nature of capitalism," and thus socialists must "fight with all their strength against naval and military armament" and work toward the abolition of permanent armies. There was Jaurèsian praise for the international congress in Brussels and its "untiring fight against militarism through . . . its endeavors to make military organization democratic." And there was a tip of the hat to Hervé: "In case of the threat of an outbreak of war, it is the duty of the working classes and their parliamentary representatives in the countries taking part, fortified by the unifying activity of the International Bureau, to do everything to prevent the outbreak of war by whatever means seem to them most effective, which naturally differ with the intensification of the class war and the general political situation." It was the part about "whatever means," which did not exclude a general strike, that made Hervé leap onto a table and thrust his hands into the air in victory. At the end of the day, all factions had been appeased and the socialists had a platform for responding to war. But the excitement of the moment and the months ahead—when Jaurès and Hervé could both extol the virtues of the same piece of paper—overshadowed the fact that, to paraphrase James Joll, while this long and involved resolution contained something for everybody, it committed nobody to anything.[87]

◆ ◆ ◆

To look back on the first decade of the twentieth century, one might see Stuttgart looming as a kind of symbol for French antimilitarism in general: among the working classes, everyone was conscious of it, although no one was really committed to doing anything unless it affected him or her directly. Hervé's renown and the massive outflow of leftist propaganda did not ensure that workers would put down their tools in the event of a war and rise up against their capitalist oppressors. Nor did it guarantee, for example, that arsenal workers in Tulle (Corrèze) would blow up their factory, as they said they would and encouraged others to do, in 1905.[88] Hervé and Hervéism were certainly the most pronounced symptoms of the very real injustices felt by ordinary working people. And although they came to serve as powerful symbols of the possibilities for concerted action, the range and reception of the Hervéist program were subject to circumstances largely out of the program's control. Peter Stearns's label of revolutionary syndicalism as a "cause without rebels" is thus too simplistic.[89] Antimilitarism had supporters in France, but the dedication of these workers was more of an individual and local matter than an ideological and doctrinal one. The propaganda was there, but it only touched them when they needed it to.

Not long after Stuttgart, while Hervé was still at what historians would later describe as the peak of his renown, a police report explained his importance thus: "Gustave Hervé, whom it would be necessary to invent if he did not exist, has done Society the immense service of forcing these people [the radical elements] to unfurl their flag openly, and to render any confusion impossible for those who intentionally are the most blind."[90] In other words, Hervé had compelled the Left to take a stand on antimilitarism, regardless of what role individual leaders felt it should play in their broader movement. Not only was he causing strife in leftist ranks and a split between radicals and socialists in Parliament, but Hervé alone had made antimilitarism a topic of major moment, discussed at international congresses and in local Bourses du Travail. His ideas may only have been superficially received, but they were widespread, and his antagonists, at least, took them seriously.

A similar observation was made in 1907 by the AIA leaders Tissier and Amette, who recognized that whatever problems the short-lived AIA had encountered in securing a consistent support base, it had achieved one thing that could never be precisely measured or accounted for: "It has prepared people's minds for the present movement; if it has not constructed a house that can contain many tenants, it has built a facade sufficient to frighten the government and bourgeoisie. There is nothing behind this facade, yet it is because of this cardboard wall that Clemenceau tirelessly hounds the few rebels against the army, and even that these few agitators exist."[91] Antimilitarism may have lacked the manpower to stop an international war, but its prevalence in working-class political culture continued to have an impact in numerous, often more immediate, ways.

5. GLORY TO THE 17TH!

"In the army itself," Émile Faguet wrote in his 1908 book *Le Pacifisme*, "antipatriotic propaganda has penetrated, it seems, profoundly, more profoundly than elsewhere; without doubt it is on the army, as is natural, that the antimilitarist propaganda has borne the largest effort."[1] Faguet was not a stupid man. The author of numerous works of literary and historical criticism, a professor at the Sorbonne, a member of the Académie Française, Faguet was a tireless scholar with interests that ranged from seventeenth-century poetry to nineteenth-century philosophy.[2] Often too he delved into contemporary questions. In *Le Pacifisme*, Faguet evaluated the nature and implications of all the antiwar currents sweeping Europe. His Darwinian argument essentially came down to this: patriotism, which emanated from the culture and traditions of a country, was the keystone to national survival. Once antipatriotism had worked its way into the institutions and values of a people, then that society was doomed to be conquered by a stronger one. In France, Faguet argued, sentiments against the *patrie* and its military were on the rise, prompting him to write a book about the dangers that could lie ahead.

The question of whether antipatriotic and antimilitarist doctrines and passions pierced the French military is a complicated one. In one sense, as Faguet had recognized, the answer is resoundingly affirmative and the evidence for it overwhelming: the rise of military indiscipline and disrespect toward officers, antimilitarist tracts in the barracks, demonstrations at railroad stations during the fall departure of conscripts, "trivial excuses for a chorus of the *Internationale* in the canteen, the sarcastic comments and the refusal to salute." All this, continues Douglas Porch, "drained the confidence of officers and NCOs [Noncommissioned Officers] forced to cope with unenthusiastic conscripts plunged into sullen revolt."[3] It is what Raoul Girardet has described as a "crisis of conscience" and David Ralston as the "pathological sensitivity" that gripped the military in the face of outside criticism and a loss of respect for the institution from within.[4] Whatever one calls it, the beginning of the twentieth century found the French army in a profound state of malaise.

Reservists, lacking a long-term commitment to the military, provide the best example of this new mood. In 1903 Driant wrote that many simply took it for granted that their training would include a demonstration against their treatment by the officers. In 1905, a hundred reservists in the 121st Territorial Regiment took the train back to Béziers without permission in order to "avoid the rain."[5] In July 1907, *Le Matin* and *La Petite République* reported that a reserve second lieutenant on a training mission to Lons-le-Saunier (Jura) presided over an antimilitarist meeting organized by a local socialist group.[6] That September *L'Écho de Paris* reported that a reservist had treated the flag carried by a passing regiment as a rag.[7] "The reserve call-up only served to demonstrate the progress of antimilitarist doctrines among several of them," declared the most important military journal of the day, *La France Militaire*, in September 1906.[8]

Indiscipline, misbehavior, and a general rowdiness and recalcitrance did not elude the regulars either. In January 1903 sixty-five soldiers of the 33rd Regiment rioted and shattered barrack windows. Similar outbursts, often punctuated with shouts of "down with the army!" and "long live socialism!," occurred in Angoulême, Epernay, Rennes, Rochefort, Tours, and Clermont-Ferrand, although these cities were not cited in the 1907 reports as being particularly active antimilitarist centers.[9] In May 1906, police reported that several soldiers guarding the *affiche rouge* signers at Clairvaux prison were smuggling out brochures for them.[10] In January 1911, an investigation of the 12th Army Corps at Limoges concluded that servicemen in nearly all the regiments had received antimilitarist circulars similar to those from the local Employers' Federation of Masonry and Stone. In his report to the prefect of the Haute Vienne, Division General Pelecier warned that the Sou du Soldat resolved to establish in the army a "veritable organization that would function in the case of war . . . to paralyze mobilization."[11]

Although Limoges was a "red city" with a strong socialist presence, a region did not have to be noted for its leftist leanings to harbor unruly soldiers. In response to Clemenceau's 1907 directive, the prefect of the generally conservative Ile-et-Vilaine described an antimilitarist center in the garrison town of Vitré, as well as a group in St.-Ouen (outside Paris) that allegedly bribed soldiers to desert with money and clothes. A soldier named Versepuy confessed that he had fallen prey to a reservist from this group, and during an interrogation he named three former soldiers as antimilitarist partisans.[12]

Although such evidence for the spread of antimilitarism among soldiers appeared incontrovertible, Porch has emphasized that it would be wrong to pin on them too many assumptions about an overall decline in military discipline. These were, generally, isolated incidents, many of which arose out of immediate frustrations such as a heavy workload or the harsh punishment of a comrade. The "mutiny of the 53rd" in Perpignan, for example, turned out to be no more than a show of support for a sympathetic colonel thought by his men to have been unduly disciplined. Still, the disorder it caused in the citadel courtyard demonstrated a new willingness on the part of reservists to act on their frustrations.[13] If anything was different, it was the perception of what was permissible within the context of military culture. "The attitude of the soldiers has completely changed in the last two years," observed Madame Racaud, canteen keeper of the 17th Regiment: "Often in the canteen things became unbearable. . . . They rioted, breaking and shattering everything while singing the *Internationale*. . . . Bad manners, disorder and excitement were everyday occurrences."[14]

The fact is, it was not merely that antimilitarist ideas abounded, but that they had arrived just as the military was going through its most trying time since the advent of the Republic. Not only had the Dreyfus Affair humbled the *arche sainte,* but it pointed up the military's awkward adjustment to the new form of government. One of the best examples of this began in 1901, when War Minister General André abolished promotion committees and general inspections in favor of a system of index cards, or *fiches,* on which he recorded the political leanings of each officer. In this way André consolidated power over military promotion into his own ministry, away from the politicians. Although the French army had traditionally been a bastion of conservative politics with close ties to the church, this attempt to promote republican officers—with all the trappings of a personal espionage system—had by 1904 become a major political scandal that brought down André and the Combes ministry. By emphasizing political connections, the *affaires des fiches* had further undermined military ideals such as excellence, self-respect, hierarchy, and autonomy.[15]

The Dreyfus Affair and *affaire des fiches* were crucial to the overall decline in military prestige. Writing on civil-military relations in January 1900, Commandant de Civrieux complained: "My uniform, once respected, is no more than a flunkey's suit."[16] The political corruptness of promotions—which meant it could take twelve to fifteen years to become a lieutenant, but only given the right political connections—undercut the allure of a military career. So did the decreased material advantages—an officer barely earned enough to support a family. In *L'Officier contemporain* (*The Contemporary Officer*, 1911), Captain d'Arbeux wrote: "Ten or twenty years ago the officer with his mind set on marriage attired himself in dress uniform and white gloves in order to seek out his prospective father-in-law. Today he scarcely dare confess he is an officer, and begs to be excused this youthful indiscretion."[17] The diminished romance of military life was accentuated by the fact that more battles were fought against the working class than against foreign invaders. General Sonnois "burst with indignation" over the army's role as a domestic police force, and he urged soldiers' families to "protest energetically" against this "scandalous abuse of the army's requisitioning right."[18]

Perhaps the best indicator of this rising dissatisfaction with military life was the precipitous drop in the number of men who chose it as their career. Candidates for Saint-Cyr fell 60 percent between 1897 and 1911, from 1,920 to 871. From 1900 to 1911 the number of noncommissioned officers who re-enlisted decreased from 72,000 to 41,000.[19] In 1907, 36 percent of the territorials failed to report for service. From 1907 to 1909 desertions more than tripled (from 5,000 to 17,000). Cases of disciplinary court-martials doubled between 1906 and 1911.[20]

All this spoke of a crisis—"of idleness and of weariness, of doubt and of discouragement"—that had settled over the military.[21] Morale was at an all-time low. Riven with political entanglements and clinging to the Alsace-Lorraine myth, army life began to take on a sort of mundane complacency that was barely recognizable and entirely disagreeable to those who made it their career. "We spent entire weeks," Major Simon wrote, "adjusting the straps around revolver holsters and canteens, seeing to it that the former run between the first and second tunic buttons and the latter between the second and third tunic buttons. . . . On the range, what mattered was not to hit the target frequently, but to adopt the precise posture called for by regulations, even if the marksman's physique made this uncomfortable for him."[22] In 1907 William-Georges Clément wrote that the "good soldier, or at least someone who is considered as such, is he who makes a square bed and kit pack, who polishes his leathers, who washes and arranges his linen, it is in a word the type of soldier who is well-behaved, timid and orderly."[23] In *La Transformation de l'armée* (1909), General Metzinger deplored the inattention given to the army's moral needs.[24] "A veritable crisis of the officers' cadres is in the making," exclaimed Claude Ares in *La Décadence intellectuelle de l'armée*.[25]

As politics interfered with army morale, so too did it with preparations for war. Petitions to upgrade military matériel such as chemical explosives and automatic weapons met with stiff resistance in Parliament. In 1905 a military reform law reduced compulsory service from three to two years and decreased the number of reservist training days from two periods of twenty-eight days to twenty-three days and, later, to seventeen days. The effective size of the army diminished from 615,000 to 504,000.[26]

Yet it was not politicians alone who made life difficult for those entrusted with the management of war—French military authorities themselves seem to have slipped into a kind of technological torpor in which they failed to recognize the importance of innovations that would alter warfare completely, heavy artillery and the machine gun above all. Instead they clung to the idea of a single, all-out offensive (*offensive à outrance*), coupled with vague notions about superior French military *esprit*, in their ruminations and preparations for the next war. As officers became more administrators than fighting men, they lost touch with the exigencies of planning a war against the rapidly industrializing and demographically exploding Germany. "The École de Guerre [War College] was not a laboratory where the army's elite boiled up tactical doctrine," writes Porch, "but a school where future staff men learned the nuts and bolts of military administration."[27]

Antimilitarists aside, the French military in the early 1900s was in a battle of its own. Not surprisingly, several contemporaries inferred from this that the army itself bore part of the blame. In his brochure *D'où vient l'antimilitarisme? Pourquoi y-a-til des antimilitaristes? L'armée telle qu'elle est!* (*Where Does Antimilitarism Come From? Why Are There Antimilitarists? The Army Such as It Is!*), William-Georges Clément wrote: "Antimilitarism today is the result of what officers do not know how to cultivate: the morale of the troops! There are antimilitarists because we have had and we still have too many bad officers!"[28] The senator and ex-officer Charles Humbert believed: "Nothing is indeed more urgent and nothing will any longer be effective—in annihilating the monstrous efforts of the men who seek to undermine the bases of patriotism and turn our conscript classes into such antimilitarist mobs—than finally to work seriously to protect the health of the soldier, his well-being, and to give all our officers the confidence and ardor from which heroic devotions are born."[29] The problem, in other words, lay within the military culture itself. Improve it, and antimilitarism will go away or, at least, truly become irrelevant.

The Cléments and Humberts, however, were the exception, as most military leaders, conservative politicians, and even journalists used the issue to wage their own war on the French Left. In the press in particular, journals from the nationalist *L'Éclair* (a competitor with *L'Écho de Paris* that had print runs of over 100,000) to the moderate *Le Journal* and *Le Petit Parisien* (the latter with its million-plus readers) began covering nearly every incident of indiscipline they could find, from a young worker in Grand-Croix who would not return to his regiment after reading antimilitarist brochures[30] to the refusal of a lieutenant and professor of civil procedure in Caen to carry the flag.[31] "It is a new column—sad column!—that we must henceforth open in the French press," wrote Georges Doutremont in the first of a series on antimilitarism in the army for *L'Écho de Paris*.[32] From January to May 1907, Doutremont attacked "the progress of antimilitarism" in the army: "Hardly a day without a lamentable series of acts of indiscipline, of insults to servicemen, even to the flag! . . . It is now a gangrene that menaces the entire army. It is necessary to apply the red light quickly if we wish there always to be a France." Rather than blaming the army, Doutremont called for more arrests, insisting that Jaurès and Hervé "held the government under their yoke." In April he reiterated André Chéradame's report in *L'Énergie Française* on an alleged soldiers' network that spread antimilitarism from within the caserne.[33]

When War Minister General Picquart irresponsibly remarked, "Antimilitarism does not exist in the army. Antimilitarism stops at the gate of the casernes. . . . I challenge anyone to cite me one sole case of indiscipline, of refusal to serve, of rebellion," Doutremont gladly accepted the challenge. He devoted two full articles to venting against Picquart: "It is puerile to deny antimilitarism in the army, since it exists in the nation. It is not a question of quibbling, but to combat energetically a profound evil that menaces the existence of our army and our country. To deny this peril, obviously, is to confess [the War Minister's] powerlessness, or his fear, or wish to do nothing to divert it."[34] *L'Éclair* argued that the "shameless audacity" of Picquart masked a true commitment to doing something, and offered "formal proof" that the war minister had undertaken his own, clandestine investigation of the antimilitarist situation.[35] Faguet called Picquart's statement "a white lie designed to reassure public opinion."[36]

If Picquart was not willing to give antimilitarists credit for the military's problems, they were well prepared to take it for themselves. As early as October 1901 the anti-Millerandist *Le Petit Sou* proclaimed: "Socialism gains on the army. It is a truth recognized by everybody, and the capitalist bourgeoisie is terrified of the forests of bayonets that increasingly threaten its privileges and livelihood."[37] By February 1908, Paris police could report:

> The majority of *compagnons* appear very satisfied at the results of the antimilitarist propaganda. Many claim to know, via young comrades presently in uniform, that antimilitarism has spread greatly at the very heart of the regiments, where acts of insubordination and even open rebellion grow. The "Internationale" has become the song of the road and the barracks. Numerous NCOs, among whom might well be some officers, could be socialists, even anarchists. In brief the *compagnons,* as well as the socialists, infer from these facts—perhaps exaggerated but above all at least partially real—that from now on the army no longer exists, so to speak, as a force of anti-revolutionary action.[38]

This was a confident assessment, soon to be disproven in Draveil and Villeneuve-Saint-Georges. Yet how else should antimilitarists have reacted? Each humiliation for the army, each individual act of indiscipline, whatever the cause and however minimal the severity, gave them a new opportunity to flaunt their successes. In 1907, the mutiny of the 17th Regiment marked the culmination of this campaign of distortion.

The Midi Uprisings

The 1907 wine growers' revolt in the Midi has been called the largest peasant uprising since the French Revolution.[39] Like the Revolution, long-term economic hardships combined with spur-of-the-moment organization to produce demonstrations that overwhelmed the government. The four departments—the Gard, Aude, Hérault, and Pyrénées-Orientales—had, over the course of the century, adjusted their economies to the almost exclusive production of a cheap red wine. By the early 1900s, rampant overproduction, competition from Algerian and Spanish imports, and above all the fraudulent addition of sugar and water sent prices plummeting throughout the region. Property values dropped by as much as 90 percent, forcing some landowners to sell their grapes directly from the vine. In 1903 mass protests by vineyard workers began to spread. In 1905 viticultural defense committees sprung up in the Narbonnais and Bittérois (Hérault) to combat *fraudeurs*—

the fraudulent wine producers perceived as having brought the regional economy to its ruin.[40]

In early March 1907, in the hillside village of Argelliers, twenty kilometers north of Narbonne, the café and small vineyard owner Marcelin Albert organized a meeting of the local viticultural defense committee. On March 11 the committee's eighty-seven members, mostly small wine growers like Albert, marched to Narbonne singing "war to the *fraudeurs* without mercy." The demonstrations soon became as regular as Sunday picnics, only much, much larger. In small towns such as Bize, Ouveillan, and Coursan, upward of a thousand people turned out. On Sunday, May 5, 80,000 gathered in Narbonne; 120,000 in Béziers a week later; 170,000 in Perpignan on May 19; 220,000 in Carcassonne on May 26; nearly 300,000 in Nîmes on June 2; and more than 500,000—the largest provincial demonstration in French history—in Montpellier on Sunday, June 9.[41] In the Midi of 1907, gender and class barriers crumbled in the face of severe economic hardship, creating an "interclass front against the government."[42]

On June 18, Clemenceau, who had been locked in a parliamentary debate over how to respond to the crisis, ordered the arrest of Albert, Ernest Ferroul (the socialist mayor of Narbonne), and other leaders of the viticultural defense committee. In so doing he had gravely underestimated not only the Narbonnais' loyalty to their mayor, but their hatred for the troops brought in from outside the region, in particular the pompously adorned cavalrymen. There were confrontations between angry citizens and their foreign invaders throughout the next day, including the serious injury of a captain when demonstrators threw a bottle. But it was on the evening of June 19 that the situation turned into a "bloody carnival" as the cavalrymen, bombarded with rocks and other debris, went on a shooting rampage that left one dead and nine seriously wounded, including a fourteen-year-old boy. The following day (June 20), with Narbonne "bathed in hate," the population went after the "assassins." A crowd marched on the Hôtel de Ville and some revolvers went off, either from the 139th Regiment positioned in front of the building or from the crowd. We will probably never know who fired first, but two salvos delivered by the soldiers rendered this point moot for the five killed. Another dozen lay seriously wounded, as news of the massacre spread quickly.[43]

Meanwhile in Béziers, the 17th Infantry, which was recruited directly from the region, was growing restless over a possible barracks change. Not known for its perfect disciplinary record, the regiment was to be transferred on June 18 to nearby Agde (less than twenty-five kilometers away), rumor had it, in order to get it out of harm's way. Having learned of the transfer in advance, the soldiers encouraged civilians to prevent their departure, and on the day of the transfer a large crowd blocked the barracks shouting: "Don't leave! Rifle butts in the air! Down with Clemenceau! Down with Picquart!" It managed to delay the regiment until 2:00 A.M., when a detachment of gendarmes and cavalrymen cleared the road out of town.[44]

At Agde, a town built out of the dark volcanic stone quarried from nearby Mont St.-Loup, conditions could not have been more ominous. On arrival the troops were met by civilians who took up where the Béziers protesters had left off. Because the only satisfactory caserne in town was already taken by the permanent garrison of the 17th, the company had to occupy a ramshackle convent and disused barracks, which did little to boost troop morale. Further complicating matters, the Bourse du Travail occupied the ground floor of the old caserne. A day later, June 20, the news from Narbonne "added fuel to the flames."[45]

The "revolt" of the 17th Infantry was really more panic than revolt, but that did not make it any less legitimate to either the antimilitarists *or* the military. Convinced that the bloody fate that had befallen protesters in Narbonne was now being carried out in Béziers, soldiers and civilians united against the officers. Two local cafés offered the soldiers free drinks, urging them to "protect civilians." By evening there was talk of a mutiny. According to the canteen manager, a soldier told her: "Tonight, we will revolt. We will be led by the people of the Bourse du Travail. They will lead us to the *Quartier-Neuf,* to the powder magazine. We will take the cartridges and march on Narbonne." Once officers got wind of a planned march to Béziers and then Narbonne, Colonel Ploque ordered his men "to stop this act of indiscipline by all means." Yet when the revolt broke out that evening most of his officers were lounging in a café, many in civilian dress.[46]

The local population, by contrast, was poised for action. Their chance came at 9:00 P.M., when a joint patrol of police and soldiers tried to round up conscripts lingering in the cafés. On encountering a crowd of soldiers and civilians demanding that the caserne be set on fire, the patrol split up and the police headed home. The soldiers, trailed by the crowd, also made for their quarters in the Bourse du Travail building. Now there is no direct evidence of contact between *bourse* leaders and the 17th, but a crowd near the building provided the spark for the revolt. According to witnesses, a few minutes after entering the barracks twenty to thirty soldiers emerged, armed and agitated, into the welcoming arms of the civilians. "We will go to Narbonne to drive off the cavalrymen who have killed our brothers," they shouted, waving their rifle butts in the air.[47]

A group of civilians and mutinous soldiers, including men from the convent and permanent garrison, now acted like any revolutionary crowd: they made for the arsenal. Soldiers and officers who tried to resist them were shoved aside amidst frenzied shouts of "they are killing our parents!" Someone threw a rock that struck Lieutenant-Colonel Boé in the jaw. A local butcher reportedly yelled at him: "You are no longer anything here. It is I who command." By the time the soldiers had pillaged the magazine and distributed twelve thousand cartridges, the officers indeed were powerless to do anything more "than pray, even beseech." Later that night some five hundred men, accompanied by civilians, were back on the road to Béziers.[48]

"Excitement is high amongst these servicemen owing to the alarming news from Narbonne. . . . The situation is extremely serious." Thus read a telegram sent by the Agde police commissioner at 11:40 P.M. to the prefects in Montpellier, Béziers, and to the head prefect in Paris himself, Clemenceau. Headed off by Major Bouyssou in the early hours of June 21, the soldiers balked: "We want to go to Béziers. They are murdering our parents, we are going to defend them." Bouyssou let them pass: "These poor souls had the glowing look of fanatics marching with an unflinching air, their gaze fixed directly in front of them, into the distance, without looking at you, without responding to you, without appearing to understand you." At the head of the 81st Infantry, General Lacroisade next tried to persuade the soldiers to give up their "awful spectacle." Although he also failed, Lacroisade did make contact with the men, and this is important. In the heat of their anger and at the peak of their power, the soldiers promised him that, once in Béziers, they would head straight for the caserne. Many used the occasion to vent frustration with the poor food and lodging at Agde. None, however, made reference to antimilitarist doctrines. Worried about their families, stirred by Agde locals and the Narbonne shootings, or just plain tired of the miserable situation in the barracks, the soldiers had decided to go home.

The entrance into Béziers marked the end of the "panic of the 17th" simply because it confirmed that the fears of the mutinous soldiers had been unfounded. Although the town held a demonstration against the Narbonne massacres that same evening, the soldiers had not fired their guns. In fact the protesters and officers had reached a truce of sorts in which their captain, Luiggi, allowed them to fly the flag at half-mast (in honor of the Narbonne dead) and agreed to call off the gendarmes. Appeased, the citizens of Béziers assured the soldiers that all was in order, and they urged them to return to duty. Their fears put to rest, the men of the 17th, weary from the twenty-two kilometer march through the night, went to bed.

The mutiny did not officially end, however, until the details of the surrender could be worked out. Throughout the day there were tense moments and hurried calls to Clemenceau, as the soldiers threatened to take up their arms if the government brought in more troops or meted out harsh punishment. But by late afternoon on June 22, after receiving vague assurances from Paris that there would be no "individual" punishments, and having been given permission from the general that, as long as they were back in the caserne before noon the next day, they could go home for dinner, the men of the 17th gave up their struggle. The next day they returned to Agde. And although authorities held to their promise of no individual reprimands, the regiment as a whole did not get off lightly. It was subsequently transferred to Gap in the Hautes Alpes, from where 589 soldiers were sent directly to the garrison in Gafsa, Tunisia.[49]

The "revolt of the 17th" sits uncomfortably in a study of antimilitarism. There seems to have been no clear ties between the mutinous soldiers and the revolutionaries; the role of the Bourse du Travail is vague and unsubstantiated; and the mutiny itself was only unpredictable insofar as degree. On this issue of origins, historians generally agree that the revolt was driven more by local events and regional solidarity than by any tangible commitment to antimilitarist doctrines. The shouts of the soldiers during their march to Béziers attests to this as much as their relief on learning that their families were unharmed. The conditions of the barracks; the timing of the Narbonne shootings; the agitation and influence of the local population, all made for a crisis waiting to happen.[50]

This interpretation is backed by Louis Vilarem, the commandant-major of the 17th and an "excellent officer, respected by his men," according to Guy Bechtel.[51] In *Pour mes soldats* (*For My Soldiers*), Vilarem described the mutiny as an "energetic protest against the Narbonne massacres taken in direct support of the nearby people of Béziers, who were believed to be menaced by the same fate as the Narbonnais." He insisted that the disturbance had no connection with the Agde Bourse, and had neither an antimilitarist nor antipatriotic character. Instead Vilarem is sympathetic to his soldiers, suggesting that their action represented the understandable human dimension of a protest against the "yoke of military service." Had it been motivated by antimilitarist doctrines, he argues, then the men's ire would have been directed at their officers: "Now at no time did the soldiers of the 17th mistreat, menace, or insult any of their officers."[52]

Yet antimilitarism was in the air, and nothing did more to confirm the depth to which army morale had sunk, or to heighten the anxiety of officers and political leaders, than the mutiny of the 17th. The response of Vilarem was the exception; in several reports, officers faulted the soldiers for their poor discipline and the "dregs of the nation" for pushing them to revolt.[53] Many directly implicated the Bourse du Travail and other "exterior elements," as did General Galliéni, who directed the inquiry.[54] After painting the Bittérois character as "lazy, sensual, extremely vain, adaptable, and fake," political by nature but afraid of force and punishment and totally lacking any moral sense or respect for authority, battalion chief Bouyssou came to his point: "With this character that I have just tried to depict, this population must receive the socialist and antimilitarist doctrines eagerly. Not acknowledging any restraint and any authority was perfectly suited to its independent and arrogant nature."[55] General Coupillaud of the 33rd Division also had a regional interpretation: "I do not hesitate to affirm that the wine crisis was a pretext for an explosion of antimilitarism in a region ripe—through the weakness of its military sentiments and a certain cowardice—for becoming prey to bold leaders. . . . Far from the dangerous frontier, sheltered from invasion . . . the taste for military things is little developed."[56] The general of the 15th Corps (Marseille) blamed the inferior moral and physical quality of Midi men, which made them "little inclined to bend to military discipline."[57] A less racist explanation may have been the antistatism in the region that one could trace to the time of Louis XIV;[58] or the fact that, in 1848–1851, the Aude, Hérault, and Pyrénées Orientales had put down strong leftist roots. For most military leaders, however, the men of the 17th were simply predisposed and overexposed to antimilitarist propaganda.

Although there is no solid evidence that direct ties between the soldiers and outside agents or leftist organizations caused the revolt, there were endless theories that some indefinite force played a crucial part.[59] *L'Éclair*, which used any excuse available to criticize the Republic, reported that the rebellion had been directed from Paris and then used to justify the military occupation of Béziers. A similar thesis won over Vilarem, who suggested that special government agents were employed to encourage a revolt and thus distract civilians from the Narbonne shootings. The plan only got out of hand, he argued, when the soldiers decided to take up arms. General Coupillaud said he saw an automobile parked in front of the *bourse* during the three days prior to the revolt, and he inferred: "Without any doubt [the auto] brought orders or instructions, then disappeared." A journalist insisted that "a dozen bicyclists" outside the *bourse* on June 20 had incited the men. None of these conspiracy theories have ever been proven. The only thing we know for sure about the revolt of the 17th is that, for antimilitarists, its timing and circumstances could not have been better even *if it were planned.*[60]

Almost as soon as the mutiny was over, antimilitarists began to appropriate it as their own. In meetings to plan a protest against Bastille Day festivities, syndicalist leaders exalted the "valiant soldiers of the 17th."[61] During the actual demonstration in Paris, police arrested several protesters (including Almereyda) for yelling "long live the 17th!"[62] One of them, a Paris pharmacist named Marie-Auguste Lucas, sported a hat with the tribute: "Béziers—17è de ligne—15 juin 1907," and carried several letters signed "The friends and collaborators of *La Guerre Sociale.*"[63] For Hervé, the Midi uprising was a clear indication "that antimilitarist propaganda has conquered the army, that the guard dog is no longer safe, that, circumstances becoming propitious, the army, except the cavalry, could well imitate the French guards of 1789 and the soldiers of Generals Lecomte and Clément Thomas on March 18, 1871."[64]

The "legend of the 17th" continued to grow all out of proportion with what had really happened, and it continues to this day to serve as symbol and myth for leftists and internationalists.[65] It has been preserved most recognizably in the song "Glory to the 17th!" by the anarchist Montéhus, a revolutionary songwriter and antimilitarist in his own right. The refrain from this contemporary classic goes:

> Hail, hail to you
> Brave soldiers of the seventeenth.
> Hail, brave young soldiers,
> Everyone admires you and loves you.
> Hail, hail to you,
> To your magnificent gesture.
> You would have, by firing at us,
> Assassinated the Republic![66]

Along with the "Internationale," this became the virtual antimilitarist anthem in France—sung during demonstrations and meetings, intoned by undisciplined conscripts, even appealed to in courtrooms. It did more than anything else to adapt the 1907 mutiny to the agenda of the antimilitarists. And it did so, as the song said, by paying homage to the Republic.

The revolt of the 17th was just the symbol that struggling antimilitarists needed to prop themselves up in the period of the AIA's decline and the heavy-handed administration of Clemenceau. As officers and journalists pointed fingers at the Left for its role in the rebellion, antimilitarists capitalized on this "proof" of their penetration of the military to play up their "exploit." The glorification of the mutinous soldiers was something the revolutionaries knew well how to manage, and in no time they had turned a revolt in which they had no direct role into, in Porch's words, a "prize for perseverance, a myth to dazzle the faithful."[67]

It bears reemphasizing, however, that antimilitarists did not create the legend of the 17th alone. They received crucial, if unwitting, aid from enemies and allies alike, who used the revolt to vent their frustration with the lenient "bourgeois" Republic. The severity with which the war minister dealt with the officers of the 17th (a note was placed in their files about their lacking the "energy and mental toughness" to end the revolt), helped build the incident from a local disruption to an all-out mutiny.[68] *L'Éclair* invigorated the myth (and generated an uproar) when it published several pieces on the uncivilized living conditions of the mutinous soldiers in their North African desert exile. A few did in fact die from exposure to the harsh climate and from the brutality of the officers who reigned in the remote caserne, which was more proof for the anti-Republican Right that the government itself was the source of the malaise that had descended on the traditionally monarchical and hierarchical military.[69]

At the other end of the political spectrum, Jaurès paid homage to the insurrection in front of five thousand workers at the Tivoli Vauxhall: "It is not by *affiches*, by puerile declamations, that these noble and courageous soldiers refused to commit murder against their destitute brothers. Their refusal has been clear, brutal, striking. It will serve as a warning to this capitalist bourgeoisie that hurls citizens against one another and believes itself capable, in desperation, of smothering the proletariats' claims in blood." The audience responded with cries of "long live the 17th!" On June 30, 1907, the Socialist Party published a manifesto extolling the "noble and courageous resistance of the soldiers of the 17th [as] the greatest social act in 35 years" (that is, since the Commune). In supporting the regiment, mainstream socialists transformed the men of the 17th into heroes, and Montéhus's song "Glory" into a hymn that could be sung by Jaurès and Hervé alike.[70]

Yet the reality of Jaurès's argument was more complex. His main point was that, antimilitarists or no antimilitarists, the revolt had resulted from the disgusting, yet persistent state of affairs in which the government employed locally recruited soldiers to control working-class disruptions in their own hometowns. This was essentially the same position that Jaurès had advocated during the *affiche rouge* affair, when he praised the signers for confronting a situation that was not being resolved through legal avenues of political pressure and popular protest. The main difference was that in 1905 Jaurès had sided with the Hervéists, whereas now he was siding with the soldiers. Antimilitarist propaganda for him was meaningless compared with the fact that, of their own free will, the rebels had placed their sense of civil rights over their obedience to the bourgeois state.

Jaurès's argument touches on the broader question of where to draw the line between soldier and citizen. There has been a good deal written on this question, much of it by political scientists interested in issues such as the decisions that faced soldiers in Vietnam or the formation of a European defense union.[71] Leonard Smith's study of France's Fifth Infantry Division in World War I shows that its command structure was more pliable and subject to the needs and even whims of soldiers than historians have assumed.[72] The Midi revolts thus seem to be an ideal case study because all evidence indicates that regional conditions combined with local recruitment to produce the volatile situation. In an interview for *Le Matin*, the twenty-three-year-old mutineer Henri Pascal said that he and his comrades had been at once "victims of those who wanted to help us [the civilians] and of our leaders' duplicity.... We were terribly upset to be the instruments of repression set against our parents and ourselves. Nevertheless, we had no seditious thoughts. They are wrong to allege our mutiny had been planned. What happened is that we were fooled."[73] The second verse of "Glory to the 17th!" likewise expresses the dilemma of blind, patriotic devotion and a civic-minded consciousness:

> Like the others you love France
> I am sure about it, even, you love her well
> But under your madder-colored trousers
> You have remained citizens

In 1907, the soldier-citizen dilemma would never have been so severe if the regiments used in the Midi had not been recruited from the Midi. Local recruitment was not a new problem, but when the republican regime came to power in the 1870s, leftist politicians renewed efforts to incorporate men into "those units which are closest to their homes," as a July 7, 1904, resolution stated. Their argument was that this would speed mobilization, cut the cost of transferring troops, and improve regimental cohesion. On October 3 the War Ministry decreed that, except for Paris, Lyon, and Marseille, soldiers would serve in local regiments.[74]

Although the goals of the republican military reformers were laudable, the problems of local recruitment soon proved to be overwhelming. In addition to the fact that the men could not keep their loyalty to the regiment separate from their innate sense of regional kinship, Porch has argued that the locally based units undercut the authority of officers and NCOs. This manifested itself in a variety of ways: the difficulty of punishing a soldier from an influential local family; a tendency to look the other way during a popular protest, as officers tried to do in Agde; and the competing authority of local civil servants such that, as one colonel remarked, "the word almost everywhere is avoid trouble." The result was to impede effective command and further damage the officers' self-respect, producing a general decline in leadership that reflected on the troops. Adolphe Messimy, the Radical Party spokesman for military affairs and future war minister, lamented in his 1907 budget report: "It is beyond question that in regiments recruited locally, local questions end up sabotaging all possibility of serious military training and education. . . . Is it possible to deny leave to the son of . . . the amiable host who entertained you the night before?" As Porch argues, liberal republican politics had sunk their claws into the venerable French army.[75]

Whether one accepts this thesis or prefers the "nation in arms" view of earlier writers such as Paul-Marie de la Gorce, Richard Challener, and David Ralston (the list could also include Eugen Weber) that the republican regime, at least in the long run, went far to root out reactionary elements from the army and mobilize the *patrie,* a fundamental significance of the mutiny remains: it brought into vivid relief many of the military's larger problems of falling prestige and professionalism. A series of directives to improve the social standing of officers and the living conditions of conscripts that began appearing in the early 1900s did ameliorate the situation and eventually bring the army to a tacit acceptance of its status in the Republic. But this did not necessarily solve its image problem. The circumstances surrounding the outbreak of war would prove the best, if tragic, remedy for that.

With regard to the antimilitarist propaganda, it was only relevant insofar as a symbol or rallying cry for the impetuous soldiers. They raised their rifle butts into the air because that's what they knew, not necessarily because they sympathized with the revolutionaries. In his masterful study of the army and society in Languedoc, Jules Maurin has shown that for 80 percent of the soldiers in the region, military service went off "without a hitch." Most cases of insubordination (only 0.55 percent of conscripts in Béziers) were a result of either personal circumstances, such as religion or family, or of the "real-life experience of military service," rather than a result of any strong identification with a cause or doctrine.[76] Just as workers were most sensitive to the economic and political issues that touched them directly, soldiers were moved by the incidents they faced daily in the caserne and in their lives.

Desertion

Nonetheless, at the highest levels the antimilitarists remained veritable scapegoats for the army's troubles. In 1912, Messimy unleashed a long debate in the Chamber of Deputies when he blamed the propaganda for a drastic increase in desertion and insubordination. According to his "brutal statistics," from 1890 to 1900 an average of 1,900 men deserted, with another 4,000 insubordinates. "But since 1900, since the moment the CGT accentuated its propaganda by the Sou du Soldat, which is—one of our colleagues told me the other day, and he had proof—which is an agency of desertion, of encouragement to insubordination, and nothing else," that average rose to 2,200 deserters and 5,000 insubordinates between 1902 and 1904, and to 2,600 and 10,000, respectively, from 1909 to 1911. By then 80,000 men, or more than two wartime army corps, had dodged the 1889 conscription law.[77]

These were remarkable, even alarming, statistics that could not have landed on *any* high-ranking official's desk without generating concern for the army's reliability. A December 1912 report would concur with the war minister: "One might wonder with anguish how many deserters and insubordinates there would be on the day of a mobilization given the recent and continual incitements of anarchists, socialists, and the CGT."[78] What was Messimy's evidence that antimilitarists were the main culprits behind this sharp rise in desertion and insubordination? Were there any direct links between the deserters and local syndicalist leaders?

The question of whether or not to encourage desertion was the ultimate ethical dilemma for antimilitarists, because it pitted a personal choice against a collective strategy. In December 1907 several antimilitarists received a one-year prison sentence and a one hundred franc fine for a placard inciting conscripts: "Desert! . . . desertion in this epoch of abasement and general spinelessness is a beautiful act of revolt, a superb affirmation of moral liberation."[79] In the *Nouveau manuel du soldat,* Yvetot had advocated desertion insofar as he recognized that some soldiers would be unable to tolerate the base humiliations of military life. This did not mean that syndicalists supported desertion in principle, but it did give the appearance of an option. Thus, for example, with the passage in 1912 of the Millerand-Berry Law, which made it easier to send insubordinates to African battalions, Union des Syndicats secretaries Savoie and Delpech advised desertion, "*if need be,*" for those who fell under the new law.[80] When Messimy accused the *bourses* of being "desertion agencies," Merrheim replied: "We state clearly, with precision, that we [the CGT] are against desertion."[81]

The only real pro-desertion position was represented by the neo-Malthusian journal *L'Anarchie*.[82] Its mandate was simple: "To fight against the army, to want to do away with it, is to desire the complete elimination of soldiers; therefore no longer be soldiers."[83] In an article that appeared after the massacre of workers in the Paris suburb of Villeneuve-St.-Georges, *L'Anarchie* practically blamed Hervé for the deaths, because he was too preoccupied with what to do in the case of war rather than with what the peace-time soldier should be doing: "These *sans-patrie* are all soldiers and consequently de facto patriots. . . . It is obvious that all these antimilitarists have never understood that the best way to suppress the army would first be not to create it."[89] *L'Anarchie* called Hervé (the "bizarre Sans-Patrie") and other "revolutionaries" cowards; argued that life abroad was not as difficult as socialists made it out to be; and accused the "antimilitarist soldier" of being "a man who has not dared to make his actions agree with the ideas he pretends to profess."[85]

L'Anarchie's rival, *Le Libertaire,* advocated a pragmatic approach to desertion and addressed the problems of living abroad such as language, work, and social alienation. Yet even if these problems were to be overcome, the journal viewed each deserter as a loss for the antimilitarist cause: "Desertion is not a means of struggle. It is vanished energy, an annihilated force." *Le Libertaire* did not deny an individual's choice to desert, but its attitude toward those who did was hardly ambivalent either: "If all [those] whose character does not enable them to submit to the passive obedience of the caserne, whose pride recoils at the subjugation, the vulgarity [of military life] . . . if all those desert, so be it. They have thus acted as they please. But from the viewpoint of 'propaganda,' of 'effect,' their act amounts to nothing."[86] The "pure" anarchists of the Fédération Communiste Anarchiste (FCA), a successor to the AIA, did not make desertion a major plank of their program, although many advocated it. In October 1912 the *affiche* "today insubordinate, tomorrow rebellious, later deserter" struck a strong antipatriotic, pro-desertion chord, and the group's national secretary, Louis

Lecoin, received a four-year prison sentence for printing pro-desertion material. Yet others felt it was a "double blade" because most men who fled their regiment tried to return to France.[87]

For the Socialist Party, the issue of desertion was never really at stake because antimilitarism began with army reform and international cooperation. Hervé, with a few exceptions, did not favor it as a means of propaganda, and Jaurès, Vaillant, and Guesde did not even consider it. If they had anything to add to the issue, it appeared in an October 1913 article in *Le Conscrit* in which Compère-Morel urged conscripts unfortunate enough to be in the first class (where military service increased from two to three years): "Go to the caserne!" The socialist aim of eliminating permanent armies would take "men of will, energy, and character," he argued, not the kind who deserted.[88]

Although antimilitarists accepted desertion in varying degrees, most did not actively promote it as doctrine. This had not always been the case. In the 1890s Jean Grave wrote: "If, in spite of everything, the blood mounts to your brain, making you 'see red?' Well, there is only one way: to not set foot in this prison.... If you want to remain men, do not be soldiers; if you do not know how to stomach the humiliations, do not put on the uniform."[89] By 1909 Grave had toned down his language, suggesting that desertion was an "affair of temperament" rather than a form of protest.[90] Although calls for desertion might resonate after working-class uprisings, as in the July–August 1908 issues of *La Guerre Sociale* that garnered a judicial investigation, most antimilitarists in the early 1900s considered desertion "an absolutely personal and private matter." Thus to encourage desertion, Charles Desplanques wrote in Grave's *Les Temps Nouveaux,* was a "serious mistake" with respect both to the individual and to propaganda in general.[91] In this attempt to compromise the idea with the act, antimilitarism was less a code for conduct than a means of expressing personal frustration.

The issue of so-called desertion agencies first emerged in the summer of 1908 with the "Daveau Affair." Daveau had been a sailor in the port of Toulon when he decided to jump ship and flee to Belgium. But he quickly had a change of heart and turned himself over to French authorities. The war council in Lorient sentenced Daveau to two years in prison, and the incident probably would have gone unnoticed if not for one thing: during his interrogation, Daveau claimed that his desertion to Anvers, by way of Paris, had been assisted by an anarchist group in Toulon.[92]

Daveau testified that he had made his own decision to desert out of fear of being sent to a disciplinary company, and that the antimilitarists provided him with the means to do so. This included money, civilian clothing, letters of reference for his Belgian contacts, and a liaison to meet him at the train station in Paris. Daveau named one person specifically—the worker Victor Busquère, a former delegate to a local antimilitarist committee and the Toulon correspondent for *La Guerre Sociale* in 1906–1907. Police searched Busquère's residence and, based on a tip, investigated the Jeunesse Libre and Bar Paul, a drinking establishment whose owner allegedly facilitated the desertion of his soldier-customers. Although nothing incriminating turned up, *L'Écho de Paris* contended that the affair uncovered the existence of a "true desertion agency" in Toulon. The virulent, right-wing *Action Française* claimed to possess "irrefutable proof" of a "liberation enterprise" in the city.[93]

It is useful at this juncture to return to Jean Masse's study of antimilitarism in the Var. Masse went back to the Almereyda/Jourdain speech in Toulon in 1904 to test whether there was a link between their promotion of desertion and the desertion of sailors from the port city. A 1908 report found the ties to be tenuous at best, although Masse does not rule out the possibility that some militants sheltered deserters. The police found no reason to believe the Jeunesse Libre weighed heavily in the military milieu, but were still not prepared to relax their repressive measures. The group's "platonic acts," after all, occurred with astonishing regularity, and often involved such feats as breaching military buildings at night. Toulon experienced such a barrage of antimilitarist propaganda that the mere hint of it, as in a problem at the local arsenal, sent writers for *L'Écho de Paris* into a state of frenzied hyperbole. Masse believes a "moral climate, systematically hostile to the military institution, had been created in the years 1905–1914." But in 1908 there was no hard evidence that the military had succumbed to it.[94]

Part of the reason there were relatively few desertions in Toulon, Masse contends, lay in the city's particular military structure. The army garrison there, due to its proximity to North Africa, was used primarily to house colonial regiments. These regiments consisted of men who had chosen a military career; not the type, in other words, who were strongly susceptible to antimilitarist propaganda. Another factor was that one of the units there recruited heavily from Corsica, which had remained less permeable to the revolutionary vicissitudes emanating from mainland France. A 1913 report described the Corsican recruits as "ignorant of syndical questions." Moreover, like their famous predecessor Napoleon Bonaparte, many saw the military as a means for career advancement. Finally, the important naval base in Toulon seems hardly to have been targeted by antimilitarists at all, and Masse provides some insightful reasons for this: first, the naval forces did not have working-class blood on their hands because they did not intervene in strikes; second, the navy's means of recruitment was such that those who served in it, like the Bretons at the Toulon base, were typically there because of their skills and remained aloof from the Provençal workers; and, finally, the "indisputable prestige of the Fleet," evidenced in the glorification of its colonial conquests.[95]

In the Daveau case antimilitarists did have a role to play, although most were not sure what it actually was. One of the main points of this study has been that, right up to 1914, government and military officials regarded antimilitarism with utmost seriousness. At times—after the Midi revolts or during the Moroccan crises—their vigilance manifested itself as outright fear for the nation's security; a fear Messimy exhibited in 1912. The issue of "desertion agencies" demonstrates just how unwilling authorities were to take for granted any potential threat to the army. By September 1908, the government had responded with a full inquiry into whether a "central desertion agency exists in Paris, and if this agency has branches in the ports of war."[96]

As we have come to expect, the results of this inquiry were dismal for antimilitarists. Although small groups existed in each of the cities surveyed (Paris and the naval ports of Cherbourg, Brest, Lorient, Rochefort, and Toulon), the only clear link with a "desertion agency" was through *La Guerre Sociale*. Officials judged the Cherbourg group as "insignificant," and described the three groups in Brest as lacking vitality and perhaps no longer even operative because they had no office, funds, members, or meeting place. In Lorient, a group created by Yvetot in 1905–1906 had already dissolved. In Toulon, the complicity of the Jeunesse Libre in the desertion of locally stationed servicemen and marines could not be established "in a precise fashion." As for Busquère of Daveau fame, he had perhaps once assisted desertions but he was no longer in the business and was short on funds. The most soldiers could expect from him were the addresses of militants such as Yvetot and Hervé. In Rochefort the antimilitarist group had disbanded two years earlier, so that the only remaining possible link with the revolutionary Left were the twenty-one members of the Jeunesse Syndicale, all of whom worked at the arsenal![97]

In Paris the sole group designated as a "central desertion agency" turned out to be "none other than *La Guerre Sociale*." Former AIA secretary Almereyda seems to have been the journal's main culprit given that he was active among provincial antimilitarists and responsible for distributing the journal nationally. Still, contrary to what many had thought, in particular a reporter close to the first maritime war council of Brest, "no one in *La*

Guerre Sociale circles believes the paper is affiliated with the large German espionage agency in Brussels," or any agency seeking to weaken the French army through such means. The reporter was forced to conclude that the journal's efforts probably never went beyond propaganda: "We have not been able to collect any proof establishing that [its] affiliates had taken personal steps in the vicinity of such or such servicemen in order to induce them to desert."[98]

The case of the "desertion agencies" illustrates well how the anxiety over antimilitarism overshadowed the reality. As decisive as the above report looks, one or two incidents tied to a handful of militants kept the question of "desertion agencies" alive through late 1912. A notable episode occurred in December 1909, when a deserter named Gosset from the 6th Colonial Regiment in Brest tried to repatriate himself. Gosset attested that his desertion had been aided by Gaston Delpech (secretary of the administrative commission of the Bourse du Travail and former AIA treasurer), Violette (secretary of the jewelers' *syndicat*, editor at *La Guerre Sociale,* and member of the tenth section of the AIA), and Louis Garreau (secretary of the paper *syndicat* and committee member of the CGT, AIA, and *La Voix du Peuple*), although all vehemently denied any role. Delpech, despite a long record of advocating sabotage and a general strike in case of war (military and civilian), abjured his support for desertion altogether: "As far as I am concerned, these legal proceedings are like a bad joke. I even wonder if the desertion they attribute to us isn't a police scheme to discredit the *syndicat* organizations. . . . I declare that, personally, I am absolutely opposed, in principle, to desertion."[99]

The customary investigation and interrogation (under Article 242 of the military justice code titled "Provocation to Desertion")[100] determined otherwise. Although the inquiry did not unearth a "desertion agency" in Paris "in the rigorous sense of the word," it counted the Gosset affair as the first "material proof" that revolutionary leaders in the capital, especially those belonging to the Union des Syndicats de la Seine, the Fédération Révolutionnaire, and *La Guerre Sociale,* provided a ready source of counsel and capital for potential deserters. The revolutionaries allegedly met in the Restaurant Coopératif of the 3rd arrondissement, where they arranged transit to Belgium. According to *L'Humanité,* Gosset had been directed from a similar restaurant in Brest to a small café where he met Violette and Delpech, from whom he expected to receive money to go abroad. When they refused and denied being a "desertion agency," and set the luckless soldier packing, Gosset, having fled on his own, returned to seek his revenge. The article further described him as a "shady individual" who spoke at the interrogation with a "raspy, alcoholic voice," and "had already deserted four times and did not need advice to desert a fifth [time]." Regardless, authorities sentenced Garreau and Violette to one year of prison without reprieve.[101]

What is peculiar about the "desertion agencies" is that from the outset antimilitarists vehemently denied having anything to do with them. This is not at all consistent with how readily the Left adopted the mutiny of the 17th as a revolt of its own making. When the deputy secretary of the Rouen Bourse, Léon Torton, was accused by a locally based soldier of having facilitated his desertion, *La Guerre Sociale* sarcastically and adamantly denied that the *bourse* had any part in it (including Torton's escape to Belgium, where he was sentenced to two years prison in absentia): "It is the antimilitarists who persuaded him to desert. Oh! he has resisted; his entire French soul outraged! But the antimilitarists got him drunk; and when he had lost his senses, the *misérables* forced him onto a train that took him away from his caserne and rushed him irredeemably into disgrace!"[102] In response to the Gosset affair, the Union des Syndicats de la Seine blamed "the hand of the police" and the "complicity of a so-called deserter by the name of Gosset" for a plot to imprison syndicalists. At the protest meeting, Secretary-General Léon Jouhaux of the CGT described it as an attempt to discredit and, eventually, dissolve the CGT, adding that French syndicalism as a whole was ideologically opposed to desertion: "Those who desert are lost for syndicalist action."[103] *La Guerre Sociale* concurred: "It is the propaganda of our friends in the caserne who prepare us for the 17ths—without which no revolution is possible."[104]

For Jouhaux and Hervé, "desertion agencies" served little purpose—military life was already so miserable that some soldiers would opt to leave on their own accord; if any more were encouraged to desert there would not be enough men to lead the military insurrection. For the public powers, on the other hand, there was no question that, "in effect . . . soldiers who intend to desert are sent to Paris by anarchists and syndicalists in the provinces."[105] Not until December 1912, when another "meticulous" inquiry failed to prove the existence of "desertion agencies," did officials acknowledge that if antimilitarists aided deserters, it was "at their request only."[106] Messimy had been only too eager to blame the CGT for the rise in desertion and insubordination. The formidable antimilitarist presence in French political and social life unquestionably provided a certain immeasurable incentive for disgruntled soldiers. But the decision to flee (and probably in most cases the arrangements for the flight) was clearly their own.

There were several causes for the increase in desertions, and Messimy must have been aware of most of them. Porch writes that the main cause was the two-year law of 1905, which for the first time stipulated that Frenchmen living abroad had to report for military service. Another was that statistics on "deserters" included reservists who had changed address and thus missed their annual training notice.[107] In *Les Voeux de l'armée* (*The Army's Vows* 1908) Charles Humbert insisted that the primary reason for the increase was the liberal and frequent application of amnesty laws. There had been four amnesties in the previous nine years, and laws in 1904 and 1906 lowered the age from 35 to 30 at which a deserter had to fulfill his military duty. Once married, he was exempt altogether.[108] It was not uncommon for deserters to beg mercy for their "peccadilloes of youth" and directly request to be reinstated in the army. A group photo from Belgium accompanied one such plea for forgiveness: "Since [deserting], we have reflected. The experience has shed light for us on the significance of our ill-considered act. We suffer from being distant from the *patrie*, and beg you to appeal to Parliament for an amnesty for all military offenses."[109] This took a lot of pluck, which alone renders antimilitarism more of a sideshow than a significant factor behind the rise in desertion. Humbert's verdict on this "evil" was that it resulted from "that which we have pardoned, amnestied, as an insignificant crime: the act of shirking a sacred obligation that weighs on everyone."[110] Yet again, honest attempts to uphold the liberal Republic had clashed with the parallel need for a strong, and strongly supported, military.

Military Syndicats

In April 1909, in the midst of the panic over "desertion agencies," a similar conflict surfaced over *syndicats* in the military itself. It centered on a group founded in February 1902 (and approved by the interior minister a year later) known as Solidarité Militaire. The organization essentially operated as a mutual aid society for active and retired soldiers, providing financial and personal support during funerals, illnesses, and injuries, and generally strengthening moral and fraternal ties between the older and younger men. From 1903 to 1909 membership in Solidarité Militaire skyrocketed from 732 to 8,875, and its net worth grew to over sixteen thousand francs. And in 1908 NCOs threatened to report sick (that is, go on strike) if Parliament failed to pass pension legislation for their widows and orphans. Almost immediately, this federally sanctioned association faced accusations that it had a "dangerous syndicalist allure" and advocated "energetic measures" of a revolutionary nature such as the military strike.[111]

This initial report, however, was skeptical. In 1908 "certain members" had misinterpreted the statutes and tried to influence the professional interests of soldiers in Solidarité Militaire. But the misunderstanding was soon cleared up and the group's bulletin declared its singular commitment to mutualist questions. This might have neatly ended the matter if the press had not taken it up. Shortly after police concluded that there was no evidence of a revolutionary syndicalist component in Solidarité Militaire, *L'Écho de Paris*, *La Démocratie Sociale*, *Les Nouvelles*, and the ardently nationalist and highly successful *La Patrie* were alleging that "syndicalist tendencies" had wrought an "immense transformation" in the army, and within a few years these tendencies would undermine its professionalism and independence.[112] *Les Nouvelles* published a three-part series that claimed Solidarité Militaire was in reality a *syndicat* of noncommissioned officers, and its president, General Pédoya, fomented rebellion by organizing officers to demand just compensation for their service. "Let's console ourselves by keeping in mind that General Pédoya no longer holds a high rank," the last article stated, "and let's hope that the army will never be in danger of seeing this former soldier, disciple of the CGT, settled in the rue St. Dominique."[113]

These harsh appraisals of Solidarité Militaire did not fall on deaf ears. A year later, the notion of an "officers' *syndicat*" had gained acceptance from military and government leaders, including former War Minister Etienne and General Noix. "Now, a strike in the officers' corps?" wrote Noix in *L'Armée Moderne*, "but that would mean the end of the army."[114] In October 1911 War Minister Messimy sent a "very confidential" note to the interior minister alerting him to a *société amicale* of colonial officers, probably from the Midi, whose monthly meetings and persistent efforts on behalf of troop officers and subalterns "visibly tends toward the organization of a veritable *syndicat*." Paris police investigating these societies added that: "Young NCOs are ready to take energetic action when the time comes. By this they mean a military strike in a revolutionary situation."[115]

Yet when Messimy launched a secret inquiry into the Solidarité Militaire it revealed, at best, some frustrated officers willing to organize illegally in order to combat the "anonymous, colossal, and irresponsible forces" of the centralized, capitalist state. Revolutionaries they certainly were not.[116] In October 1912 the Commissaire Spéciale Près le Gouvernement Militaire of Paris wrote the director of the criminal department that his section had searched in vain for an NCO *syndicat*. Although he admitted that changes since the advent of the Republic had led to a real decline in the condition of the military and the stature of NCOs, "antimilitarist and anarchist ideas have nevertheless encountered amongst NCOs only very, very rare and indeed only weak echoes." The conclusion of this high-level report was that the officers sought security not because they hated the army and had become imbued with antimilitarist ideas, but because they lacked the kind of confidence in the future that had once typified military careerists.[117]

Still, as long as rumors abounded, the reports multiplied, and vice versa. In July 1911 police arrested Sergeant Bonafous of the 83rd Infantry in Toulon on charges of railway sabotage. He belonged to Solidarité Militaire, of which the officers wrote: "Now, this society is a center of syndicalist action in the army."[118] By late January 1913 the group's membership had reached ten thousand (a third of the total number of career NCOs), with one hundred sections around the country.[119] Maybe the *affaire des fiches* had gone too far—officers, many now believed, had become full-fledged socialist revolutionaries. In April 1914 *La France* reported that Jaurès presided over a banquet attended by several hundred officers who came to hear "the good antimilitarist word."[120] In the first quarter of 1911, *L'Action Française* and *La Libre Parole*, both known for their pro-military, anti-foreigner *revanchisme*, viewed the purported coming of syndicalism to the army as the Republic's final, deadly blow to that institution: "This syndicalist attempt is only the beginning of the last phase of the crisis, only the violent upheaval of a deep evil from which the army suffers, and with which some truly crazy and guilty politicians have knowingly infected it."[121] Lieutenant-Colonel Driant, now a deputy from Nancy and a member of the army commission, added: "What is certain is that the military *syndicat* is the fatal culmination of the regime to which the army has submitted for the past ten years."[122] But verily, the only certainty was that what democracy tolerated, the military still found intolerable.

◆ ◆ ◆

The influence of antimilitarism on the army was greatly exaggerated by leftist and republican enemies who saw the propaganda, heard the rhetoric, knew the stakes, but failed to weigh in the facts. The right-wing agendas of journalists and others made the Left easy prey, even if evidence for serious antimilitarist sympathies in the army was limited. But such arguments have little relation to what people felt, read, and worried about at the time. In the first decade of the twentieth century, two facts remained constant: the army, traditional pillar of France, was still groping to find its way into the mainstream ethos of the Third Republic; and antimilitarists were doing everything they could to make it that much harder to do so.

The Narbonne shootings and subsequent mutiny had the same effect on antimilitarists that the *affiche rouge* affair did: it united disparate factions and induced a surge in propaganda laying claim to their righteousness. For the coming eve of the national fête (July 13), syndicalists began making plans to "assert their disaffection from the republican regime," their way of expressing frustration with the policies of Clemenceau and Briand that led to Narbonne.[123] As always, the moral language of antimilitarism served them well: "It is up to you, mothers, to raise your children with the ideas of the rebellious soldiers of the 17th. It is up to you to say *no*, I do not want him to become a murderer."[124] The mutiny had become for the CGT, as the June 1907 *affiche* "government of murderers" stated, "the justification of our antimilitarist propaganda." The syndicalists may have stretched the truth by taking so much credit for the revolt, but it was hard to argue with their claims for its justifiability: "The peasants of the 17th have grasped how right we are to proclaim that the bourgeoisie not maintain an army only for war at home."[125] A month later in Lyon, twenty-two people were accused of "provocation to murder and disobedience" for the *affiche* "bravo! the antimilitarist army." Their offense had been to retest the limits of antimilitarist ethics: "But do better [than the 17th], and do not let your bullets remain in your cartridge pouch." The spirit of the *affiche rouge* lived on.[126]

Symbols such as the 17th Regiment, "desertion agencies," and "military *syndicats*" proved tremendously useful for antimilitarists seeking to legitimize their activities and "keep up appearances" in the true nineteenth-century meaning of that phrase. But ultimately they were just that—symbols—and could never tell the full story of what stirred inside the individual soldier. In the Midi it was a deep, inborn loyalty to the fertile wine country of one's youth. During war it may be an intangible devotion to a *patrie* that only her defilement by a foreigner could bring out. Whatever it was, in the early twentieth century the grave problems faced by the military and the enduring existence of antimilitarism spoke more of prolonged personal and political frustrations than of any massive transformation in French consciousness. For all of the evidence that antimilitarism had penetrated the caserne, and for all the worries that reservists were untrustworthy and may not fight, military life went on, recruits showed up for training, and France prepared for war.

Eugen Weber has written that "much of the fear of antimilitarism was based on ignorance of antimilitarists." Insiders, soldiers themselves, often had very different stories to tell from those on the outside, who invariably harbored set notions about what they would find. Weber thus provides the example of the young writer René Benjamin, a reservist during the autumn 1908 maneuvers. Benjamin wrote that his fellow soldiers could all recite from their Hervéist manuals with perfunctory precision, but predicted that "on the day of mobilization they would be so scared of the gendarmes that they would be the first to part for the front. Antimilitarism is almost popular, a part of our workers' make-up; but antimilitarists are just poor chaps who will behave very well provided they are marched up to the line of fire in good step."[127] This rather condescending view, which spoke of antimilitarists and not merely antimilitarist leaders, achieved what cartons of police reports could not: it explained the basic difference between how people act and, under more trying circumstances, how they might really behave.

The same could be said for the military experience of Albert Lecup. Lecup had been an ardent Hervéist, an entry in the Carnet B, and an irritable, restless conscript in the 110th Infanty Regiment that incorporated him in 1910. But by the time the war came, he had become a fervent patriot and unit leader with the rank of sergeant-major. Lecup describes his transformation in *Avant le dernier cantonnement* (*Before the Last Billet*), an insightful look at how the military was perhaps more forgiving with its recruits than it might have been under a different government. For example, Lecup's commanders, who knew of his background, granted his request to remain at the caserne during a miners' strike in Lens, and they seem only to have prodded him in a light, good-natured way to become an obedient soldier and even officer. The turning point for this soldier-revolutionary comes when he turns out to be an excellent shot and earns the rank of *1ère tireur* (first marksman). Suddenly, Lecup finds himself at a crossroads: "Inscribed on this famous Carnet B, am I going to accept or refuse this small stripe in red wool?" He accepts the decoration, and now there is no turning back.[128]

Another insider, the reservist Henry de Larzelles, wrote several letters on his military experiences in which the discussion of antimilitarism among barrack comrades figures prominently. The fact that these doctrines were the topic of impassioned after-hours debate in the caserne at all is indicative of a certain pervasive appeal. But de Larzelles remained wholly unconvinced that they had altered the realities of France's preparedness for war, as he wrote on April 7, 1907:

> The French are disciplined by temperament, in spite of their *frondeuse* [rebellious] appearance, and those who knowingly refuse to submit to their duties as citizens are the rare exceptions. This is why the antimilitarists will see their disarmament projects fail pitiably, [and] their

appeals to desertion remain in vain. This is why, despite the disorganization of the opposing parties, despite the class antagonism, everyone, at the moment of danger, would feel great solidarity and march on the enemy like a single man, without distinction of origin, without new opposition from contradictory ideas.[129]

In an entry written shortly after he left the service, de Larzelles's opinion remained steadfast: "I return home convinced that the disorganization believed to be advanced has in fact never existed, that our nation is far from being weakened by intestine strife, and that it only awaits the hour of *revanche* to awaken, fortified and unified, before the enemy."[130]

Antimilitarism was in the casernes and on the minds of conscripts. It pierced the army and pervaded the consciousness of anyone who had experienced the harshness of military regimentation or the presence of troops sent in to prevent unrest in their own backyards. But human habits and traditional loyalties were not easily broken by a decade or so of leftist propaganda, and many could sense this even when that propaganda was at its height. "Man?" wondered Charles Humbert soon after the Midi revolts and in the midst of an upsurge of revolutionary activity: "Man? He is still the same. In effect, the stupid and cowardly antimilitarism has not even touched him. He functions well; he is robust, resistant, capable of all endeavors asked of him and of all the successes we can possibly prepare for him."[131]

6. ANTIMILITARIST WARS I

The Battle Within

The journalist Georges Doutrement did not mince words when, in 1907, he wrote assertively in *L'Écho de Paris:*

> Whoever stops to seriously ponder the methods used in today's social and antimilitarist demonstrations will see the mark of an activity that is not limited to the simpleminded agitators. One senses above them a mysterious force, clairvoyant and organizing, that directs and conducts their acts.[1]

Once Doutrement had found a story in antimilitarism, he pursued it with all the relentlessness of an investigative reporter and wrote it up with the verve of a French belletrist. Antimilitarism was a highly organized, rapidly expanding "movement" that united the various factions of the loosely defined French Left and needed to be stopped immediately. That was the message Doutremont felt impelled to deliver.

It was in the courtroom that antimilitarists were particularly adept at presenting a united front. During the trial for signers of the "government of murderers" *affiche,* for example, Jaurès sided with the revolutionary syndicalists when judicial officials arbitrarily singled out the twelve (out of seventy-seven) most prominent for indictment, including Victor Griffuelhes, Alphonse Merrheim, Émile Janvion, and Émile Pouget. Under the *L'Humanité* headline "Absurd Prosecutions," Jaurès reminded authorities that socialist deputies had also circulated a manifesto against the Narbonne massacres, and that their biased treatment would only aggravate all working-class representatives: "To decapitate the workers' organizations, to strike those who try to lend some cohesion to the proletariat, is the work of a blind reactionary who worsens social anarchy on the pretense of healing it . . . it only irritates and justifies such anger."[2] Jaurès had backed revolutionary syndicalists before, most notably during the *affiche rouge* trial. Likewise the enthusiasm he and Hervé shared at Stuttgart, and his involvement in efforts to secure Hervé's release from prison in 1911, gave the impression that even a pragmatic socialist could join forces with elements of the extreme Left. In the public sphere—on trial, at congresses, and in widely circulating journals such as *L'Humanité* and, periodically, even *La Guerre Sociale*—antimilitarism often did seem to speak with a cohesive, indeed "clairvoyant," voice.

Yet Doutremont did not represent a very objective viewpoint. If he and others on the Right had not just "seriously pondered" antimilitarism but actually probed into the affairs of the Left, as the police did, then they might have noticed (although not necessarily admitted to) conflicting evidence concerning the content and coherence of the propaganda. To disentangle the complicated workings of the antimilitarists, it is necessary to examine them from their own standpoint as socialists, syndicalists, and anarchists, as opposed to viewing them through the distorted prism of their enemies. For example, at the peak of antimilitarist renown in the aftermath of the mutiny, the CGT rejected the SFIO's offer to hold joint protest meetings on July 13. Although syndicalists did allow socialists to speak at "their" meetings, under no circumstances would they permit any name or affiliation to appear on the announcement. What to an outsider might have seemed the perfect opportunity for the Left to come together on antimilitarism instead devolved into a conflict of ideology.[3] As one revolutionary summarized the feelings of syndicalists toward their "allies": "The socialists are no longer antimilitarists because they have become partisans of the state."[4]

The mantle of true antimilitarism had been worn by specific groups before. We saw how libertarians such as Lorulot and Libertad refused to support the AIA because it harbored such "unrevolutionary" elements as socialists and syndicalists. Years later, Lorulot's outlook was still intransigent: "The antimilitarism of the socialists is not—and cannot be—integral. Only anarchists, denigrators of authority, logically combat its basic manifestation as militarism; only they can repulse the dogma of the *patrie,* and thus break the cadres of all the oppressive collectivities of human individuality."[5] This notion that anarchists alone could advance the antimilitarist cause manifests itself in the different offshoots of the AIA, including the Fédération Communiste Révolutionnaire and the Fédération Communiste Anarchiste. By September 1907, police could report the confusing situation in which "the antimilitarists now call themselves anarchists, and even pretend to be the best anarchists, while the anarchists repulse the antimilitarists . . . who they say play foolishly at the martyr."[6] A few months later a report identified 3,780 anarchists and 2,157 antimilitarists in France who "would constitute a danger for public order." The latter were mostly socialists and syndicalists.[7]

Socialists, with their moderate Jacobin leaders and direct participation in government, were equally prone to criticize and even thwart the efforts of their supposed "allies." The same month Jaurès supported the syndicalists on trial for the "government of murderers" *affiche,* his journal lauded the guilty verdict returned against Almereyda and Merle for provoking servicemen to disobedience: "This country has enough Hervés, Merles, and Vigos. . . . We need an army to defend our border."[8] In a similarly confident and condescending tone, J.-P. Granvallet condemned syndicalists for placing the "political" issue of antimilitarism before their real duty on behalf of workers: "It is better not to put the cart before the horse or to build a house beginning with the loft." He felt "it would take a great deal of willpower to find in antimilitarism a question for *syndicats.*"[9] Guesde shared this sentiment wholeheartedly:

> We do not have the right to say to a metallurgist or a glass worker: you will not enter the metallurgists' or glass workers' union if you do not support boycotting, if you are not for sabotage, if you are not for antimilitarism or antipatriotism. . . . You do not have the right to divide against itself, by extraneous considerations, the profession which your duty is to unite, or if you do you end up precisely with what I deplore, with what I affirm and you deny, with skeletons of *Syndicats.*[10]

Certainly not all socialists were in agreement here, and divisions within the "unified" party contributed as much to weakening the antimilitarist Left as did the dissension between "allies." Although Guesdists regularly lambasted the CGT for subordinating real, working-class issues to its antimilitarist agenda, Lagardelle scolded fellow socialists for not following the example of revolutionary syndicalism, "the perfect realization of the class struggle." In *Le Mouvement Socialiste,* he argued that the opposition of mainstream socialists to the antimilitarism and antipatriotism of the CGT would only lead to further gridlock and sterility in the party.[11] In a sense, he was right. Hervé was an ongoing dilemma for socialists. In October 1907 Guesde and Lafargue introduced a journal specifically to combat him.[12] A year later at the national congress in Toulouse, delegates who tried to avoid the divisive issue of antimilitarism found the conflicts it engendered always near the surface. As Gravereaux wrote: "The gulf separating the official socialists from the syndicalists swells deeper in the course of discussion." Someone had to be the scapegoat for the party's problems, and that someone invariably was Hervé. "In socialism there is a worm," stated Compère Morel, "we see here some men who restrain themselves, but once home, ambushed behind their journals, they restart their denigrating work against the Socialist Party. Go with the anarchists. As for us, we will remain with French and international socialism."[13]

The public powers, although no less anxious about antimilitarism in 1908 than they had been in 1905, were more likely than the conservative press to concede these ideological crosscurrents and even to see them as a source of weakness for the Left. The December 1907 convictions led to this observation: "At the last antimilitarist trial, it was easy to notice how much the antimilitarists, belonging to different groups, have few sympathies between them, few connections. The young people who appear before the [Court of] Assizes are members of the local 'jeunesses révolutionnaires' and have more ties with the pure socialist groups, who hardly like them, than with the anarchists, who do not like them at all."[14] Had Hervé and Gohier not been in the defense, it continued, then "one might have thought these young men were not at all in sympathy with the ideas of the AIA, or with the libertarian or antimilitarist journals: *La Guerre Sociale, Les Temps Nouveaux, Le Libertaire, L'Anarchie.* We saw neither Almereyda, nor Méric, nor any CGT member and not a single socialist."[15] The next May, Lyon officials ascribed "the rivalries that divide the leaders of the movement" for the disintegration of local anarchist and antimilitarist groups.[16] What it really came down to was this: the categories of revolutionary or reformist, anarchist or syndicalist, and socialist or Hervéist overshadowed what everyone wanted to label, conveniently, antimilitarist.

It is no great revelation that ideological differences wreaked havoc for the Left; this has been a constant theme of the literature on the prewar period in France and in Europe in general.[17] "What is striking if one tries to take it as a whole," writes Jean Touchard, "is the extreme division of the Left, or rather the near total lack of a leftist mindset with regards to antimilitarism."[18] Syndicalists pinned their hopes on a general strike in the case of war. Hervéists advocated insurrection, both military and civilian. Anarchists promoted sabotage and, in some cases, desertion, and they were not always content to wait around for a war to overthrow the state. Finally, mainstream socialists looked to forms of international cooperation and to measures such as the reduction of military service and creation of a citizens' militia; and they proudly proclaimed their Jacobin patriotism. There was, obviously, considerable overlap between these groups, and within each the fault lines could be gaping. What concerns us here, however, is not simply the range and roots of antimilitarist antagonisms, but also the ability of the Left to formulate and execute unified responses to specific abuses of military/governmental power. How and how well, in other words, did antimilitarists overcome their divisions to achieve common goals? In the case of the anarchists, the answer is with great difficulty indeed.

Anarchist Dissension

As the AIA stumbled, the numerous attempts to reorganize it came primarily from extreme elements that had little success cooperating even with "mainstream" leaders such as Hervé. Georges Durupt of the Jeunesse Syndicaliste organized meetings in early 1908 to reestablish the AIA, but soon encountered trouble when he criticized the socialists and *La Guerre Sociale* for not supporting the faltering organization.[19] As far as Hervé was concerned, his journal did not belong to any sect, the AIA or otherwise, and it had enough of its own court cases that it did not need to take on those of the anarchists. "In sum," police reported, "Hervé did not want to have anything to do with the International Antimilitarist Association."[20]

One might make the case that if more socialists and syndicalists had come to the AIA's rescue it could have bolstered itself, if only in image, for a while longer. When Durupt was sentenced to three years in prison in late 1908, the new secretary Violette did try to attract non-anarchists on the condition that they leave party politics out of their antimilitarist discussions.[21] Yet however sincere these efforts, they were by now wholly impractical, and many were clamoring for a purely anarchist organization to lead the war on militarism. Speaking at an anarchist congress in Amsterdam in August 1907, Robert de Marmande, founder of La Liberté d'Opinion, argued that the AIA had been doomed precisely *because* it neglected its anarchist origins: "The program of the AIA contained a certain character that had to be exhausted rather early. Antimilitarism is not a doctrine. There are anarchist conceptions where antimilitarism finds its place quite naturally. Anarchism has planted, sowed, and sprouted the revolt all over."[22] It took the new founders of the AIA a few years longer to accept the truth in this. Although *La Guerre Sociale* accorded the group a column (*L'Humanité* refused), it did not, according to police, rejoice in the AIA's reconstitution. In fact Almereyda, AIA founder and an editor at *La Guerre Sociale,* urged the anarchists to relax their propaganda, at least until he could be amnestied.[23]

It was not until February 3, 1909, that police could finally acknowledge what they had already ascertained: "Born in difficulty, the AIA no longer exists."[24] The AIA had not conceded defeat easily, and its decline did not halt anarchist efforts to establish an organization that would attract syndicalists and left-wing socialists. "A revolutionary Fédération will have much more weight," declared Violette, who predicted that once the Socialist Party divided, the Fédération Révolutionnaire would absorb its most extreme elements.[25] In its April 11, 1909, "declaration of principle," the Fédération Révolutionnaire recommended that its members "take part in the syndicalist movement and support in it only the plans and manifestations of Direct Action (strikes, boycotts, sabotage, antimilitarism, antipatriotism) . . . that in themselves have a revolutionary character."[26] Although the group defined itself as a "political" organization devoted to overthrowing the capitalist government,[27] it was really no more than a revolutionary wing of French syndicalism that at its peak may have attracted five hundred members nationally.[28] As Hervé recognized when he set off a controversy by writing in *La Guerre Sociale* that the group only existed on paper, its prospects were not great. The police harbored few illusions either: "These people do not have any real importance because they are not taken seriously in the socialist milieu, and are regarded as a negligible quantity by syndicalists."[29]

As long as socialists and syndicalists paid little or no heed to the Fédération Révolutionnaire, libertarian anarchists who wished to strike out with their own group had a free hand to do so. The result was the Fédération Communiste Révolutionnaire (FCR), later known as the Fédération Communiste Anarchiste (FCA), founded in November 1910 by the left wing of the original Fédération Révolutionnaire. As with its forebears, antimilitarism was viewed as a means to achieve larger goals. But the new group distinguished itself in a way that also highlights differences among antimilitarists in general: sabotage.[30]

Mobilization Sabotage: Anarchists and the CGT

According to the July 1914 report "Les Projets de sabotage de la mobilisation" (Projects for Sabotaging Mobilization), both the CGT and independent anarchist groups had, by 1910 and independent of Hervé, taken serious initiatives concerning what do in the event of war. The June 4, 1911, congress of the FCA adopted full-fledged sabotage plans that included precise instructions for destroying rail and telegraph lines, dynamiting viaducts, tunnels, coal reserves, and embarkation quais, destroying war matériel, and assassinating officers.[31] In 1912 *Le Mouvement Anarchiste* became instrumental in spreading sabotage tips. The article "Useful Formulas" (signed "an engineer") gave technical information on how to debilitate a cannon or Lebel gun, halt locomotives, and suppress the press and its war propaganda. With these formulas, the November 1912 issue stated, "a few comrades could immobilize hundreds of cannons in just hours."[32]

This may appear as so much folly from our perspective, but the public powers monitored sabotage plans closely, particularly once the *Brochure rouge* (*Red Brochure*) appeared in 1913. Named for its red cover (with the title "In Case of War"), the *Brochure rouge* was a detailed thirty-five-page (including bibliography) enumeration of all sabotage acts that revolutionaries could "easily" commit during mobilization. Prepared clandestinely through the combined efforts of anarchists and the CGT, its first and, from all evidence, only print run totaled just two thousand copies. Most copies, however, managed to avoid the close police surveillance and make their way to various *syndicats*, to anarchist groups in Bezons, and, ironically, to conservative towns in western France such as Saintes, Nantes, Niort, Rochefort, Lorient, and la Roche-sur-Yon. Several showed up in Lyon following the pamphlet's prosecution in May 1913.[33]

After an introduction that urges workers to take the upperhand ("ACT!") as soon as war is declared, the *Brochure rouge* divides into three parts: "Theoretical Propaganda," "Revolutionary Tactics," and "Mobilization Sabotage." Part one reviews and surpasses the antipatriotic formulas of Yvetot's *Nouveau manuel du soldat*, concluding: "Little soldier, you are of the people. Remain with the people and kill your leaders." It is in part two that one first learns how the people will carry out the insurrection: small bands of armed revolutionaries will go into action as soon as war is declared; their task is to destroy all lines of communication, expropriate funds, silence the press, shoot political and military leaders, and seize the military forts. "To act rapidly, not to split up, to organize the 'taking of the heap'; to put aside all false sentimentality."[34]

In part three the reader is entrusted with the technical know-how necessary to accomplish the sabotage mission. Subsections ranging from electric tramways to telephone cables, bridges and viaducts, and railroads and mines give precise instructions on how to blow up, rupture, set fire, or in any way possible destroy, disrupt, and disable the major lines of transport and communication and the main fuel sources so crucial during war. There are even detailed diagrams that illustrate, for example, how a bridge can be put out of commission. And although some of the authors belonged to the publishers' *syndicat*, they included a section on how to disable the press. In the bibliography one finds references to works on making explosives, including entries on "dynamite" and "chlorate" in the *Nouveau Larousse illustré*.[35]

How seriously should we consider the *Brochure rouge* and the effusive anarchist propaganda to sabotage mobilization? The point of this sketch is not to prove the futility of their undertakings or reemphasize the general lack of support for them, but rather to show just how serious were these small bands and, in turn, how serious the public powers were in their regard of them. The transformation of anarchist ideas into printed matter such as the *Brochure rouge* was less an effort to salvage the antimilitarist "movement" than to reaffirm the anarchist commitment to it, particularly in the case of war. Yet in the process of standing their ground, anarchists also incurred the wrath of authorities, who outlawed the *Brochure rouge* and, based on the archival record, must have sent spies to virtually every FCA meeting from 1911 to 1914. Never mind that anarchists struggled to regroup after the AIA's decline, they had penetrated the syndicalist milieu and created their own image of a serious threat to mobilization:

> Each anarchist is a deserter, a "saboteur"; we knew this and we surveyed their acts and gestures with solicitude. But the law of 1884 on the professional *syndicats* has made this surveillance very difficult. The anarchist was afraid of the special laws of 1893–94 [*lois scélérates*]; and if he has not become a common criminal, he has become a revolutionary syndicalist; he has infiltrated the workers' organizations; he became master of the CGT. And it is thus that his action has become the most harmful.[36]

It was the anarchist-influenced CGT, then, that authorities recognized as possessing the organization and commitment to hinder an international war. As Becker writes: "Indeed, from congress to congress, from international crisis to international crisis, by its motions, its campaigns of meetings, by *affiches*, by press, over the last ten years the CGT has not ceased to affirm its positions against war and the means by which to oppose it."[37] It began with an *ordre du jour* at the Bourges congress (1904), which, in the midst of the Russo-Japanese War, encouraged workers to "keep themselves out of the conflicts between nations and save their energy for the true syndicalist combat against capitalism." We have already seen how the Algeciras conference following the first Moroccan crisis and the subsequent Amiens congress

(1906) provoked appeals from the CGT to insurrection and social revolution, and affirmed their separation from "corrupt socialist parliamentarians." In August 1909, at an international congress in Paris, Yvetot declared: "Our dream would be to bring our foreign comrades the formidable example of opposing a declaration of war with a declaration of a general strike, which would mean social revolution."[38]

When the second Moroccan crisis threatened war in June 1911, the CGT again presented itself as a partisan of insurrection. Numerous meetings combined an outcry against war with the ongoing campaign against the high cost of living that war would exasperate.[39] Syndicalists distributed handbills protesting the dangerous diplomatic maneuvers of the "colonial bandits," and on July 27 the *affiche* "against the war" proclaimed in democratic fashion that "war is only possible with the consent of the people."[40] Articles both in *La Voix du Peuple* and in the CGT's new daily journal, *La Bataille Syndicaliste*, were brought before the examining magistrate for "harm and defamation toward the army, and military provocations aimed at turning [soldiers] from their duties."[41] On August 4, 1911, Yvetot told delegates to an international meeting: "I have a proposition to make to you. I fear that you will not be patriots (laughs). I come to suggest that you be patriots, that you be the first to march when the Government gives you the signal by declaring a general strike, and that you respond to the order for mobilization with a veritable insurrection." A few weeks later, in spite of a downpour and a sizable police force, a crowd of twenty thousand (sixty thousand according to *La Bataille Syndicaliste* and *L'Humanité*) met at Aéro Park on the outskirts of Paris to affirm their hatred of the "government's war" and their commitment to the general strike.[42]

The antiwar fervor peaked in early October, when the CGT convened a *congrès extraordinaire* of the *bourses* and various federations specifically to resolve the issue of the attitude of the proletariat in the case of war. It was high time. The majority of the delegates, with the exception of the National Miners Federation and a group of postal workers, still were unprepared to act on the decisions taken at Marseille and Toulouse. In response, the congress unanimously passed an elaborate *ordre du jour,* the heart of which was that "at any declaration of war the workers should, without delay, respond by the revolutionary general strike."[43] It would apply this call to arms thus:

1. A circular will be addressed by the CGT to each *syndicat,* asking them to prepare their members, as of tomorrow, to apply the decisions taken at the opportune moment;

2. Each Fédération should immediately concern itself with finding the best means to realize the General strike, in its profession or in its industry;

3. Each Bourse du Travail, Union des Syndicats, and independent *syndicat* should institute a general strike subcommittee at the center of their organization. . . . These subcommittees will have the task . . . of intensifying the antimilitarist and antipatriotic propaganda.[44]

Any lack of antimilitarist unity was easily overshadowed by the CGT's latest attempt, at the height of the Moroccan crisis, to plan a war strategy:

> In the presence of the diplomatic difficulties of the day, on the eve perhaps of mobilization and a European war, the Confédération does not hesitate to assign responsibilities to each organization and to dictate its last orders for the day conflict would break out. . . . One would think he was dreaming in reading such things. What! The Republic has tolerated the existence of the CGT by pretending to consider it a Union of Syndicats; and it is at the moment the country courts the greatest dangers that it openly advocates sabotage and revolt and prepares the defeat! Never before had the Confédération published such audacity and announced so clearly that it had hatched a veritable plot against the nation![45]

Nor did the temporary abatement of international tensions after the Moroccan crisis lead to a corresponding pacification of the CGT. Over the next year Yvetot and Jouhaux toured the countryside to spread syndicalist propaganda in favor of mobilization sabotage. Their threats were repeated by delegates at the Havre congress in 1912, and on November 23–24 a new *congrès extraordinaire* convened in Paris to plan a general strike against war.

"Sabotage is not a Legend," proclaimed Yvetot in *La Voix du Peuple*. The piece was a direct and embittered response to Jaurès's assertion in *L'Humanité* that syndicalism was the "fundamental negation of sabotage." For "citizen Jaurès," as Yvetot unflatteringly referred to the socialist leader, sabotage had no place in working-class politics. For Yvetot, it was tremendously useful in attacking the government, especially when combined with strikes. "If the government does not like it," he boasted, "that's because it hits it in its weak spot. . . . If the politicians do not like it, that's because it compromises their importance." Sabotage was no mere means of action; it was a form of intimidation.[46]

The revolutionary Left generally supported Yvetot's arguments. *La Guerre*

Sociale called the Socialist Party's condemnation of sabotage a "serious political mistake," accusing Jaurès of being completely out of touch with the working classes. *Le Libertaire, La Bataille Syndicaliste,* and *Les Temps Nouveaux* joined in the one-sided debate in September to October 1913; a debate that, in truth, had more to do with workers' rights than with what they should or should not do in the case of war. Most of these articles do not even mention antimilitarism, and they often discuss sabotage as if it were some abstraction of principle rather than a political and social reality. "The Worker and Sabotage," for example, loosely defines sabotage as total devotion to work: "When we say to the worker . . . 'Excel at your job': that is sabotage. When the railway man strictly enforces the rules: that is also sabotage."[47] Regardless of the language, antimilitarist enemies saw the threats and accompanying congressional resolutions as evidence of elaborate plans to stop mobilization and destroy the nation. *La Liberté* warned that mobilization sabotage was no longer the theory of crazies, but an openly conducted enterprise of "bandits," most of whom ran around in the legally sanctioned CGT.[48]

The Socialist Dilemma

Jean-Jacques Becker has labeled socialist antimilitarism "an indecisive pacifism" precisely because its efforts to prevent war did not necessitate that it destroy the Republic and its institutions.[49] Jaurès may have been reasonably tolerant of Hervé because he believed all opinions in the party should be aired, but he never questioned the integrity of the nation-state. In a public debate with the Sans-Patrie in 1905, Jaurès urged socialists to accept the reality, indeed the overwhelming force of the *patrie:* "All nations, each endowed with its own individual spirit, language, literature, sense of life, memories, hopes, passions, soul, and genius, must comprise the great communist society of the future."[50] Moreover, Jaurès's high regard for democratic, revolutionary France constantly informed his thinking on the nation's special role in creating this future socialist world: "If we, French socialists, if we were indifferent to the honor, security, and prosperity of France, we would not only be committing a crime against the *patrie,* but a crime against humanity; for France, and a free France great and strong, is necessary to humanity. . . . If France declined, reactionary [forces] would rise."[51]

The question that gnawed at socialists such as Jaurès and made them look "indecisive" concerned how to reconcile this humanistic Jacobin patriotism with the antimilitarism that was fundamental to their collectivist ideology.

In this regard, three tenets generally defined the party's agenda: (1) abolition of permanent armies and replacement with a citizens' militia, the "nation in arms"; (2) complete denunciation of wars of aggression (although acceptance of the need to defend the *patrie*); and (3) international solidarity of the proletariat. With the help of a young officer named Henry Gérard, Jaurès undertook in 1907 a vast study of French and European military matters in an effort to forge a reorganization scheme for the army that fit in with his hopes for a more democratic, socialist, and above all humane future.

The result, *L'Armée nouvelle* (*The New Army*, 1911), was hardly just another ideological venture into the affairs of state. Rather, this two-volume, nearly six-hundred-page work is a carefully researched and clearly, if repetitively, written attempt by one of Europe's great intellectuals to develop a full-scale plan for national defense and, by association, international peace. It was premised on Jaurès's real fear of what war between France and Germany would be like. He wrote with conviction about German plans for a definitive offensive that would quickly crush the opposition, even if it meant massive casualties for her own men. And he railed against the influence of German militarist thinking in France, arguing that "irreparable disaster" would be done to the army's "spirit, as its national independence," if it were to be but "a weak imitation of militarist Germany." Jaurès's main contention was that despite universal conscription, the Republic had not created a *nation armée* à la revolutionary tradition. Instead, its distinction between "active" and "reserve" units had produced an officer corps largely closed off from French society both intellectually and morally (he calls the War Office "a heavy bureaucracy in which arrogance and egoism rose as its ideal declined"), while the reserves, which constituted the bulk of French forces, were ill-trained and underequipped. The *patrie*, Jaurès believed, was courting suicide if it applied an offensive strategy using the active army against the larger, professionalized German forces.[52]

Jaurès's "new army" would overcome these problems by integrating qualified citizens into a "plainly national and plainly defensive" force. Taking a cue from the Swiss militia system, Jaurès proposed a universally conscripted reserve army that was to be recruited and trained locally for approximately three months. These million-plus reserve citizens would be "elevated," in his words, into "the great and veritable active army":

> If France wants to live honestly and be assured of eternity, if she wants to serve her ideal with a national force that will discourage all potential aggressors, it is necessary that she demand a military institution in

which all valid citizens are trained, educated, [and] prepared for war; it is necessary that the artificial and dangerous distinction between active and reserve [units] be abolished. . . . It is only by a completely defensive strategy, soon transformed into an irresistible offensive, that all the energies of France can be put to work for her well being.

Moreover, only by integrating her citizens into a *nation armée* could France truly become a *nation juste,* in which the army would never again serve as a "too convenient instrument in the hands of the powers of repression," as at Fourmies, Narbonne, and elsewhere. As an assimilated institution of French people, Jaurès's army was a model for the socialist state, infused with the passion of all its classes, including the bourgeoisie.[53]

Two points about Jaurès's study should be emphasized: first, that the book fit into a clear conception of his socialist and antimilitarist principles; and, second, that his work was not just a set of ideas but a serious proposal that he introduced in the Chamber of Deputies on November 14, 1910. In *L'Armée nouvelle* and in the military bill that embodied its arguments, Jaurès presented a plan for military restructuring that gave priority to the moral and political needs of citizens. If the book was perhaps too quick to denigrate "militarist and absolutist Germany" before the moral force of revolutionary France, its strength was to ask directly what citizens needed to give their government in exchange for guaranteed security, freedom, and justice. "When we want a defensive strategy for France," Jaurès wrote, "it is because we want a defensive [political] policy for her, a policy of peace and equity." What he most admired about the Swiss militia was its liberty of thought and action, its democratic rather than hierarchical virtue. And although the socialist leader clearly writes from a leftist ideological perspective, in his work he is less imposing his views than highlighting their universal, republican attributes: "It is not a question of officers subscribing to such and such a formula or social organization. It is a question of them recognizing the impressive treasure of moral force contained within working-class socialism, smitten as much with national liberty as human solidarity." It is thus that Jaurès understood antimilitarism, be it his own or that of those to his left, better than anyone else of his time:

> These accents on virile directness and courageous pride will only ring again in men's hearts when the military institution, broken of all the stains, of all the violence of the spirit of caste and class, washed of all aggressive nature, will be no more than the supreme protection and supreme recourse of a society smitten with peace and searching for

justice. It is the vigorous antimilitarist proletariat of today that will be the first to understand these words and to thrill to their tone.[54]

Despite the humane and seemingly universal appeal of *L'Armée nouvelle*, neither the antimilitarists left of Jaurès nor the republicans on his right gave him the support he needed to realize the "new army." Debate over its implementation, although widespread, never even made it to the floor of the Chamber of Deputies. By placing his faith in the reserves, Jaurès's ideas simply ran counter to most professional military thinking.

Yet it was his supposed allies that most disappointed the socialist leader. Guesdists accused Jaurès of placing himself at the service of the War Ministry by treading into the arena of military and strategic planning, where they questioned his competence. In *La Bataille Syndicaliste*, Francis Delaisi called Jaurès's project a direct affront to working-class antimilitarism. He predicted that the Jaurèsian army would essentially create a situation in which a child would find "militarism at school," and that this so-called army of the people, in truth organized and led by professional officers and intellectuals, would be "the most ingenious system to subjugate militarily one class to another."[55] Socialists outside France failed to embrace the plan as well. Max Schippel, a revisionist in the SPD, wrote sarcastically: "You cannot put a cannon in the bed of every former gunner and give each old sea dog a little warship to put in the farmyard trough or wash tub."[56]

For those left of Jaurès, their antimilitarism could never conceive of a role for the bourgeoisie, and they did not distinguish between offensive and defensive wars so long as workers were used to fight them. Marcel Cachin (town councillor of Paris), Jean Morin (general councillor of the Seine), the influential deputy Marcel Sembat, and others used party meetings to promote more aggressive solutions to prevent war. At a large rally at Pré Saint-Gervais organized by the Fédération de la Seine and the Parti Socialiste on November 16, 1912, Morin implored workers: "The moment is serious; Europe is on the eve of a major war; you must overcome your cowardliness: Well! Rather than go serve as cannon fodder for the sole benefit of capitalism, we have to respond to the government's call by complete silence, to refuse to obey any mobilization order, and to go into the streets for the final insurrection." Sembat announced: "We are a lot closer to the Commune than you ever thought!"[57] On November 21 a group of socialists at the party's *congrès extraordinaire* recommended legal means to oppose war, but added that "the proletariat is justified if, after having recognized the inefficacy of these means, it resorted to the General Strike and insurrection." Various socialist leaders summoned their comrades to sabotage mobilization by whatever means possible right through to the outbreak of World War I. The aforementioned report "Les projets de sabotage de la mobilisation" is a reaction to this, and a warning about where it could lead: "By the progressive contamination of the working-class milieus, a completely new mentality has been created . . . that seems infinitely dangerous, since its consequence would be to make it impossible for France to mobilize and defend herself against the invader. The revolutionaries cannot ignore the fact that they thus prepare, for France alone, defeat and dismemberment."[58]

And yet despite the ominous predictions, only the Hervéists attempted the transition from principle to practice on the question of sabotage. During the April 1908 elections Hervé called for a general strike and insurrection in case of war, and soon thereafter he began looking for a new organizational outlet altogether: "Rather than constantly crying about the failure of parliamentarism, let's try to begin work on the need for insurrectional organization, so that when a crisis suddenly appears tomorrow no one will be able to talk of the failure of revolutionary action."[59] He took a major step toward forming such an organization when, in the same year Jaurès was pushing his "nation in arms" vision, he finally decided to split with the "party of electoral action and parliamentarism" and form his own *parti révolutionnaire*.[60] At a meeting on March 8, 1909, two hundred Hervéists adopted an insurrectional manifesto that declared: "The role of the Socialist Party is to organize, with all the revolutionary elements of the country, an energetic minority that, by its example, will prevent the CGT from becoming less extreme as its numbers swell, and from slipping into the social peace reformism of the British or German *syndicats*."

Unable to make socialists give a "capital place to antimilitarism," Hervé pushed ahead with a special Organisation Révolutionnaire, or Organisation de Combat. On October 19, 1910, writing from prison, he called on the Left "to group all the revolutionary temperaments of the country into a formidable band." As he later put it: "The question is not to stir a general embrace . . . but the anti-parliamentarians [syndicalists] and the revolutionary or libertarian anarchists have the same kind of propaganda, especially in the cities, where their revolutionary activity, far from scaring away workers, attracts a fair number of them." Nor was this simply a matter of improved cooperation. Hervé saw the new organization as an "urgent, imperious need," or as he sometimes put it, "a question of life or death" that even the imprisonment of all the editors at *La Guerre Sociale* could not stop. The Organisation Révolutionnaire was nothing less than

Hervé's last gasp effort to group the Left into an impenetrable antimilitarist front.[61]

And how could it possibly fail? As soon as Hervé announced plans for a *parti révolutionnaire*, the anarchists and revolutionary syndicalists Tissier, Almereyda, Marie, Jobert, and Sébastien Faure gave it their full backing. His close association with Yvetot also proved useful. Moreover, Hervé had learned to cast his net widely. An early announcement for the Organisation Révolutionnaire spoke of the "indispensable" need to "defend the little public and individual liberty against the arbitrariness and oppression of the Government, its magistrates, police forces, and its roughneck soldiers."[62]

The most distinguishing aspect of Hervé's initiative was its commitment to sabotage mobilization by "gaining ground in the professional military milieus, which we must, at all costs, infiltrate."[63] For the FCR/FCA and CGT, as we have seen, sabotage was an article of faith. And, according to police, it was on the rise. Between October 1, 1910, and June 30, 1911, there were 2,908 acts of sabotage.[64] So why—when both the comprehensive reports "L'Action revolutionnaire en France" and "La Lutte contre le sabotage" (The Struggle Against Sabotage) viewed the rise of this "association of criminals" as a serious threat—were Hervé's efforts to expand the revolutionary arm of the Socialist Party into the syndicalist and anarchist milieus received with such little enthusiasm, and in some cases outright disdain, by these factions?[65]

We have seen part of the answer already in terms of the distrust many revolutionaries harbored toward Hervé. The anarchists decided to wait until the party actually existed and had undertaken serious action before linking their fate to it. Several argued that it would require a heroic effort for them to cast their lot with a group of socialists.[66] An article that labeled Hervé "The Impenitent" had this to say about his desire for a revolutionary party: "He can no longer continue thus. On the whole, he only abetted the destruction of his political party, without any benefit for the collectivist ideal. What he lost was the chance to pause and recover with a staff that could help him rejuvenate and restore the appearance of a revolutionary party.... This good Hervé! He is always on a honeymoon with his elected socialists. He will ruin them."[67]

The CGT, meanwhile, viewed itself as a party in its own right and felt its autonomy threatened by Hervé. Besides, there were several new groups (the FCR/FCA, Jeunesse Révolutionnaire de la Seine, Comité de Défense Sociale, and Groupe des Libérés des Bagnes Militaires) that comprised syndicalists and anarchists and appeared poised to advance the antimilitarist cause. In early 1910, moreover, Hervé vanished from the scene for more than two years after receiving a four-year prison sentence for an article that lauded one Jacques Liabeuf, a shoemaker who was sentenced to death for murdering a policeman in revenge for a vagrancy conviction. Over most of the next two years, while writing from prison, Hervé would accumulate an additional two years and three months of sentences along with fifteen hundred francs in fines.[68]

Even with Hervé temporarily out of the picture, the mistrust of each others' motives and the stubborn self-reliance of the various groups of the revolutionary Left created tension between leaders and, in turn, resistance to formal cooperation. This is essentially the only way to understand the inability of the revolutionaries to answer Hervé's calls for a union from socialists to anarchists. As one might expect, slight ideological and strategical differences played a role, but that role entered in with the establishment of the various groups in the first place. On important issues such as mobilization sabotage, the revolutionaries were a lot closer than they may have been willing to admit.

As long as the propaganda continued and the authorities continued to feel threatened by it, most antimilitarists, their notch firmly secured in French political and social life, were complacent about broadening their ideas and activities into the kind of organization that Hervé envisioned. It is not enough to say that they lacked commitment, supporters, or even ideological consistency, but more essentially that few felt compelled to step out of their familiar anarchist, socialist, or syndicalist trappings in order to pursue jointly their larger antimilitarist goals, in particular the prevention of war. A crucial factor here was their capacity to respond to the government when a situation arose that offended the moralities of antimilitarists universally. The Aernoult-Rousset Affair, a blatant case of disciplinary injustice in a North African military prison, constituted just such a situation.

The Aernoult-Rousset Affair

On July 2, 1909, Albert Aernoult, age twenty-two, died at Djenan-ed-Dar (Algeria) while serving in a disciplinary company of the African battalions. A military dispatch reached his parents in Romaineville two days later: "Your unfortunate child," the captain of the 1st Company of the 1st African Battalion began coolly, "whose behavior left much to be desired, went into a violent rage on July 2, and in this state of cerebral overexcitement in which he placed himself, had the stroke that carried him off." Just days earlier Aernoult had written his parents that he was in fine health. His friends and family were stunned. No one was really satisfied with this "official" explanation.[69]

The circumstances that led Aernoult to the infamous African battalions were equally disconcerting. A road worker by trade, he was participating in a strike of the local road workers' union when authorities arrested him in a *chasse au renard* (literally, a fox hunt). After ten miserable months in jail, Aernoult was easily persuaded by Conseiller d'État Voisin to join the army. The army, however, meant the African battalions, and it appears that this was not made clear to Aernoult. An unruly and plainly unhappy conscript, he was soon transferred to a disciplinary company. Two years after his arrest, Aernoult was dead.[70]

The annals of history would have long since forgotten this poor, unskilled laborer from Romaineville if not for one man in his company: Émile Rousset. Rousset claimed to have witnessed Aernoult being beaten to death by his commanding officers, Lieutenant Sabatier and Sergeants Beignier and Casanova. Imprisoned for his impetuosity, Rousset refused to keep quiet. He wrote Aernoult's parents and some Parisian journals directly, inspiring *Le Matin* to publish a protest article against the circumstances surrounding Aernoult's death. On November 12, after *L'Humanité* and *La Guerre Sociale* had taken up the issue, the socialist deputy Allemane interpellated the war minister on the cause of death, which Allemane attributed to "hazings" on the part of Aernoult's superiors. The minister ordered an inquiry, but it was only a formality and reaffirmed death by stroke. On November 15 the deputy Veber read a letter in the Chamber of Deputies signed by fifteen of Aernoult's comrades alleging that he had succumbed to the blows of his officers. That, however, was as far as the protest would get in the chamber. An *ordre du jour*, passed by the decisive margin of 431 to 133, ended the interpellation "pure and simple." The case was closed.[71]

But the "affair" had just begun. As long as Rousset continued to speak out on behalf of the dead soldier, the military could not easily bury him. And as long as there were antimilitarists, Rousset did not have to feel that he acted alone. The tension burst into open confrontation when Rousset went before the war council of Oran, supposedly to present his account of Aernoult's death, but in reality to stand trial for refusing to obey orders and for insulting his superiors. On February 2, 1910, he was sentenced to five years in prison.

The news spread quickly, reaching socialist delegates at the Nîmes congress by telegraph. In an impressive show of solidarity, they immediately voted a motion protesting "with indignation" the sentence against Rousset, "guilty in the eyes of the disciplinary *chaouchs* (servants, in Arabic) of having denounced the crime they themselves committed." The congress insisted on a new inquiry, and *L'Humanité* started a fund to finance the exhumation and return of the corpse to France, which Aernoult's parents fervently desired.[72] Soon the entire French Left, with journals ranging from *L'Humanité* to *Les Temps Nouveaux*, was holding meetings, pasting *affiches,* and planning protests. Socialists, syndicalists, and anarchists all shared three reasonable goals: first, the return of Aernoult's remains; second, the liberation of Rousset; and third, the closure of the Algerian military prisons. The question was whether they could work together to achieve them.[73]

The first indication of success in unity came in March, when the Comité de Défense Sociale (CDS) launched the violent *affiche* "down with Biribi."[74] The CDS, which traced its origins to 1905 and to anarchist groups such as Freedom of Opinion, prided itself as a "body of defense against the enterprises of power and the machinations of the police." The CDS had previously organized meetings to support the militant syndicalists arrested in 1908 for the Villeneuve-St. Georges crisis.[75] But it was the "down with Biribi" *affiche* that put the CDS at the forefront of antimilitarist activity. The signers accused the army of committing a second crime (Rousset's sentence) in order to hide the first, and adapted the moral imperative of the *affiche rouge* in their appeal:

> Soldiers! if you feel yourselves threatened, menaced by Biribi, do not hesitate, desert! If you have not had time to desert, if you departed for the prisons where torture and death await you, remember that the military crimes already committed legitimate all reprisals against the head murderers—these officers and *chaouchs* who torture and kill and whose execution in one day of revolt would be greeted with enthusiasm by all men smitten with freedom. They are the executioners, you have bayonets, use them![76]

This time circumstances allowed for acquittal of the sixteen signers. Biribi existed, and there was clear evidence both from the attending physician, who found external signs of physical violence to Aernoult's body, and from Rousset's own testimony, that an injustice had taken place. The defense had hinged its argument on the simple, ethical principle that when legal means failed to resolve the problem of military prisons, revolutionary ones became acceptable. The attorney Joseph Hild insisted that the *affiche* represented a legitimate "cry of indignation and revolt," and praised the defendants for not being "afraid to risk their own freedom merely to ensure the triumph of the eternal ideas of Justice and Humanity."[77] Following the trial, *La Guerre Sociale* declared Biribi indefensible: "It only lives on in silence and in a state of oblivion."[78] This righteous posturing appealed broadly to the French Left, which felt that the case not only called on them to speak out but gave them a moral incentive to act.

Although there is probably no better example of an issue that brought antimilitarists together than that of military injustice in the notoriously corrupt African battalions, even the Aernoult-Rousset Affair could not completely free itself of the internecine squabbles that practically defined the Left. In July *La Voix du Peuple* and *La Guerre Sociale* printed special editions devoted entirely to the affair, but Hervé could not resist chiding the CGT for failing to organize a "vast peaceful protest against Biribi."[79] This was a serious critique, particularly because Aernoult himself had belonged to a *syndicat*. Not only had the anarchist CDS released the first major *affiche*, two months later Émile Aubin's newly constituted Groupe des Anciens Disciplinaires/Groupe des Libérés des Bagnes Militaires would steal headlines with the poster "decorated murderers." The powerful CGT, it seemed, had yet to put itself on the line for Rousset.[80] Hervé also criticized his fellow socialists for not taking seriously enough their resolution at Nîmes and for failing to collect the money to retrieve Aernoult's remains.[81]

Yet if the Aernoult-Rousset Affair had any positive legacy for the antimilitarist Left, it was that it eventually produced a serious and successful effort to work together for a specific cause: the return of Aernoult's remains and, during his funeral rites, a mass demonstration against military prisons. This process began in June 1910, when *L'Humanité* sent its editor, Alfred Kurz, to Algeria to arrange for the body's delivery to France and its burial in Romaineville, as Aernoult's parents had requested of the Interior Ministry.[82] The plan was to organize a large demonstration in the capital on Sunday, June 26, which, in the presence of the corpse and *tout-Paris*, would signal to the public powers the united stance of syndicalists and socialists against military injustice. The syndicalists, however, opposed the idea in favor of their own procession, which they predicted would be "far more important" and which the socialists would want to join "in order to avoid a deplorable comparison."[83] What prevented the whole project from collapsing was the refusal of the Algerian authorities to exhume the body on the grounds that "it is normal practice not to authorize body transport during the hot sea-son."[84] Grandjouan responded with an *affiche* depicting the republican symbol of Marianne slouching in her throne with Aernoult's remains at her feet and a caption that read: "She who sends her poorest and most destitute sons to die in Africa is no longer a mother, she is a step-mother."[85] It was just this sort of blatant attempt to repulse the antimilitarists that was likely to backfire, creating instead "the pretext of a rapprochement between the SFIO and the syndicalists in view of a violent protest campaign against the attitude of the government."[86] That September, the CDS, Union des Syndicats de la Seine, and SFIO formed a *commission mixte* (joint commission) to plan an even larger demonstration in Paris and the provinces.[87]

Now authorities became really concerned. One report expressed fear that "all the revolutionaries of the day will go [to this demonstration] armed."[88] Others worried that the demonstration would "cement an *entente* between the CGT and the PSU."[89] As long as the situation was perceived as being so explosive, the body would have to remain in Algeria. Aernoult's parents were thus forced into the humiliating position of having to readdress the war minister, while socialists and syndicalists sent delegates to Interior Minister Briand to request authorization to return the corpse. Briand refused, but on the grounds that they needed the body in Algeria in order to undergo a medico-legal examination. At last there was to be justice: Lieutenant Sabatier and sergeants Beignier and Casanova were to stand trial in Oran on charges of voluntary murder.[90]

If the antimilitarists had their Dreyfus Affair, then the Aernoult-Rousset case was definitely it. As with the hapless Captain Dreyfus, *L'Humanité* pointed out, the question at hand was "the honor of the army." In this role Captain Allix played the parts of Commandant du Paty de Clam and General Mercier (two leaders heavily implicated in intrigues against Dreyfus) put together. Charged with Rousset's initial examination, Allix had urged him to rescind his accusations with promises that the case would then be closed. The trial in Oran was a travesty like the Rennes court-martial. Before it even opened, *L'Humanité* predicted that the war councils would be nothing but a "show of justice."[91] Rousset, whom the leftist press revered, had forced the army into a cycle of dishonesty and prevarication. That the accused were acquitted in September 1911 surprised no one: "By order they had sentenced Dreyfus! By espirt de corps and because Aernoult was a poor devil whose death in truth should have gone unnoticed, his torturers were just acquitted."[92]

Yet, as in the Dreyfus Affair, the longer the case went on the thicker the plot became. Although Rousset had been pardoned in April 1911 and rejoined the African battalions, in August he was accused of murdering the soldier Brancoli. Thus when Rousset appeared before the Oran war council to testify against the officers he had imputed in Aernoult's murder, he did so as a suspect in his own right. Three months later (December 9, 1911), the military tribunal of Algeria sentenced Rousset, on the flimsiest evidence, to twenty years of hard labor. Aernoult's affair was now just as much Rousset's.

Despite these reversals, antimilitarists were determined to honor the memory of their fallen comrade with a large demonstration. It was over two years since Aernoult's death when, in December 1911, the CDS finally received permission to return the corpse to France. This concession had not come easily for a government haunted by the specter of huge, nationwide demonstrations by the revolutionary Left. It thus moved cautiously. Although the CDS had hoped the remains would be disembarked in Marseille, where the large working-class population would make it an ideal place for a demonstration, authorities mandated the body enter through the more isolated Port-Vendres, about ten kilometers north of the Spanish border.[93]

Regardless of the conditions, antimilitarists were not to be denied this time. In the few frantic weeks prior to the February date set for the demonstration, socialists, syndicalists, and anarchists put aside their differences, just as the public powers had feared, and prepared one of the largest rallies in French history. Back in September 1910 police had observed that each antimilitarist organization sought "to draw it over to its side, which is to say, to turn a profit from the projected demonstration."[94] Now the joint commission was showing signs of genuine cooperation. All the major journals, including *L'Humanité*, *La Guerre Sociale,* and *La Bataille Syndicaliste,* pleaded "to all the proletarian organizations to affirm their disgust for the murderers and their hatred of the military judges"; *L'Humanité* reached out "to all those who, socialists or not, find there are enough victims [of military injustice]."[95] For the day of the funeral, Jaurès's journal gloated: "Never, perhaps, were there such throngs of meetings by syndicalist groups. Never, perhaps, was there more unanimity in the joint effort." He predicted a huge turnout.[96] The forces of reaction did as well. *La Patrie* ominously expected the demonstration would be the "*tout-Paris révolutionnaire,* anarchist, socialist, and antimilitarist."[97]

On February 11, 1912, the long anticipated demonstration took place. By all accounts it was a tremendous success: "Never since those [funeral rites] of Victor Hugo has Paris seen anything similar." Like a "human sea" the procession began at the Gare de Lyon (where the remains arrived), moved up the

Boulevard Diderot to the Place de la Nation, and made its way to Père-Lachaise Cemetery via the avenue Philippe-Auguste and the boulevard Ménilmontant. All along the route, demonstrators carrying emblems of their organizations, from the black flag of the FCR to the red banners of the socialist sections, sang the "Internationale," the "Carmagnole," "Glory to the 17th!" and the newest revolutionary refrain "Glory to Rousset."[98] Reliable sources estimated 100,000 to 200,000 people took part in what *La Libre Parole* described as a "veritable mobilization of the revolutionary and anarchist forces of Paris."[99] Demonstrations also took place in Marseille, Saint-Etienne, Lorient, Angers, and Niort. In Orléans a red crown inscribed "to comrade Aernoult, murdered by the *chaouchs* of the Third Republic" was placed at the base of the Joan of Arc statue.[100] *L'Humanité* summed up the day thus: "It is therefore really the entire proletariat of the great city, conscious and active, that stands with us, rises to our appeal, to the appeal of the social organizations, and to that of its *patrie*."[101]

If antimilitarists had allowed their differences to interfere with the planning of the demonstration in its early stages, those differences were not apparent on February 11. The twenty thousand who entered Père-Lachaise and represented virtually every leftist faction listened respectfully to speeches by socialist, syndicalist, and CDS representatives who appealed to the working classes as a whole and avoided the ideological language that had led socialists to walk out of a meeting of the joint commission months before. There were no disruptions other than a scuffle as the demonstrators were trying to leave, and police made only twenty-six arrests. It was a day, one might say, of emotions rather than opinions; passion rather than politics. Aernoult's parents were on hand to give their son his final rites, and when Madame Aernoult began to cry, countless pairs of eyes teared up as well. "A few days like that of Aernoult's obsequies is worth more than twenty years of propaganda," concluded a police report.[102]

Always a keen observer of the Left, Gustave Hervé, who had seen his own efforts to form a united antimilitarist front fall by the wayside, easily grasped the meaning of the demonstration. In an article published that very day, as he languished in jail, Hervé argued that the rally's most important outcome was the union between socialists, syndicalists, and anarchists in the Paris region: "What a single organization could not do, the three combined will do." He continued:

> When we preach the "disarmament of hatreds," it is not for the pleasure of prompting a general embrace or frustrating the necessary au-

tonomy of the syndicalist, socialist, or libertarian organizations . . . it is merely so that, during great occasions like today, entente . . . is not rendered impossible by petty squabbles, cliques, and by doctrines poisoned at the outset by fierce individual quarrels. If today's demonstration reveals to everyone, in a concrete fashion, the advantages of entente and union, we will not have wasted our time preaching "the disarmament of hatred" in the past year.[103]

For now Hervé could feel vindicated. But what did unity actually accomplish at Père-Lachaise? Rousset, after all, was still a condemned man. The military prisons in Africa had not magically disappeared. And perhaps most sadly was that Aernoult had died without a single statement of remorse from the republican government. On the contrary, less than two months before the demonstration Georges Berry introduced a modification to an earlier law on suspension from the army which, after further adjustments by the socialist war minister Alexandre Millerand, became the infamous Millerand-Berry Law. Pushed through the Chamber of Deputies with surprising ease on March 25, 1912 (partly because the socialists had left the room to protest Wilm's speech on the taxi strike), the law was a direct attack on the purported influence of antimilitarism in the military. Promulgated December 9, 1912, it created the following conditions for immediate dispatch to an African battalion: (1) individuals sentenced to at least three months in prison for provocation to desertion or insubordination; (2) individuals sentenced two or more times (total duration of at least two months) for defamation or harm toward the army and navy, and for provocations toward servicemen aimed at deterring them from their military duties and obedience toward superiors.[104]

Although the Millerand-Berry Law emerged out of Millerand's larger plans to bolster army cohesion and increase officer stature in the wake of the second Moroccan crisis, its implications for the Left were vast. Viewed as a direct attempt to silence antimilitarists, the "new *loi scélérate*," or as *Le Populaire du Midi* (and many other journals) called it, "law of infamy,"[105] engendered nationwide protest by syndicalists, socialists, and such offshoot groups as the Comité Féminin de Protestation Contre la Loi Millerand-Berry et les Bagnes Militaires and the Comité d'Entente Pour l'Action Antimilitariste.[106] The CGT complained that the law struck directly at workers' dignity and liberties;[106] *L'Humanité* said it had "raised the indignation of the working world." *La Voix du Peuple* deemed the law "a crime, a repugnant forfeit," while *La Bataille Syndicaliste* criticized socialists for not protesting enough. The CGT organized 112 meetings against the law, 22 of them in the Seine department, and its 1912 congress in Le Havre authorized a vigorous campaign to repeal it.[107] The FCR anarchists were still more accusatory, damning the socialists for being accomplices to the law because one of their own had helped write it: "To the powerless socialism, to the opportunist revolutionarism [syndicalism], we will victoriously oppose anarchist agitation, brutal without doubt, but frank, loyal, an enemy of all compromise and bargaining."[108]

Despite this setback, the affair was not over for the Left as long as its other half was under a sentence of hard labor. Moreover, important new evidence had surfaced—on his deathbed, Brancoli confessed that it was not Rousset who had struck him. His own insalubrious past aside (accusations of robbery and pederasty, among others), Rousset was starting to look like the very embodiment of that fine delineation between the rights of the citizen and the prerogatives of the state. Amidst the numerous and nationwide activities organized on his behalf, at least three thousand attended a meeting at the Cirque de Paris on October 1, 1912.[110] The goal was clear: freedom for Rousset and an end to the military prisons. When *La Guerre Sociale*'s Eugène Merle went to Algeria to visit Rousset, he returned declaring "we recognized Christ in him immediately." The antimilitarists had found their savior.[111]

As a direct result of united antimilitarist agitation, the government freed Rousset and, as soon as he set foot on French soil, the Left gave him a hero's welcome. The secretary-general of the CDS personally met Rousset's boat in Marseille, and from there members shuttled him to the local Bourse du Travail. From Marseille he was taken to Lyon, where crowds were so large that police imprisoned him temporarily just to prevent a major disruption.[112] In Paris, thousands of workers at the Salle Wagram wildly cheered their hero and promised to continue the fight against the war councils. Indeed in the coming years Rousset was to play a large role in that fight, appearing as guest of honor at meetings and rallies, a kind of token survivor of an outdated army, most of whose victims could never hope to escape their African exile.

◆ ◆ ◆

There are two ways of looking at the Aernoult-Rousset Affair that can, more generally, help in understanding the successes and failures of the Left in confronting the state with a unified program of moral antimilitarism. On the one hand, were it not for the activities of the CDS, in conjunction with socialists and the CGT, there would have been no affair to begin with. A syndicalist *affiche* reported in Périgueux beseeched soldiers "not to forget that it was the workers who unveiled the military crimes."[113] The large crowds at Aernoult's funeral service and the celebrations of Rousset's freedom affirmed the real force that antimilitarism had in French society. The affair became at once a powerful example of military abuse and a political weapon with ethical overtones that enabled the Left to overcome ideological and personal differences and compelled the government to meet some of its demands.

Yet the affair had another side as well, the side of petty rivalries and persistent hostilities that came from both deeply rooted ideological differences and mistrust as to strategical commitment. Beneath the rallies and meetings there remained a thick layer of resentment between groups that sought to use the issue for their own purposes. Even Rousset's return summoned these conflicts to the surface. On Rousset's arrival in Marseille, CDS leader de Marmande made him read the statement: "The organized working class freed me from prison, but I do not owe it anything because it used my case to prove its strength."[114] This was an undisguised attack on socialists and on the CGT; reassertion through coercion of the notion that only anarchists were true antimilitarists. As such, it evoked angry response. *La Guerre Sociale* set off an acrimonious debate when it accused the libertarians and syndicalists of the CDS (many affiliated with *La Bataille Syndicaliste*) of having a "pet craze": "They are violently, passionately anti-socialist." *La Bataille* defended the CDS with the old argument that it transcended all political parties and groups, and it reaffirmed its mistrust of socialists, Hervé in particular.[115]

As promising an issue as Aernoult-Rousset was for the Left, it did not, in the end, bring it any closer to realizing Hervé's ideal of a permanent, revolutionary antimilitarist front from socialists to anarchists. What it did do was allow the Left, at least for the short term, to show its strength and determination in fighting blatant abuses of power and hierarchy on the part of the government and military. This was nothing to scoff at. Although Hervé was perhaps exceptional in recognizing that antimilitarism did not even stand a chance of stopping international war without cooperation across leftist boundaries, smaller battles could be won with even superficial collaboration. A telling statement in *Le Libertaire* captured the significance of this perfectly: "As much as the CGT—perhaps more than it—we hate the politicians of the PSU. But if they appeal to the socialist crowds in order to protest some great governmental infamy, our duty is to be there. We ourselves have to join closely with these crowds because their action merits our association. . . . The events should oblige socialists, syndicalists, and anarchists to act in unison each time the goal pursued is common to them."[116]

◆ ◆ ◆

"Nevertheless," concluded a May 1911 report after finding more division than cohesion between leftist elements, "if a unique revolutionary party does not exist in France, there are numerous groups, in Paris and the provinces, that carry out active revolutionary and antimilitarist propaganda. . . . It is through brochures, conferences, and theater that this agitation manifests itself, supported by rounds of propaganda created in an almost uninterrupted fashion on all points of the territory."[117]

Did unity matter? Maurice Guichard, who wrote a series on antimilitarism for the conservative *La France,* did not seem to think so. In his 1913 analysis of anarchists, syndicalists, and socialists—"three parties equally of the extreme left, equally revolutionary, [that] profess, in France, antimilitarist doctrines and undertake propaganda on their own behalf"—Guichard discovered "three large fractions of the revolutionary party," each contributing a fundamental component to the antimilitarist whole. Socialists provided the political element, bringing antimilitarist doctrines before the Chamber of Deputies and the general public. At the other extreme were the anarchists, who were defined by their antipatriotism and operated outside the army, thus encouraging resistance to it. Finally, the syndicalists took their propaganda directly into the casernes and prepared soldiers and conscripts to disobey their commanding officers. Antimilitarism worked so well indeed *because* of its variegated parts.[118]

By contrast, George Bonnamour of *L'Éclair* and André Tardieu of the literary *Revue des Deux Mondes* interpreted the successes of antimilitarism as an imbalance of revolutionary elements that favored the anarchists:

> The anarchists, carrying through their plan of 1895, are at the head of the workers' movement and, by the same token, of parliamentary socialism enslaved to the *syndicats*. The men of direct action, struck down by the law of 1894 [*scélérates*], have barricaded themselves behind the law of 1884 [establishing the *syndicats*]. The Confédération Générale du Travail . . . is their main instrument. These socialist, syndicalist, and anarchist groups of all shades, with their combative agencies (Jeunes gardes, Jeunesses, etc.), are in constant communication and understand one another.

Tardieu concluded:

> In sum, the workers' socialist organizations and others are in clear agreement with the anarchist organization that for the last fifteen years has infiltrated them thoroughly. Against the army and the *patrie;* for insubordination, desertion, insurrection in the case of war, assassination of officers, and mobilization sabotage: *voilà* the terrain of this accord. After the unity of instrument, the unity of doctrine is established.[119]

Similarly, Bonnamour's "Inquiry into Antimilitarism" (1911) blamed anarchists for the preponderance of antimilitarist ideas not only in working-class milieus, but in French intellectual life as well.[120]

The question remains: Did antimilitarists need to be unified in order to engage the government and military effectively? In light of the reactions of Georges Doutremont, Maurice Guichard, André Tardieu, and George Bonnamour; in light of the continued vigilance of public officials and the fears registered by military leaders; and in light of their prominent successes in the courtroom and on the streets, few antimilitarists seemed as concerned as Hervé over the need for a united, revolutionary "movement." Yet there can be little doubt too that their own pride and achievements overshadowed the complexity of their larger goal: to prevent international war. In his critique of the divisions between revolutionaries and the disarray of the Left during the Balkan Wars, FCA leader Edouard Boudot estimated: "If the revolutionary forces had been organized, if homogeneity had taken hold between the active men of our groups, we could have created a movement with some possibilities for success on the day war was declared."[121] Boudot may have been right, but as he also probably recognized when he spoke only of "some possibilities of success," many more factors would have to go into the equation besides that of unity. In the years before the war, the political situation in France was to turn against antimilitarists even as the socialists gained strength in the Chamber of Deputies. The question still must be put, then, as to whether we judge antimilitarism for its ability to face down these challenges or for its capacity to stop an international war. As the Aernoult-Rousset Affair demonstrated so well, antimilitarism was more than just another divisive ideology—it was a real working force for an enhanced measure of political and social justice.

7. ANTIMILITARIST WARS II

The Battle Without

When Radical Party leader Joseph Caillaux became prime minister in June 1911, the antimilitarist Left could not have been too displeased. Here was a man who showed few signs of his forerunner Georges Clemenceau's fierce, right-wing patriotism, who hailed from a party with a large rural and small-town base whose voters traditionally begrudged military service, and who was intensely dedicated to Franco-German reconciliation. Caillaux had been a treasury official before his rapid political ascent, and as prime minister he hoped to draw on his banking connections to strengthen relations with Germany through international business. Here was a man, in short, who despite being a banker appeared more ally than enemy to the Left.

Events, however, quickly undid any illusions about who was on whose side in the ongoing struggle against militarism. Caillaux had barely taken office when Berlin sent the gunboat *Panther* to the Moroccan port of Agadir, allegedly to protect the interests of German nationals. But this aggressive act was actually carried out in defiance of Morocco's conversion into a French protectorate by Caillaux's predecessor. The new prime minister responded by ceding Germany a large piece of the French Congo in exchange for a free hand in Morocco, but he did this *without* informing his foreign minister. An enraged Chamber of Deputies ratified the transfer but then overthrew Caillaux less than six months into his ministry. In the wave of nationalist and anti-German sentiment that followed, the so-called nationalist revival that had been gaining in France since the first Moroccan crisis received definitive political confirmation when the patriotic Lorrainer Raymond Poincaré was named head of state.

Caillaux's botched Moroccan diplomacy and the boost it gave nationalists are part of the oft-told story of how, in the years before World War I, French political leadership began to drift rightward and, correspondingly, to act as if war was imminent by legislating military expansion, solidifying alliances, and even passing measures to raise morale. Yet while scholars of World War I have labored over every detail of the diplomatic and political maneuverings leading up to August 1914, they have largely neglected the domestic dimension of security. How did the renewed militancy of the government, the "nationalist revival," and the growing anticipation of war by political elites affect the ideas and activities of antimilitarists? In the complicated picture of how France prepared for war, the significance of domestic security can be illustrated by the lesser known fact that, eight days after the Germans threatened Morocco and with Europe on the brink of war, the once-promising Caillaux ordered a search of the Paris offices of the Bourse du Travail and had three syndicalist leaders arrested for inciting soldiers to disobedience.[1]

The Affair(s) of the Sou du Soldat

Caillaux's search of the Paris Bourse was really an excuse for what had long been in the making: a direct strike against the Sou du Soldat and the antimilitarist propaganda in the casernes. The main target was the masonry and stone *syndicat,* and the three arrests were its leaders—Pierre Viau, Augustin Baritaud, and Ferdinand Dumont. Why this particular union? One reason was that its membership explosion from five hundred in 1905 to fifteen thousand by 1912, coupled with its leadership in protests and strikes favoring the nine-hour day and wage increases, had brought national recognition.[2] But the main reason was that this revolutionary *syndicat* had a well organized Sou du Soldat fund. Each January 1 and May 1 the union sent five to ten francs to affiliated soldiers with messages such as "on this occasion, [the Fédération] thinks about its comrades attired against their wishes in military uniform, and reminds them that this uniform . . . carries the stigma of the murder of workers who were guilty only of wanting to alleviate the exploitation of man by man."[3] According to a dossier found during the search, more than five hundred soldiers in the masonry *syndicat* alone received this material. And authorities believed this was only the tip of the iceberg. Because an *ordre du jour* at the Toulouse congress (October 1910) encouraged *syndicats* to establish Sou du Soldat funds and appraise *bourse* administrators of their member-soldiers, the institution saw a renaissance. Numerous groups, including the Union des Syndicats de la Seine and the *bourses* in Bourges and Saint-Malo, now regularly took part. By December 1911, the CGT was praising the Sou du Soldat as "a syndicalist institution that honors the working class."[4]

It was less the language of the circulars, typically more subdued than the *affiches*, that bothered officials so much as it was their presence "at the heart of the army." In January 1911 a memo from the interior minister to the prefects contended that with the Toulouse decision "ferments of disorganization have been introduced into the army," and it recommended "very close" surveillance of the *bourses* and *syndicats*.[5] A month later the commander of the 12ème Army Corps in Limoges, General Pelecier, reported that an investigation of his unit revealed that numerous soldiers had received the circulars, and he concluded that "the Sou du Soldat fund aimed to create a veritable organization within the army that would function, in the case of a strike or war, to paralyze mobilization or challenge any measures to maintain order."[6] By May the interior minister was urging prefects "*to survey this movement in the most active fashion.*"[7] In June, War Minister Goiran warned of "certain civil organizations" that spread antimilitarism in the army through letter-circulars inciting soldiers to indiscipline. He urged army commanders to exercise "exemplary disciplinary repression against clearly characterized antimilitarist acts."[8]

All this activity was a sure sign of an impending government crackdown. Yet while authorities had tried to stop the syndicalists behind these circulars before, the public prosecutor's office had always hindered their efforts because the provocation was not direct and thus could not fall under the 1881 law. By July 1911, the government had found a loophole, applying instead the 1894 *lois scélérates*. It was this anti-anarchist legislation, in short, that became the basis for the search and arraignments.[9]

The Left was incredulous. For the simple, righteous act of aiding their working-class comrades under arms and for summoning them to think twice before pulling the trigger on strikers, three syndicalists were being tried for anarchist propaganda![10] A letter to *L'Humanité* interpreted Caillaux's move as the inauguration of a "reign of terror" against the working classes.[11] For *Le Radical* and *La Bataille Syndicaliste*, this "assassination" was "proof of the little importance the Third Republic attaches to the liberty and dignity of workers."[12] A CDS *affiche* appealed to all political prisoners detained by the Republic: "They strangle our liberties, let's defend them!"[13] *La Bataille Syndicaliste* argued that what really had been sacrificed was the "prestige" and "favor" of the Republic.[14]

In defense of the Sou du Soldat, the Left relied on the humanistic language of individual rights rather than on violent antimilitarist threats. What Yvetot had once referred to as a potent instrument for antimilitarist propaganda was now no more than "a small sum, rather meager, rather modest, that could help [soldiers] forget the thousands of physical and above all moral torments of life in the caserne." In *La Bataille Syndicaliste* he whitewashed the revolutionary purpose that first marked the Sou du Soldat, outlining four "articles of faith" that he now attached to it: (1) military rules should come after human law; (2) officers' orders should not suffocate those of one's conscience; (3) before being a slayer of men, one should become the dispenser of justice and avenger of the oppressed; (4) strikers are not the enemy, but those who command, oppress, and exploit are.[15]

Put this way, it is easy to see why the affair of Viau, Baritaud, and Dumont, also known as the Sou du Soldat Affair, became a catalyst for the Left. Circulars protested the arrests as "the immense crime that put France on the verge of ruin."[16] In the Paris region alone forty-one *syndicats* announced that they had a Sou du Soldat fund, and in a show of solidarity with the masons these *syndicats* demanded that they too be prosecuted. Thirteen unions in Bordeaux did the same, as did others in Lyon, Marseille, Saint-Etienne, and Toulon.[17] Conferences, meetings, and incessant propaganda across France culminated with a demonstration at the Palais de Justice and a public meeting in Paris on January 10, 1912, the designated court date for the three defendants.

The striking thing about these protests is how minor a part the accused played in them. Like Marcel Thomas's book *L'Affaire sans Dreyfus* (*The Affair without Dreyfus*), in which the beleaguered Captain Dreyfus plays only a bit part in his own affair, the issue of the *lois scélérates* virtually drowned out the plight of Viau, Baritaud, and Dumont.[18] Announcing the "suicide of the Third Republic," *La Guerre Sociale* predicted: "The application of the *lois scélérates* to the militant syndicalists is the last straw to break the camel's back."[19] It was due to these laws that the three spent six months in prison awaiting trial, so it seemed to make more sense to focus on the laws than on the accused themselves. On the day of the trial, the CGT distributed flyers that gave a complete history of the laws and referred to them as "monstrous anachronisms" in a regime that calls itself republican, yet only mentioned Viaud, Dumont, and Baritaud once in its tirade against the government's lack of progress since the Dreyfus Affair. As *L'Humanité* recognized, "their trial had disappeared before that of the *lois scélérates*."[20]

Because of the nature of the offense, the Sou du Soldat Affair was one of those issues that put the entire antimilitarist Left at odds with the government. Although estimates vary, thousands of workers protested the trial, and as many as six thousand packed into the Manège St. Paul to hear syndicalist leaders appeal for a just society.[21] And although some conservative journals reported that the agitation planned by the CGT, Union des Syndicats de la Seine, and Fédération National du Bâtiment "had not been the great day these organizations had counted on," the trial, which the government set back a week due to the throngs roaming around the Palais de Justice, ended in a meaningless guilty verdict where Viau, Baritaud, and Dumont were sentenced to six months in prison, exactly the period that they had just served.[22] The three walked out of the courtroom and into a café across the street that very day. *L'Humanité* called the outcome a "gesture of revolt, [but] a sentence of acquittal."[23]

Most importantly for antimilitarists, this imagined victory for the forces of reaction resulted in exactly what it was intended to prevent: new life had been breathed into the Sou du Soldat. As originally conceived, the Sou du Soldat depended on the initiative of each individual *syndicat*, a division of labor that inhibited its rapid and uniform diffusion. Now the CGT began distributing antimilitarist material via the larger federations. The national metallurgy, railroad, and building organizations quickly complied, the latter printing a brochure of "practical information" on the fund's "goal, principle, [and] operation."[24] At the local level, collection boxes were placed in restaurants, cafés, and the like to facilitate donations.[25]

The spread of the Sou du Soldat clashed again with the right-leaning government when the Fédération des Syndicats d'Instituteurs (primary school teachers), which had been affiliated with the CGT only since 1909, voted at their congress in Chambéry (August 1912) to create a fund. The furor was magnified by the fact that schools were traditionally bastions of republican and patriotic zeal, particularly because reforms in the 1880s made primary education free compulsory, secular, and, thus, highly nationalistic. Even the designation *instituteur*, which replaced terms such as "schoolmaster" or "rector" during the French Revolution, reflected the notion that it was a teacher's role to *institute* (educate) the nation. Could they too be infected with antimilitarism? Were the youth of France being indoctrinated with revolutionary rather than republican spirit?[26] From the regional council in the Ain, former War Minister Messimy was first to sound the alarm:

"We are ardently attached to the lay school, and it is precisely because I am convinced that it is necessary for children to go through secular school . . . that I care to rise up against these saddening facts."[27]

On August 23, Minister of Public Education Guist'hau addressed a circular to prefects ordering them to dissolve their *syndicats* by September 10. While the Morbihan union complied, several departments, including the Maine-et-Loire, Charente, and Seine, resisted the directive and received full backing by the CGT for doing so. To symbolize its defiance, the CGT called on André Chapolin, secretary of the Syndicat des Instituteurs de la Seine, to preside over its first meetings at the Havre congress (September 16–22, 1912). Not a welcome gesture to the public powers, they proceeded to prosecute the departmental *syndicats* of the Seine, Bouches-du-Rhône, Maine-et-Loire, and Rhône. Despite the gallant efforts of defense attorney Pierre Laval, the government dissolved these unions.[28]

Yet there was more to come. Every Friday from November 8 to December 13 the Chamber of Deputies entertained heated debate over what Paul Pugliesi-Conti, the "nationalist" deputy of the Seine, referred to as the "veritable overflowing of anarchy and revolutionary spirit that marked the Chambéry Congress."[29] On November 29, Louis Dubois argued that the *instituteurs'* actions proved that the teachers of France had fallen into a worrisome state of malaise: "One can judge them as one likes, but one fact remains undeniable, which is that the *instituteurs* are not happy; that they are not admitting their true situation; that they are in revolt; that they advocate anarchy."[30] Moreover, according to Pugliesi-Conti, their attitude was having a profound impact on French schoolchildren: with 6,000 unionized *instituteurs* and approximately 20 students per class, "that comes to 120,000 French youth shaped by 'delinquent' teachers each year."[31]

By far the sharpest voice of indignation came from Messimy, who once called the Sou du Soldat a "dishonor to the French language." Messimy never doubted that the CGT had the potential "to play a very important role, very useful, very efficacious, and truly very fruitful," but to his great chagrin it had chosen a different path: "The skill of the CGT has been to hide behind an innocuous name and under the cover of a sort of mutuality a work [the Sou du Soldat] that aims . . . to pursue antimilitarist and antipatriotic propaganda ardently; even to form, wherever possible, centers of this propaganda in the regiments themselves." Messimy proceeded to prove his point by recounting the history of the Sou du Soldat, arguing that this "powerful . . . very rationally conceived" organization actually sought, "which is no great secret to anyone, to interrupt mobilization in times of war." The Sou du

Soldat, he concluded, "could be the most useful, the most efficacious of the works of mutuality and working-class solidarity; but it is not . . . it is the most efficacious means of CGT antipatriotic propaganda, which includes action against the State, the nation, and the army."[32]

Messimy's tirade in the Chamber of Deputies reconfirmed the existence of a large gap between official estimations of the CGT and real understanding of it and, by extension, its antimilitarism. In defense of the teachers, several socialist deputies took the moral high ground, arguing that it was their "right" and duty" to express themselves: "If you do not want them to frequent the Bourses du Travail, to belong to the CGT, which *bourses* do you want them to frequent? The Bourse of [moral] Values!"[33] On the other side, the Right accused the new generation of *instituteurs* of being corrupters of youth and saboteurs of the patriotic ideal. In Ernest Psichari's novel *L'Appel des armes* (*The Call of Arms*), a student has to be coaxed away from his *instituteur* father before he can be converted to the militant nationalism spreading among young, primarily urban Frenchmen in the period.[34]

One thing was certain: rational arguments about the ethical purpose of the Sou du Soldat had little effect on the nationally charged political climate of the day, as the government's dissolution of the teachers' union soon proved. Although the overreactions of the public powers grew with each antimilitarist incident, what they overlooked was that their own vociferous responses often clouded important realities. One reality was that at its pre-1914 peak the teachers' *syndicats* comprised only 4 percent of France's 120,000 *instituteurs*.[35] Another, as Jacques and Mona Ozouf show, was that patriotic (although not warmongering) ideals suffused the primary school texts of the period.[36] A third reality was that antimilitarists thrived on the attention, as Yvetot recognized: "The best proof that our work is good, useful, [and] fruitful is the determination our enemies put into trying to stop it."[37] In the end the only way that *instituteurs* would prove that there was a difference between their conceptualization of the Sou du Soldat and that of the government was when over one-quarter (35,000) of them fought in 1914–1918, and 8,419 died, as their dossiers recorded, *sur le champ d'honneur*.[38]

The Nationalist Revival

One of the main themes of this study has been the chasm between official perceptions of antimilitarism and the real meaning and sources of power behind the various "antimilitarisms" that coexisted in this period. At no time before the First World War did this chasm seem to yawn so widely as it did in the years 1911 to 1914. What had happened, particularly if most researchers find only decline and discord on the Left in the immediate prewar period? Historians have long debated the significance of France's "nationalist revival." For Eugen Weber, a "change of atmosphere" took place from 1905 to 1914 as moderate bourgeois and even left-wing republican parties migrated toward more traditional, nationalist forces as a result of international crises culminating in Agadir, the growing political power of the SFIO, and social unrest in general. Antimilitarism certainly played a role here, although Weber does not emphasize it.

What Weber does examine is the crucial popular element of the "nationalist revival," which signaled a reversal from the disfavored view of the military going back to the Dreyfus Affair and the *affaire des fiches*. Demagogues such as Paul Déroulède of the *revanchiste* Ligue des Patriotes, Édouard Drumont of the viciously anti-Semitic *La Libre Parole,* and Charles Maurras of the royalist Action Française may have been few in number and concentrated in the capital, but their ideas reverberated with an important component of the French youth, bourgeoisie, and intellectuals. What Jean-Jacques Becker terms the "sociology of nationalism" included the students Henri Massis and Alfred de Tarde, whose 1913 inquiry "into the opinions and lifestyles" of their generation, titled *Les jeunes gens d'aujourd'hui* (*The Young People of Today*), celebrated war and "energetic action" as regenerative forces for spiritually starved French youth.[39] Becker's typology also embraces the replacement of the nineteenth-century vogue for antimilitarist novels with Maurice Barrès's works of "integral nationalism," the so-called Alsatian novels *Au Service de l'Allemagne* (1905) and *Colette Baudoche* (1909), Charles Péguy's and Ernest Psichari's work on the "mystique of the army" and allure of war, and the neo-Catholicism of Péguy, Alfred de Mun, and Roger Martin du Gard.[40]

Although France as a whole may have been no more nationalistic because an elite minority found in the army and church a remedy for what it perceived as the social and political ills of the Republic, this "small sharp voice" had, according to Weber, its "great booming echo" in French political and military life.[41] It was in this period, when war seemed imminent and socialists in France and Germany were staging some of their largest antiwar demonstrations,[42] that major military decisions were taken that would directly affect the next war. In particular, in addressing the need for a more coherent command structure the newly appointed chief of staff General Joseph Joffre endorsed the Plan XVII strategy—an invasion through Alsace-Lorraine that put to rest any illusions that France would fight only a defensive war against

Germany. Poincaré's 1912 cabinet, as did the governments of Briand and Louis Barthou that succeeded his election to president in January 1913, strengthened France's political and military alliance with Russia to ensure that Germany would face immediate attack on both fronts.[43]

Poincaré's foreign policies were widely accepted in 1912 because they appeared as a direct reaction to German aggression. Even socialists understood this and helped secure his presidential election.[44] But on the domestic front Poincaré made changes that did *not* appear essential to the peaceful pursuit of national defense, and it was against these measures that the full ire of antimilitarists came to bear. Gerd Krumeich has argued that Poincaré purposely linked foreign and domestic issues in a "policy of moral unification," citing a speech he gave at Dunkirk in fall 1912, shortly after returning from talks in St. Petersburg, in which he referred to "political confidence and this unity of national feeling" as direct complements of military strength. With his war minister Millerand, Poincaré set out to instill this "national feeling" in several ways. One was a decree stipulating that soldiers give "total obedience" and "constant submission" to their superiors. Another, the Millerand-Berry Law, aimed at bolstering cohesion in the ranks and rooting out antimilitarism.[45] And although Niall Ferguson may term Poincaré's establishment of a national holiday to commemorate Joan of Arc a symbolic gesture in an already exaggerated "nationalist revival," it was just such small public acts that made war more plausible and, ultimately, acceptable to French citizens in 1914.[46]

In fact it was in the public sphere that Poincaré/Millerand undertook their most divisive action by reestablishing *retraites militaires*. Prohibited since the Dreyfus Affair, these weekly military forays from the caserne and into the streets of Paris (usually held on Saturday nights) were enthusiastically embraced by citizens anxious to exhibit their latent patriotic energy with effusive marches and rallies. Their success was more than Millerand had anticipated, which in itself attests to a certain "nationalist revival." But what Henri Contamine has described as "a kind of militarist demagogy invented by the Minister of War" quickly, and predictably, became a target of the Left.[47]

Antimilitarists reacted to this show of nationalist ardor and military bravado by attempting to disrupt it outright. Anarchist and syndicalist groups urged their members to follow the marches and try, literally, to out-shout the demonstrators and military bands. Some even furnished lead sticks and truncheons to knock down the police agents protecting the demonstrators. Yet it appears the *retraites* produced few serious incidents. At their worst, in

August 1913 approximately 500 marchers from the group Friends of the *Retraite* clashed with some 350 syndicalists, anarchists, and Jeunes Gardes révolutionnaires at the Place de la Concorde. Police made several arrests and reported property damage of 2,500 francs, but the cost to army prestige was likely minimal.[48]

The groups that caused havoc during the *retraites* were typically from the extreme Left; the rest were content to stay home and protest from their journals. Socialists of the Conseil Fédéral de la Seine decided not to advocate participation in the protests, and Jaurès refused to publish the time and location of the *retraites* in *L'Humanité*.[49] What really rankled antimilitarists was not simply that there were nationalist demonstrations taking place in Paris and other towns, but the very *idea* of these demonstrations as legally sanctioned acts of outright bellicosity and militarist provocation was cause for offense. The *retraites* themselves only attracted a few hundred people; indeed, the evening before Aernoult's funeral rites, one took place that the next day's events would overshadow completely.[50] But it was the fact that the government, with an ex-socialist minister of war, had established the gatherings—in flagrant violation of any tacit program to ensure national security and a peaceful purpose—that was beyond the comprehension of antimilitarists: "At this moment it is not only the revolutionaries who should protest, it is everyone who calls themselves republicans and rebukes, like us, the chauvinistic incitements."[51] This sentence from *La Guerre Sociale* reveals as much about the national identity of antimilitarists as it does the government's shifting policies of aggressive nationalism.

The Waning of Revolutionary Syndicalism

The *retraites militaires,* the Millerand-Berry Law, and Poincaré's foreign policy and military reforms all were signs of the times, but the language of the Left's responses signaled another change taking place as well: revolutionary antimilitarism—in particular its antipatriotic protests—was in decline. The "flag in the dung heap" appeals of the Hervéists and anarcho-syndicalists could not well sustain themselves in post-Agadir France, and critiques of Poincaré's foreign and domestic policies became less ideological and more practical in light of the perilous international situation. In a long essay in *Les Temps Nouveaux,* Jean Grave wonders if the "renaissance of chauvinism" and the Left's "general spinelessness" with regard to the latest military burdens proved the sterility of antimilitarist efforts. Yet rather than give a one-sided interpretation of the leftist cause, he proves to be open-minded about the innumerable ways in which militarism and war are detriments to society as a whole, looking at it from as much a capitalist as an anarchist perspective. Although Grave still favors some form of social revolution, his model is what the people together did to protect their newly won liberties in 1792: "Which proves that, in order to defend a country, it is not necessary to reduce it to militarism, but simply to give it something tangible to defend."[52]

Both international and domestic factors had a hand in subduing some of the more confrontational language of antimilitarism. After German police almost arrested Yvetot in Berlin for a peace demonstration (July 1911), his relief on being back on French soil (he had to return covertly) showed no bounds, as he exulted "salut à ma patrie!" in *La Bataille Syndicaliste*.[53] Freedom of expression in Wilhelmine Germany, with a political system one historian has described as "an autocratic, semi-absolutist sham constitutionalism," *was* different.[54] As an August 1, 1911, report stated: "On their return from Berlin, CGT members are saying that the Berlin syndicalists made it clear to them that in the case of war they could not act easily and would be restricted to verbal protests."[55] From a domestic perspective, Madeleine Rebérioux shows that the insurrectional movements of Lagardelle and Hervé began to lose momentum after 1911 due to social reform (which improved workplace relations through the creation of the Labor Ministry in 1906), the unionization of civil servants (which made the state a better ally of the Left), and increased industrial concentration (which lent force to socialist arguments for nationalization).[56]

The shifting domestic and international currents had perhaps their most direct consequences for the CGT, particularly its already precarious revolutionary wing. The turn of political events in 1911 (what Susan Milner refers to as "a 'bad' year for the CGT") forced the CGT to increase its antiwar propaganda even as its leaders began to move away from the aggressive, insurrectional policies that had characterized revolutionary syndicalist dominance.[57] Thus at the Havre congress in 1912, the socialist Charles Rappoport observed: "In the past, antimilitarism and antipatriotism were considered by many as essential tasks of the CGT. Now these principles are being restrained. In theory antimilitarism is maintained, but it produces no enthusiasm amongst the majority."[58]

The question historians have tried to understand is whether antimilitarism, and in particular the ongoing protests against war, was really a serious means of rallying the working classes, which simply fell apart in 1914. Or was it rather, as Milner sees it, maintained essentially as an elaborate bluff to disguise the troubles of the CGT, both nationally and internationally, a bluff that was only called in 1914. Although there is some validity to both of these positions, neither of them take into account the fine-tune adjustments made by antimilitarists prior to the war, as we have already begun to see. Only by continuing to study antimilitarism for what it was, rather than what it would not be, can we appreciate the role it did play, and persisted in playing, in French social and political life through August 1914 and even after.

Clearly syndicalist leaders were growing weary of the revolutionary excesses that had made the CGT the focal point for organized insurrectional activity. Although this was not reflected in the special antimilitarist issues of *La Voix du Peuple*, which continued to print the standard argument that defending the *patrie* was akin to sacrificing one's liberties in the name of the bourgeoisie,[59] an "Encyclique syndicaliste" issued August 20, 1912, decried antipatriotism as "an hysterical reaction that was foreign to any idea . . . a bastard production of overdone publicity."[60] Criticism of the revolutionary elements within the CGT had been building since 1908, when Griffuelhes denounced the pitfalls of "revolutionary romanticism" and "rabble-rousers" such as his colleague Yvetot and the staff at *La Guerre Sociale*.[61] Léon Jouhaux, who replaced Griffuelhes as head of the CGT in July 1909 (after revolutionaries ousted the newly elected reformist Louis Niel), brought with him the opinion that the organization had strayed from its social and economic mandate.[62]

An instrumental force in efforts to "free the CGT from the antimilitarist excesses of the anarchist milieus" was Alphonse Merrheim, secretary of the Metalworkers' Federation.[63] In his study of Merrheim, Nicholas Papayanis argues that Merrheim's "public posture" evidenced "an uncompromising antimilitarism and an apparent commitment to the general strike to prevent war," but in private he was increasingly pessimistic about such action. Although Merrheim warned fellow syndicalists of the nearness and dangers of war; sponsored the Marseille statement on the general strike (1908); and proposed antimilitarist resolutions at Le Havre (1912) and other congresses through 1914, he maintained that antimilitarism was less an ideological issue for the working classes than one of economics and, at times, just good politics. His Marseille resolution won out, according to this argument, because it steered clear of divisive issues and emphasized worker education rather than actual commitment to a general strike in the case of war.[64]

Most historians, including Jacques Julliard and Jean-Jacques Becker, have emphasized the ambiguous intentions of CGT leaders such as Merrheim and the lack of a definitive plan for war as anticipating the "failure" of 1914. In no case does this seem more true (and do more to reinforce Milner's argument that antimilitarism concealed the CGT's deeper troubles) than for the *congrès extraordinaire* of November 23–24, 1912. With its single-item agenda of "organizing war resistance," the *congrès* has been referred to by Becker and Annie Kriegel as the climax of the CGT's antiwar campaign.[65] Yet in the end the event could only reaffirm the CGT's commitment to the idea of a general strike, and relinquish all responsibility for its coordination to the local organizations. As Merrheim interpreted the resolution: "We wanted to make clear to the working class that as soon as war was declared, there would be no CGT, no signal for action. People outside Paris, in all the provincial centers, must get rid of this idea; they must not expect a call to action, but as soon as mobilization is announced, workers should refuse to obey and go instead to their local Bourse du Travail to see what is to be done."[66] This, rather than the events of 1914, was doubtless the death knell for syndicalist efforts to resist war by means of a revolutionary general strike. Yet it was not the end of the "idea" of the general strike as a means to rally workers, nor the "ideal" of antimilitarism as a means to counter governmental injustice and nationalist jingoism. In this regard, the most important outcome of the *congrès extraordinaire* was its decision to call a 24-hour nationwide general strike against war for Monday, December 16, 1912.

In her account of the *congrès extraordinaire*, Milner contrasts perceptions of this strike by the French Left in general and CGT leaders in particular. For the former, she argues, it was sure indication that the CGT had heightened its antiwar campaign; an interpretation supported by the CGT's emphasis on the Marseille resolution in its propaganda bombardment during the weeks leading up to the planned protest. December 16, in this view, was no less than a trial run for the CGT's war plans. By contrast, according to Milner, CGT leaders, despite pronouncements to the contrary, saw the strike as a preventive action—a means to display publicly the workers' hatred of war and their resolve to avoid it at all costs. Thus Jouhaux spoke for all syndicalists when he wrote: "The important thing is not to decide what to do in the event of war; it is necessary, above all, to prevent war."[67]

What was the government's attitude? A police report from November 28, 1912, as well as reports from the Interior Ministry on December 10 and 16, put the public powers in the camp of those who looked on the general strike as nothing less than a full-scale dress rehearsal for the CGT's plans to paralyze mobilization in the event of war. Interior Minister Steeg beckoned prefects to follow the strike preparations closely, disperse illegal gatherings (he closed down all Bourses du Travail), and send to him detailed reports on the "frame of mind" of the working-class organizations in their departments. He also threatened "serious disciplinary measures" against any public service agent or worker not at his job on December 16.[68] Although the resolution passed by the *congrès extraordinaire* hedged on the CGT's responsibility for organizing a general strike during mobilization, thereby disappointing many anarchist groups,[69] the government interpreted December 16 according to the most sinister aims: "The CGT has surely shown that it did not have the goal, with pacifist intention, to oppose an offensive or defensive war; it affirmed that its sole concern was to oppose mobilization and profit from the circumstance to provoke a civil war. . . . It goes without saying that purely anarchist groups are actively behind this propaganda."[70]

Much of the evidence for this official view came from the numerous meetings in Paris and the provinces in the weeks before December 16 (twenty-two meetings outside Paris alone). During these gatherings, which were closely monitored by police, it was not uncommon for syndicalists to declare that they would not go "like sheep to the slaughter," or that their wives would lay down on the railroad tracks to stop the trains headed for the front.[71] An article in *Le Travailleur du Bâtiment* titled "Oppositional Measures to Mobilization" favored seizing the opportunity of war to carry out a social revolution.[72] In *La Bataille Syndicaliste* a caption declared: "Your mobilization, we don't give a damn! We will respond by immobilization."[73] The prefect of Finistère, convinced that revolutionary syndicalists and anarchists held the upper hand in his department, called for the establishment of a police state with military reinforcements in Brest.[74]

In evaluating the buildup to the general strike and the outcome of December 16, one must bear in mind the day's two-fold purpose. Foremost, in the midst of the Balkan crisis, syndicalist leaders fashioned it as an urgent protest against a war they perceived not only as a growing likelihood but as a potentially unmitigated disaster. An article in *La Voix du Peuple* made this point sharply. After analyzing the military strength of the great powers and comparing it to the situation in 1870, it offered one of the most powerful and prophetic warnings of the era: "Think of the frenzy of killing and carnage that these murderous hordes would set loose upon each other. . . . Consider that on land, as on sea, the cries of pain, the groans of the dying, the screams of rage and the howls of the wounded would dominate the roar of the cannons and would only die down to give way to centuries of hatred, and to ideas of vengeance between the peoples of Europe."[75] Another piece in the issue ("Shame on Europe! Shame on Modern War!") favored the general strike not specifically to stop war but to halt the "progress of civilization" altogether, by which it meant "advances" such as "extra-rapid warfare [and] mechanical killing." An *affiche* in Amiens called the one-day strike "a small sacrifice" compared to the horrors that war between the great powers would bring. Throughout France, *affiches* proclaimed it "indispensable" for workers to take part in the strike since a butchery the likes of which the world had never seen was otherwise unavoidable.[76] In 1912 antimilitarists were being more realistic about war than most military and political leaders would be in all of 1914–1918.

Still, the question of how many workers were willing to make the "small sacrifice" of a day's labor to protest something that had not yet happened remained to be seen. The second purpose of the strike—to put on display what workers had long threatened by bringing the normal daily operation of France, Paris in particular, to a standstill—was thus the real test. *La Bataille Syndicaliste* dubbed it a "precursor gesture" that would give the CGT the strength to carry out another strike at the first mobilization order.[77]

According to this second objective, the December 16 general strike must be considered a failure. Despite the bold language of the meetings leading up to it and the urgent appeals in the journals, there was considerable apathy in the ranks. Most workers in the large PTT union (the state-run post, telephone, and telegraph service) showed no enthusiasm; some even called the strike a shame for the *syndicat*.[78] In Saint-Etienne, a revolutionary syndicalist stronghold, delegates to a December 6 meeting of the *bourse* agreed with the need for active, incessant antiwar propaganda, but not for a general strike.[79] In most regions the feeling was similar—the sacrifice of a day's labor, with potentially harsh repercussions, appealed to workers less than did disobeying the CGT.

Throughout France the strike fell short of its organizers' expectations. According to government sources, only about 30,000 workers in Paris and 50,000 in the rest of the country took part (the CGT naturally put the numbers much higher).[80] And although several industries did feel the strike's effect, and it should not be dismissed entirely, most prefects confirmed that the day proceeded relatively smoothly. On December 16 they reported "absolute calm" in Cantal, "no manifestation of any kind" in Calvados, a "few workers taking part" in the strike in the Haute-Garonne, and complete failure in the Aube. In Brest there were 60 absences out of 650 workers in the arsenal (the norm for Mondays was 50). In Lyon, despite a last minute decision by tramway workers to participate in the strike, service continued and the city remained calm. The prefect of the Alpes-Maritimes wrote that "the moral effect produced by this demonstration has been null." In the

Ardennes, near the German border, the towns of Mohon, Mezières, and Sedan remained calm, despite numerous *affiches* placed by the CGT.[81]

There were, however, noteworthy exceptions. In the Loire, where an extremely repressive decree prohibited marches, meetings, banners, and the like, several industries still missed a sizable portion of their workforce.[82] In Firminy, for example, although the police commissioner posted a formidable force of gendarmerie, cavalry, and armed infantrymen, 118 out of 195 miners and 200 out of 300 builders refused to work. Yet the commissioner reported that the day was otherwise quite normal. In Saint-Etienne approximately one-fourth of the miners and two-thirds of the glassworkers did not report for work, and several hundred met at a boules game (local authorities had closed the *bourse*). Overall, however, the day "unfolded in great peacefulness" according to *La Tribune*.[83] For Paris, Julliard found the strike had "honorable success." The building unions and automobile chauffeurs came out in force, but most reports and articles rate the effect on the city as minimal.[84] On the whole, apart from the miners in Alès, Decazeville, Montceau-les-Mines, and Douai, "the strike only resulted in negligible work stoppage, slightly more than that of a normal Monday."[85]

The failure of the strike was clear to all, the question was how to respond to it. While Jouhaux praised December 16 as a "historic date in the syndicalist movement,"[86] *Le Petit Parisien,* which examined the strike's impact in each quarter of Paris, concluded: "The general physiognomy of the capital was not changed at all yesterday morning."[87] *L'Écho de Paris* judged that "the general strike attempt collided with the indifference and even hostility of the great majority of workers."[88] The minister of the interior, who had put his prefects and gendarmerie on the highest alert, was self-congratulatory: "Thanks to the steadfastness of the public powers, this strike . . . did not produce the effect expected."[89] But probably the most telling observation was the honest one made by the usually unflinching Georges Yvetot, who in the same issue of *La Bataille Syndicaliste* where Jouhaux praised the strike, wrote: "The response to the menacing attitude of the criminals capable of unleashing a general conflagration of indescribable horror should have been a precursor act worthy of the cause that motivated it and the people who evoked it. It was not that."[90]

As Yvetot knew, December 16 was more theater than threat, although it confirmed an important shift in the CGT's antimilitarist struggle: the ideological appeals of the beginning of the century were giving way to more pragmatic language and strategies to oppose war. The theme of the general strike was less the exploitation of capitalism than it was the potential for catastrophe, which Poincaré's policies seemed to bring closer every day. Seen in this way, December 16 was more important as a response to the times than a protest against the conditions of the working classes. Yet this distinction had little bearing on public powers bent on ensuring that France was as prepared for war domestically as she was internationally. Despite the evident contraction of revolutionary syndicalism and its antipatriotic rhetoric, French authorities proved their unflappable determination to repress any activities that constituted a menace to public order, particularly in the case of mobilization. Moreover, the syndicalists managed to keep up appearances well enough to make this seem necessary: "The failure of the general strike of December 16 has not discouraged the militants. In spite of the press reports, which they describe on this occasion as "venal" and "sellouts to the government," they sing victory to the CGT and to the Union des Syndicats de la Seine."[91]

Becker has written that syndicalism "incontestably fabricated antimilitarists." If anything had really come out of December 16, it was reaffirmation of the gap between syndicalist leaders and their constituents. Yet a big factor for this was not simply the lack of committed antimilitarists, but the decline in syndicalist support overall, evidenced by the precipitous drop in the number of unionized workers from 687,463 in 1911 to about 300,000 in 1914. In the Building Federation of the Seine alone, the numbers shrank from 40,000 to 17,000, and a similar decline occurred in the metal federation and automobile factory *syndicats*. Moreover, the circulation of *La Bataille Syndicaliste* by 1914 had fallen to the point that the CGT daily almost disappeared.[92] The 1914 May Day demonstration, according to an official report, "passed completely unnoticed."[93]

The causes of the CGT's waning support and its transition to a more reformist posture in the midst of the "nationalist revival" were the subject of a July 1914 report that the government attributed to a director within the CGT.[94] The explanations therein include the lassitude of "revolutionary" action; fear of new betrayals after government agents were discovered in the CGT ranks; suspicion of "syndicale civil servants"; greater resistance from employers; and a lack of financial resources. Jouhaux wondered what he could do "to free the working majority from its torpor."[95] The final factor was repression. Each time Yvetot left jail he may have boasted, as he did in November 1908, that he would take up his antimilitarist propaganda more vigorously than ever, but what good did that do when he was sentenced to over ten years of prison between 1904 and 1914 (he was invariably released early by amnesty)?[96] Hervé himself spent four years behind bars from 1906 to

1912.[97] As Dominique Bertinotti shows, convictions for antimilitarist crimes were on the rise in 1912, and orators or journalists who defamed the army could draw an average of eight months in prison and a fifty to three thousand franc fine.[98] There can be no doubt, then, that all of these issues were sources of aggravation for syndicalist leaders and apathy for their constituents, who as we have already seen needed something more concrete than ideology to rally them to the antimilitarist cause. Still, none of these explanations is very satisfying when it comes to understanding the startling transformation of the most renowned revolutionary of them all: Gustave Hervé, the Sans-Patrie.

Hervé's rectification du tir

Although unscrupulous politicians are deservedly criticized for their opportunistic migrations from Left to Right (or vice versa) and, often, back again, the transformation of Hervé is more baffling in that it had nothing to do with personal advancement. Nor, as Hervé himself argued, did it represent a transformation so much as an evolution, or what he called a *rectification du tir*, a "correction of aim." Whatever one calls it, Hervé's journey—from antipatriot to patriot, from revolutionary promoter of insurrection in the case of war to staunch nationalist who voted against a socialist resolution for a general strike—came to pass between 1911 and the outbreak of World War I, and it shocked his enemies and allies alike.

Hervé's change had both political and tactical elements. There was the "disarmament of hatreds" mentioned previously, as Hervé extended his plea for cooperation between socialists and syndicalists to Radicals on his right, and vowed to become a force for unity in his party rather than its nemesis. "Antipatriotism," he declared, had been a "pedagogical mistake"; Hervéism was now "no more than enraged pacifism."[99] After the stupendous electoral victory of German socialists in 1912, Hervé also took back his earlier (in Stuttgart in 1907) criticism of the SPD ("a machine for voting") and began to look seriously at the potential for parliamentary action to better the conditions of the working classes.[100] From a tactical standpoint it was in jail that Hervé first realized the hopelessness of insurrection without the support of at least part of the army. The "guard dog" of the capitalist class would have to become the ally of the working class; or in Hervé's own formulation, socialists would have to "conquer" the army. In an article published shortly after he left prison in July 1912 (thanks again to an amnesty for all political prisoners), Hervé referred to this as "revolutionary militarism," and justified it with reference to the armed insurgents of France's revolutionary past.[101]

For the "New Hervéism," as *Le Libertaire* condescendingly labeled the first sign of Hervé's transformation, the struggle against militarism and the working-class revolutionary struggle were separate issues.[102] In *L'Alsace-Lorraine* (1913) he argued that the most important factor for peace was not insurrection, but rapprochement between France and Germany and a definitive resolution of the territorial question. Hervé's proposal—autonomy for Alsace-Lorraine in exchange for a slice of Madagascar or the Congo—is less relevant than his new-found obsession with the geopolitical, rather than ideological, issue. So dramatic was the shift that the steadfast anarchist Louis Lecoin would fantasize in his memoir *De Prison en prison* (*From Prison to Prison*) about murdering Hervé, "for whom he would have gladly slashed himself before 1912."[103] When Paul Déroulède died in February 1914, Hervé actually saw fit to praise him for, much like himself, having the courage to defend his ideals, even if they were naïve and misguided: "Do I dare confess that I have always had a weakness for Déroulède? Yes, I know: the suppression of the Commune, Boulangism, the Dreyfus Affair, the stupid and abject anti-Semitism, his senile bigotry. . . . All the same, he was the bravest of the brave . . . at a time when political leaders seemed afraid of their own shadows."[104]

As the threat of war increased, so did Hervé's feeling that cooperation between rather than contention with the national governments was the only way to prevent a catastrophe. At the SFIO's tenth congress in Brest (March 23–25, 1913), during debate over the three-year military service law, Hervé suggested that Germany and France settle the issues of armaments and Alsace-Lorraine forthwith. His utter failure to stir colleagues in this direction attests to his diminished influence in the party. Yet by this time Hervéism had taken on new meaning. Not only had he given up on the idea of an insurrection in the case of war (except for offensive wars, at least for another year), but he had abandoned hope in the revolutionary antimilitarist cause altogether. "When I defended insurrection," Hervé declared at a Socialist Party congress in Paris (July 14–16, 1914), "I thought I could count on some insurrectionists, and [yet] I noticed myself that there would not be any on the day war was declared."[105]

Hervé's observation was perfectly consistent with his *rectification*, which by fall 1912 had admitted that to revolt or strike once war was declared would already be too late, as "the nationalist wave and governmental terror" would submerge it.[106] Still, the whole purpose of the Paris congress, held in the feverish aftermath of the assassination of Austrian Archduke Francis Ferdinand and in advance of an international meeting scheduled for August in Vienna, was to decide on a socialist strategy for war. Moreover, there was newfound optimism among some delegates in light of the moderate Bebel's death the year prior, and the corresponding emergence of a revitalized revolutionary wing in the SPD under the leadership of Karl Liebknecht and Rosa Luxemburg. The congress concluded with passage of the Vaillant-Keïr-Hardie amendment, supported by Jaurès, which judged an international general strike and strong public action "particularly efficacious" means "to forestall and prevent war, and to compel governments to resort to arbitration." Once again Hervé found himself on the losing side, only this time his usual battle with Guesde concerned who could denounce the motion most forcefully. A narrow majority gave it their support, and France went to war having achieved one of the original goals of the Sans-Patrie, without his own endorsement.[107]

"I am persuaded that it is not I who has changed, but the circumstances."[108] Hervé's attempt to explain his departure from antipatriotism and insurrection deserves serious attention. How *had* the circumstances changed, and for whom? The nationalist revival; the realization that the Germans would not follow an insurrectional movement initiated by France; and the CGT's declining strength certainly had an impact. Yet many hardened revolutionaries forged ahead with their antimilitarist programs and doctrines and resented Hervé's "betrayal." Yvetot, still secretary of the Fédération des Bourses, sensed the winds of change in his comrade in early 1911 and broke with him then. *La Bataille Syndicaliste,* founded that same year, was in large part a reaction against the "new Hervé." With Hervé's hope to "conquer the army" and Jaurès's desire to remake it, the CGT now stood alone in seeking the army's destruction. As *La Bataille* put it: "As long as there are armies, governments and the privileged will use them to oppose the people. This is why we do not want an army in any form."[109] Likewise *Le Bonnet Rouge,* created in November 1913 by Hervé's coworkers Almereyda and Merle, was modeled on the original *Guerre Sociale* and represented a definitive end to their collaboration. At a particularly raucous gathering of some thirty-five hundred anarchists and syndicalists in Paris on September 25, 1912, Hervé had to brave violent heckling and flying furniture in attempt to explain his *rectification*. For many of those present, it was without doubt Hervé *himself* who had changed.[110]

So how can the change be explained? After eliminating theories of governmental repression or that he had been "bought off," Becker and Rotstein locate a better answer in Hervé's character and temperament. In particular, both stress his tendency to subjugate ideas and doctrines to base instincts and political understandings.[111] What this ultimately allowed Hervé was the ability to recognize the historical context and moral value of his ideas, rather than simply their ideological worth in the realm of working-class politics. Most significantly for our purposes, he succeeded in doing so three years before the war brought his fellow revolutionaries to the same conclusion. Hervé the antimilitarist was, by nature, a realist whose grasp of politics and history led him into closer alliance with the Republic well before August 1914 confirmed this alliance for all antimilitarists. When the situation changed, when the nationalist revival received political backing from the Poincaré government and it became obvious that the antimilitarist Left still had not adapted itself to this development through the formation of a united front and the formulation of a universal strategy, then it was not hard for Hervé to concede that the struggle against war, *in the way he had been fighting it,* was essentially lost.

Hervé's *rectification,* in short, was recognition of the reality and moral authority of the Third Republic. Despite the many trials and convictions, antimilitarism and Gustave Hervé flourished in France precisely because their absolute commitment to combating governmental injustice could be exercised in relative freedom. This did not simply end when Hervé began to "correct his aim," it only took on a new, less confrontational form. When the revolutionary working-class organizations let him down, Hervé turned to the idea of republican democracy to protect the rights of citizens and forestall international war. "I had a dream," he wrote on the eve of the Bastille Day 1913 military review, in the middle of the fiery debate over the three-year law, "the CGT and the Socialist Party, the two single organized and disciplined popular forces, had formed a bloc. Neither of the contracting parties had let its autonomy be alienated before the nationalist wave. . . . As July 14 approached, in all the *syndicats* and party sections the watchword had spread like wildfire: 'Everyone to the [military] review to shout down the three-year law!' " After a long digression on his dream, Hervé awakens: "Unfortunately, we will not go to Longchamp to shout down the three-year law. We are not yet unified enough, nor organized enough, nor disciplined enough, nor courageous enough to wage such a battle." Yet rather than giving in, Hervé now looks for more mainstream support: "It is because we still have neither the strength nor courage to combat and stop, by the proletarian bloc alone, the nationalist wave that is unraveling upon us, that I am for the other bloc, the modest republican bloc that has proven itself threefold already."[112] From socialist revolutionary to republican ally, the evolution of Gustave Hervé always took place within the context of democratic citizenship.

The Three-Year Law

Just days after Hervé published the above article calling for republican unity, the government passed landmark legislation increasing compulsory military service from two to three years. Introduced in March 1913 by the Briand administration, the "three-year law" was sold to left-wing republicans and the general public as an essential measure to protect France from German attack. Between 1911 and 1913, Germany had passed three military laws that, whether one accepts or not Krumeich's argument that they were directed at France, expanded the active army substantially. In comparison with its rival, France was dwarfed in both size and population, and it had a standing army of 540,000 men compared to Germany's 870,000. From its inception, in other words, the three-year law presupposed the growing possibility of war.[113]

It is on the basis that the three-year law would increase not only the probability of war but also its destructiveness that socialists, syndicalists, and anarchists fought it tooth and nail. Even before the government officially introduced the bill, the CGT began mobilizing workers against it: "Inaction would permit the execution of a program that would culminate in war." In May an *affiche* urged: "A grave danger threatens us! To avoid it, a great effort is indispensable. . . . Against this *coup de force* we must put up irresistible élan."[114] In one of his many speeches against the three-year law, Jaurès declared that it was a war of adventure and arrogance "to which our regime inevitably leads us."[115] The FCA denounced the law's real profiteers—arms manufacturers, journal directors, political and military leaders—who sowed seeds of mutual hatred by demanding an ever-escalating state of military preparedness. The group printed some one hundred thousand copies of its fifteen-page brochure "Contre les armements, contre la loi de 3 ans, contre tout militarisme" (Against Armaments, Against the Three-Year Law, Against All Militarism). Yvetot likened the struggle to a "marvelous trampoline" off which the CGT's antimilitarist propaganda would rebound to new heights. Jouhaux wrote: "Never has a more favorable hour sounded for working-class agitation."[116]

Socialists, syndicalists, and anarchists posted *affiches*, disseminated petitions, distributed brochures, held rallies, and often overcame internal divisions in a wave of support against "a crime in preparation," "an abuse of confidence," another governmental betrayal.[117] In many respects, they achieved a facade of cooperation in their separate endeavors to block the legislation. One report observed that reformist socialists were in accord with revolutionary antimilitarists, and that the socialists would support the syndicalists. Although nearly all revolutionary syndicalists and anarchists remained uncomfortable with rapprochement, the flagging CGT increasingly found itself under the wing of the SFIO during protests. Several meetings planned by the local *bourse* and Socialist Party brought together thousands, such as the one attended by Guesde, Jaurès, and Jouhaux on June 9 in Roubaix.[118]

These collaborative efforts were most evident during three large demonstrations at the Pré Saint-Gervais outside Paris. On Sunday, March 16, upward of one hundred thousand people from the FCA, CGT, and SFIO protested the "criminal eventuality of war [and] the new military burdens under which they want to crush the country." The *ordre du jour* stated that the purpose of the three-year law was not "to consolidate the peace" but "to make a military conflict between the German and French people inevitable."[119] A few days later, after the government thwarted CGT plans to demonstrate at Père-Lachaise in honor of the Commune heroes, the Comité Confédéral gave in to socialist initiative for another demonstration at the Pré St.-Gervais. On May 26 some one hundred thousand heard Jaurès, Vaillant, Sembat, and others attack the government for its irresponsible reaction to the international crisis.[120] The importance of these rallies was not simply that they overcame some of the traditional strife between leftist groups, but that despite the difficulties of revolutionary syndicalism, the defection of Hervéist socialism, and the much-touted development of a "nationalist revival," working-class antimilitarism could still be a force to reckon with given a just and reasonable cause.

Moreover, it no longer had to rely on antipatriotic rhetoric for effect. Although the propaganda did include sharp statements against the "bourgeois" *patrie* as well as calls for an insurrection in the case of war, the protests against the three-year law more often took the form of an attack on the government, in particular the ministers Barthou (premier since April 1913) and Millerand. Without making any calls for social revolution, an FCA *affiche* warned: "The overzealousness of *our* government could have ... the worst consequences for world peace."[121] For the republican and socialist Left, one of the law's main offenses was its contravention of the cherished idea of the "nation in arms." As a clearly offended Jaurès stated in his hometown of Castres: "If, by a potential calamity which we are doing all we can to avoid,

Germany tried to attack France without mobilizing its reserves, I could rejoice in it, because the six or 700,000 Germans who would come would find before them an entire people . . . 2,500,000 Frenchmen. The problem does not involve doing an extra year of [military] service, but in assuring a complete and rapid mobilization."[122] *La Bataille Syndicaliste,* which had condemned Hervé's transformation, reinterpreted the *patrie* thus in its protests against the law: "You will respond to the second-rate patriots that the *patrie* has a meaning for you: Which is that it should be a foyer of emancipation and not a caserne and jail. It is up to you [workers] to defend the cause of humanity against the new barbarism."[123]

Krumeich argues that revolutionary syndicalists had hoped to use the three-year law to revive their cause, but instead found the tables turned on them by the more powerful socialists. The relatively few CGT demonstrations in Paris and the low attendance at one held July 13 indicate that revolutionary syndicalism, which never had as large a following as it appeared, faired poorly during these protests.[124] Yet this evidence for the diminished prestige of the CGT is only one aspect of the transformation taking place on the antimilitarist Left, and not the most important one. As we just saw, in addition to Hervé's personal *rectification,* there were already perceptible changes in the language of these protests, which now seemed more bent on disproving the government's military policy than simply on disproving the government. The emphasis of so many historians (Krumeich, Becker, Julliard, Lefranc) on the weakening of the CGT and its lack of a definitive plan for war has come all too often at the expense of a more thoroughgoing examination of what antimilitarists were really saying in 1913. It is clear from the propaganda and sheer size of the socialist-dominated rallies that antimilitarism still had a role to play in the struggle to improve social justice and diminish the likelihood of war, even if it was increasingly clear that this role would not be enough to stop war with an insurrection. That was the naïve utopia clung to until the end by only a handful of militants. It is thus not the best measure by which we can judge antimilitarism.

◆ ◆ ◆

In contrast to the changes taking place on the antimilitarist left, the government's attitude toward it, and toward the CGT above all, hardly wavered. This became most evident when authorities blamed syndicalists for initiating a series of military uprisings between May 17 and 23 in several garrisons in eastern France. The disruptions originated in Toul when some three hundred soldiers marched through town shouting "down with the three years!," singing the "Internationale," and insulting officers who tried to control them. More than twenty-five hundred soldiers joined in the next day, and similar disruptions followed in Paris (Neuilly, Clignancourt), Belfort, Nancy, Verdun, Saint-Dié, Epinal, Commercy, Bourges, and Rodez, where two battalions tried to exit the caserne. Both local and state officials acted quickly, making inquiries into the uprisings and, in some cases, searching soldiers' belongings for incriminating propaganda or organizational plans. By May 25, over twenty men had been sent to African battalions; many more were court-martialed and imprisoned. Several officers were demoted for not acting decisively to squelch the demonstrations.[125]

As we have come to expect, however, these measures, not to mention the clear linkage between the protests against the three-year law and the government's recent decision not to grandfather in second-year recruits, would not nearly assuage everyone that the threat to the military was under control. *Le Temps, Le Journal, Le Matin, L'Écho de Paris, Le Figaro, L'Éclair,* and *La Libre Parole,* among others, called on authorities to take stringent action against syndicalist influence in the army. *L'Écho de Paris* and *Le Temps* used the incidents to remind readers of the long history of antimilitarism in the CGT. *Le Matin* affirmed bluntly: "They are convinced in high places that the maintenance of the class [for an extra year of military service] did not cause the [disruptions in the casernes], but the long-awaited opportunity of a long prepared for movement [did]." On May 22 the journal published what was clearly a forged CGT circular, "found" in the Toul barracks and supposedly instigating the revolt. General Pau stated in an interview: "We are not in the presence of a military mutiny, but of a movement of political origin."[126] The inspector general called the uprisings the "logical culmination" of the propaganda of the CGT, SFIO, and FCA, and urged the Sûreté (criminal investigation department) to "attack the evil at its root."[127] War Minister Etienne declared in the Senate that the government was convinced that the uprisings had been planned in advance, and that it must act to "stamp out" syndicalism "at its roots." Senators applauded.[128]

Then on the morning of May 26, in what *La Bataille Syndicaliste* would describe as a "general mobilization" at the prefecture of the police,[129] officials armed with an investigatory commission from examining magistrate Drioux searched over six hundred syndicalist and socialist offices for evidence of their complicity in the "mutinies."[130] The nationwide search included the Maison des Fédérations, the building, metallurgy, leather and hide, and jewelry federations; *syndicats* heavily involved in the anti-three-year-law campaign, such as the masons, road workers, carpenters, and electricians; and the seats of radical journals such as *L'Action*. Police literally turned upside-down the residences of Yvetot, Jouhaux, and Pierre Monatte, among others.[131] In the words of a disgusted Jaurès, the searches were "stupefying madness" on the part of the "regime."[132]

Although officials found no evidence that the military uprisings were part of some grandiose syndicalist plan, they persisted in accusing the CGT of forging relations with soldiers that were "tight, direct, patent." On May 29 Barthou called the CGT's acts "illegal, wicked, and criminal," and sought legislation to ensure they never recurred. On July 23 the minister of the interior instructed local police commissioners to furnish him—as quickly as possible and after "a very discreet inquiry"—with a list of revolutionaries, antimilitarists, and anarchists among the reservists. That same month police arrested numerous revolutionary syndicalists for allegedly having instigated the "mutinies," and imprisoned eighteen of them, including Yvetot, for "inciting soldiers to disobedience" (all but two were acquitted on March 26, 1914). In early September 1913 the Sûreté issued another memo, almost replicating that in July, in a renewed effort to track down antimilitarists in the regiments. In most departments the reports came back with few names, and although *La Bataille Syndicaliste* and other journals denied the charges vehemently, nothing could convince the public powers otherwise: "The prolonged antimilitarist and antipatriotic propaganda of the CGT, in which the Sou du Soldat was only one form, has ended by planting a most unsettling frame of mind in the army."[133]

◆ ◆ ◆

What I have called the "battle without"—the struggle for antimilitarists to maintain influence in light of the renewed militancy of the government, the "nationalist revival," and the growing sense of the imminence of war— continued right through August 1914. Regardless of the waning strength of the CGT, the ongoing governmental repression now spreading to groups such as the teachers' *syndicat*, and the lamentable lack of coordination, antimilitarists adapted to their circumstances to remain the most active force in the nation working to elevate military justice and prevent war. The modification of Hervé and moderation of antipatriotism did not upset this goal, but merely redirected some elements of the Left onto a more openly accommodating course.

By contrast, military and political authorities proved far less adaptable, maintaining excessive pressure on antimilitarists and continuing to misunderstand their capacity for collective action. Yet perhaps this was to the

Left's credit. If one considers the significance of antimilitarism—its relentless and periodically successful efforts to combat blatant military injustice, effusive displays of nationalist fervor, a longer conscription period, and the growing likelihood of a catastrophic war—then the government's wary extrapolation of the Left's ability to stop war with a workers' insurrection makes more sense. Although repression, disunity, and waning support did not help antimilitarists, neither did they keep them from reining in the "nationalist revival" with displays of popular solidarity far larger than any the Right ever organized. For the representatives of the working classes, whether revolutionary or reformist, the bottom line, as *La Bataille Syndicaliste* put it a day after the insulting search of its offices, was that "the CGT will continue its protest work despite the blows of authority because it is conscious of expressing the popular will, of fulfilling a useful and profoundly humane function."[134]

This was the far more significant reality of antimilitarism than the fact that it somehow "failed" to disrupt world war, as scholars have emphasized ad infinitum. Despite the false accusations that syndicalists had fostered the military revolts in May 1913, it was they, along with the FCA and new groups such as the Defense Committee for Prosecuted Soldiers, that spearheaded the campaign to free the mutinous soldiers.[135] It was *La Bataille Syndicaliste*, moreover, that launched a national subscription for these unfortunate men, and mandated the Defense Committee to "look after the fate of the citizen-soldiers punished for having protested against the maintenance of the class [in service for an extra year], and assure these victims of repression, as well as their families, material aid and moral comfort."[136] In February 1914, at the CGT's behest, nine thousand workers convened in the salle Wagram (Paris meeting hall) to protest the three-year law, the imprisonment of their leaders, and the detainment of the "mutineers" in African military prisons. Nor were such protests merely for show. After the socialist electoral triumph in the spring of 1914, repeal of the three-year law was just a matter of time.[137]

Right through the outbreak of the war, antimilitarism remained high on the agendas of working-class organizations, and the government likewise maintained its firm grip. Regardless of the moderation of antimilitarist language and leaders in response to the changing domestic and international environments and in recognition of their true strength, antimilitarists had succeeded superbly in establishing a real means by which ordinary people could express their own moral politics. Indeed, it was precisely this ethical element of antimilitarism that government and military authorities never fully understood. This is why, less than a month after the raids on CGT offices across France, Yvetot was still capable of writing that the public powers could never just dissolve the CGT because it was an "idea," and ideas cannot just be dissolved "like a piece of sugar." This idea, of "solidarity" and a "social future," was, in the end, an idea about creating a better, and fairer, France; an idea, that is, that followed in the same tradition as all French revolutions since 1789.[138]

EPILOGUE

En Avant!

On August 2, 1914, the first day of French mobilization, Gustave Hervé addressed an open letter to War Minister Messimy in *La Guerre Sociale*. "When I was twenty years old," he began,

> I obtained an excuse from military service because I had to support my family and was nearsighted. In spite of my nearsightedness and my forty-three years, I am perfectly capable of fighting. . . . I beg you to place me in the first infantry regiment leaving for the front. After having been thrown out of the university, disbarred from practicing law, sentenced to over eleven years in prison on the grounds that I lacked patriotism, since all my criminal acts, like those of my party and of the CGT, consisted of foreseeing and trying to prevent today's catastrophe, I am sure that you will agree with me that the Republic owes me this great reparation. Long live France! That is all.[1]

How had Hervé, the very symbol of the antimilitarist aspirations of the revolutionary Left, come to embrace the nation he had spent over a decade blaspheming? How had he reached the point of literally begging the war minister to allow him, regardless of his utter lack of military training, to join the army heading for the front? Hervé was not antimilitarism and antimilitarism was certainly not Gustave Hervé, but this question is part of the larger one we asked at the beginning of this study and that bears repeating now: how was it that the French Left, which succeeded in creating the most antimilitarist culture and society in pre–World War I Europe, came to accept and, in many instances, support war in 1914?

The short answer, the one that reflects most historiography to date, is that there was little else it could do because the Left had "failed" to build a following that was strong and united enough to confront the powerful French state. The CGT was in decline: "The pale image of an ardent and virile utopia that over a few years had excited a handful of courageous men but which, like any utopia, had to disappear before the realistic imperatives [of war]."[2] There was also the incertitude of socialists concerning what to do in the event of war, and the fear that their German counterparts did not share their commitment to antimilitarism. Historians have additionally focused their cases for the "capitulation" of the Left on the threat of repression and imprisonment; the relatively superficial penetration of antimilitarism into working-class and military milieus; and the strategical and ideological differences that kept the Left from developing a unified "movement." Finally, scholars have emphasized that antimilitarism was defused in the end by the suddenness with which war descended on Europe, and the positive diplomatic efforts taken by the French government to prevent an assassination in faraway Sarajevo from unraveling the precarious balance of power and hurtling the alliance system into a major conflict.[3]

To fuel this argument that the war caught the CGT both unaware and, most important, unprepared, many syndicalist leaders would later admit that their propaganda had not been as effective as they may have thought, or pretended to think, at the time. Georges Dumoulin, who served briefly as CGT head in 1914, wrote after the war: "Our antimilitarist propaganda, more for show than really serious, fooled us. The success, the acclamations of the meetings, blinded us. We fooled ourselves by nourishing our pride on the boisterous congresses with their puffed up motions full of self-importance. We believed that the masses were behind those who did not want to be less revolutionary than Yvetot."[4] At the onset of the war, Yvetot himself lamented: "Ah! if our propaganda, so disparaged, had brought forth fruit, if the generous ideas that supported us in making it had been understood, no one would even wonder whether they should leave [for the front]: the government would no longer dare order it. . . . they would declare [war] impossible."[5] Alphonse Merrheim wrote in August 1914: "We were completely helpless, completely terrified." And the CGT's executive committee gave its own succinct interpretation: "We considered ourselves the vanquished."[6]

Although the increasingly prominent obstacles faced by the revolutionary Left no doubt made it difficult to organize a war resistance movement, the very premise of this work has always been that its successes in terms of antimilitarism are in many ways more revealing than its so-called failure in terms of preventing war. In other words, this book has maintained that there was more to the story than merely these well-attested and significant problems faced by French leftist leaders. This missing element comes through in the emphasis the later chapters in particular have placed on how *l'antimilitarisme* served as a crucial means by which the Left fought governmental injustice in military matters, and was recognized for its role in trying to thwart war simply by virtue of the fact that governing authorities took it so seriously. This was a role the Left continued to play right up to the final, precious moments of peace, and it is the aim of these concluding pages to judge how consistent it was playing that part when, toward the end of the July diplomatic crisis that preceded hostilities, peace seemed to be such a fleeting fancy.

From Crisis to Cooperation: July–August 1914

What was the nature and meaning of the propaganda and activities of the antimilitarist Left in the days immediately preceding the outbreak of World War I, the final days of an era in European history? This question alone could be the topic for a book-length study, and indeed it was an important part of the first chapters of Alfred Rosmer's work *Le Mouvement ouvrier pendant la guerre* (1936). One of Rosmer's enduring contributions was to follow, "day by day," the journal that had taken over as the official organ of the CGT—*La Bataille Syndicaliste*. The striking thing he finds about *La Bataille* is that, unlike the gradual changeover of Hervé and *La Guerre Sociale,* it went the furthest the fastest, "from the general strike without restrictions . . . to the Union Sacrée [Sacred Union] without reservations." Did this represent a "collapse," as Rosmer calls it, or rather reflect a larger transformation of the Left that merely was finalized in August 1914?[7]

Working-class resistance to war redoubled after Sarajevo and during the flurry of diplomatic maneuverings that followed. From the onset of the July crisis to the outbreak of hostilities, socialists, syndicalists, and anarchists engaged in an eleventh-hour frenzy of antiwar activism that made them the most outspoken force for peace in the nation. In immediate response to Austria-Hungary's July 23 ultimatum to Serbia, the CGT's executive committee reconfirmed all its previous resolutions concerning the attitude of workers in the case of war, undertook an extensive campaign of meetings and demonstrations to pressure the government to ensure peace, and reminded workers: "If need be, the declaration of war should be . . . the watchword for the immediate cessation of work."[8] On July 27 Léon Jouhaux and Georges Dumoulin, respectively the secretary and adjunct secretary of the CGT, met in Brussels with the head of the General Commission of German Trade Unions, Karl Legien, in an ultimately unsuccessful attempt to unite their forces to protest war. Just two days later, also in Brussels, socialist delegates of the International Bureau met to assess the situation and, they hoped, coordinate a plan of action. In this moving, final prewar encounter of the major European socialist leaders, they urged the proletariat of all countries "not only to pursue, but above all to intensify their demonstrations against war, for peace, and for a negotiated resolution of the Austro-Serbian conflict."[9] They also decided to advance the next international congress from August 14 in Vienna to August 9 in Paris. Even the anarchists planned a congress for August–September 1914 to address international entente and the abolition of permanent armies.[10]

The most important efforts made to salvage peace that did not rely on international cooperation, as in the case of the Socialist Party, came from the CGT, especially its new voice, *La Bataille Syndicaliste*. Although one report found syndicalist leadership to be "without direction at the present time," it added that *La Bataille* was now the best measure of what syndicalists planned to do.[11] The journal did not disappoint. On July 26 it printed the CGT's aforementioned commitment to honor the decisions of past congresses, followed by an appeal by Jouhaux for a working-class effort to halt the "threatening war—with its slaughters, massacres, famine, the epidemics it brings, [which] would mean a formidable retreat, perhaps the end of a civilization, definitely the destruction of all our hopes."[12] The next day, according to the report "On the Attitude of the CGT and the Union des Syndicats de la Seine during the Crisis Period that Preceded Mobilization and since the Opening of Hostilities," some thirty thousand militants held a "particularly moving" protest in Paris against the chauvinistic attitudes leading the nation to war.[13] Demonstrations quickly spread to the provinces.

On July 28, the day Austria declared war on Serbia, syndicalists meeting in what one member described as an "atmosphere of fear" took up the issue of a demonstration in conjunction with the socialists, and planned a manifesto and nationwide meetings. Published in *L'Humanité* the following day, the manifesto asserted that war could still be avoided provided the workers' protest was formidable enough. On July 31, the CGT printed yet another manifesto in *La Bataille Syndicaliste* insisting, "peace remains possible," and calling for a "voice of reason" at "these moments of anguish, during which the lives of millions of human beings hang in the balance."[14] Even as it was becoming clear that syndicalists held no power over the fast-paced course of international events, they continued to assert their moral authority as if they might yet have the final word.

"At the CGT, they are beginning to regain courage." This is how the public powers described syndicalism in the July 31 report "La Campagne contre la guerre à la CGT" (The Campaign against War at the CGT).[15] Despite the menace of the Carnet B, Yvetot returned to Paris after a trip to Tulle and Toulouse, and Jouhaux remained in the capital, although like many syndicalists he did not sleep at home for fear of arrest. There was still talk of insurrection at this late date, and the news of antiwar demonstrations in the provinces gave many confidence that the campaign was finally bearing fruit. In Brest, at the behest of the Bourse du Travail and Socialist Party, more than five thousand marched through the streets shouting down the nationalist warmongers.[16] Some syndicalist leaders even felt that the government, which at first had responded to the antiwar activity by barring socialists and syndicalists from public rallies and threatening them with arrest, was now showing some leniency. "If the international crisis continues for a few more days," stated the July 31 report, then syndicalists "will certainly succeed in mobilizing public opinion for a twenty-four hour protest strike; and if this twenty-four hour strike succeeds, we could be certain of the success of another strike on the day of mobilization that would unfold with all its consequences, sabotage, and violence. . . . In truth, one repeats at the CGT, nothing is lost."[17]

Regardless of French syndicalism's internal troubles and the manifest realities of its antimilitarist campaign in general, CGT leaders succeeded in conveying, up to forty-eight hours before mobilization, a certain confidence and coordination with regard to their ability to combat the government's relentless slide toward disastrous war. This was bolstered by the parallel activities of the socialists, whose persistent opposition to war and important influence in government now appeared a more pragmatic means of stemming the international tide than placing an ideological barrier between workers. The CGT was still unwilling to give up its independence, but on July 31 Jaurès encouraged syndicalists to renounce the idea of an insurrection (although not a general strike) and organize a major demonstration in Paris. Socialist leaders proposed the rally be held August 9, and a syndicalist commission including Jouhaux, Dumoulin, and Merrheim entered into negotiations with the SFIO. Soon pressure grew to advance this "monster meeting" to Sunday, August 2, the very day, ironically, that socialist leaders in Paris would declare their participation in the national defense. Yet if syndicalist-socialist negotiations were nullified by Russian mobilization, this last-minute effort to organize a joint protest could not have come about unless working-class representatives firmly believed that they could have achieved something by it. The one thing antimilitarist leaders never, to the very end, doubted, was that the workers' movement alone possessed the capacity to keep the nation out of war. They believed in themselves because of their past successes, not their failures.[18]

As the government's commitment to her military alliance with Russia became increasingly clear, and as attempts by the Poincaré administration to appear pacific and conciliatory began to look suspicious, antimilitarist propaganda grew more forceful in its appeal for working-class solidarity. "Since it is [the working classes], actually, who in truth are responsible for world peace, it is necessary that they be constantly ready to impose it," wrote Jouhaux on July 26.[19] "The will and action of the workers is above diplomacy," read a *Bataille Syndicaliste* headline on the 28th.[20] On July 30, in response to the government's prohibition of a syndicalist meeting, the CGT and Union des Syndicats proclaimed their "unshakable attachment to the cause of humanity," declaring "the best chance for international peace lies in the hands of the working class."[21] On August 1, *La Bataille Syndicaliste* continued to express faith in the manifest purpose of the working classes to stop war. In the article "Do Not Panic," which ran shortly after Jaurès's assassination the previous evening in an effort to assure workers that "the moment is serious, but not desperate," Jouhaux exhorted: "Once more we repeat that the best chance for peace lies in the hands of the working class, which should not let itself be dragged outside the profoundly human role that has been assigned to it."[22] The very day these lines appeared in print, Jouhaux would meet with Interior Minister Louis Malvy, and in exchange for the release of syndicalists imprisoned by "some overzealous prefects," assure him that the CGT would not interfere with the general mobilization that was now all but inevitable. Malvy, meanwhile, had already defied the advice of Clemenceau and ordered his prefects to suspend arrests for the Carnet B. On August 2 the CGT relayed its decision to workers, "establishing undeniably," in Philippe Bernard's rendition of these events, "the failure of the executive committee's efforts in favor of peace."[23]

Yet despite these facts, the crucial, typically overlooked reality is that working-class leaders continued, in the final days before "the end of a world" (the dramatic title of Bernard's book), to view their role in impeding war as destiny; a destiny no longer based in antipatriotic or revolutionary ideals but in those of serving humanity. This is an important shift from earlier propaganda that focused on war as an abuse of workers at the hands of the bourgeoisie. Although such language did not vanish completely by this late date, it was almost wholly overshadowed by an incessant stress on the negative aspects of war itself—its cruelty, its indifference to human life, and its capacity to reverse the "progress" of European civilization, which included the bourgeoisie. As war became more imminent, antimilitarism was becoming less directly a means to secure a better future for the working classes than to prevent this "challenge thrown against Progress and Humanity," as an *ordre du jour* from the PTT workers put it, from ruining what they already had. On July 28 *La Bataille Syndicaliste* warned that a European war "would be a horrifying carnage, a grandiose slaughter in which blood would run in streams. The almost total extermination of people and of things, a renewal of ancient barbarity without precedent."[24] In the same issue, the matter-of-factly titled article "Let's Abolish Wars" went into explicit detail about all the death and destruction war would wreak, and in reference to Norman Angell's *The Great Illusion* implored: "War is suicide before being homicide. If I go off to fight I am unaware if I would kill, but I am certain that I will not come back, at least such as I am. Complete or partial, everyone who leaves for the [military] camps implies an individual suicide."[25] Just as the Sou du Soldat propaganda had urged workers cum soldiers not to forget that they were "above all" men, the prewar propaganda urged men, in general, not to forget their humanity.

This shockingly sober portrayal of the approaching conflict ran counter to popular notions that the war would be "over by Christmas." *La Bataille Syndicaliste* painted a bleak and, sadly, more accurate picture: "War . . . is the unleashing of all the hideous instincts, the most bloody, the most vile, the most miserable. . . . These cadavers, they will be yours tomorrow! These women, these children, these elderly people, they will be yours tomorrow! It's war!" The more than 1.3 million French dead and 630,000 war widows by 1918 would make this even more true than the *La Bataille* writers might have imagined. On July 27, the article "On the Brink of the Abyss" announced prophetically that "the unleashing of a cataclysm that will surpass in horror what men with the fullest imagination could never conceive of hangs by a thread. . . . It is the end of the mobilization. It is the burial, pure and simple, of humanity."[26] In the days before the "collapse" of the antimilitarist Left, its pleas were less to salvage revolutionary ideals than to preserve the spirit and human decency of all Europeans, then and for the future.

When the last hope for peace gave way and France mobilized on August 2, the reaction of syndicalists and socialists was not so much a "capitulation" as a reconciliation to the fact that they had tried everything but had been unable to restrain the surge of international events. As a CGT manifesto that day put it, "if the efforts of [the workers' International] do not seem to have resulted in what we had the right to expect, what the organized working class had hoped for, it is because events submerged us." This was by no means self-exoneration; the very next sentence read: "It is also, we should say at this decisive moment, because the proletariat has not been unanimous enough in understanding the continuous efforts needed to preserve Humanity from the horrors of a war."[27] The mood at CGT offices, as some syndicalist leaders themselves prepared to leave for the front, was somber, even to the point of despondency. Certainly there was a profound sense of failure; a feeling that all their efforts—the ceaseless demonstrations and *affiches*, the articles and resolutions—had somehow come to naught the moment Poincaré gave his speech on the *union sacrée*.[28] But if the idea that it had "failed" was the only reality, then the CGT's unanticipated and seemingly overnight shift in favor of the government makes even less sense. If the antimilitarist Left had not been able to reconcile itself to the war, then it may have continued its protest from behind the front lines.[29]

The fact that it did not continue, and that it was barely opposed in this decision, is the main reason that a comprehensive and chronological study of antimilitarism in pre-World War I France has been essential. For if this work has succeeded in altering our perceptions of what antimilitarism meant at the time, it is because it has highlighted just how crucial this radical leftist response to social and political injustice was in consolidating the democratic values of the Third Republic. Eventually and, in fact, ironically, it was this very success that assuaged even the most extreme antimilitarists and permitted their acceptance of the war. But by 1914 that seemingly sudden change of course had been facilitated by years of gradual realization, however grudgingly, of shared values with the admittedly imperfect Republic. Although only a handful of militants such as Hervé would acknowledge it before the guns of August, the "republican moment," as Philip Nord has aptly labeled the accession of democratic, public identity among the French, had slowly taken hold of her most leftist citizens as well.

It is thus far too simplistic, not to mention ahistorical, to view the Left's acceptance of war as stemming solely from the nature of that war itself. Such a scenario is akin to the following: imperial Germany, bastion of Prussian militarism and political authoritarianism, source of the treasonous dismemberment of Alsace-Lorraine, had invaded neutral Belgium and was attacking democratic and republican France. National defense was incumbent on every citizen if the nation was to maintain its dignity and autonomy and continue to serve as a beacon of justice for all civilization. In the case of the Left, governmental opposition gave way to a reassertion of Jacobin patriotism. And political, social, and even religious differences faded quickly in the spirit of national unity. The *union sacrée* was born.[30]

Although Jean-Jacques Becker has already gone far to dispel the illusion of the *union sacrée* as a magical dissolution of the multifold oppositions within French society, there persists an element of believability to this fanciful version when applied to the presumably radical conversion of the revolutionary Left.[31] As an October 1914 report explained it, "all political, philosophical or sentimental consideration must give way to the brutal fact of German aggression."[32] Jouhaux himself mounted the rostrum at Jaurès's obsequies on August 4, in the presence of Maurice Barrès, to declare on behalf of the CGT: "We rise up in order to drive back the invader, in order to safeguard the patrimony of civilization and of noble ideology that we have bequeathed history."[33]

Rosmer pinpoints a precise change in language in *La Bataille Syndicaliste* from the edition of August 1 to that of August 2. Whereas the syndicalist daily had managed to maintain its position against war on August 1, once mobilization became a reality a new understanding of the conflict materialized: "That the name of the old emperor Francis-Joseph be cursed!" The next day, August 2, the journal included "William II and the pangermanists" in its denunciation of those responsible for the war.[34] On August 4, an editorial in *La Bataille* asserted: "Obvious too is our role: against the right of the fist, against Germanic militarism, it is necessary to save the democratic and revolutionary tradition of France."[35] In *Le Bonnet Rouge*, Editor-in-Chief Almereyda ran the headline "To Arms, Citizens!" on August 3, and printed the "Marseillaise" on the front page. In "Our War," he defended the *patrie* he had once disparaged: "France is within her rights. It is no longer the time for essays on the horrors of war. It is the time for action. . . . The present war is a holy war. Our cause is the cause of the independence of peoples, it is the cause of liberty, what our fathers went into combat and died for while singing." Having made the connection between traditional France ("our fathers") and the present conflict, Almereyda proceeded to draw a parallel between the antimilitarist campaign in which he had played so prominent a part and the war in which he was now so anxious to fight:

We have not renounced our dream of universal fraternity. On the contrary, at the present tragic hour what emboldens our hearts is the conviction that this war brings with it precisely the realization of this great dream. Out of the war of '70–71 came the Republic. Out of the present war will come the German Republic. And out of the German Republic will soon emerge the United States of Europe, which is to say certain peace at last, and a permanently open route to social progress.[36]

What had taken place in the space of a few short days was a complete reconceptualization of war, not of antimilitarism. Rosmer writes that war had now come to represent the "decisive struggle between militarism and democracy, between civilization and barbarism."[37] Of added import for our purposes is that this "struggle," World War I, would serve as the bridge between revolutionaries of the French past and present. The war, in sum, became the new means by which antimilitarist citizens believed they could carry on their decades-long campaign for a more just order.

◆ ◆ ◆

In his study of Gustave Hervé and *La Guerre Sociale* during the summer of 1914, Michel Baumont pinpoints a similar, if more reticent, reconfiguration of the meaning of war. Although Hervé had long since reconciled himself to the impracticality of an insurrection and the fact that, "to the misfortune of humanity, our poor socialist International is not yet capable of stopping war" (July 18), it was not until confronted with the impending German offensive that he sought justification for outright support of the conflict. Under the banner headline "Neither Insurrection! Nor General Strike! DOWN WITH WAR!," Hervé wrote on July 29: "We must say it out loud, first of all because it's the truth, second because it's in our political interest that, under the present circumstances, we will not sabotage the national defense." In the same issue he gave a clearer idea of what it was they were defending: republican and socialist France. On July 31 Hervé sounded the infamous revolutionary call, "the *patrie* in danger." The next day, in commemoration of his fallen colleague whose own position permitting defensive wars Hervé had come to accept, he wrote:

National Defense above all!
They have murdered Jaurès.
We will not murder France![38]

France, by now, had come to have special meaning for the Sans-Patrie. As much as he wished to avoid seeing Europe "plunge itself up to the neck in a bloodbath and dive headfirst into barbarism," as he wrote on August 4, Hervé found solace in the idea of defending the France of *liberté, égalité, fraternité* against German political backwardness and militarist brutality. Thus the war had a clear purpose for Hervé—the creation of a German Republic and a Republic of the United States of Europe—as well as a clear enemy: "If we fight each other, the German people should understand that it is not them we have something against, but rather the Prussian military caste that has unleashed the storm."[39] Over a year later Hervé could still justify the by then stalemated and tragically destructive conflict: "This war, it is a war against war, it is a war on militarism in its most odious and grotesque form: Prussian militarism." On January 1, 1916, as the first signs of organized resistance to the war began to appear, *La Guerre Sociale* became *La Victoire*, and one of France's most outspoken revolutionaries became one of her staunchest citizens.[40]

◆ ◆ ◆

In a *thèse de droit* defended May 26, 1913, that examined the themes of patriotism and militarism during the socialist and syndicalist congresses of the previous decade, the doctoral candidate Louis Gravereaux concluded:

> If in the final analysis one wonders what the attitude of the proletariat would be on the day the *patrie* would be threatened, the response is impossible to formulate. Obviously, the doctors of antipatriotism will affirm that the working class will not "march." What do they know about it? We think, on the contrary, that humanitarian considerations will be abandoned on this day, and that syndicalists, revolutionaries, and reformists will "march."[41]

Gravereaux was both right and wrong. Over a year before the outbreak of the Great War, he predicted the behavior of the proletariat correctly. But did the workers "march" at the expense of humanitarian interests or in the name of them? Despite their deep understanding of the massive bloodletting that awaited Europe, antimilitarists accepted the war with Germany for the same reason that they had pursued their own struggle with France: to defend the rights of citizens in a democratic society. Through all the customary language of revolutionary working-class political culture that suffused the propaganda, antimilitarism ultimately worked, flourished, and put the government on edge because it was a forceful means to address grave injustices committed by the state against her people. To argue that it simply "failed" or "collapsed" in 1914 is to make the same mistake the government made in assessing it. Antimilitarism, whether it targeted capitalism, the army, war, or patriotism itself, never became the self-standing ideology that its leaders hoped it would and that its enemies imagined it was. But it succeeded brilliantly as a rallying cry against social and political inequities on behalf of ordinary citizens.

Once the government decided not to implement the Carnet B and the revolutionary Left could take account of the situation, it was this very reality that imposed itself on its subsequent actions.[42] In response to the war, the CGT and the Socialist Party went out of their way to alleviate the sufferings of the nation. On September 6 they jointly founded the Commission d'Action du Parti Socialiste et de la CGT, which aided the government in such crucial tasks as provisioning the troops, informing families of their wounded and dead, providing clothes and gifts for soldiers, and organizing ambulances and convalescent homes. And although these measures were to pertain to workers in service, the Commission d'Action earned the confidence of the public powers and the praise of the population, according to a report on the CGT written after mobilization.[43] Moreover, syndicalists who were not mobilized encouraged workers to make themselves useful to the military health services.[44] The Maison des Syndicats of the 15th arrondissement offered its clinic;[45] and the great hall of the new Maison des Syndicats building at 33 rue de la Grange-aux-Belles, once the nerve center for revolutionary planning in France, was filled with beds and put at the service of the Red Cross.[46] "We do not have to reaffirm the horror of a war we did everything we could to prevent," Yvetot wrote confidently in late August, "but we have to ward off, other than by resolutions, the misery that rages everywhere as a consequence of the war."[47]

CGT secretary Jouhaux recognized the importance of such humanitarian impulses from the first days of the fighting, when he used the pages of *La Bataille Syndicaliste* to encourage local *bourses* and *syndicats* to set up soup kitchens and other organizations of solidarity. Such actions, he wrote, "are the only practical means we have in our hands to give an element of continuity to our groups. Syndicalism must not die."[48] The irony is that the antimilitarist Left had to accept the war in order to sustain its fight against it. But the reality is that in so doing it had, at last, forsaken its own revolutionary ideals, and conceded its place in *la patrie française*.

NOTES

Introduction: "The Revolution That's Coming"

All translations are mine unless otherwise noted.

1. Gaston Dru, *La Révolution qui vient, enquête sur le syndicalisme révolutionnaire* (Paris: Édition de L'Écho de Paris, 1906).
2. See Niall Ferguson, *The Pity of War* (New York: Basic Books, 1999); and John Keegan, *The First World War* (New York: Knopf, 1999).
3. Philip Nord, *The Republican Moment: Struggles for Democracy in Nineteenth-Century France* (Cambridge, Mass.: Harvard University Press, 1995), pp. 191, 217.
4. Charlotte C. Wells, *Law and Citizenship in Early Modern France* (Baltimore: Johns Hopkins University Press, 1995); Renée Waldinger, Philip Dawson, and Isser Woloch, eds., *The French Revolution and the Meaning of Citizenship* (Westport, Conn.: Greenwood Press, 1993); Rogers Brubaker, *Citizenship and Nationhood in France and Germany* (Cambridge: Harvard University Press, 1992).
5. Brubaker, *Citizenship and Nationhood*, pp. 85–113.
6. Jean Jaurès, *L'Armée nouvelle* (Paris: Imprimerie Nationale, 1992).
7. From Michael Howard, *The Lessons of History* (New Haven, Conn.: Yale University Press, 1991), pp. 59–60. Bernhardi's book went into seven editions.
8. Ferguson, *Pity of War*, pp. 25–26.
9. Georges LeFranc, *Le Mouvement socialiste sous la troisième république, 1875–1940* (Paris: Payot, 1963), p. 200.
10. Jean-Jacques Becker, *Le Carnet B: Les pouvoirs publics et l'antimilitarisme avant la guerre de 1914* (Paris: Éditions Klincksieck, 1973), pp. 175–80.
11. Jean-Jacques Becker, *1914: Comment les français sont entrés dans la guerre* (Paris: Presse de la Fondation Nationale des Sciences Politiques, 1977), p. 579.
12. Cited in Roger Picard, *Le Mouvement syndical durant la guerre* (Paris: Presses Universitaires de France, 1927), p. 48.
13. Ibid.
14. Georges Lefranc, *Le Mouvement syndical sous la troisième république* (Paris: Payot, 1967), pp. 147–86.

15 See Jean-Jacques Becker and Annie Kriegel, *1914: La Guerre et le mouvement ouvrier français* (Paris: A. Colin, 1964).
16 Jacques Julliard, "La CGT devant le problème de la guerre, 1900–1914," *Le Mouvement Social* 49 (October–December 1964): 47–62.
17 Peter N. Stearns, *Revolutionary Syndicalism and French Labor* (New Brunswick, N.J.: Rutgers University Press, 1971). See also Michel Winock, "Le Pacifisme à la française, 1789–1991," *L'Histoire* 144 (May 1991): 39.
18 Michel Auvray, *Objecteurs, insoumis, déserteurs: Histoire des refractaires en France* (Paris: Stock, 1983), p. 151.
19 Susan Milner, *The Dilemmas of Internationalism: French Syndicalism and the International Labor Movement, 1900–1914* (New York: Berg, 1990).
20 Becker, *Le Carnet B*, p. 180.
21 Milorad M. Drachkovitch, *Les Socialismes français et allemand et le problème de la guerre, 1870–1914* (Geneva: Librairie E. Droz, 1953).
22 *Le Soir*, September 27, 1906.
23 Roger Chickering, *Imperial Germany and a World without War* (Princeton, N.J.: Princeton University Press, 1975), pp. 358–61.
24 Sandi E. Cooper, *Patriotic Pacifism: Waging War on War in Europe, 1815–1914* (New York: Oxford University Press, 1991), pp. 74–75, 133.
25 *L'Action*, April 6, 1903(?). This radical, anticlerical journal was launched March 30, 1903.
26 *Le Conscrit*, January 1902.
27 Victor Dave, *Pacifisme et antimilitarisme* (Paris: Petite Bibliothèque, n.d. [although the date must be after 1907 because it refers to the socialist International that year]), pp. 20, 30–31. See also Peter Brock, *Pacifism in Europe to 1914* (Princeton, N.J.: Princeton University Press, 1972), pp. 489–90.

1. Origins of War: The Roots of Antimilitarism in the Third Republic

1 Stéphane Audoin-Rouzeau, in *1870: La France dans la guerre* (Paris: A. Colin, 1989), examines the war's role in the development of national identity and citizenship in the nineteenth century; a process that culminated in World War I. My study examines how some of the most disaffected groups in France came to see themselves as part of the national whole as well.
2 Émile Zola, *The Debacle* (London: Penguin, 1972), p. 66. See also Guglielmo Ferrero, *Le Militarisme et la société moderne* (Paris: Stock, 1899), which emphasizes the generational propagation of a militarist tradition in France.
3 See Guillaume de Bertier de Sauvigny, *La Restauration* (Paris: Flammarion, 1955), pp. 14–17.
4 Jean Rabaut, *L'Antimilitarisme en France, 1810–1975: Faits et documents* (Paris: Librairie Hachette, 1975), pp. 17–18.
5 Louis Bergeron, *France under Napoleon* (Princeton, N.J.: Princeton University Press, 1981), p. 118. About half were killed or died from their wounds; the rest were prisoners who never returned. See also Martyn Lyons, *Napoleon Bonaparte and the Legacy of the French Revolution* (London: Macmillan, 1994), p. 46.

6. Michael Howard, *War and the Liberal Conscience* (London: Temple Smith, 1978), p. 36.
7. Ibid., pp. 39–40.
8. Cooper, *Patriotic Pacifism*, pp. 16–17, 21–22, 24.
9. Ibid., p. 24. Approximately six hundred delegates and over a thousand spectators took part in the congress.
10. Ibid., pp. 24–25, 87.
11. Jean-Jacques Becker and Stéphane Audoin-Rouzeau, *La France, la nation, la guerre: 1850–1920* (Paris: Sedes, 1995), pp. 218–19.
12. Cooper, *Patriotic Pacifism*, p. 238. By 1914 more than two hundred thousand copies of Bertha von Suttner's *Die Waffen Nieder!* were in circulation, along with a million copies in other languages.
13. Madeleine Meyer-Spiègler, "Antimilitarisme et refus du service militaire dans la France contemporaine, 1945–1962" (thèse de doctorat, Paris: Bibliothèque de la Fondation des Sciences Politiques, 1969), ch. 1.
14. Ibid.
15. Ted W. Margadant, *French Peasants in Revolt: The Insurrection of 1851* (Princeton, N.J.: Princeton University Press, 1979), pp. 8–10.
16. Michel Winock, *Le Socialisme en France et en Europe* (Paris: Éditions du Seuil, 1992), p. 324.
17. Despite its name, the Thiers government made peace with the Prussians. It was the Paris communards and Gambetta's government-in-exile that attempted to defend France. Stewart Edwards, *The Communards of Paris, 1871* (Ithaca, N.Y.: Cornell University Press, 1973), p. 30.
18. Edwards, *The Communards*, pp. 44–46, 48–49. *Affiches* from before and during the Commune attest to this.
19. George Woodcock, *Anarchism: A History of Libertarian Ideas and Movements* (New York: Meridian, 1962), p. 290. The International was banned in March 1872 and all socialist activities were suppressed.
20. See Raoul Girardet, *La Société militaire dans la France contemporaine, 1815–1939* (Paris: Librairie Plon, 1953); and Douglas Porch, *The March to the Marne: The French Army, 1871–1914* (Cambridge, Eng.: Cambridge University Press, 1981), pp. 25–27. The "one-year volunteers" paid 1,500 francs to cover training costs.
21. Girardet, *La Société militaire*, p. 175. See also Jean-Pierre Bertrand, *Les Soldats seront troubadours* (Paris: Les Presses D'Aujourd'hui, 1979), pp. 60–61, which views the 1872 law as the "instigator of a new social space."
22. Abel Hermant, *Le Cavalier Miserey, 21e chasseurs* (Paris: Charpentier, 1887), pp. i–ii. See also Rabaut, *L'Antimilitarisme en France*, p. 28. For examples not covered below: Christian Charron, "L'Antimilitarisme et son expression littéraire à la fin du XIXè siècle en France, 1886–1902" (thèse pour le doctorat de troisième cycle, Bordeaux, 1977); Claude Digeon, *La Crise allemande de la pensée française, 1870–1914* (Paris: Presses Universitaires de France, 1959), p. 361; Porch, *March to the Marne*, pp. 54–55.
23. Henri Fèvre, *Au Port d'armes* (Paris, 1887); Lucien Descaves, *Sous-offs, roman militaire* (Paris: Tresse et Stock, 1889), p. 139.
24. Louis Lamarque, *Un An de caserne* (Paris: P.-V. Stock, 1901), pp. 187, 65–66, 133.

25 Ibid., pp. 128–29.
26 Girardet, *La Société militaire*, p. 217. For a contemporary account, see A. Corre, "Le Militarisme," in *Almanach de la question sociale*, ed. A.-J. Crollard (Paris: Pauteur, 1892): Instead of understanding that the army should be a meeting of citizens, equal in their human rights . . . we continue to submit the soldier to a system of excessive subordination, a veritable bondage in the shadow of a military code that stems directly from old monarchic ordinances" (cited in Winock, *Le Socialisme*, p. 332).
27 Georges Darien, *Biribi, discipline militaire* (Paris: Albert Savine, 1890), p. x: "*Biribi* is not a novel expounding a social thesis, it is the sincere study of a piece of life, a raw fragment of existence." In 1907 the book was reissued as *Biribi, armée d'Afrique*. Similarly, Paul Vignée d'Octon wrote anticolonial works based on his experiences as a navy doctor: *Terre de mort—Soudan et Dahomey* (Paris: Lemerre, 1892); *La Gloire du sabre* (Paris: Flammarion, 1900); *Les Crimes coloniaux de la troisième république* (Paris: La Guerre Sociale, 1911).
28 Girardet, *La Société militaire*, p. 248.
29 These included the future antimilitarists C.-A. Laisant and Georges Darien, which illustrates why the distinctions between Right and Left are still blurred in this period. Both men denounced Descaves for his unpatriotic book, then went on to attack the army during their anarchist careers. See Georges Darien, *Georges Darien and Édouard Dubus, Les Vrais sous-offs, réponse à M. Descaves* (Paris: A. Savine, 1892), pp. 9–10.
30 Rabaut, *L'Antimilitarisme en France*, p. 29. See Lucien Descaves, *Sous-offs en cours d'assises* (Paris: Tresse et Stock, 1890).
31 Girardet, *La Société militaire*, ch. 5. *Arche sainte* can mean arch saint or, with more religious symbolism, ark of the saint.
32 Ibid., p. 179.
33 Meyer-Spiègler, *Antimilitarisme et refus du service militaire*, p. 15.
34 Rabaut, *L'Antimilitarisme en France*, p. 31.
35 "Un An de caserne," *Le Petit Sou*, July 9, 1901.
36 Lamarque, *Un An de caserne*, p. vi.
37 Winock, *Le Socialisme*, p. 322. Winock believes the literature had an important impact on leftist politicians, citing René Vallery-Radot, "L'Esprit militaire en France depuis cent ans," *Revue Bleue*, February 8, 1890.
38 Hermant, *Le Cavalier Miserey*, pp. 89–90.
39 Zola, *The Debacle*, p. 7 (from the introduction by Leonard Tancock). Anatole France's later novels exhibit growing skepticism toward military and patriotic values. See *Monsieur Bergeret à Paris*, and *Le Mannequin d'osier*. See also Meyer-Spiègler, *Antimilitarisme et refus du service militaire*, pp. 19–24.
40 Winock, *Le Socialisme*, pp. 321–22, n. 3, quotes René Vallery-Radot on the emergence of a new generation "raised in peacetime and that did not know what the invaded soil was." Germany acquired all of Alsace except Belfort and one-third of Lorraine.
41 John F. V. Keiger, in *France and the Origins of the First World War* (New York: St. Martin's Press, 1983), pp. 15, 39–40, 71–72, argues that while Alsace-Lorraine still informed diplomatic negotiations, the "generation of *revanche*" had largely diminished by the mid-1890s. Even the region's people resisted Germanization less and debated autonomy as a means of Franco-German rapprochement. See also Becker,

42. Rabaut, *L'Antimilitarisme en France*, pp. 45–66.
43. Edward L. Shorter and Charles Tilly, *Strikes in France, 1830–1968* (London: Cambridge University Press, 1974), pp. 47, 62, 147.
44. Boucher de Perthes, *Hommes et choses*, pp. 166–67, cited in Jean Grave, ed., *Guerre-militarisme* (Paris: Les Temps Nouveaux, 1902).
45. Porch, *March to the Marne*, p. 106.
46. Frederic H. Seager, *The Boulanger Affair: Political Crossroads of France, 1886–1889* (Ithaca, N.Y.: Cornell University Press, 1969), p. 33.
47. *Cri du Peuple*, April 25, 1884.
48. Zola used the strike at La Ricamarie (1869) as a model for the uprising in his novel *Germinal*. See Susanna Barrows, *Distorting Mirrors: Visions of the Crowd in Late-Nineteenth-Century France* (New Haven, Conn.: Yale University Press, 1981), pp. 28–29.
49. "Viande à Mitraille," *La Révolte*, May 15, 1891. "L'Armée," *Le Socialiste*, May 13, 1891. Lafargue was Karl Marx's son-in-law.
50. Michel Collinet, "Le Saint-Simonisme et l'armée," *Revue Française de Sociologie* (April–June 1961): 38–47.
51. Drachkovitch, *Les Socialismes français et allemand*, pp. 2–3, 55–56.
52. Alain Dalotel, Alain Faure, and Jean-Claude Freiermuth, *Aux Origines de la commune: Le Mouvement des réunions publiques à Paris 1868–1870* (Paris: F. Maspero, 1980).
53. Winock, *Le Socialisme*, p. 325.
54. Ibid., pp. 326–27. See also Drachkovitch, *Les Socialismes français et allemand*, pp. 53–55.
55. Winock, *Le Socialisme*, pp. 331–35. In *Catéchisme du soldat* (1894), Maurice Charnay defines an officer as "a kind of soldier, who does by inclination what the others do by force." Cited in *Crosse en l'air: Le Mouvement ouvrier et l'armée, 1900–1914* (Paris: Maspero, 1970), p. 15. See also "Semaine militaire," *Le Parti Socialiste*, August 19–26, 1893.
56. Winock, *Le Socialisme*, pp. 328, 335–38.
57. The Liebknecht-Vaillant resolution stated that "only the creation of a socialist order . . . will put an end to militarism and assure definitive peace"; referred to the Socialist Party as "the veritable and unique party of peace"; urged workers "to act energetically and incessantly against all vague impulses of war and the alliances that favor it"; and allowed that, in principle, a strike "is the only means to avert the catastrophe of a general war." *La Bataille*, August 23, 1891.
58. *L'Égalité*, August 20 and 27, 1891.
59. Archives de la Préfecture de la Police (PP) BA30, Congrès Internationale de Bruxelles, Rapport Général, September 25, 1891.
60. Winock, *Le Socialisme*, pp. 340–58, 371.
61. D. W. Brogan, *The Development of Modern France, 1870–1939* (London: Hamish Hamilton, 1967), p. 428. The sentence continues "and what was true of the SFIO was truer still of the CGT."

62 Winock, *Le Socialisme*, p. 361; Alexandre Zevaès, "Patrie et patriotisme," *Le Parti Socialiste*, January 31, 1892; *Le Parti Ouvrier*, April 19–20, 1891.
63 Maurice Charnay "Catéchisme du soldat," in *Crosse en l'air*, pp. 9–19.
64 Winock, *Le Socialisme*, p. 338.
65 Yolande Cohen, *Les Jeunes, le socialisme et la guerre: Histoire des mouvements de jeunesse en France* (Paris: L'Harmattan, 1989), p. 168.
66 PP BA913, December 23 and November 26, 1886. A December 24 report stated: "In reality, the 'League' is far from having the importance ascribed to it. Its core consists of a band of young good-for-nothings for whom anarchy is above all the free exercise of their bad instincts."
67 *La Souveraineté*, July 24, 1887.
68 Roland Andréani, "L'Antimilitarisme en Languedoc méditerranéen avant la première guerre mondiale," *Revue d'Histoire Moderne et Contemporaine* 20 (January–March 1973): 106.
69 Archives Départementales (AD) Loire 19M 2, Jeunesse Antipatriote (1891).
70 Edward P. Fitzgerald, "Émile Pouget, the Anarchist Movement, and the Origins of Revolutionary Trade-Unionism in France, 1880–1901" (Ph.D. dissertation, Yale University, 1974), pp. 188, 243–48. The journal continued, "with interruptions and variations," until April 1900.
71 Émile Pouget, *Le Père peinard* (Paris: Éditions Galilée, 1976), pp. 262–95. Fitzgerald, "Émile Pouget," pp. 191–92, estimates the journal printed eighty-five hundred to fifteen thousand copies.
72 Claude Bellanger et al., *Histoire générale de la presse française*, vol. 3 (Paris: Presses Universitaires de France, 1972), p. 245.
73 Ibid., p. 379.
74 PP BA1495.
75 AD Loire 19M 32, "L'Antimilitarisme et l'antipatriotisme en France" (December 1, 1912), p. 17.
76 Cited in Drachkovitch, *Les Socialismes français et allemand*, pp. 47, 52; Jean Maitron, *Le Mouvement anarchiste en France, des origines à 1914*, vol. 1 (Paris: Gallimard, 1975).
77 PP BA913.
78 PP BA1495.
79 PP BA913. Officials estimated attendance at 1,000.
80 PP BA1495, from a flyer found in the caserne de Lourcine (April 1891).
81 PP BA913, Paris, September 7, 1886.
82 Drachkovitch, *Les Socialismes français et allemand*, pp. 17–18. See also Marie Fleming, *The Anarchist Way to Socialism: Elisée Reclus and Nineteenth-Century European Anarchism* (Totowa, N.J.: Rowman and Littlefield, 1979), p. 226.
83 Archives Nationales (AN) F7/13323.
84 James Joll, *The Anarchists* (Cambridge, Mass.: Harvard University Press, 1980), pp. 179–80.
85 Gérard Noiriel, *Workers in French Society in the Nineteenth and Twentieth Centuries* (New York: Berg, 1990), p. 93.
86 Joll, *The Anarchists*, pp. 180–82; Woodcock, *Anarchism*, p. 319.
87 AN F7/13567.

88 Woodcock, *Anarchism*, pp. 319–20.
89 Ibid., pp. 320–21; Joll, *The Anarchists*, pp. 182–83.
90 Jacques Julliard, *Fernand Pelloutier et les origines du syndicalisme d'action directe* (Paris: Seuil, 1971), pp. 117, 420–22.
91 Woodcock, *Anarchism*, p. 304. See also Fitzgerald, "Émile Pouget," pp. 55–96, 75–93.
92 Fitzgerald, "Émile Pouget," pp. 80–93.
93 Ibid., p. 278–83. Pouget was certainly not the first to suggest that anarchists take their ideas into the unions, but his example shows how readily it happened. See also Jean Maitron, ed., *Dictionnaire biographique du mouvement ouvrière française* (Paris: Éditions Ouvrières, 1964–1993), vol. 14, pp. 300–1.
94 Cohen, *Les Jeunes*, p. 172.
95 André May, *Les Origines du syndicalisme révolutionnaire: Évolution des tendances du mouvement ouvrier, 1871–1906* (Paris: Jouve, 1913), pp. 106–8.
96 Jacques Bainville, *La Troisième république, 1870–1935* (Paris: Fayard, 1935), pp. 201–32.
97 René Garmy, *Histoire du mouvement syndical en France, des origines à 1914* (Paris: Bureau d'Éditions, 1933), p. 220.
98 Jean Touchard, *La Gauche en France depuis 1900* (Paris: Seuil, 1977), p. 78.
99 Cohen, *Les Jeunes*, p. 169.
100 AN F7/12887 Paris, October 18, 1898.
101 Eric Cahm, *The Dreyfus Affair in French Society and Politics* (London: Longman, 1996), p. 96.
102 Sébastien Faure, *Les Anarchistes et l'affaire Dreyfus* (Paris: Fourneau, 1993), p. 16.
103 Jean-Denis Bredin, *The Affair: The Case of Alfred Dreyfus* (New York: George Braziller, 1986), pp. 295, 524–26; Zeev Sternhell, *La Droite révolutionnaire, 1885–1914: Les Origines françaises du fascisme* (Paris: Seuil, 1978), and *Ni droite ni gauche, l'idéologie fasciste en France* (Paris: Seuil, 1983).
104 Michael Burns, *Rural Society and French Politics: Boulangism and the Dreyfus Affair* (Princeton, N.J.: Princeton University Press, 1984).
105 Eugen Weber, *France, fin de siècle* (Cambridge, Mass.: Belknap, 1986), pp. 122–23.
106 Victor Méric, "Vive l'armée," *Le Libertaire*, June 5–12, 1902.
107 Bredin, *The Affair*, pp. 517–27; Becker, *La France, la nation, la guerre*, p. 187.
108 AN F7/13324, Individual note No. 126 on Gaston Goirand of the agricultural workers *syndicat* in Marsillargues (Hérault).

2. Antimilitarist Armies: Structures and Strategies

1 Christopher Andrew, *Théophile Delcassé and the Making of the Entente Cordiale* (New York: St. Martin's Press, 1968), pp. 302–8.
2 Howard, *Lessons of History*, pp. 97–112. For English translation, see Jan Gotlib, *The Future of War in Its Technical, Economic, and Political Relations; Is War Now Impossible?* (New York: Doubleday & McClure, 1899).
3 Domela Nieuwenhuis, *Rapport: Sur le militarisme et l'attitude des anarchistes et socialistes révolutionnaires en cas de guerre entre les nations* (Paris: Les Temps Nouveaux, 1913); "L'Agitation antirusse," *Patrie*, February 4, 1905; Jaurès, *L'Armée nouvelle*, p. 43.
4 Howard, *Lessons of History*, p. 101.

5 Charles Albert, "La Guerre et l'opinion," *Les Temps Nouveaux,* February 10–16, 1900.
6 "L'Agitation: Groupe de propagande antimilitariste de Paris," *Le Libertaire,* March 16–23, 1901. The group was founded by the anarchist Gaston Dubois-Desaulle, author of *Sous la casaque: Notes d'un soldat* (Paris: P.-V. Stock, 1899), and *Camisards, peaux de lapins et corps disciplinaires de l'armée française* (Paris: Éditions de la Reine Blanche, 1901). The placards (February 1900, December 1900, and January 1901, respectively) were prosecuted in Bourges, Nancy, and Nîmes.
7 PP BA1511.
8 PP BA1495, November 19, 1902.
9 The German socialist Karl Liebknecht speculated that "the League probably never extended its influence beyond the borders of France," in *Militarism and Anti-militarism* (Glasgow: Socialist Labour Press, 1917), p. 103. Cohen, *Les Jeunes,* pp. 188–90, argues that the league was founded to support desertion.
10 PP BA1495, see flyer listing speakers for the December 14, 1902, meeting, where attendance was estimated at 140. Other participants included the anarchists Charles Malato, Gaston Dubois-Desaulle, and Georges Yvetot. Allemane was general treasurer.
11 Ibid. Posters such as "a bas la justice militaire!" had cartoon panels depicting instances of military abuse and accompanied by a description of its doleful outcome: "aucune poursuite" or "acquittement." For example, an officer punches a soldier in the mouth and the caption mocks the military court's verdict: "The accused did not strike but simply 'collided with' the injured [soldier]." Several drawings were done by the artist Félix Vallotton.
12 Ibid. See also "La Défense du soldat," *Le Libertaire,* February 13, 1903.
13 PP BA1495, February 8 and July 13, 1903.
14 *Le Libertaire,* June 10–17, 1904.
15 AN 14AS 39 (Archives Sociales).
16 Nieuwenhuis, *Rapport: Sur le militarisme.*
17 *Bulletin de l'Association Internationale Antimilitariste,* October 1, 1906.
18 *L'Ennemi du Peuple,* July 1–16, 1904. The other countries were Holland, Belgium, England, Spain, Austria, and Switzerland. The minutes published here indicate that the French delegation put forth the resolution for the association's creation. PP BA1511, April 26, 1906, claims the French initiated the congress.
19 E. Armand, *Le Refus de service militaire et sa véritable signification,* rapport présenté au congrès antimilitariste international d'Amsterdam, Juin 1904 (Paris: Édition de l'Ère Nouvelle, 1904), p. 8.
20 *L'Ennemi du Peuple,* July 1–16, 1904. Women were admitted into the AIA from the beginning (Article 8), and three female delegates were at Amsterdam. The morning session of June 27 instructed women that "their true place is beside those who want to destroy the monster that devours men." In *Aux Femmes* (Paris: L'Homme Libre, 1904) Urbain Gohier appealed to "all the honest women who are worthy of being lovers, spouses and mothers" to declare "war on war, and as a consequence war on militarism." For a brief look at feminism and antimilitarism, see Jean Rabaut, *Féministes à la belle époque* (Paris: France-Empire, 1985), pp. 128–32.
21 Ten centimes remained with the local section and five each went to the national and international committees. The group's logo depicted two tense hands breaking a rifle.

22 *L'Ennemi du Peuple,* July 1–16, 1904. *Le Libertaire,* July 1–7, 1904, published the complete statutes of the AIA.
23 *L'Action,* September 14, 1904.
24 PP BA1511, September 15, 1904.
25 AN F7/12890, July 27, 1905. See "Le Congrès national de l'AIA," *Le Libertaire,* July 23–30, 1905.
26 PP BA1511, October 27, 1905. Arrondissements and suburbs listed are: 4th, 5th, 10th, 11th, 12th, 14th, 15th, 17th, 18th, 19th, and 20th; Asnières, Argenteuil, la Garenne-Colombes, Gargan-Livry, Montreuil-sous-Bois, Nogent-le-Perreux, and Saint-Denis. *Le Libertaire* regularly printed blurbs on new sections.
27 PP BA1495, July 4, 1905.
28 PP BA1511, meetings of October 1 and 6 and August 19, 1905.
29 Ibid., meetings of October 1 and 27, 1904.
30 André Lorulot, "AIAT-isme," *L'Anarchie,* October 19, 1905. Libertad, "La Bonne discipline," *L'Anarchie,* November 30, 1905. *L'Anarchie,* founded in April 1905 and lasting until 1914, preached "individualism," emphasizing personal initiatives such as desertion.
31 PP BA1511, September 11, 1904.
32 PP BA1511, August 17, 1904.
33 *Le Libertaire,* July 23–30, 1905. See also PP BA1511, meeting of April 23, 1905, when Almereyda calls attention to the serious financial problems.
34 PP BA1495, July 4, 1905.
35 PP BA1511, April 26, 1906.
36 "Le Congrès national de l'AIA," *Le Libertaire,* July 23–30, 1905.
37 Ibid. See also AN F7/12890, August 11, 1905.
38 Maitron, *Dictionnaire biographique,* pp. 345–46.
39 AN F7/13324. See also PP BA1511, April 26, 1906, for a comparison between the AIA and CGT.
40 *La Voix du Peuple,* January 1903.
41 Ibid., January 1904.
42 Ibid., March 6–13, 1910, October 1907, February 1908, and September 1908.
43 AD Loire 19M 32, "L'Antimilitarisme et l'antipatriotisme en France" (Situation au 1er déc. 1912), p. 26.
44 AD Loire 19M 33, "Une Oeuvre de la CGT: Le Sou du soldat" (Situation au 1er déc. 1912), pp. 1–3. See AN F7/13581, for the debate over the creation of the Sou du Soldat.
45 Ibid., pp. 3–4.
46 One sou = five centimes.
47 AD Loire 19M 33, pp. 4–5. See also Becker, *Le Carnet B,* pp. 22–25.
48 Becker, *Le Carnet B,* pp. 24–25.
49 AD Loire 19M 33, pp. 5–7.
50 Ibid., p. 7.
51 *Le Petit Sou,* May 4, 1902.
52 "Les Ouvriers soldats," *L'Aurore,* May 4, 1902.
53 "Lettre ouverte à M. André, Général et Ministre," *La Voix du Peuple,* May 11–18, 1902.
54 AN F7/13323, Chambre des Députés, January 16 and 22, 1903. The "cercles Catho-

liques" enabled soldiers to continue their education and provided them with paper, stamps, and money from their Sou du Soldat fund.

55 AD Loire 19M 33, pp. 7–8.
56 Georges Yvetot, *Nouveau manuel du soldat: La Patrie, L'armée, La guerre*, 4th ed. (Paris: Fédération des Bourses du Travail, 1902), pp. 3–4.
57 Becker, *Le Carnet B*, pp. 69–71.
58 Yvetot, *Nouveau manuel*, pp. 4–7.
59 Ibid.
60 Ibid., pp. 28–32.
61 Becker, *Le Carnet B*, pp. 69, 75.
62 AN F7/13323, September 3, 1905.
63 AD Loire 19M 32. Becker, *Le Carnet B*, pp. 51, 188. This resolution, along with Griffuelhes's proposal proclaiming the independence of the CGT vis-à-vis the Socialist Party (the Charte d'Amiens), was a victory for revolutionary syndicalists over the reformists. See Drachkovitch, *Les Socialismes français et allemande*, pp. 134–35.
64 Meyer-Spiègler, *Antimilitarisme et refus du service militaire*, pp. 46–48. The term *contre-armée* (against army) comes from an article in *La Revue Blanche* by Charles Péguy.
65 Leo A. Loubère, "Left-Wing Radicals, Strikes, and the Military, 1880–1907," *French Historical Studies* 3 (Spring 1963): 102–3.
66 Alain Brossat and Jean-Yves Potel, eds., *Antimilitarisme et révolution (1): Anthologie de l'antimilitarisme révolutionnaire* (Paris: Union Générale d'Éditions, 1975), p. 77.
67 Cohen, *Les Jeunes*, p. 185.
68 Ibid., pp. 186–88.
69 The French term *pioupiou* is slang for "young soldier" or "Tommy." The British equivalent is "Tommy Atkins."
70 "Ne désertez pas," *Le Conscrit*, January 1903; "Camarade," *Le Conscrit*, January 1902; Rabaut, *L'Antimilitarisme en France*, p. 73. See also "Le Conscrit," *Le Petit Sou*, October 30, 1901; "A Celui qui part," *Le Conscrit* (February 1906), in *Crosse en l'air: Le Mouvement ouvrier et l'armée, 1900–1914* (Paris: F. Maspero, 1970) and Claude Willard, *Les Guesdistes: Le Mouvement socialiste en France, 1893–95* (Paris: Éditions Sociales, 1965), pp. 556–57.
71 John Merriman, *The Agony of the Republic: The Repression of the Left in Revolutionary France, 1848–1851* (New Haven, Conn.: Yale University Press, 1978), pp. 191–214. For an amusing look at why the Yonne was a center for antimilitarism, see *L'Écho de Paris*, February 24, 1906.
72 Cohen, *Les Jeunes*, pp. 177–80. See also Jean-Jacques Becker, "Antimilitarisme et antipatriotisme en France avant 1914: Le Cas de Gustave Hervé," in *Enjeux et Puissances* (Paris: Sorbonne, 1986), p. 102.
73 Maurice Rotstein, "The Public Life of Gustave Hervé" (Ph.D. dissertation, New York University, 1956), pp. 2–3; Michael Roger Scher, "The Anti-patriot as Patriot: A Study of the Young Gustave Hervé" (Ph.D. dissertation, University of California at Los Angeles, 1972). Recently, the first full-length biography of Hervé has appeared: Gilles Heuré, *Gustave Hervé: Itinéraire d'un provocateur* (Paris: La Découverte, 1997).

74 Becker, "Antimilitarisme et antipatriotisme en France," p. 104. See also Maitron, *Dictionnaire biographique*, vol. 13, p. 48.
75 Maitron, *Dictionnaire biographique*, vol. 13, pp. 47–53.
76 Ibid., pp. 47–48.
77 Rotstein, "The Public Life of Gustave Hervé," pp. 8–13.
78 Maitron, *Dictionnaire biographique*, p. 50.
79 Raymond Escholier, ed., *Souvenirs parlés de Briand* (Paris: Librairie Hachette, 1932), pp. 35–53. As foreign minister, Briand helped initiate the Kellogg-Briand Pact (1928), in which sixty-two nations agreed to "renounce [war] as an instrument of national policy." William R. Keylor, *The Twentieth-Century World: An International History* (New York: Oxford University Press, 1984), pp. 125–26.
80 Rotstein, "The Public Life of Gustave Hervé," pp. 17–18.
81 Gustave Hervé, "L'Anniversaire de Wagram," *Le Travailleur Socialiste de l'Yonne*, July 20, 1901.
82 Maurice Dommanget, "Gustave Hervé et l'affaire du drapeau dans le fumier," *Révolution prolétarienne* 92 (1955): 22–24. Othon Guerlac, in *Les Citations françaises: Recueil de passages célèbres, phrases familières, mots historiques* (Paris: A. Colin, 1931), p. 291, lists "*le drapeau dans le fumier*" (flag in the dung heap) alongside quotes by the likes of Zola and Hugo.
83 Heuré, *Gustave Hervé*, pp. 38–39.
84 Péguy defended Hervé in terms of political liberty, calling the verdict a "political acquittal." See Éric Cahm, *Péguy et le nationalisme français: De l'affaire Dreyfus à la grande guerre* (Paris: Cahiers de l'Amitié Charles Péguy, 1972), pp. 27–28; and Jacques Viard, *Les oeuvres posthumes de Charles Péguy* (Paris: Cahiers de l'Amitié Charles Péguy, 1969), pp. 63–72.
85 Rotstein, "The Public Life of Gustave Hervé," pp. 23–24.
86 Louis Gravereaux, *Les Discussions sur le patriotisme et le militarisme dans les congrès socialistes* (thèse de droit, Paris, 1913), pp. 69–72. See also Rotstein, "The Public Life of Gustave Hervé," pp. 26–27.
87 Gustave Hervé, *Histoire de la France et de l'Europe: L'Enseignement pacifique par l'histoire* (Paris: Bibliothèque d'Éducation, 1903), pp. v–vi; Rotstein, "The Public Life of Gustave Hervé," pp. 31–32. See also "Un Livre d'Hervé interdit," *L'Avant-Garde*, August 27, 1905.
88 Rotstein, "The Public Life of Gustave Hervé," pp. 33–36. See also Drachkovitch, *Les Socialismes français et allemand*, p. 89.
89 Paul Lafargue, *Le Patriotisme de la bourgeoisie* (Paris: L'Emancipatrice, Imprimerie Communiste, 1913). See also "L'Armée et la bourgeoisie," *L'Humanité*, December 4, 1906.
90 Gravereaux, *Les Discussions*, pp. 74–88.
91 Gustave Hervé, *Leur patrie* (Paris: L'Auteur, 1906). This book appeared in English translation as *My Country, Right or Wrong?* (London: A. C. Fifield, 1910).
92 Ibid., chaps. 3–12, p. 95. On symbolic representations of the Republic, see Maurice Agulhon, *Marianne au pouvoir* (Paris: Flammarion, 1989).
93 "En Cas de guerre," *L'Avant-Garde*, February 4, 1906; *La Guerre Sociale*, July 10–16, 1907.

94 Hervé, *Leur patrie*, p. 133.
95 Ibid., p. 223. Madeleine Rebérioux, in "Les Tendances hostiles à l'etat dans la S.F.I.O., 1905–1914," *Le Mouvement Social* 65 (October–December 1968), views Hervéisme as one *antiétatist* (antistate) current that reemerged in the unified Socialist Party in response to its increasing parliamentary tendencies.
96 Hervé, *My Country, Right or Wrong?*, pp. 210–13.
97 Ibid., pp. 210–34. In less than four years, 127,000 copies of the journal had inundated the primarily rural Yonne.
98 Hervé, *Leur patrie*, p. 169.
99 "Contre le sabre," *Le Libertaire*, July 8–15, 1900. The "few isolated individuals" are Urbain Gohier and Dubois-Desaulle, who published *L'Armée contre la nation* and *Sous la casaque: Notes d'un soldat*, respectively.
100 Becker, "Antimilitarisme et antipatriotisme en France," p. 106; Rebérioux, "Les Tendances," p. 29, calls *La Guerre Sociale* a "crossroads journal" between socialists and syndicalists. Bellanger, *Histoire générale de la presse française*, vol. 3, p. 296.
101 Hubert Lagardelle, "Enquête sur l'idée de patrie et la classe ouvrière," *Le Mouvement Socialiste*, nos. 160, 161: August 1–15, 1905, pp. 433–70; nos. 162, 163: September 1–15, pp. 36–71; nos. 164, 165: October 1–15, pp. 202–31; nos. 166, 167: November 1–15, pp. 320–37.
102 *Le Mouvement Socialiste*, nos. 162, 163: September 1–15, 1905, pp. 40–41; nos. 164, 165: October 1–15, 1905, pp. 227–31. The French thinker Georges Sorel proposed direct action in the form of a general strike as both the ultimate weapon and "social myth" needed to inspire workers to agitate for major social change.
103 Eugen Weber, *The Nationalist Revival in France* (Berkeley: University of California Press, 1959), p. 31.
104 AN 14AS 39.
105 Cited in Gordon Wright, *France in Modern Times* (New York: W. W. Norton, 1987), pp. 303–4.
106 See Samuel R. Williamson, *The Politics of Grand Strategy: Britain and France Prepare for War, 1904–1914* (London: Ashfield, 1990), p. 52, on the "chaos that was the French Navy and Army" at this time.
107 Paul Kennedy, *The Rise and Fall of the Great Powers: Economic Change and Military Conflict from 1500 to 2000* (New York: Vintage, 1989), p. 224.
108 "En Cas de guerre," *L'Avant-Garde*, February 4, 1906.

3. Enemies and Allies

1 PP BA1511, 1512. Police found the poster in most of the arrondissements of Paris and many communes of the Seine.
2 Ibid.
3 PP BA1512, "L'Appel à la désertion," October 8, 1905. See also "Arrestations et perquisitions," *L'Action*, October 9, 1905.
4 *L'Avant-Garde*, January 4, 1906. For a complete account of the proceedings, see *Le Libertaire*, January 6–13, 1906.

5   John Merriman, *The Red City: Limoges and the French Nineteenth Century* (New York: Oxford University Press, 1985), p. 213. In 1906, 438,500 workers took part in 1,309 strikes, a record that would endure until the 1914 war. See also Sternhell, *La Droite révolutionnaire*, p. 322.
6   "L'Appel à la désertion," *L'Éclair*, October 8, 1905. The laws were enacted in response to the anarchist attacks of 1892–1894.
7   Ibid., for the complete list.
8   PP BA1512. See also "Contre l'arbitraire," *L'Humanité*, March 5, 1906, which harshly criticized the "arbitrary" use of the laws ("the most Draconian of western Europe") against the *affiche rouge* (as well as *La Voix du Peuple* and *Le Conscrit*), "the pretext of which is the antimilitarist propaganda."
9   "L'Affaire des antimilitaristes aux Assises de la Seine," *L'Action*, December 27, 1905.
10 AN F7/12910, *Débats*, December 24, 1905. See *Le Libertaire*, January 6–13, 1906, for the full version of Jaurès's speech.
11 Porch, *March to the Marne*, p. 107.
12 Merriman, *The Red City*, pp. 234–36.
13 PP BA1511.
14 Brossat and Potel, *Antimilitarisme et révolution*, p. 76. See also Roland Andréani, "Armée et nation en Languedoc méditerranéen, 1905–14" (thèse de troisième cycle d'histoire, Montpellier, 1975), p. 144.
15 Sylvain Humbert, *Le Mouvement syndical* (Paris: Librairie Marcel Rivière, 1912), pp. 66–67.
16 Urbain Gohier, *L'Antimilitarisme et la paix: Plaidoirie prononcée en cour d'Assises de la Seine, le 28 décembre 1905* (Paris: Chez l'Auteur, 1906), p. 24.
17 Becker, "Antimilitarisme et antipatriotisme en France," p. 103. Hervé's speech took forty-seven pages of his work, *Mes crimes, ou onze ans de prison pour délits de presse* (Paris: Éditions de La Guerre Sociale, 1912).
18 "Antimilitaristes," *Le Matin*, December 30, 1905.
19 "Le Procès des antimilitaristes," *Le Journal*, December 28, 1905.
20 Hervé, *Mes crimes*, pp. 76–77.
21 "Antimilitaristes," *Le Matin*, December 30, 1905.
22 "Antimilitaristes," *Le Matin*, December 30, 1905. Almereyda also argued that antimilitarism, in particular the AIA, was international in its propaganda and humanitarian in its appeal.
23 *Le Libertaire*, January 6–13, 1906. The other acquitted signer was the Greek revolutionary Amilcare Cipriani, who also expressed the desire "to share the fate of my comrades." See his article "Mon antimilitarisme," *La Petite République*, November 14, 1905.
24 *Le Journal*, December 29, 1905. England's expeditionary force would, of course, be an important factor in halting the German attack in 1914.
25 See *Le Libertaire*, January 6–13, 1906, for Seligman's closing speech.
26 *Le Temps*, January 1, 1906.
27 See Maitron, *Le Mouvement anarchiste en France*, pp. 371–72; and Porch, *March to the Marne*, p. 110.

28 AN F7/13323, "Les Bourses du Travail et l'antimilitarisme," October 1907. Several reports viewed the *affiche rouge* outcome as a devastating, if not fatal blow for the AIA. Almost a year later, the report "La Situation actuelle de l'antimilitarisme" began: "The AIA has almost disappeared after the sentences pronounced by the Seine jury, December 30, 1905" (AN F7/13324, Paris, April 3, 1907). Another concluded that although the signers were amnestied six months later, "these severe sentences sowed disarray in the midst of the AIA; several of these groups took back their independence" (AD Loire 19M 32). Only a few months after the sentences, a police commissioner concluded they had "brought about the quasi disappearance of all these groups" (PP BA1511, Paris, April 26, 1906).

29 The amnesty of July 14, 1906, liberated Hervé. Those serving only a one-year sentence were released on parole on June 23, 1906, thanks to a partial amnesty. See Rotstein, "The Public Life of Gustave Hervé," p. 51.

30 *Les Temps Nouveaux,* January 5, 1906.

31 In addition to the journals cited above, articles appeared in *La Libre Parole, Le Gaulois, La Liberté, L'Action, Le Petit Parisien,* and *La Patrie,* to name a few.

32 Public Record Office (PRO), Foreign Office (FO) 371 69, Despatch nos. 316 and 490, pp. 532–39. A German foreign office report refers to "the trial against Hervé and comrades." Auswärtiges Amt (AA), Allgemeinen Angelegenheiten Frankreich R 6601, Militärbericht Nr. 10, Paris, February 22, 1906.

33 Rotstein, "The Public Life of Gustave Hervé," pp. 44–45.

34 *Le Petit Parisien,* October 1, 1906. See also PP BA1512. On his release from prison, Hervé allegedly said that he was happy to leave, but "we are ready to go back there, you can quote it!" (*Le Matin,* July 15, 1906).

35 Drachkovitch, *Les Socialismes français et allemand,* p. 90.

36 Becker, "Antimilitarisme et antipatriotisme en France," p. 104.

37 Rotstein, "The Public Life of Gustave Hervé," pp. 52–54.

38 Jules Guesde, *Questions d'hier et d'aujourd'hui* (Paris: V. Gard et E. Brière, 1911), pp. 39–46, 49–50, 52; and Drachkovitch, *Les Socialismes français et allemand,* pp. 93–95.

39 Becker, "Antimilitarisme et antipatriotisme en France," p. 105.

40 Drachkovitch, *Les Socialismes français et allemand,* pp. 90–91.

41 Charles Péguy, *Notre jeunesse* (Paris: Cahiers de la Quinzaine, 1957), pp. 173–74. For a harsh critique of Hervé, see Péguy, *Oeuvres complètes de Charles Péguy, 1873–1914* (Paris: Gallimard, 1952), pp. 261–85; and Viard, *Les Oeuvres postumes,* pp. 171–75. During Hervé's trial for the "dung heap" article, Jaurès had praised him for showing that "the true France is the France of philosophy, peace, and the Enlightenment." See Harvey Goldberg, *The Life of Jean Jaurès* (Madison: University of Wisconsin Press, 1962), p. 310.

42 AA Frankreich R 6601, No. 1050, Paris, December 9, 1905.

43 Cited in Drachkovitch, *Les Socialismes français et allemand,* p. 91. According to AD Loire 19M 32, this protest appeared on October 1907 and was signed by eighteen socialist deputies.

44 AN F7/13323. Later, in an interview for *Le Matin* (May 11, 1907), Guesde sounded a more optimistic note: "The direct action and antimilitarism as some understand it are maladies that the party will liberate itself from like it cured itself of others."

45 Albert Thomas, *La Politique socialiste* (Paris: M. Rivière, 1913), p. 33.
46 AN F7/13323, *Principaux actes d'antimilitarisme (1900–09)*.
47 AA Frankreich R 6601, Militärattaché Nr. 46, Militärbericht Nr. 10, Paris, February 22, 1906.
48 AN F7/12890, December 30, 1905.
49 PP BA1512. The *affiche* went up on the night of Feb. 11–12, 1906. See also "Manifestation au palais," *Le Petit Parisien*, April 6, 1906.
50 AD Loire 19M 32, pp. 37–38.
51 AN F7/12890, January 30, 1906.
52 AN F7/13323, 13324, "Les Bourses du Travail et l'antimilitarisme," October 1907. The "freedom of opinion" group was founded in Paris in February 1906.
53 AN F7/13324, February 14, 1906.
54 PP BA1511, 889, July 6 and 15, 1906. Twenty to thirty diehard supporters did turn up.
55 PP BA1511, September 8, 1906.
56 AN F7/13324, September 19, 1906. This report suggested that the initiative for a successful reconstitution would have to come from the youth.
57 PP BA1511, November 5–20, 1906. According to Méric's recollections, some one hundred thousand copies of *Lettre à un conscrit* were printed. See Victor Méric, "Vieilles choses, vieilles histoires: Souvenirs d'un militant," *Nouvelle Revue Socialiste* (December 5, 1925): 99.
58 AD Dordogne 1M 76.
59 PP BA1780, November 19, 1906; December 5, 1906.
60 PP BA1495.
61 AN F7/13323, "Les Bourses du Travail et l'antimilitarisme," October 1907.
62 *Le Matin*, April 4, 1907. The daily had a circulation of 665,000 in 1907. Bellanger, *Histoire générale de la presse française*, p. 311.
63 Bibliothèque de Documentation Internationale Contemporaine (BDIC), Université de Paris, Nanterre, "Les Antimilitaristes au cour d'Assises de la Seine (plaidoirie de McJacques Bonzon)," *Revue des Grands Procès Contemporain* 25 (June 24, 1907): 479–84. Hervé was also a defense attorney at this trial. See also PRO FO 371 255, No. 21323, Despatch No. 326, Paris, June 27, 1907, pp. 102–4.
64 AN F7/13324, *Verdict des douze*, Paris, June 26, 1907.
65 Archives de Paris (AP, Ville Moisson) D.3.U.6., p. 102. That same month a design by Grandjouan in *Le Conscrit* came before the Seine tribunal. It depicted a group of soldiers, rifles aimed at their officers, with the legend: "Dare now to give the command to fire." It was in response to the application of the *lois scélérates* against these two journals *and* the *affiche rouge* that "Contre l'arbitraire" appeared in *L'Humanité*, March 5, 1906 (see n. 8).
66 Humbert, *Mouvement syndical*, pp. 66–70. The socialist René Viviani defended the CGT's right to exist against Pugliesi-Conti. See AN F7/13568, transcript from Chambre des Députés—1er Séance du 23 octobre 1908. The chamber debated the CGT's legal rights on December 1, 1905, May 7–8 and 11–14, 1907, and January 13, 20, and 27, 1911.
67 AN F7/12890, CGT—February 26, 1906, and March 1, 2, 1906.
68 AN F7/13323, "Les Bourses du Travail et l'antimilitarisme." See also AN 14AS 136;

Frédéric Stackelberg, *Mystification patriotique et solidarité prolétarienne* (Paris: Éditions de La Guerre Sociale, 1907).

69 AN F7/13567, 13323, *Action antimilitariste*, September 3, 1905.

70 See Joan W. Scott, "Mayors versus Police Chiefs: Socialist Municipalities Confront the French State," in *French Cities in the Nineteenth Century*, ed. John Merriman (London: Hutchinson, 1982), pp. 237–45. Scott argues that in the 1890s the socialist municipal councils "provided protection from the police, the repressive arm and most immediate exemplification of state power." The actions of socialist mayors were more vigilantly controlled by the prefects in the 1900s.

71 AN F7/13567, "La Propagande révolutionnaire dans les Bourses du Travail," Paris, March 17, 1905.

72 Ibid.

73 Ibid. There are some discrepancies between this report and "Les Bourses du Travail et l'antimilitarisme" (F7/13323). In the latter, these towns are listed as having lost *departmental* subsidies: Châteauroux, Issoudun (500 francs), La Pallice (port of La Rochelle), Marmande (300), Villeneuve-sur-Lot (800).

74 AN F7/13323, 13326.

75 AN F7/12890, 13323. For the German viewpoint, see the *Vorwärts* article that appeared in French in *La République Sociale*, March 8, 1906 (AD Aude).

76 AN F7/12890, CGT—February 15–16, 1906.

77 Robert Michels, "Les Socialistes allemands et la guerre," *Le Mouvement Socialiste*, February 10, 1906, pp. 129–39. Michels represented the revolutionary wing of German socialism.

78 *Débats*, February 22, 1906. See also *Revue Socialiste*, January–February 1906, pp. 86, 213–18, which cites *La Voix du Peuple* stating that German syndicalists responded negatively to Griffuelhes's idea for a joint demonstration out of the conviction that it would lead to their dissolution.

79 AN F7/13323, see article by Jean Girardet, editor of *Gil Blas*.

80 *Le Journal*, February 15, 1907. The others were Dutch and Belgian.

81 Carl Schorske, *German Social Democracy, 1905–1917: The Development of the Great Schism* (Cambridge, Mass.: Harvard University Press, 1955), pp. 69–70. See also Volker Berghahn, *Militarism: The History of an International Debate, 1861–1977* (Warwickshire: Berg, 1981), pp. 23–26.

82 Schorske, *German Social Democracy*, pp. 72–73.

83 "Le Péril antimilitariste," *La République Française*, October 5, 1906.

84 "Par Delà les frontières," *Le Conscrit*, no. 6, n.d.

85 L'abbé Desgranges, *Le Sillon contre l'antimilitarisme: L'abbé Desgranges contre Gustave Hervé* (Joigny: Librairie Tissier, 1906). Abbé Jean Desgranges was a staunchly antisocialist/republican priest who participated in some 2,100 *conférence contradictoires* throughout France. See Merriman, *The Red City*, pp. 189–90, 193–94.

86 Paul Levy, "Les Deux antimilitarismes," *L'Aurore*, February 16, 1907. See also "L'Antimilitarisme en Allemagne," *La Guerre Sociale*, March 20–26 and June 12–18, 1907.

87 Robert Michels, "Le Prochain congrès socialiste internationale," *Le Mouvement Socialiste*, July 1907, p. 45. See Félicien Challaye, *Syndicalisme révolutionnaire et syndicalisme réformiste* (Paris: Félix Alcan, 1909), pp. 98–99.

88 Victor Camboulin, *Pour l'armée, réponse à l'antimilitarisme* (Alger-Mustapha, 1906), p. 6.
89 Commandant Driant, *Vers un nouveau Sedan* (Paris: Librairie Félix Juven, 1906), p. 144. This work was immediately translated into German. Gaston Jollivet, *Le Colonel Driant* (Paris: Delagrave, 1918), p. 116, calls it a "cry of anguish."
90 J. Harouée, *La Détresse de l'armée* (Paris: Victor-Harvard et cie., 1904), pp. 1–3, 143.
91 Ibid., pp. 461–66, 1–3.
92 Galinier Osman, *La Raison d'être des armées au XXème siècle: Les véritables causes de guerres possibles,* extrait de conférences données par l'auteur, June 29, 1907 (Oran: Imprimerie du Progrès, 1907), p. 32.
93 Camboulin, *Pour l'armée,* pp. 3–5.
94 André Chéradame, *L'Antimilitarisme?* (Paris: Alix, 1906).
95 James Joll, *The Second International, 1889–1914* (Oxford: Alden and Mowbray, 1974), pp. 115–16.
96 Camboulin, *Pour l'armée,* p. 1.
97 PRO War Office (WO) 33 363. This survey was initiated by Charles à Court Repington, military correspondent for *The Times* (London).
98 Cited in Becker, *Le Carnet B,* pp. 81–82.
99 PP BA1780, Intérieur sûreté à Gouverneur Alger et préfets, September 9 and October 14, 1907.
100 Becker, *Le Carnet B,* pp. 105–8.
101 Ibid., pp. 111, 108.
102 Ibid., pp. 111–12, 116.
103 AN F7/13323, "Les Bourses du Travail et L'antimilitarisme," October 1907.
104 Jacques Julliard, *Clemenceau, briseur de grèves: L'Affaire de Draveil-Villeneuve-Saint-Georges, 1908* (Paris: René Julliard, 1965).
105 PRO FO 371 256, No. 33534, pp. 130–37. See *Journal Officiel de la République Française,* October 7, 1907, pp. 7015–20.
106 *La Patrie,* September 30, 1905.
107 "Les Progrès de l'antimilitarisme," *L'Écho de Paris,* January 15, 1907.
108 AA Frankreich R 6601, No. 1050, Paris, December 9, 1905.

4. Antimilitarist Militants: The Question of Commitment

1 André Lorulot, "L'Antimilitarisme en province," *L'Anarchie,* April 12, 1906.
2 AA Frankreich R 6601, Militärbericht Nr. 10, Paris, February 22, 1906.
3 Lorulot, "L'Antimilitarisme en province." Lorulot wrote "that is the question!" in English.
4 AN F7/12890, Paris, January 13, 1906.
5 It was Malato's idea to draft an *affiche* "identical to that of the condemned *affiche*" (*Le Libertaire,* January 6–13, 1906). Paris officials first reported the *affiche* on February 13, 1906 (AN F7/12890).
6 PP BA1512.
7 AN F7/13324, Paris, October 12 and 17, 1905, November 30, 1905.

8. Laurent Tailhade, *Pour la paix* and *Lettre aux conscrits* (Amiens: Édition le Goût de l'Être, 1987). See the introduction by Thierry Maricourt (pp. 5–10).
9. *L'Action*, October 9, 1905; and Tailhade, *Pour la paix*, pp. 5, 8–9. Tailhade retracted his name and thus was not among those who stood trial. He broke with libertarian anarchism on account of the *affiche rouge*.
10. *Le Libertaire*, January 6–13, 1906.
11. AP D.3.U.6., 102 (Non-lieu correctionels). The case became known as the Affaire Aleix after the first name on Numietska's list—Charles Aleix.
12. Ibid.
13. Ibid. The source of the Yonne article is not identified.
14. Ibid.
15. PP BA1512, Paris, March 14, 1906.
16. PP BA1495, July 4, 1905, October 1905.
17. PP BA1511, Paris, April 26, 1906.
18. AN F7/13324, "L'Antimilitarisme dans la région de l'est," Paris, April 3, 1907.
19. Ibid., "L'AIA à Lyon," September 21, 1907 (Le Préfet du Rhône à Monsieur le Président du Conseil, Sûreté Générale—2è Bureau).
20. Ibid., Nancy, September 26, 1907.
21. Ibid., "L'AIA," October 14, 1907.
22. PP BA1511, Paris, October 12, 1907.
23. Ibid.
24. Ibid., Paris, April 26, 1906, October 12, 1907.
25. AD Loire 19M 32, pp. 31–33.
26. *Le Libertaire*, September 20, 1907.
27. PP BA1511, Paris, October 12, 1907.
28. AN F7/13324, "La Situation actuelle de l'antimilitarisme," Paris, April 3, 1907. See also PP BA1511 on the futile efforts to reform the AIA, especially April 24 and May 4, 1908. Tissier soon fulfilled this prophecy, abandoning anarchism to become an editor for *La Guerre Sociale* (December 18, 1907). Grandidier, always sympathetic to syndicalism, was secretary of the Saint-Denis Bourse. Maitron, *Dictionnaire biographique*, vol. 15, p. 237, and vol. 12, p. 318.
29. AN F7/13324, "L'Antimilitarisme dans la région de l'est."
30. Émile Pouget, *Les Bases du syndicalisme* (Paris: Éditions de La Guerre Sociale, 1910).
31. Gaston Dru, *La Révolution qui vient*, p. 11.
32. Lefranc, *Le Mouvement syndical*, p. 100.
33. Julliard, "La CGT devant la guerre," p. 51.
34. AN F7/12525, Paris, October 19, 1908.
35. F. F. Ridley, *Revolutionary Syndicalism in France, the Direct Action of Its Time* (Cambridge, Eng.: Cambridge University Press, 1979), pp. 176–79. Although most workers did not belong to a union, the *syndicats* still influenced them and could draw on their support. The transient nature of many jobs, union dues, and so forth helped keep the numbers down. For a different reading on the strength of revolutionary syndicalism, see Val R. Lorwin, *The French Labor Movement* (Cambridge, Mass.: Harvard University Press, 1966), pp. 43–46.

36. The reformist federations included the printers, textile workers, railroad workers, and miners. For information on Keufer's Fédération du Livre, see Lefranc, *Le Mouvement syndical*, pp. 409–10, especially the table "Les Effectifs de la CGT à la veille de la guerre de 1914."
37. Drachkovitch, *Les Socialismes français et allemand*, pp. 140–41.
38. Henri Dubief, *Le Syndicalisme Révolutionnaire* (Paris: A. Colin, 1969), pp. 14, 44; J. Hampden Jackson, *Clemenceau and the Third Republic* (New York: Macmillan, 1948), p. 155. Clemenceau employed spies to gather information on the CGT. See also Julliard, *Clemenceau*, pp. 145–66.
39. Ridley, *Revolutionary Syndicalism*, pp. 176–77.
40. Humbert, *Le Mouvement syndical*, p. 97. Reformists were continually suppressed in their attempts to change the voting system.
41. Cited in Drachkovitch, *Les Socialismes français et allemand*, p. 133.
42. Pierre-A. Carcanagues, *Sur le mouvement syndicaliste réformiste* (Paris: Librairie C. Reinwald, 1912), pp. 113–64. One respondent said: "I am, in my way, antimilitarist, you see, but not in the Hervéist sense of the word."
43. AN F7/13323, "Les Bourses du Travail et l'antimilitarisme (Situation au 10 Octobre 1907)." See also AD Loire 19M 32, p. 45, which reports that 93 (out of 153) *bourses* were signaled by prefects as centers of anarchism and antimilitarism as of January 1, 1912. This represents a clear increase in the spread of propaganda in under five years, although the report does not delineate the level and nature of the antimilitarist activity in nearly the detail of the earlier report.
44. Ibid.
45. Merriman, *The Red City*, p. 245. See also Rémy Cazals, *Avec les ouvriers de Mazamet* (Paris: F. Maspero, 1978), for examples of cooperation between socialists and the CGT in this industrial town in the Tarn.
46. AN F7/13323, "Les Bourses du Travail et l'antimilitarisme."
47. Dominique Bertinotti, "L'Antimilitarisme à travers *La Bataille syndicaliste* (thèse de troisième cycle, Paris I, 1975), pp. 183–84.
48. AN F7/13567. This report, also from late 1907, goes by department rather than city. There are discrepancies between these reports, but in general the Nord region is not specified for harboring active antimilitarist *bourses*.
49. Ibid. These are relatively the same as the five "zones" identified by Julliard ("La CGT devant la guerre," p. 56), with the addition of the individual departments. Several reports in late 1907 attempted to assess the regional breakdown. They are not perfectly consistent, and the text represents areas where there was the most consensus.
50. Michael Hanagan, *The Logic of Solidarity: Artisans and Industrial Workers in Three French Towns, 1871–1914* (Urbana: University of Illinois Press, 1980), pp. 192–94.
51. Eugen Weber, *Peasants into Frenchmen: The Modernization of Rural France, 1870–1914* (Stanford: Stanford University Press, 1976), pp. 293–96.
52. Ibid., pp. 292–302.
53. Charles Tilly, "Did the Cake of Custom Break?" in *Consciousness and Class Experience in Nineteenth-Century Europe*, ed. John Merriman (New York: Holmes and Meier, 1979), pp. 17–44.

54 Weber, *Peasants into Frenchman*, p. 297.
55 Jean Masse, "Aperçus sur l'antimilitarisme ouvrier dans le département du Var avant 1914," *Cahiers d'Histoire* 13, no. 2 (1968): 204–6.
56 This sector consisted of mining, clothing industries, food production, and industry directly linked to agriculture such as the manufacture of paper, soap, spirits, and corks.
57 Masse, "Aperçus sur l'antimilitarisme"; Andréani, "L'Antimilitarisme en Languedoc méditerranéen."
58 Tony Judt, *Socialism in Provence, 1871–1914* (Cambridge, Eng.: Cambridge University Press, 1979), pp. 85, 94, 97–98. Judt judges that anarchists "failed to establish themselves in the Var," although he does grant that they were not completely nudged aside by the political successes of socialism. Masse insists anarchism was "formerly if not strongly implanted" in the region.
59 Masse, "Aperçus sur l'antimilitarisme," pp. 193–96.
60 Judt, *Socialism in Provence*, pp. 56–57. There were three arrondissements in the Var and Toulon had its own seat.
61 Masse, "Aperçus sur l'antimilitarisme," p. 196.
62 Ibid., pp. 194–97.
63 AA Frankreich R 6601, Militärbericht Nr. 10, Paris, February 22, 1906.
64 Henri de Noussane, *Enquête sur l'antimilitarisme à Toulon* (Paris: "L'Écho de Paris," 1906), pp. 20–21.
65 Judt, *Socialism in Provence*, pp. 217–38, argues that Var peasants had a good understanding of the socialist ideology that they turned to in the late nineteenth century, as well as how it related to their interests. In other words, they embraced socialism and Guesdism not simply because of the traditional Radical party politics in the region, but in response to their own economic situation.
66 Masse, "Aperçus sur l'antimilitarisme," pp. 206–7.
67 Andréani, "L'Antimilitarisme en Languedoc méditerranéen."
68 Laura Levine Frader, *Peasants and Protest: Agricultural Workers, Politics, and Unions in the Aude, 1850–1914* (Berkeley: University of California Press, 1991), pp. 114–15.
69 Andréani, "L'Antimilitarisme en Languedoc méditerranéen," p. 113. See also "Armée et nation en Languedoc méditerranéen," p. 145.
70 AD Aude 5M 97, Parti Anarchiste en Aude.
71 AD Aude 5M 94, Parti Socialiste, *La Dépêche*, October 21, 1907.
72 AN F7/13567, La Propagande révolutionnaire dans les Bourses du Travail (late 1907, early 1908).
73 Ibid., Propagande antimilitariste et révolutionnaire (October 1911).
74 Ibid., La Propagande révolutionnaire dans les Bourses du Travail.
75 AN F7/13323, Nord—63/102.
76 Jules Maurin, *Armée-guerre-société: Soldats Languedociens, 1889–1919* (Paris: Publications de la Sorbonne, 1982), p. 172. The Béziers anarchist traveled the city on his bicycle singing antimilitarist songs.
77 Becker, *Le Carnet B*, pp. 93–101.
78 Ibid., p. 101.
79 AD Haute Vienne 1M 193, Limoges, March 18, 1905.

80 "L'Antimilitarisme des travailleurs: La Cause première," *Révolution,* March 2, 1909.
81 Rotstein, "The Public Life of Gustave Hervé," pp. 55–58.
82 Becker, "Antimilitarisme et antipatriotisme en France," p. 107.
83 Ibid. See also Maitron, *Dictionnaire biographique,* vol. 13, p. 51; and Hervé, *Mes crimes,* p. 279.
84 Becker, "Antimilitarisme et antipatriotisme en France," p. 107.
85 Rotstein, "The Public Life of Gustave Hervé," pp. 71–72.
86 Rabaut, *L'Antimilitarisme en France,* pp. 92–94.
87 Joll, *The Second International,* pp. 206–8, 140–42.
88 Girardet, *La Société militaire,* p. 232.
89 Stearns, *Revolutionary Syndicalism and French Labor.*
90 PP BA1495, Paris, October 3, 1907.
91 PP BA1511, Paris, October 12, 1907.

5. Glory to the 17th!

1 Émile Faguet, *Le Pacifisme* (Paris: Société Française d'Imprimerie et de Librairie, 1908), p. 316.
2 Stanley J. Kunitz and Vineta Colby, eds. *European Authors, 1000–1900: A Biographical Dictionary of European Literature* (New York: N. H. Wilson, 1967), p. 271; Sir Paul Harvey and J. E. Heseltine, eds., *The Oxford Companion to French Literature* (Oxford: Clarendon Press, 1959), p. 264; Edward Berenson, *The Trial of Madame Caillaux* (Berkeley: University of California Press, 1992), p. 182.
3 Porch, *March to the Marne,* p. 114.
4 Girardet, *La Société militaire,* ch. 7; David B. Ralston, *The Army of the Republic: The Place of the Military in the Political Evolution of France, 1871–1914* (Cambridge, Mass.: MIT Press, 1967), pp. 252–53.
5 Porch, *March to the Marne,* pp. 114–15.
6 *La Petite République* and *Le Matin,* July 10, 1907.
7 *L'Écho de Paris,* September 6, 1907.
8 Porch, *March to the Marne,* p. 115.
9 Ibid., pp. 115–16.
10 PP BA1495, Paris, May 11, 1906.
11 AN F7/13333, XIIè Corps D'Armée, État Major, 1ère section, Limoges, January 31, 1911.
12 AN F7/13324, Rennes, October 28, 1907.
13 AN F7/13323, *L'Humanité,* July 29, 1907.
14 Porch, *March to the Marne,* pp. 115–16.
15 Paul-Marie de la Gorce, *The French Army: A Military-Political History* (New York: George Braziller, 1963), pp. 53–54.
16 Porch, *March to the Marne,* p. 123.
17 Cited in de la Gorce, *The French Army,* pp. 49–50.
18 AN F7/12910.
19 De la Gorce, *The French Army,* p. 50.
20 Alistair Horne, *The French Army and Politics, 1870–1970* (London: Macmillan, 1984), p. 28.

21 Girardet, *La Société militaire*, p. 267.
22 De la Gorce, *The French Army*, p. 54.
23 William-Georges Clément, *D'Où vient l'antimilitarisme? Pourquoi y a-t-il des antimilitaristes? L'Armée telle qu'elle est!* (Paris: Chez l'Auteur, 1907), p. 42.
24 Général Metzinger, *La Transformation de l'armée, 1897–1907* (Paris: Société d'Édition Belleville, 1909), p. 61.
25 Claude Ares, *La Décadence intellectuelle de l'armée* (Paris: Jouve, 1912), p. 117.
26 De la Gorce, *The French Army*, pp. 54–57; and Horne, *The French Army and Politics*, p. 28.
27 Porch, *March to the Marne*, p. 220.
28 Clément, *D'Où vient l'antimilitarisme?*, pp. 5–9.
29 Charles Humbert, *Les Voeux de l'armée: Nos soldats, nos officiers, notre armement* (Paris: Librairie Universelle, 1908), pp. 298–99. See also his *Chinoiseries militaires* (Paris: Henri Charles-Lavauzelle, 1909), pp. 293–94; and A. Messimy, *Considérations générales sur l'organisation de l'armée* (Paris: Henri Charles-Lavauzelle, 1907), pp. 182–83.
30 *Le Journal*, October 12, 1906; *L'Éclair*, June 11, 1907.
31 *Le Petit Parisien*, October 4, 1907.
32 "Les Progrès de l'antimilitarisme," *L'Écho de Paris*, January 15, 1907.
33 Cited in Faguet, *Le Pacifisme*, p. 317.
34 Georges Doutremont, *L'Écho de Paris*: "Les Progrès de l'antimilitarisme," January 15, 1907; "L'Antimilitarisme," March 1907; "Le Péril antimilitariste," April 27, 1907; "L'Antimilitarisme est un rêve," May 6, 1907.
35 "L'Antimilitarisme dans l'armée," *L'Éclair*, June 11, 1907.
36 Faguet, *Le Pacifisme*, p. 317.
37 Jean-Bertrand, "L'Armée socialiste," *Le Petit Sou*, October 3, 1901, p. 1.
38 PP BA1495, Paris, February 19, 1908.
39 Frader, *Peasants and Protests*, p. 140. See also Félix Napo, *1907: La Révolte des vignerons* (Toulouse: Privat, 1971), p. 60.
40 Jean Sagnes, "Les Grèves dans l'Hérault de 1890 à 1938," in *Économie et société en Languedoc-Rousillon de 1789 à nos jours* (Montpellier: Centre d'histoire contemporaine du Languedoc-méditerranéen et du Roussillon, 1978), pp. 251–74; Harvey J. Smith, "Agricultural Workers and the French Wine-Growers Revolt of 1907," *Past and Present* 79 (1978): 100–25.
41 Frader, *Peasants and Protests*, pp. 139–41. At the Carcassonne rally, issues of *La Guerre Sociale* were handed out. See Napo, *1907*, p. 62.
42 Frader, *Peasants and Protests*, p. 140.
43 Guy Bechtel, *1907: La Grande révolte du Midi* (Paris: Éditions Robert Laffont, 1976), pp. 176–214.
44 Napo, *1907*, p. 128; Porch, *March to the Marne*, p. 118.
45 Bechtel, *1907*, p. 236.
46 Ibid., pp. 237–38.
47 Ibid., pp. 238–39. See also Maurice Le Blond, *La Crise du Midi* (Paris: Bibliothèque Charpentier, 1907), p. 379. The *crosse en l'air* (rifle butts in the air) was a gesture of

disrespect made, for example, by the escort who returned Louis XVI to Paris after his attempt to flee during the Revolution.
48 Bechte, *1907*, pp. 240–42; Porch, *March to the Marne*, p. 118.
49 Bechtel, *1907*, pp. 246–53; Napo, *1907*, pp. 132–38.
50 Andréani, Bechtel, Napo, Porch, and Frader see the mutiny in terms of regional solidarity rather than antimilitarist doctrine.
51 Bechtel, *1907*, pp. 255–56.
52 Louis Vilarem, *Pour mes soldats: La Vérité sur la mutinerie du 17è d'infanterie* (Paris: Éditions de l'oeuvre, 1910).
53 Napo, *1907*, p. 138.
54 Maurin, *Armée-guerre-société*, p. 172. See AN F7/12794, 12920, and Archives Militaires (AM) Vincennes, Fonds Gallieni 6N 41, report from Le Général Gallieni, Gouverneur Militaire de Lyon, Commandant le 14è Corps d'Armée à MG, September 27, 1907.
55 *Journal Officiel*, October 4, 1907, p. 988.
56 Ibid., pp. 985–86.
57 From Porch, *March to the Marne*, p. 120.
58 See William Beik, *Absolutism and Society in Seventeenth-Century France: State Power and Provincial Aristocracy in Languedoc* (Cambridge, Eng.: Cambridge University Press, 1985).
59 This is similar to the 1917 mutinies. See Guy Pedrocini, *Les Mutineries de 1917* (Paris: Presses Universitaires de France, 1967).
60 *Journal Officiel*, October 4, 1907, p. 983. Coupillaud put the number of bicyclists at over one hundred.
61 Andréani, "Armée et nation en Languedoc méditerranéen," p. 161. See also AN F7/12910; according to *La Patrie*, July 14, 1907, there were over one hundred protest meetings in Paris and the provinces.
62 PP BA1780, Paris, August 8, 1907.
63 AN F7/13323, *Le Radical*, July 18, 1907. I assume the date June 15 was a mistake. The mutiny took place on June 20–21.
64 Cited in Faguet, *Le Pacifisme*, p. 319. Soldiers under Lecomte and Thomas sympathized with the revolutionary crowd during the Paris Commune.
65 Andréani, "Armée et nation en Languedoc méditerranéen," p. 161; and Bechtel, *1907*, p. 258.
66 Rabaut, *L'Antimilitarisme en France*, p. 101.
67 Porch, *March to the Marne*, p. 119.
68 AM 6N41, Paris, November 6, 1907.
69 Bechtel, *1907*, p. 259.
70 Brossat and Potel, *Antimilitarisme et révolution*, pp. 92–93.
71 See, for example, Samuel P. Huntington, *The Soldier and the State: The Theory and Politics of Civil-Military Relations* (Cambridge, Mass.: Harvard University Press, 1957); and Morris Janowitz, ed., *Civil-Military Relations: Regional Perspectives* (London: Sage, 1981).
72 Leonard V. Smith, *Between Mutiny and Obedience: The Case of the French Fifth Infantry Division during World War I* (Princeton, N.J.: Princeton University Press, 1994).

73 "Leur excuse," *Le Matin*, July 2, 1907; *Le Journal de Genève*, July 3, 1907. Pascal deserted to Geneva on learning that his regiment would be sent to Africa.
74 Porch, *March to the Marne*, p. 119.
75 Ibid., pp. 122–25. Messimy was war minister from July 1911 to January 1912. He was reappointed to the post on June 14, 1914.
76 Maurin, *Armée-guerre-société*, pp. 309–14.
77 *Journal Officiel*, November 29, 1912, p. 2875.
78 AD Loire 19M 32, p. 66.
79 *L'Humanité*, December 31, 1907; *L'Action*, January 1, 1908.
80 *La Bataille syndicaliste*, June 7, 1912. Cited in Bertinotti, "L'Antimilitarisme à travers *La Bataille syndicaliste*, pp. 72–73.
81 "Parti Socialiste (SFIO)—CONTRE LA GUERRE," *L'Humanité*, November 30, 1912.
82 Maitron, *Le Mouvement anarchiste en France 1*, pp. 276–78, 347, 373. *L'Anarchie* appeared from April 13, 1905 until 1914.
83 André Lorulot, "Antimilitarisme et désertion," *L'Anarchie*, August 3, 1905.
84 Levieux, "L'Outil de meurtre," *L'Anarchie*, September 17, 1908.
85 Hael, "Faut-il aller au régiment???," *L'Anarchie*, October 6, 1910.
86 Victor Méric, "Déserteurs," *Le Libertaire*, August 23–30, 1902.
87 Auvray, *Objecteurs, insoumis, déserteurs*, pp. 139–40. AN F7/13332, Paris, August 18, 1913, Congrès Anarchiste Communiste. See also AN F7/13055 (May 31, 1912), and 13056 (Congrès Anarchiste Communiste, Paris 1913).
88 *Le Conscrit*, October 1913.
89 Jean Grave, *La Société mourante et l'anarchie* (Paris: Tresse et Stock, 1893), p. 170.
90 Jean Grave, "Que faire," *Les Temps Nouveaux*, January 30, 1909.
91 Charles Desplanques, "La Désertion," *Les Temps Nouveaux*, December 26, 1908.
92 AN F7/13324.
93 *L'Écho de Paris*, September 13, 1908; *L'Action Française*, September 14, 1908.
94 Masse, "Aperçus," pp. 197–200. See *L'Écho de Paris*, August 16, 1908. See also Henri de Noussane, *Enquête sur l'antimilitarisme à Toulon et la désorganisation de la défense nationale* (Paris: L'Écho de Paris, 1906).
95 Masse, "Aperçus," pp. 203–4.
96 AN F7/13323, Paris, September 25, 1908.
97 Ibid.
98 Ibid.
99 AN F7/13324, Paris, December 2, 1909.
100 "Every non military or non combatant who . . . provokes or furthers desertion is punished by a court of competent jurisdiction to a prison sentence of two months to five years."
101 *L'Humanité*, May 28 and December 8, 1910. Delpech's case was dismissed for lack of evidence.
102 *La Guerre Sociale*, December 21, 1910.
103 AN F7/13324, from the CGT poster "manoeuvres policiers."
104 *La Guerre Sociale*, December 21, 1910.
105 AN F7/13324, December 22, 1910, regarding the Torton affair.
106 Ibid., December 3, 1912.

107 Porch, *March to the Marne*, p. 113.
108 Humbert, *Les Voeux de l'armée*, pp. 130–37.
109 *Le Journal*, December 19, 1910.
110 Humbert, *Les Voeux de l'armée*, p. 136.
111 AN F7/13330, La Solidarité Militaire, April 15, 1909. See also Porch, *March to the Marne*, pp. 198–200.
112 *La Patrie*, April 28, 1909; *L'Écho de Paris*, May 5, 1909; *La Démocratie Sociale*, December 4, 1909; *Les Nouvelles*, January 11–13, 1910.
113 *Les Nouvelles*, January 13, 1910. The War Ministry is on the rue St. Dominique.
114 *L'Armée Moderne*, February 18, 1911.
115 AN F7/13330, Paris, October 13, 1911. Porch, *March to the Marne*, p. 199.
116 AN F7/13330, Paris, October 13, 1911.
117 Ibid., October 24, 1912. See Porch, *March to the Marne*, pp. 199–200.
118 Ibid., Paris, July 25, 1911.
119 Ibid., Paris, January 27, 1913.
120 Les Socialistes et l'armée," *La France*, April 24, 1914.
121 *L'Action Française*, March 5, 1911.
122 *La Libre Parole*, January 29, 1911.
123 AN F7/12910, Paris, June 25, 1907.
124 Ibid., Roanne (Loire), July 14, 1907.
125 AN F7/12910.
126 Ibid., Lyon, July 22, 1907. Twenty defendants were acquitted by the Lyon court. *L'Humanité* (December 1, 1907) announced "acquittement triomphal" and praised Hervé's defense. See also AN F7/13324.
127 Weber, *Nationalist Revival*, p. 46.
128 Albert Lecup, *Avant le dernier cantonnement* (Arras: Imprimerie Central de l'Artois, 1974), pp. 11–12.
129 Henry de Larzelles, *Lettres d'un réserviste* (Paris: H. Charles-LaVauzelle, 1907), pp. 140–41.
130 Ibid., p. 183.
131 Humbert, *Chinoiseries militaires*, pp. 359–60.

6. Antimilitarist Wars I: The Battle Within

1 *L'Écho de Paris*, April 27, 1907.
2 *L'Humanité*, February 19, 1908.
3 AN F7/12910, July 12, 1907.
4 Ibid., July 6 and 12, 1907.
5 André Lorulot, *L'Idole patrie et ses conséquences* (Paris: Éditions de "l'Anarchie," 1910), p. 16. Lorulot was sentenced to three months in jail by the Court of Assizes of Douai (Nord) for this work.
6 AN F7/12910, Paris, September 14, 1907.
7 AN F7/13323, Paris, February 29, 1908.
8 *L'Humanité*, February 25, 1908.
9 J.-P. Granvallet, "Antimilitarisme syndical," *Le Socialisme*, September 5, 1908.

10 Jules Guesde, "Le Parti Socialiste et la Confédération du Travail," in *Bibliothèque du mouvement socialiste*, ed. Hubert Lagardelle (Paris: Marcel Rivière, 1908).
11 Hubert Lagardelle, "Chronique politique et sociale: Antimilitarisme et syndicalisme," *Le Mouvement Socialiste*, January 15, 1906, pp. 121–26.
12 PP BA 1495, Paris, October 3, 1907. The journal was *Le Socialisme*. Leslie Derfler, *Paul Lafargue and the Flowering of French Socialism, 1882–1911* (Cambridge, Mass.: Harvard University Press, 1998), p. 260, argues that Lafargue was increasingly sympathetic toward Hervéism.
13 Gravereaux, *Les Discussions*, p. 105.
14 AN F7/13324, January 1, 1908.
15 Ibid.
16 Ibid., Lyon, May 21, 1908.
17 See Schorske, *German Social Democracy*; Touchard, *La Gauche en France*; Joll, *The Second International*; and Georges Haupt, *Aspects of International Socialism, 1871–1914* (Cambridge, Eng.: Cambridge University Press, 1986).
18 Touchard, *La Gauche en France*, p. 84.
19 PP BA1511, Paris, May 30, 1908.
20 Ibid., December 22, 1908. See also *La Guerre Sociale*, December 16–22, 1908.
21 PP BA1511, December 20, 1908.
22 AN F7/13053, Congrès Anarchiste d'Amsterdam, August 1907, p. 42.
23 PP BA1511, reports of January 4, 6, and 22, 1909. See de Marmande's articles "À la Fédération Révolutionnaire" (April 14, 1909), and "Les Anarchistes et la Fédération Révolutionnaire" (April 7, 1909) in *La Guerre Sociale*. Almereyda was in jail for his articles in *La Guerre Sociale*.
24 PP BA1511, AN F7/13324, February 3, 1909.
25 PP BA1511, January 24, 1909; and PP BA1514, February 26, 1909. The Fédération included Jeunesse syndicalistes; former AIA members; libertarians of the 18th and 19th arrondissements; Jeunesse Révolutionnaire of Lyon, Marseille, and Anger; the Avignon anarchists; and the anarchist group of Amiens, Germinal. See reports of March 31 and April 4 and 28, 1909.
26 AD Loire 19M 32, p. 19.
27 PP BA1511, March 12, 1909.
28 PP BA1514.
29 PP BA1511, BA1514, April 17, 1909.
30 PP BA1513 (June 8, 1912), BA1514; and AD Loire 19M 32.
31 AN F7/13053, "Les Menées anarchistes," 1912. See also "Note—Sur la participation de plus en plus grande des anarchistes aux crimes et délits de droit commun" (January 1912); and PP BA1514, Paris, June 6, 1911.
32 AN F7/13065, "Les Projets de sabotage de la mobilisation"; and AN F7/13328, *Le Mouvement Anarchiste*, "Useful Formulas," prompted a police search of the residences of editors Henri Combes and Georges Durupt, who fled the country. The manager Ruff was arrested. Their disappearance was a "mortal blow" to the journal according to a June 1913 report (AN F7/13053).
33 AN F7/13348. "Les Projets de sabotage de la mobilisation" (July 1914), gives a concise analysis of the brochure (AN F7/13065).

34 AN F7/13348, *Brochure Rouge*, pp. 1–8, 14.
35 Ibid., pp. 14–35.
36 AN F7/13065, "Les Projets de sabotage de la mobilisation" (July 1914).
37 Becker, *Le Carnet B*, p. 51.
38 AN F7/13065, "Les Projets de sabotage de la mobilisation" (July 1914).
39 PP BA1491; for example, the meeting of September 22, 1911.
40 AN F7/13325, 13065.
41 *La Voix du Peuple*, September 2, 1911; "L'Abattoir," *La Bataille Syndicaliste*, October 30, 1911. *La Bataille Syndicaliste* first appeared on April 27, 1911.
42 *La Bataille Syndicaliste* and *L'Humanité*, September 25, 1911.
43 AN F7/13583, Conférence du 1er Octobre. See also Becker, *1914*, p. 87.
44 AN F7/13567, "Les Agissements de la CGT depuis 1er Oct. 1911." See also *La Bataille Syndicaliste*, October 2, 1911. About one hundred delegates "from all corners of France" attended the congress.
45 AN F7/13583, Conférence du 1er Octobre.
46 "Le Sabotage n'est pas une légende," *La Voix du Peuple*, September 27, 1913; "Le Principe d'erreur," *L'Humanité*, September 20, 1913.
47 "Le Parti socialiste et le sabotage," *La Guerre Sociale*, August 30, 1911; "Jaurès et le sabotage," *La Guerre Sociale*, September 17, 1913; "M. Jaurès et le sabotage," *Les Temps Nouveaux*, September 26, 1913; "Le Sabotage ouvrier," *La Guerre Sociale*, October 8–14, 1913; "L'Ouvrier et le sabotage," *La Bataille Syndicaliste*, October 1, 1913; "L'Ouvrier consciencieux et honnête pratique le sabotage intelligent," *La Bataille Syndicaliste*, October 3, 1913; "Sabotage et Politique," *Le Libertaire*, October 4, 1913.
48 "Le Banditisme antimilitariste," *La Liberté*, June 18, 1913. See AN F7/13336, 13325 for reports on incidents of sabotage.
49 Becker, *1914*, p. 99.
50 Goldberg, *The Life of Jean Jaurès*, pp. 351–52, 543 (n. 168).
51 Annie Kriegel, *Aux Origines du communisme français, 1914–1920: Contribution à l'histoire du mouvement ouvrier français* (Paris: Mouton, 1964), p. 49.
52 Jaurès, *L'Armée nouvelle*, especially pp. 54, 98, 389.
53 Ibid., especially pp. 96, 98, 176–77, 391.
54 Ibid., especially pp. 179, 292, 52, 196.
55 Jean-Noël Jeanneney's introduction to Jaurès, *L'Armée nouvelle*, pp. 29–30.
56 Goldberg, *The Life of Jean Jaurès*, p. 388.
57 AN F7/13328, June 17, 1912.
58 AN F7/13065, "Les Projets de sabotage de la mobilisation" (July 1914).
59 *La Guerre Sociale*, June 15–21, 1910.
60 AN F7/13054, "L'Action révolutionnaire en France" (May 1911).
61 AD Loire 19M 32, p. 9; *La Guerre Sociale*, December 14 and 21, 1910. See also AN F7/13054, 13065, "La Lutte contre le sabotage"; and *La Guerre Sociale*, September 14–20, 1910.
62 Cited in AN F7/13054, "L'Action Révolutionnaire en France" (May 1911).
63 AD Loire 19M 32, p. 9.
64 AN F7/13054, 13065, "La Lutte contre le sabotage."
65 AN F7/13054, "L'Action révolutionnaire en France" (May 1911).

66 PP BA1513, May 19, 1912.
67 Eugene Martin, "L'Impénitent," *Bulletin de la Fédération Révolutionnaire Communiste*, January 15, 1912.
68 *La Guerre Sociale*, January 12, 1910. Heuré, *Gustave Hervé*, pp. 176–83.
69 AN F7/12909, "L'Affaire Aernoult-Rousset" (Paris, December 8, 1910). See also AN F7/13331, 13332, 13333, 12908, and PP BA1495, 927, 882, 1780.
70 Ibid.
71 Ibid., and F7/13331, Paris, March 23, 1910.
72 AN F7/13331, February 28, 1910.
73 AN F7/12909, Paris, December 8, 1910.
74 "Biribi" was the term of contempt used to describe the North African military prisons or disciplinary companies.
75 AN F7/13054, "L'Action révolutionnaire en France" (May 1911).
76 AN F7/13331, *L'Humanité*, March 23, 1910.
77 Joseph Hild, *A Propos de Biribi: Une Affaire antimilitariste: Plaidoirie devant la Cour d'Assises de la Seine* (Rodez: Imprimerie Forveille, 1913), pp. 12, 19. Defendants included editors for *Le Libertaire, Le Temps,* and *La Guerre Sociale*.
78 AN F7/13331, *La Guerre Sociale*, July 13, 1910.
79 *La Guerre Sociale*, July 6–12, 1910; *La Voix du Peuple*, June 26–July 3, 1910.
80 AN F7/13054, "L'Action révolutionnaire en France" (May 1911); F7/13332, PP BA1495, 1780, 927. On July 3 the CDS held a meeting that attracted 1,200 participants, including Aernoult's parents and Rousset's brother. Founded in May 1910 by men who had endured disciplinary companies, the Groupe des Libérés des Bagnes Militaires worked for the suppression of these companies. Aubin was a former battleship sailor and member of the electricians' union.
81 *La Guerre Sociale*, March 9, 1910.
82 PP BA927.
83 AN F7/12908, 13331, Paris, June 15, 1910.
84 AN F7/12908, Paris, December 10, 1910. The governor general deemed all exhumation between June 1 and September 30 a danger to public hygiene.
85 Alain Gesgon, *La Mémoire murale politique des français* (Paris: La Conciergerie, 1984), p. 20.
86 AN F7/13331, June 1910.
87 AN F7/12909.
88 PP BA927, Paris, September 19, 1910.
89 Ibid., December 1, 1910.
90 *L'Humanité*, December 16 and 22, 1910.
91 *L'Humanité*, December 28, 1910.
92 "Triumphe militariste," *L'Humanité*, September 14, 1911.
93 PP BA927, December 8, 1911.
94 AN F7/13331, September 26, 1910.
95 "Au Peuple de Paris," *La Guerre Sociale*, February 7, 1912; "Aux Obsèques d'Aernoult," *L'Humanité*, February 9, 1912.
96 *L'Humanité*, February 11, 1912.

97 *La Patrie,* February 11, 1912.
98 PP BA927, February 12, 1912.
99 *La Libre Parole,* February 12, 1912.
100 *Le Matin,* December 12, 1912.
101 *L'Humanité,* February 12, 1912.
102 PP BA927, February 12, 1912.
103 "Les Bienfaits de l'union," *La Guerre Sociale,* February 11, 1912.
104 Francis Delaisi, *Contre la loi Millerand* (Paris: Temps Nouveaux, 1912); "Les Origines de la loi d'infame," *L'Humanité,* December 6 and 10, 1912; "La Loi d'infamie," *La Guerre Sociale,* 31[?] 1912. Only the parts of the law that applied specifically to antimilitarists are given here. See also Georges Bonnefous, *Histoire politique de la troisième république: L'Avant-guerre, 1906–1914* (Paris: Presses Universitaires de France, 1965), p. 309.
105 AN F7/13330, *La Bataille Syndicaliste,* May 31, 1912.
106 PP BA1780, August 14, 1912; see AN F7/13331 on the Comité Féminin.
107 AD Dordogne 4M 206, Perigueux, July 26, 1912.
108 *L'Humanité,* July 8 and 15, 1912; *La Voix du Peuple,* June 30, 1912; *La Bataille Syndicaliste,* July 12, 1912.
109 "La Nouvelle scélérate," *Bulletin de la Fédération Révolutionnaire Communiste,* May 20, 1912.
110 PP BA882.
111 AN F7/13331, September 1, 1912.
112 AN F7/12909, *La Bataille Syndicaliste,* October 6, 1912.
113 AD Dordogne 1M 76.
114 AN F7/12909, October 6, 1912.
115 "Pourquoi Rousset n'est pas venu à Paris," *La Guerre Sociale,* October 9, 1912; "Réponse à La Guerre Sociale," *La Bataille Syndicaliste,* October 19, 1912; "Réponse à une réponse," *La Guerre Sociale,* October 16–22, 1912.
116 "Si la guerre éclate. . . . nous serons prêts," *Le Libertaire,* November 16, 1912.
117 AN F7/13054, "L'Action révolutionnaire en France" (May 1911).
118 Maurice Guichard, "L'Organisation antimilitariste," *La France,* May 25, 1913.
119 André Tardieu, "La Campagne contre la patrie," *Revue des Deux Mondes,* July 1, 1913, pp. 88, 95.
120 Georges Bonnamour, "L'Oeuvre des intellectuels," *L'Éclair,* January 3, 1911; "L'Oeuvre de la CGT," *L'Éclair,* January 4, 1911. For a response, see Eugène Péronnet, "L'Antimilitarisme," *Le Libertaire,* January 14, 1911.
121 PP BA1513, November 6, 1912.

7. Antimilitarist Wars II: The Battle Without

1 AN F7/13333, 13334, and PP BA1431. See Général Percin, *Le Combat* (Paris: Librairie Félix Alcan, 1914), on efforts to make war more comprehensible to ordinary Frenchmen.
2 Becker, *Le Carnet B,* pp. 28–29.
3 AD Loire 19M 33, "Une Oeuvre de la CGT: Le Sou du Soldat" (December 1, 1912).

4 Ibid., pp. 10–16. Towns with a local fund included Auxerre, Bourges, Dun-sur-Auron, Fougères, La Guerche, Lorient, Méhun-sur-Yèvre, Niort, Rennes, St.-Amand (Cher), St.-Nazaire, Vierzon, and Marseille.
5 AN F7/13332, Paris, January 24, 1911.
6 AN F7/13334, Limoges, February 7, 1911.
7 AN F7/13332, Paris, May 8, 1911.
8 AM 5N6, Paris, June 8, 1911.
9 AD Loire 19M 33, pp. 16–20.
10 PP BA1431. See *La Bataille Syndicaliste,* August 11, 1911, for trial coverage.
11 *L'Humanité,* July 7, 1911.
12 *Le Radical, La Bataille Syndicaliste,* July 9, 1911.
13 PP BA882, Paris, August 12, 1911.
14 AN F7/13334, "Les Policiers à la bourse"; *La Bataille Syndicaliste,* July 7, 1911.
15 *La Bataille Syndicaliste,* July 8, 1911.
16 AD Loire 19M 33, pp. 20–26.
17 Ibid., pp. 23–26.
18 Marcel Thomas, *L'Affaire sans Dreyfus* (Paris: Fayard, 1961).
19 *La Guerre Sociale,* January 10, 1912.
20 PP BA1431, Paris, January 10, 1912; and "Le Procès des lois scélérates," *L'Humanité,* November 11, 1912. Baritaud was considered a revolutionary and militant syndicalist, although his name did not appear on the list of principal revolutionaries in Paris, as did those of Dumont and Viau. Dumont was on the Carnet B.
21 PP BA1431; AD Loire 19M 33 estimates twelve thousand demonstrators.
22 *Le Petit Journal,* January 11, 1912.
23 *L'Humanité,* January 20, 1912.
24 AN 14AS 134, "La Caisse fédérale du Sou du Soldat" (April 7–11, 1912).
25 AN F7/13334, Loire (Saint-Etienne), December 16, 1911. A report of January 4, 1912 shows that most prefects did *not* actually find collection boxes.
26 On the role of education in the creation of national identity, see Weber, *Peasants into Frenchmen,* pp. 332–36.
27 Becker, *Le Carnet B,* p. 34. See also Émile Bocquillon, *La Crise du patriotisme à l'école* (Paris: Vuibert-Noiry, 1905).
28 Ibid., p. 35. The dissolution never actually went into effect. After several appeals, an amnesty was voted and the Republic annulled the proceedings. For an example of the collaboration between the CGT and instituteurs, see "Pour les instituteurs" (AN F7/13328).
29 Ibid., p. 36.
30 *Journal Officiel,* November 29, 1912, p. 2875.
31 Becker, *Le Carnet B,* p. 36.
32 *Journal Officiel,* November 29, 1912.
33 Becker, *Le Carnet B,* p. 36.
34 Barnett Singer, "From Patriots to Pacifists: The French Primary School Teachers, 1880–1940," *Journal of Contemporary History* 12 (1977): 417–18.
35 Ibid. This makes a total of 4,800 syndicalist teachers, or 1,200 less than Pugliesi-Conti

counted. Singer points out that most of these teachers were young and from urban areas, and many were upset by the charges of antipatriotism.

36 Jacques Ozouf and Mona Ozouf, "Le Thème du patriotisme dans les manuels scolaires," *Le Mouvement Sociale* 49 (October–December 1964): 5–31.
37 *La Bataille Syndicaliste,* December 23, 1911.
38 Singer, "From Patriots to Pacifists," p. 418.
39 Robert Wohl, *The Generation of 1914* (Cambridge, Mass.: Harvard University Press, 1979), pp. 5–41.
40 Becker, *1914,* pp. 30–52.
41 Weber, *The Nationalist Revival,* p. 8.
42 In Berlin, antiwar demonstrations in 1911 and 1912 drew up to a quarter of a million people.
43 Gerd Krumeich, *Armaments and Politics in France on the Eve of the First World War* (Warwickshire: Berg, 1984), pp. 21–30. See also Christopher M. Andrew, "France and the German Menace," in *Knowing One's Enemies: Intelligence Assessment before the Two World Wars,* ed. Ernest R. May (Princeton, N.J.: Princeton University Press, 1984), pp. 127–28.
44 Krumeich, *Armaments and Politics,* p. 233.
45 Ibid., pp. 30–34.
46 Ferguson, *Pity of War,* p. 16.
47 Cited in Becker, *1914,* p. 28.
48 AN F7/13347, Paris, August 1, 8, and 11, 1913.
49 AN F7/13347, Paris, September 2, 1912.
50 Several right-wing journals noted this in their reports on the Père-Lachaise demonstration. See *La Libre Parole, Le Gaulois,* and *L'Écho de Paris,* which called it "beautiful revenge" for the previous evening (February 12, 1912).
51 *La Guerre Sociale,* August 27–September 27, 1913.
52 "La Guerre, le militarisme," *Les Temps Nouveaux,* September 13 and 20, 1913, pp. 505–18.
53 *La Bataille Syndicaliste,* July 27, 1911.
54 Hans-Ulrich Wehler, *The German Empire, 1871–1918* (New York: Berg, 1985), p. 55.
55 Cited in Bertinotti, "L'Antimilitarisme à travers *La Bataille Syndicaliste,*" pp. 93–94.
56 Rebérioux, "Les Tendances hostiles à l'état dans la S.F.I.O," pp. 35–36. On pre-1914 social legislation, see Noiriel, *Workers in French Society,* pp. 103–4.
57 Milner, *Dilemmas of Internationalism,* p. 172.
58 Krumeich, *Armaments and Politics,* p. 35.
59 See, for example, "Petit conscrit, tu seras soldat!," February 18–25, 1912, and "Leur patriotisme," September 21–28, 1912.
60 Dubief, *Syndicalisme révolutionnaire,* pp. 216–19; Milner, *Dilemmas of Internationalism,* p. 185. Jouhaux, Griffuelhes, C. Voirin, Savoie, and Bled signed the manifesto, which ran in *La Bataille Syndicaliste,* August 20, 1912.
61 Julliard, "La CGT devant la guerre," p. 52.
62 Becker, *1914,* p. 93.
63 Julliard, "La CGT devant la guerre," p. 52.

64 Nicholas Papayanis, *Alphonse Merrheim: The Emergence of Reformism in Revolutionary Syndicalism, 1871–1925* (Dordrecht: Martinus Nijhoff, 1985).
65 Becker, *Le Carnet B*. The congress was attended by 450 people representing 1,450 organizations.
66 Milner, *Dilemmas of Internationalism*, p. 191.
67 Ibid., pp. 190–91. Jouhaux quote is from *La Bataille Syndicaliste*, November 16, 1912.
68 AN F7/13328, Paris, November 28, 1912; December 10, 1912; and the report "La CGT et la sabotage de la mobilisation" (Paris, December 16, 1912).
69 Anarchists criticized harshly the ambiguity and "lack of audacity" of the *congrès extraordinaire* resolution. See AN F7/13330, especially *Le Mouvement Anarchiste*, December 1912, and *Le Libertaire*, December 9, 1912.
70 AN F7/13328, "La CGT et la sabotage de la mobilisation," December 16, 1912.
71 Ibid.
72 *Le Travailleur du Bâtiment*, December 15, 1912.
73 *La Bataille Syndicaliste*, December 16, 1912.
74 AN F7/13328, November 21 and 26, and December 9, 1912.
75 *La Voix du Peuple*, December 15–22, 1912. See also Merrheim's article in *La Bataille Syndicaliste*, December 15, 1912.
76 AN F7/13329, "A la population," Amiens, December 14, 1912.
77 *La Bataille Syndicaliste*, December 30, 1912.
78 AN F7/13328, Paris, December 2, 1912.
79 AD Loire 10M 150. On December 13 the Loire prefect, in response to reports that no definitive resolution had been taken by the department's main worker organizations on what to do December 16, wrote that he did not think the demonstrations would materialize, but worried about the "violent minority" who organized them, and recommended that they be watched "very closely."
80 *La Bataille Syndicaliste*, December 17, 1912, announced the presence of over 110,000 strikers in Paris and 600,000 in France.
81 AN F7/13328, December 16, 1912; Julliard, "La CGT devant la guerre," p. 57, quotes Merrheim's jubilant telegram on how the tramway workers *were* able to paralyze transportation in Lyon: "Magnificent solidarity, transportation stopped, general work stoppage in Lyon. Never seen similar demonstration. Over 50,000 demonstrators, without counting the onlookers."
82 AD Loire 10M 150.
83 Ibid., *La Tribune*, December 17, 1912.
84 AN F7/13329, *La Voix du Peuple*, December 19–January 5, 1912.
85 Julliard, "La CGT devant la guerre," p. 57.
86 *La Bataille Syndicaliste*, December 17, 1912.
87 *Le Petit Parisien*, December 17, 1912.
88 Cited in *La Bataille Syndicaliste*, December 18, 1912.
89 Becker, *1914*, p. 86.
90 *La Bataille Syndicaliste*, December 17, 1912.
91 AN F7/13328, Paris, December 19, 1912.
92 Bertinotti, "L'Antimilitarisme à travers *La Bataille Syndicaliste*," pp. 167–71.
93 Becker, *1914*, pp. 87–89.

94. AN F7/13574, "La Crise des effectifs syndicaux et ses causes," Paris, July 2, 1914.
95. *La Battaile Syndicaliste,* April 29, 1912.
96. PP BA1495, Paris, November 9, 1908.
97. Becker, "Antimilitarisme et antipatriotisme en France," p. 111. See Compère-Morel, *Encyclopédie socialiste,* notes, pp. 81, 152–53: "Hervé only left the prison of Clairvaux for the prison of the Santé or the Conciergerie."
98. Bertinotti, "L'Antimilitarisme à travers *La Bataille Syndicaliste,*" pp. 192–95.
99. Heuré, *Gustave Hervé,* pp. 188, 190.
100. Harold Weinstein, *Jean Jaurès: A Study of Patriotism in the French Socialist Movement* (New York: Columbia University Press, 1936), p. 175.
101. "En sortant de la Conciergerie," *La Guerre Sociale,* July 24, 1912; Rotstein, "The Public Life of Gustave Hervé," pp. 107–8. Hervé served twenty-six months of his sentence.
102. "Le Nouvel Hervéisme," *Le Libertaire,* February 4, 1911.
103. Louis Lecoin, *De Prison en prison* (Antony-Seine: Édité par l'Auteur, 1946), p. 70.
104. Rotstein, "The Public Life of Gustave Hervé," p. 118.
105. Maitron, *Dictionnaire biographique,* vol. 13, p. 52.
106. Heuré, *Gustave Hervé,* p. 198.
107. Becker, "Antimilitarisme et antipatriotisme en France," p. 109; Becker, *1914,* pp. 106–14.
108. Cited in Rotstein, "The Public Life of Gustave Hervé," p. 108.
109. *La Bataille Syndicaliste,* December 8, 1912. Cited in Bertinotti, "L'Antimilitarisme à travers *La Bataille Syndicaliste,*" pp. 68–71.
110. PP BA1513, September 26 and November 6, 1912; See also Rotstein, "The Public Life of Gustave Hervé," pp. 109–11; and Becker, "Antimilitarisme et antipatriotisme en France," p. 110.
111. Rotstein, "The Public Life of Gustave Hervé," pp. 124–25; Becker, "Antimilitarisme et antipatriotisme en France," p. 111. Heuré, in *Gustave Hervé,* p. 203, sees "the paradox of Hervé" as the consequence of "disoriented energy" from a man who now saw clearly, and with great remorse, that his earlier positions had been built on collective illusion and profound naïveté.
112. "14 Juillet 1913," *La Guerre Sociale,* July 9–15, 1913.
113. Krumeich, *Armaments and Politics;* Becker, *La France, la nation, la guerre,* p. 244–45.
114. AN F7/13336, "Contre le retour à la loi de 3 ans," February 27, 1913; *La Voix du Peuple,* May 18–25, 1913.
115. AN F7/13345, July 13, 1913, at the Pré Saint-Gervais.
116. AN F7/13336, 13056; *La Bataille Syndicaliste,* April 14 and May 7, 1913. *Contre les armements, contre la loi de 3 ans, contre tout militarisme* (Édition de propagande de la Fédération Communiste Anarchiste, May 1913).
117. AN F7/13337. On July 3, 1913, *L'Humanité* claimed to have almost 730,000 signatures against the three-year law. In Limoges, an SFIO petition was signed by 10,500 citizens (Merriman, *The Red City,* p. 245). Other anti-three-year law brochures: "Contre la loi des trois ans" (*Bataille Syndicaliste*); Jean Grave, *Contre la folie des armements* (Paris: Les Temps Nouveaux, 1913).
118. AN F7/13335.
119. *L'Humanité,* March 17, 1913. The journal estimated 150,000 to 200,000 protesters.

120 AN F7/13335, Paris, May 26, 1913.
121 AN F7/13056. Italics are mine.
122 AN F7/13336, Castres, March 17, 1913.
123 *La Bataille Syndicaliste*, March 16, 1913.
124 Krumeich, *Armaments and Politics*, pp. 64–70.
125 AN F7/13345, *Le Matin*, May 19, 1913. See also Krumeich, *Armaments and Politics*, pp. 94–102.
126 AN F7/13345, *Le Matin*, May 23, 1913.
127 AN F7/13335.
128 AN F7/13345. See also Krumeich, *Armaments and Politics*, pp. 95–96.
129 *La Bataille Syndicaliste*, May 27, 1913.
130 AN F7/13335, 13336. Besides Paris, the police made searches in Lille, Nancy, Troyes, Brest, Lorient, Orléans, Lyon, Roanne, Marseille, Bordeaux, Rouen, and Clermont-Ferrand.
131 See the picture on the cover of *La Bataille Syndicaliste*, May 27, 1913, depicting Jouhaux in his office with papers strewn all over the floor.
132 *L'Humanité*, May 27, 1913.
133 AN F7/13346, 13332, Paris, December 11, 1913.
134 *La Bataille Syndicaliste*, May 27, 1913.
135 See AN F7/13332, 13347 for examples of propaganda made on the soldiers' behalf.
136 AN F7/13348, January 9, 1914.
137 Becker, *Le Carnet B*, pp. 42–43. The war ended efforts to repeal the law.
138 *La Bataille Syndicaliste*, June 22, 1913.

Epilogue: En Avant!

1 Rotstein, "The Public Life of Gustave Hervé," p. 126. Hervé was refused permission to join the army because of his myopia. In acknowledgment of his support for the Republic, however, he was reinstated to the bar (*Le Bonnet Rouge*, August 8, 1914).
2 Drachkovitch, *Les Socialismes français et allemand*, p. 153.
3 AN F7/13348, Paris, July 29 and 31, 1914. On July 28 the syndicalist leader Bled argued: "Since the government is favorable to maintaining peace, is [it] not the duty of the workers to support it?" Jouhaux asserted: "We could not decree the general strike in France, since the government focused its efforts on the maintenance of peace."
4 Georges Dumoulin, *Les Syndicalistes français et la guerre* (Paris: Éditions de la Bibliothèque de Travail, 1921), p. 22.
5 "Guerres impossibles," *La Bataille Syndicaliste*, July 31, 1914.
6 Annie Kriegel, *Aux Origines du communisme français*, p. 60.
7 Alfred Rosmer, *Le Mouvement ouvrier pendant la guerre: De l'Union sacrée à Zimmerwald* (Paris: Librairie du Travail, 1936), pp. 95–96.
8 Becker and Kriegel, *1914*, p. 64, quote from the Congrès Extraordinaire des Bourses et Fédérations (October 1, 1911).
9 AN F7/13348.
10 AN F7/13053, Paris, July 20, 1914.
11 AN F7/13348, Paris, July 27, 1914.

12. Rosmer, *Le Mouvement ouvrier pendant la guerre*, pp. 97–98.
13. AN F7/13348. Demonstrators gathered outside the offices of *Le Matin*, which was pushing particularly hard for war.
14. Ibid., Paris, July 29, 1914; *La Bataille Syndicaliste*, July 31, 1914.
15. AN F7/13574, Paris, July 31, 1914.
16. Rosmer, *Le Mouvement ouvrier pendant la guerre*, p. 106.
17. AN F7/13574, Paris, July 31, 1914.
18. Ibid., August 1, 1914.
19. Rosmer, *Le Mouvement ouvrier pendant la guerre*, pp. 97–98.
20. *La Bataille Syndicaliste*, July 28, 1914.
21. Rosmer, *Le Mouvement ouvrier pendant la guerre*, pp. 107–8.
22. "Pas d'affolement," *La Bataille Syndicaliste*, August 1, 1914.
23. Philippe Bernard, *La Fin d'un monde, 1914–1929* (Paris: Seuil, 1975), p. 6.
24. "Honte de la guerre," *La Bataille Syndicaliste*, July 28, 1914.
25. "Abolissons les guerres," *La Bataille Syndicaliste*, July 28, 1914.
26. "Au Bord du gouffre," *La Bataille Syndicaliste*, July 27, 1914.
27. Rosmer, *Le Mouvement ouvrier pendant la guerre*, pp. 114–15.
28. On August 4 Poincaré declared: "In the war that is beginning, France . . . will be heroically defended by all its young men, who will never break the *union sacrée* before the enemy."
29. AN F7/13574, "À la CGT," Paris, August 6, 1914. Several militant syndicalists rejoined their regiments, including Lapierre, Minot, Pericat, Sene, Marchand, and Morel. Dumoulin left for Amiens on the third day; Jouhaux and Lenoir were mobilized on the twenty-first day. Yvetot, Bled, and Dumas were, like Hervé, declared unfit for service and discharged.
30. Jean-Jacques Becker, in *The Great War and the French People* (Dover, N.H.: Berg, 1983), pp. 84–85, shows how minimal war resistance was in France in August 1914. Pierre Monatte's *Pourquoi je démissionne du comité fédéral* was the only protest against the CGT's support for the government.
31. Becker, *1914*, pp. 365–485. Becker sees the *union sacrée* as a "truce" between the varying groups, political and otherwise.
32. AN F7/13348, Paris, October 31, 1914.
33. From Auvray, *Objecteurs, insoumis, déserteurs*, p. 150.
34. Rosmer, *Le Mouvement ouvrier pendant la guerre*, p. 143.
35. Ibid., p. 118.
36. *Le Bonnet Rouge*, August 2, 1914. In this piece Almereyda writes of trying to enlist in the army but being told by the interior minister that for now "men like you are more useful in Paris than at the frontier."
37. Rosmer, *Le Mouvement ouvrier pendant la guerre*, pp. 143–44, 117–18.
38. Michel Baumont, "Gustave Hervé et la 'Guerre Sociale' pendant l'été 1914 (July 1– November 1)," *Information Historique* (September–October 1968): 156.
39. Ibid., p. 157. According to one report (AN F7/13574, Paris, August 6, 1914), the CGT, inspired by the Russian revolutionary Bakounin, also fought to establish a Germanic Republic.
40. *La Guerre Sociale*, January 2, 1915. *La Victoire* had great success, printing over eighty

thousand issues by late October 1916 (Bellanger, *Histoire générale de la presse française*, vol. 3, pp. 437–38). Hervé's nationalist shift continued through the interwar years. Most famously and prophetically, in 1936 he penned *C'est Pétain qu'il nous faut* (Paris: Éditions de la Victoire, 1936).

41 Gravereaux, *Les discussions*, p. 255.

42 For an account of how the government's decision not to implement the Carnet B came about, see Annie Kriegel's long footnote in *Aux Origines du communisme français*, p. 57.

43 AN F7/13348, "NOTE—Sur l'attitude de la CGT et de l'Union Syndicale de la Seine pendant la période de crise qui a précédé la mobilisation et depuis l'ouverture des hostilités" (Paris, October 31, 1914).

44 Ibid., "La CGT la guerre" (Paris, August 6, 1914).

45 "L'Entr'aide," *Le Bonnet Rouge*, August 3, 1914.

46 AN F7/13348, Paris, August 7, 1914.

47 Rosmer, *Le Mouvement ouvrier pendant la guerre*, p. 126 (From *La Bataille Syndicaliste*, August 24, 1914).

48 *La Bataille Syndicaliste*, August 5–13, 1914.

BIBLIOGRAPHY

Archival Sources

1. ARCHIVES NATIONALES (PARIS)
Administration Général (Series F): F7 (Police): 12885–91, 12908–11, 13053–56, 13065, 13074–75, 13323–40, 13345–49, 13367, 13370–76, 13567, 13574, 13581, 13583, 13790
Archives Sociales (Series AS): 14AS 39, 14AS 134–36, 14AS 145, 14AS 222, 14AS 236, 14AS 264, 14AS 266, 14AS 480, 14AS 492

2. ARCHIVES DE LA PRÉFECTURE DE LA POLICE (PARIS)
Series BA: 882, 889, 913, 927, 1431, 1491, 1495, 1511–14, 1533, 1558, 1780

3. ARCHIVES DÉPARTEMENTALES DE PARIS (VILLEMOISSON)
D.3.U.6—Non-lieu correctionnels, 1821–1924, Cartons 5, 71, 101, 102, 112, 114, 115, 150, 152

4. ARCHIVES MILITAIRES (VINCENNES)
5N6, 5N371, 6N41

5. ARCHIVES DÉPARTEMENTALES (SERIES M)
Loire (Saint-Etienne): 10M 95, 10M 130, 10M 139, 10M 150, 10M 158, 19M 2, 19M 24, 19M 31, 19M 32, 19M 33, 19M 35, 19M 38
Aude (Carcassonne): 5M 97, 5M 94
Archives Municipales de Narbonne: *La République Sociale* (journal)
Haute-Vienne (Limoges): 1M 193
Dordogne (Perigueux): 1M 76, 4M 206.

6. BIBLIOTHÈQUE DE DOCUMENTATION INTERNATIONALE CONTEMPORAINE (BDIC), UNIVERSITÉ PARIS X–NANTERRE

7. POLITISCHES ARCHIV DES AUSWÄRTIGEN AMTS (BONN, GERMANY)
Allgemeinen Angelegenheiten Frankreich: R 6601, 6602, 6603, 6608

8. PUBLIC RECORD OFFICE (KEW, ENGLAND)
Foreign Office (FO): 371 69, 371 72, 371 255, 371 256, 371 454, 371 456, 371 897, 371 13565, 33 363, 262
War Office (WO): 33 363

Newspapers and Journals

L'Action
L'Action Antimilitariste
L'Anarchie
L'Antipatriotisme
Aux Conscrits (Association internationale antimilitariste, 1906)
L'Avant Garde
La Bataille Syndicaliste
Le Bonnet Rouge
Bulletin de l'Association Internationale Antimilitariste
Bulletin de la Fédération Révolutionnaire Communiste
Le Conscrit, organe d'agitation antipatriotique
Le Conscrit, organe de la Fédération des Jeunesses Socialistes de France
Le Conseiller Militaire (Bulletin mensuel de renseignements publié par le Sou du Soldat)
Contre la Guerre
Le Cri du Peuple
Le Cri du Soldat (Bulletin non officiel des Armées de Terre et de Mer)
L'Égalité
L'Ennemi du Peuple
La Griffe
La Guerre Sociale
L'Humanité
Le Journal Officiel
Le Libertaire
Le Monde
Le Mouvement Anarchiste
Le Mouvement Social
Le Parti Ouvrier
Le Parti Socialiste
Le Père Peinard
Le Petit Parisien
Le Petit Sou
La Petite République
La République Sociale (département de Midi)
La Revue des Grandes Procès Contemporain
La Revue Socialiste
Le Socialisme
Les Temps Nouveaux

Le Travailleur du Bâtiment (Organe de la Fédération Nationale des Travailleurs de l'Industrie du Bâtiment de France et des Colonies)
Le Travailleur Socialiste de l'Yonne
La Vie Ouvrière
La Voix du Peuple

Printed Primary Sources

Albert, Charles. *Patrie, guerre, caserne: Lettre à un prolétaire*. Paris: Les Temps Nouveaux, 1911.

André, Général Louis. *Cinq ans de ministère*. Paris: L. Michaud, 1909.

Angell, Norman. *The Great Illusion*. London: William Heinemann, 1910.

Ares, Claude. *La Décadence intellectuelle de l'armée*. Paris: Jouve, 1912.

Armand, E. *Le Refus de service militaire et sa véritable signification*. Rapport présenté au congrès antimilitariste international d'Amsterdam, juin 1904. Paris: Édition de l'Ère Nouvelle, 1904.

Bernhardi, Friedrich Adam Julius von. *Germany and the Next War*. London: E. Arnold, 1912.

Bocquillon, Émile. *La Crise du patriotisme à l'école*. Paris: Vuibert-Noiry, 1905.

Bonnamour, George. *Enquête sur l'antimilitarisme*. Paris: La Renaissance Française, 1911.

Bonnetain, F. *Autour de la caserne*. Paris: Havard, 1885.

Boudenoot, Léon. "L'Armée en 1903: Questions militaires résolues ou traitées de 1899 à 1903." *Revue politique et parlementaire* 35 (1903): 5–39.

Bourgin, Hubert. *La Guerre pour la paix*. Paris: Marcel Rivière & Cie., 1915.

Brialmont, Général. *Antimilitarisme: Causes et dangers*. Paris: Henri Charles-Lavauzelle, 1898.

Calinaud, Léon. *Antimilitariste et antipatriote, pourquoi?* Paris: Édité par les Soins de l'Union de la Voiture et de la Jeunesse Syndicaliste de la Voiture, 1912.

Camboulin, Victor. *Pour l'armée, réponse à l'antimilitarisme*. Alger-Mustapha, 1906.

Carcanagues, Pierre-A. *Sur le mouvement syndicaliste réformiste*. Paris: Librairie C. Reinwald, 1912.

Challaye, Félicien. *L'Armée internationale*. Paris: Colin, 1908.

———. *Syndicalisme révolutionnaire et syndicalisme réformiste*. Paris: Félix Alcan, 1909.

Chardon, Pierre. *Le Mirage patriotique*. Orléans: Imprimerie Ouvrière, Éditions de la Jeunesse Syndicaliste de Châteauroux (Indre), 1913.

Charmes, Francis. "Chronique de la quinzaine." *La Revue des Deux Mondes* 15 (June 1, 1913): 709–20.

Charnay, Maurice. *Catéchisme du soldat*. Paris, 1894.

Chéradame, André. *L'Antimilitarisme?* Paris: Alix, 1906.

Clément, William-Georges. *D'Où vient l'antimilitarisme? Pourquoi y a-t-il des antimilitaristes? L'Armée telle qu'elle est!* Paris: Chez l'Auteur, 1907.

Compère-Morel, Adéodat, ed. *Encyclopédie socialiste, syndicale et coopérative de l'internationale ouvrière*. "La France Socialiste," by Hubert Rouger. Paris: A. Quillet, 1912.

Confédération Générale du Travail. *Le Prolétariat contre la guerre et les trois ans, s.d.* Paris, 1913.

Contre la Guerre. Paris: Les Temps Nouveaux, 1911.

Corre, Armand. *Aperçu général de la criminalité militaire en France.* Paris: G. Steinheil, 1891.

———. *Militarisme.* Paris: Édition de la Société Nouvelle, 1894.

Couté, Gaston. *La Chanson d'un gas qu'a mal tourné.* Paris: Eugène Rey Éd., 1928.

Crosse en l'air: Le Mouvement ouvrier et l'armée, 1900–1914. Paris: F. Maspero, 1970.

Darien, Georges. *Biribi, discipline militaire.* Paris: Albert Savine, 1890.

———. *L'Ennemi du peuple, compte rendu du congrès antimilitarisme d'Amsterdam en 1904.* Paris: Réédition Champ Libre, 1972.

———. *L'Ennemi du peuple, précédé de crève la démocratie!* par Yann Cloarec. Paris: Éditions Champ Libre, 1972.

———. *L'Épaulette: Souvenirs d'un officier.* Paris: E. Fasquelle, 1905.

———. *Georges Darien et Édouard Dubus: Les Vrais sous-offs, réponse à M. Descaves.* Paris: A. Savine, 1892.

Dave, Victor. *Pacifisme et antimilitarisme.* Paris: Petite Bibliothèque, n.d.

D'Avrigny, Lucien. *L'Armée et la crise sociale.* Paris: Armée et Démocratie, 1911.

Delaisi, Francis. *Contre la loi Millerand.* Paris: Temps Nouveaux, 1912.

———. *La Guerre qui vient.* Paris: Édition de La Guerre Sociale, 1911.

Descaves, Lucien. *Sous-offs, roman militaire.* Paris: Tresse et Stock, 1889.

Desgranges, L'Abbé. *Le Sillon contre l'antimilitarisme: L'Abbé Desgranges contre Gustave Hervé.* Joigny: Librairie Tissier, 1906.

Devaldès, Manuel. *La Chair à canon.* Paris: Éd. de Génération Consciente, 1908.

Driant, Commandant E. *Vers un nouveau Sedan.* Paris: Librairie Félix Juven, 1906.

Dru, Gaston. *La Révolution qui vient, enquête sur le syndicalisme révolutionnaire.* Paris: Édition de L'Écho de Paris, 1906.

Dubois, Félix. *Le Péril anarchiste.* Paris: E. Flammarion, 1894.

Dubois-Desaulles, Gaston. *Camisards, peaux de lapins et corps disciplinaires de l'armée française.* Paris: Éditions de la Reine Blanche, 1901.

———. *Sous la casaque: Notes d'un soldat.* Paris: P.-V. Stock, 1899.

Escholier, Raymond, ed. *Souvenirs parlés de Briand.* Paris: Librairie Hachette, 1932.

Faguet, Émile. *Le Pacifisme.* Paris: Société Française d'Imprimerie et de Librairie, 1908.

———. *Le Socialisme en 1907.* Paris: Société Française d'Imprimerie et de Librairie, 1907.

Faure, Sébastien. *Les Anarchistes et l'affaire Dreyfus.* Paris: Fourneau, 1993.

Ferrero, Guglielmo. *Le Militarisme et la société moderne.* Paris: Stock, 1899.

Fèvre, Henri. *Au Port d'armes.* Paris, 1887.

France, Anatole. *Le Mannequin d'osier.* Paris: Calmann-Lévy, 1897.

———. *Monsieur Bergeret à Paris.* Paris: Calmann-Lévy, 1901.

Fried, Alfred H. *Les Bases du pacifisme: Le Pacifisme réformiste et le pacifisme "révolutionnaire."* Paris: Pedonne Éditeur, 1909.

Galinier, Osman. *La Raison d'être des armées au XXè siècle: Les Véritables causes de guerres possibles.* Oran: Imprimerie du Progrès, 1907.

Gérard-Varet, L. *L'Antipatriotisme.* Coulommiers: Imprimerie Paul Brodard, 1909.

Girard, André. *L'Enfer militaire*. Paris: Publication des Temps Nouveaux, 1911.

Girault, Ernest. "La Crosse en l'air." Alfortville (Seine): Édition du Bureau de Propagande, Librairie Internationaliste, 1906.

——. *Travailleur, tu ne voteras point! Soldat, tu ne tireras pas!* Puteaux: La Cootypographie (Société Ouvrière d'Imprimerie), n.d.

Gohier, Urbain. *L'Antimilitarisme et la paix: Plaidoirie prononcée en cour d'assises de la Seine, le 28 décembre 1905*. Paris: Chez l'Auteur, 1906.

——. *L'Armée contre la nation*. Paris: Éditions de la Revue Blanche, 1898.

——. *L'Armée nouvelle*. Paris: P.-V. Stock, 1897.

——. *Aux Femmes*. Paris: L'Homme Libre, 1904.

——. *A Bas la caserne*. Paris: La Revue Blanche, 1908.

——. *Menaces du sans-patrie Hervé, le camarade de caserne*. Paris, August 1916.

Gotlib, Jan. *The Future of War in Its Technical, Economic, and Political Relations: Is War Now Impossible?* New York: Doubleday & McClure, 1899.

Grave, Jean. *L'Anarchie, son but, ses moyens*. Paris: Stock, 1924.

——. *La Colonisation*. Paris: Les Temps Nouveaux, 1900.

——. *Contre la folie des armements*. Paris: Les Temps Nouveaux, 1913.

——. *La Société mourante et l'anarchie*. Paris: Tresse et Stock, 1893.

——, ed. *Guerre-militarisme*. Paris: Les Temps Nouveaux, 1902.

Gravereaux, Louis. "Les Discussions sur le patriotisme et le militarisme dans les congrès socialistes." Thèse de droit, Paris, 1913.

Griffuelhes, Victor. *L'Action syndicaliste*. Paris: Librairie des Sciences Politiques et Sociales, Marcel Rivière et Cie., 1908.

——. "Les Caractères du syndicalisme français." In *Bibliothèque du mouvement socialiste: Syndicalisme et socialisme*, ed. Hubert Lagardelle. Paris: Marcel Rivière, 1908.

Guennebaud, Lieutenant. *La Vie à la caserne au point de vue social*. Saint-Brieuc: René Prudhomme, 1906.

Guesde, Jules. "Le Parti Socialiste et la Confédération du Travail." In *Bibliothèque du mouvement socialiste*, ed. Hubert Lagardelle. Paris: Marcel Rivière, 1908.

——. *Questions d'hier et d'aujourd'hui*. Paris: V. Gard et E. Brière, 1911.

Guétant, Louis. *Enquête sur la guerre et le militarisme*. Paris: C. Reinwald, 1899.

Guieysse, Charles. *La France et la paix armée: La Conférence de la Haye*. Paris: Librairie de "Pages Libres," 1905.

Halevy, Daniel. *Essais sur le mouvement ouvrier en France*. Paris: Société Nouvelle de Librairie et d'Édition, 1901.

Hamon, Augustin. *Psychologie du militaire professionnel—essai sur l'influence du milieu sur la forme de la criminologie*. Paris: La Revue Socialiste, 1894.

Harouée, Jacques. *La Détresse de l'armée*. Paris: Victor-Havard et Cie., 1904.

Hermant, Abel. *Le Cavalier Misery, 21e chasseurs*. Paris: Charpentier, 1887.

Hervé, Gustave. *L'Alsace Lorraine*. Paris: Éditions de La Guerre Sociale, 1913.

——. *C'est Pétain qu'il nous faut*. Paris: Éditions de la Victoire, 1936.

——. *Le Congrès de Stuttgart et l'antipatriotisme*. Paris: Éditions de La Guerre Sociale, 1907.

——. *Histoire de la France et de l'Europe: L'Enseignement pacifique par l'histoire*. Paris: Bibliothèque d'Éducation, 1903.

———. *L'Internationalisme*. Paris: V. Giard and E. Brière, 1910.
———. *Leur patrie*. Paris: l'Auteur, 1906.
———. *Mes Crimes, ou onze ans de prison pour délits de presse: Modeste contribution à l'histoire de la liberté de la presse sous la Troisième République*. Paris: Éditions de La Guerre Sociale, 1912.
———. *My Country, Right or Wrong?* London: A. C. Fifield, 1910.
———. *La Patrie en danger*. (*La Guerre Sociale* from 1 July to 1 November 1914). Paris: Bibliothèque des Ouvrages Documentaires, 1915.
Hild, Joseph. *A Propos de Biribi: Une Affaire anti-militariste; plaidoirie devant la cour d'assises de la Seine*. Rodez: Imprimerie Forveille, 1913.
Humbert, Charles. *Chinoiseries militaires*. Paris: Henri Charles-Lavauzelle, Éditeur Militaire, 1909.
———. *Les Voeux de l'armée: Nos soldats, nos officiers, notre armement*. Paris: Librairie Universelle, 1908.
Janvion, Émile. *L'École, antichambre de caserne et de sacristie*. Paris: Éditions du Groupe de Propagande par la Brochure, 1908.
Jaurès, Jean. *L'Armée nouvelle*. Paris: Imprimerie Nationale, 1992.
———. *Pages choisies, de Jean Jaurès*. Paris: Les Éditions Rieder, 1928.
Jollivet, Gaston, *Le Colonel Driant*. Paris: Delagrave, 1918.
Jouhaux, Léon. *Le Syndicalisme français et Contre la guerre*. (Recueil d'articles et de discours liés à la campagne contre les Trois Ans.) Vol. 14, La Bibliothèque du mouvement prolétarien. Paris: Rivière, 1913.
Kropotkine, Pierre. *La Guerre*. Paris: Les Temps Nouveaux, 1912.
Lafargue, Paul. *Le Patriotisme de la bourgeoisie*. Paris: L'Émancipatrice, Imprimerie Communiste, 1913.
Lagardelle, Hubert. "Chronique politique et sociale: Antimilitarisme et syndicalisme." *Le Mouvement Socialiste*, January 15, 1906, pp. 121–26.
———. *La Grève générale et le socialisme: Enquête internationale, opinions et documents*. Paris: E. Cornély et Cie., 1905.
———. "L'Idée de patrie et le socialisme." In *Le Mouvement Socialiste* 6 (May–August, 1906).
———. *Le Parti Socialiste et la Confédération du Travail*. Paris: Marcel Rivière, 1908.
———. "Le Syndicalisme et le socialisme en France." In *Bibliothèque du mouvement socialiste: Syndicalisme et socialisme*, ed. Hubert Lagardelle. Paris: Marcel Rivière, 1908.
Lamarque, Louis. *Un An de caserne*. Paris: P.-V. Stock, 1901.
Larzelles, Henri de. *Lettres d'un réserviste*. Paris: H. Charles-LaVauzelle, 1907.
Le Blond, Maurice. *La Crise du Midi, étude historique, suivie de la publication des rapports des fonctionnaires civils et militaires sur les événements du Midi*. Paris: Bibliothèque Charpentier, 1907.
Lecoin, Louis. *Le Cours d'une vie*. Paris: Chez l'Auteur, 1965.
———. *De Prison en prison*. Antony-Seine: Édité par l'Auteur, 1946.
Lecup, Albert. *Avant le dernier cantonnement*. Arras: Imprimerie Central de l'Artois, 1974.
Le Tosca, Maurice. *Ce que c'est que d'être antimilitariste*. Alger: Édition du Journal La Pensée Libre, n.d.
Liebknecht, Karl. *Militarism and Anti-militarism*. Glasgow: Socialist Labour Press, 1917.

Longuet, Jean. *Le Mouvement socialist international*. Paris: A. Quillet, 1913.

———. *Les Socialistes allemands contre la guerre et le militarisme*. Paris: Librairie de la SFIO, 1913.

Lorulot, André. *L'Idole patrie et ses Conséquences*. Paris: Éditions de "l'Anarchie," 1910.

Marmande, R. de. *Émile Rousset et l'enquête du lieutenant Pan Lacroix: Étude d'après la correspondance d'Émile Rousset*. Paris: Librairie Schleicher, 1912.

May, André. *Les Origines du syndicalisme révolutionnaire: Évolution des tendances du mouvement ouvrier, 1871–1906*. Paris: Jouve, 1913.

Meric, Victor. *Lettre à un conscrit*. Paris: Publication de l'Association Internationale Antimilitariste, 1904.

———. "Vielles choses, vielles histoires: Souvenirs d'un militant." *Nouvelle Revue Socialiste* (December 5, 1925).

Messimy, Adolphe-Marie. *Considérations générales sur l'organisation de l'armée*. Paris: Henri Charles-Lavauzelle, Éditeur Militaire, 1907.

Metzinger, Général. *La Transformation de l'armée, 1897–1907*. Paris: Société d'Édition Belleville, 1909.

Millerand, A. *Pour la défense nationale: Une Année au ministère de la guerre (14 janvier 1912–12 janvier 1913)*. Paris: E. Fasquelle, 1913.

Monatte, Pierre. "La Légende d'Arrocourt." *La Vie Ouvrière*, December 20, 1912.

———. *Syndicalisme révolutionnaire et communisme*. Paris: Maspero, 1968.

Le Mouvement ouvrier français contre la guerre, 1914–1918. Paris: Éditions d'Histoire Sociale, 1985.

Nieuwenhuis, Domela. *Rapport: Sur le militarisme et l'attitude des anarchistes et socialistes révolutionnaires en cas de guerre entre les nations*. Paris: Les Temps Nouveaux, 1913.

Noussane, Henri de. *Enquête sur l'antimilitarisme à Toulon et la désorganisation de la défense nationale*. Paris: L'Écho de Paris, 1906.

Osman, Galinier. *La Raison d'être des armées au XXème siècle: Les véritables causes de guerres possibles*. Extraits de conférences données par l'auteur, June 29, 1907. Oran: Imprimerie du Progrès, 1907.

Pédoya, Jean-Marie. *L'Armée évolue*. Paris: Chapelot, 1908.

Péguy, Charles. "Notre jeunesse." *Cahiers de la Quinzaine*, 2, no. 2. Paris, 1910.

———. *Notre jeunesse*. Paris: Cahiers de la Quinzaine, 1957.

———. *Oeuvres complètes de Charles Péguy, 1873–1914*. Paris: Gallimard, 1952.

Percin, Général. *Le Combat*. Paris: Librairie Félix Alcan, 1914.

Pouget, Émile. *Antimilitarisme*. Almanach du Père Peinard. Paris, 1894.

———. *Les Bases du syndicalisme*. Paris: Éditions de La Guerre Sociale, 1910.

———. *La Confédération générale du travail*. Bibliothèque du mouvement socialiste. Paris: Marcel Rivière, 1908.

———. *Le Père peinard*. Paris: Éditions Galilée, 1976.

———. *Syndicat*. Paris: Bibliothèque Syndicaliste, n.d.

Le Procès des antimilitaristes, Plaidoirie prononcée le 25 Juin 1907 devant la Cour d'Assises de la Seine par Me Jacques Bonzon, avocat à la Cour de Paris. Paris: Liberté d'opinion, 1907.

Proudhon, P. J. *La Guerre et la paix*. Paris: Marcel Rivière, 1927.

Rappoport, Charles. *Socialisme de gouvernement et socialisme révolutionnaire*. Paris: Alcan-Lévy, n.d.

Rey, Étienne. *La Renaissance de l'orgueil français*. Paris: B. Grasset, 1912.

Rolland, Romain. *Au-Dessus de la mêlée*. Paris: Ollendorff, 1915.

Rullier, Jean. *L'Anti-militarisme socialiste, son origine, son développement, ses causes*. Reims: Action Populaire, 1913.

Saint Jouan. *Digues sociales: Un anarchiste au régiment*. Paris: Flammarion, 1903.

Sembat, Marcel. *Faites un roi, sinon faites la paix*. Paris: Eugène Figuière et Cie., 1913.

Severac, Jean Baptiste. *Le Mouvement syndical*. Paris: A. Quillet, 1913.

Simon, Paul. *L'Instruction des officiers, l'éducation des troupes et la puissance nationale*. Paris: H. Charles-Lavauzelle, 1905.

Sorel, Georges. *Reflections on Violence*. Glencoe, Ill.: Free Press, 1950.

Stackelberg, Frédéric. *Mystification patriotique et solidarité prolétarienne*. Paris: Éditions de La Guerre Sociale, 1907.

Suttner, Bertha von. *Lay Down Your Arms (Die Waffen Nieder!)*. London: Longmans, Green, 1894.

Tailhade, Laurent. *Imbéciles et gredins*. Paris: Robert Laffont, 1969.

———. *Pour la paix* et *Lettre aux Conscrits*. Amiens: Édition le Goût de l'Être, 1987.

Tanger, Albert. *Contre le fratricide*. Paris: Parti Socialiste Révolutionnaire, n.d.

Tardieu, André. "La Campagne contre la Patrie." In *Revue des Deux-Mondes,* vol. 16. Paris: Bureau de la Revue des Deux Mondes, 1913.

Thomas, Albert. *La Politique socialiste*. Paris: Marcel Rivière, 1913.

Tolstoy, Leo. *War and Peace*. London: Penguin, 1982.

Vaillant, Edouard. *Suppression de l'armée permanente et des conseils de guerre*. Paris: Bibliothèque du Parti Socialiste de France, n.d.

Verfeuil, Raoul. *Pourquoi nous sommes anti-militaristes?* Villeneuve-Saint-Georges: Imprimerie Coopérative Ouvrière, 1913.

Vidal, Joseph. *Histoire et statistique de l'insoumission*. Paris: M. Giard et E. Brière, 1913.

Vignée d'Octon, Paul. *Les Crimes coloniaux de la troisième république*. Paris: La Guerre Sociale, 1911.

———. *La Gloire du sabre*. Paris: Flammarion, 1900.

———. *La Nouvelle gloire du sabre (documents pour servir à l'histoire de la guerre (1re série) 1914–1918. Les Crimes du service de santé et de l'état-major général de la marine. Suivi du véritable scandale des pensions (le cas de Jean Millerand)*. Marseille: Petite Bibliothèque du Mutilé, 1922.

Vilarem, Louis. *Pour mes soldats: La Vérité sur les mutineries du 17è d'infanterie*. Paris: Éd. de L'Oeuvre, 1910.

Vingtras, J. *Socialisme et patriotisme*. Lille: Imprimerie ouvrière de P. Lagrange, 1900.

Yvetot, Georges. *Nouveau manuel du soldat: La Patrie, l'armée, la guerre*. 4th ed. Paris: Fédération des Bourses du Travail, 1902.

———. *Le Syndicalisme: Les Intellectuels et la CGT*. Paris: La Publication Sociale, 1907.

———. *La Vache a lait (lettre à un Saint-Cyrien)*. Paris: Édition de l'Internationale Anti-militariste, 1905.

Zola, Émile. *The Debacle*. London: Penguin, 1972.

Secondary Works

Agulhon, Maurice. *Marianne au pouvoir*. Paris: Flammarion, 1989.

Almond, Gabriel A., and Sidney Verba. *The Civic Culture: Political Attitudes and Democracy in Five Nations*. Princeton, N.J.: Princeton University Press, 1963.

Andréani, Roland. "L'Antimilitarisme en Languedoc méditerranéen avant la première guerre mondiale." *Revue d'Histoire Moderne et Contemporaine* 20 (January–March 1973): 104–23.

———. "Armée et nation en Languedoc méditerranéen, 1905–14." Thèse de troisième cycle d'histoire, Montpellier, 1975.

Andrew, Christopher M. "France and the German Menace." In *Knowing One's Enemies: Intelligence Assessment before the Two World Wars*, ed. Ernest R. May. Princeton, N.J.: Princeton University Press, 1984, 127–49.

———. *Théophile Delcassé and the Making of the Entente Cordiale*. New York: St. Martin's Press, 1968.

Aron, Raymond. *Paix et guerre entre les nations*. Paris: Calmann-Lévy, 1962.

———. *La Société industrielle et la guerre*. Paris: Plon, 1959.

Audoin-Rouzeau, Stéphane. *1870: La France dans la guerre*. Paris: Armand Colin, 1989.

Auvray, Michel. *Objecteurs, insoumis, déserteurs: Histoire des réfractaires en France*. Paris: Stock, 1983.

Bainville, Jacques. *La Troisième république, 1870–1935*. Paris: Fayard, 1935.

Barrows, Susanna. *Distorting Mirrors: Visions of the Crowd in Late-Nineteenth-Century France*. New Haven, Conn.: Yale University Press, 1981.

Baumont, Michel. "Gustave Hervé et La Guerre Sociale pendant l'été 1914 (1 juillet–1 novembre)." *Information Historique* (September–October, 1968): 155–63.

Beales, A. C. F. *The History of Peace: A Short Account of the Organized Movements for International Peace*. New York: The Dial Press, 1931.

Bechtel, Guy. *1907: La Gande révolte du Midi*. Paris: Éditions Robert Laffont, 1976.

Becker, Jean-Jacques. "Antimilitarisme et antipatriotisme en France avant 1914: Le Cas de Gustave Hervé." In *Enjeux et Puissances*. Paris: Publications de la Sorbonne, 1986. 101–13.

———. "L'Appel de guerre en dauphiné." *Le Mouvement Social* 49 (October–December 1964): 33–45.

———. *Le Carnet B: Les Pouvoirs publics et l'antimilitarisme avant la guerre de 1914*. Paris: Éditions Klincksieck, 1973.

———. *The Great War and the French People*. Dover, N.H.: Berg, 1985.

———. "Gustave Hervé, Vom revolutionärem Syndikalismus zum Neobonapartismus." In *Die Geteilte Utopie, Sozialisten in Frankreich und in Deutschland*, ed. Marielwise Christadler. Oplanden: Leske und Budrich, 1985.

———. *1914: Comment les français sont entrés dans la guerre*. Paris: Presse de la Fondation Nationale des Sciences Politiques, 1977.

Becker, Jean-Jacques, and Stéphane Audoin-Rouzeau. *La France, la nation, la guerre: 1850–1920*. Paris: Sedes, 1995.

Becker, Jean-Jacques, and Annie Kriegel. "Les Inscrits au 'Carnet B': Dimensions, composition, physionomie politique et limite du pacifisme ouvrier." *Le Mouvement Social* 65 (October–December 1968): 109–20.

———. *1914: La Guerre et le mouvement ouvrier français.* Paris: A. Colin, col. Kiosque, 1964.

Beik, William. *Absolutism and Society in Seventeenth-Century France: State Power and Provincial Aristocracy in Languedoc.* Cambridge, Eng.: Cambridge University Press, 1985.

Bellanger, Claude et al., *Histoire générale de la presse française.* Paris: Presses Universitaires de France, 1972.

Berenson, Edward. *The Trial of Madame Caillaux.* Berkeley: University of California Press, 1992.

Bergeron, Louis. *France under Napoleon.* Princeton, N.J.: Princeton University Press, 1981.

Berghahn, Volker. *Militarism: The History of an International Debate, 1861–1979.* Warwickshire: Berg, 1984.

Bernard, Philippe. *La Fin d'un monde, 1914–1929.* Paris: Seuil, 1975.

Bertier de Sauvigny, Guillaume de. *La Restauration.* Paris: Flammarion, 1955.

Bertinotti, Dominique. "L'Antimilitarisme à travers 'La Bataille Syndicaliste' (avril 1911–décembre 1912)." Thèse de troisième cycle, Paris I, 1975.

Bertrand, Jean-Pierre. *Les Soldats seront troubadours.* Paris: Les Presses D'Aujourd'hui, 1979.

Best, Geoffrey. *Humanity in Warfare.* New York: Columbia University Press, 1980.

Blanc, Jacques. "L'Idée antimilitariste dans les milieux anarchistes et syndicalistes en France de 1919–1924." Thèse de troisième cycle, Paris I, 1971.

Bonet, Pierre. "Montéhus." Mémoire de maîtrise, multigraphié. Paris: Centre d'Histoire du Syndicalisme, 1970.

Bonnefous, Georges. *Histoire politique de la troisième république: L'Avant-guerre, 1906–1914.* Paris: Presses Universitaires de France, 1965.

Bourgin, Hubert. *Le Parti contre la patrie.* Paris: Plon-Nourrit et Companie, 1924.

Bozon, Michel. *Les Conscrits.* Paris: Berger-Levrault, 1981.

Brécy, Robert. *Le Mouvement syndical en France: Essai bibliographique.* Paris-La Haye: Mouton, 1963.

Bredin, Jean-Denis. *The Affair: The Case of Alfred Dreyfus.* New York: George Braziller, 1986.

Brock, Peter. *Pacifism in Europe to 1914.* Princeton, N.J.: Princeton University Press, 1972.

Brogan, D. W. *The Development of Modern France, 1870–1939.* London: Hamish Hamilton, 1967.

Brossat, Alain, and Jean-Yves Potel, eds. *Antimilitarisme et révolution: Anthologie de l'antimilitarisme révolutionnaire.* Paris: Union Générale d'Éditions, 1975.

Brubaker, Rogers. *Citizenship and Nationhood in France and Germany.* Cambridge, Mass.: Harvard University Press, 1992.

Burns, Michael. *Rural Society and French Politics: Boulangism and the Dreyfus Affair.* Princeton, N.J.: Princeton University Press, 1984.

Cahm, Éric. *The Dreyfus Affair in French Society and Politics.* London: Longman, 1996.

———. *Péguy et le nationalisme français: De l'affaire Dreyfus à la grande guerre.* Paris: Cahiers de l'Amitié Charles Péguy, 1972.

Carrias, Eugène. *La Pensée militaire française.* Paris: Presses Universitaires de France, 1960.

Carroll, E. Malcolm. *French Public Opinion and Foreign Affairs, 1870–1914.* Hamden: Archon Books, 1964.

Carsten, F. L. *War against War: British and German Radical Movements in the First World War.* Berkeley: University of California Press, 1982.

Cazals, Rémy. "Antimilitarisme dans l'Aude en 1913." *Viure à l'Escola* 14 (May 1977).

———. *Avec des ouvriers de Mazamet.* Paris: F. Maspero, 1978.

———. *Les Carnets de guerre de Louis Barthas, tonnelier 1914–1918.* Paris: Éditions de la Découverte, 1987.

Ceadel, Martin. *Thinking about Peace and War.* Oxford, Eng.: Oxford University Press, 1987.

Cesarani, David, and Mary Fulbrook, eds. *Citizenship, Nationality, and Migration in Europe.* New York: Routledge, 1996.

Challener, Richard D. *The French Theory of the Nation in Arms, 1866–1939.* New York: Columbia University Press, 1955.

Chapman, Guy. "The French Army in Politics." In *Soldiers and Governments,* ed. Michael Howard. London: Eyre and Spottiswoode, 1957.

Charron, Christian. "L'Antimilitarisme et son expression littéraire à la fin du XIXè siècle en France, 1886–1902." Thèse pour le doctorat de troisième cycle, littérature française, Bordeaux, 1977.

Chatfield, Charles, and Peter van den Dungen, eds. *Peace Movements and Political Cultures.* Knoxville: University of Tennessee Press, 1988.

Chickering, Roger. *Imperial Germany and a World without War.* Princeton, N.J.: Princeton University Press, 1975.

Cohen, Yolande. *Les Jeunes, le socialisme et la guerre: Histoire des mouvements de jeunesse en France.* Paris: L'Harmattan, 1989.

Collinet, Michel. "Les Saint-Simoniens et l'armée," *Revue Française de Sociologie* (April–June 1961): 38–47.

Cooper, Sandi E. "Pacifism in France, 1889–1914: International Peace as a Human Right." *French Historical Studies* 17, no. 2 (fall 1991): 359–86.

———. *Patriotic Pacifism: Waging War on War in Europe, 1815–1914.* New York: Oxford University Press, 1991.

Daline, V. M. "La C.G.T. au début de la première guerre mondiale." *Annuaire d'Études Française* (1964): 219–53.

———. "Hervé et Domela Nieuwenhuis." *Annuaire d'Études Française* (1966): 261–67.

Dallas, Gregor. *At the Heart of a Tiger: Clemenceau and His World, 1841–1929.* London: Macmillan, 1993.

Dalotel, Alain, Alain Faure, and Jean-Claude Freiermuth. *Aux Origines de la commune: Le Mouvement des réunions publiques à Paris 1868–1870.* Paris: F. Maspero, 1980.

Derfler, Leslie. *Paul Lafargue and the Flowering of French Socialism, 1882–1911.* Cambridge, Mass.: Harvard University Press, 1998.

Digeon, Claude. *La Crise allemande de la pensée française, 1870–1914.* Paris: Presses Universitaires de France, 1959.

Dommanget, Maurice. "Gustave Hervé et l'affaire du drapeau dans le fumier." *Révolution prolétarienne* 92 (1955): 22–24.

———. *Histoire du drapeau rouge des origines à 1939.* Paris: Librairie de l'Étoile, 1967.

———. *Histoire du premier mai.* Paris: Éditions de la Tête de Feuilles, 1972.

Drachkovitch, Milorad M. *Les Socialismes français et allemand et le problème de la guerre, 1870–1914.* Geneva: Librairie E. Droz, 1953.

Dubief, Henri. *Les Anarchistes (1870–1914).* Paris: A. Colin, 1972.

———. *Le Syndicalisme révolutionnaire.* Paris: A. Colin, 1969.

Dumoulin, Georges. *Les Syndicalistes français et la guerre.* Paris: Éditions de la Bibliothèque de Travail, 1921.

Edwards, Stewart. *The Communards of Paris, 1871.* Ithaca, N.Y.: Cornell University Press, 1973.

———. *The Paris Commune, 1871.* New York: Quadrangle Books, 1971.

Ellis, Jack D. *The French Socialists and the Problem of Peace.* Chicago: Loyola University Press, 1967.

Ferguson, Niall. *The Pity of War.* New York: Basic Books, 1999.

Ferré, Max. *Histoire du mouvement syndicaliste révolutionnaire chez les instituteurs, des origines à 1922.* Paris: S.U.D.E.L., 1935.

Ferro, Marc. *La Grande guerre, 1914–1918.* Paris: Éditions Gallimard, 1969.

Fiechter, Jean-Jacques. *Le Socialisme français de l'affaire Dreyfus à la grande guerre.* Geneva: Droz, 1965.

Fitzgerald, Edward P. "Émile Pouget, the Anarchist Movement, and the Origins of Revolutionary Trade-Unionism in France, 1880–1901." Ph.D. dissertation, Yale University, 1974.

Fleming, Marie. *The Anarchist Way to Socialism: Elisée Reclus and Nineteenth-Century European Anarchism.* Totowa, N.J.: Rowman and Littlefield, 1979.

Frader, Laura Levine. *Peasants and Protests: Agricultural Workers, Politics, and Unions in the Aude, 1850–1914.* Berkeley: University of California Press, 1991.

Freymond, Jacques. *Études et documents sur la première internationale.* Geneva: Droz, 1962.

Frossard, Ludovic Oscar. *Le Parti socialiste et l'internationale.* Paris: Librairie de l'Humanité et du Parti Socialiste, 1920.

Garmy, René. *Histoire du mouvement syndical en France, des origines à 1914.* Paris: Bureau d'Éditions, 1933.

———. *Histoire du mouvement syndical en France, de 1914 à nos jours.* Paris: Bureau d'Éditions, 1934.

Georges, Bernard, and Denise Tintant. *Léon Jouhaux: Cinquante années de syndicalisme.* Paris: Presses Universitaires de France, 1962.

Gesgon, Alain. *La Mémoire murale politique des français.* Paris: La Conciergerie, 1984.

Girardet, Raoul. *Le Nationalisme français, 1871–1914.* Paris: Presses Universitaires de France, 1959.

———. "Pour une introduction à l'histoire du nationalisme français." *Revue Française de Science Politique,* vol. 8, no. 3 (1958).

———. *La Société militaire dans la France contemporaine, 1815–1939.* Paris: Librairie Plon, 1953.

Goetz-Girey Robert. *La Pensée syndicale française.* Paris: Armand-Colin, 1948.

Goldberg, Harvey. *The Life of Jean Jaurès.* Madison: University of Wisconsin Press, 1962.

Gorce, Paul-Marie de la. *The French Army: A Military-Political History.* New York: George Braziller, 1963.

Grave, Jean. *Le Mouvement libertaire, sous la troisième république.* Paris: Oeuvres Représentatives, 1930.

Gruzinska, Aleksandra. "Octave Mirbeau antimilitariste." *Nineteenth-Century Studies* 4, nos. 1, 2 (fall–winter 1975–76): 394–403.

Guerlac, Othon. *Les Citations françaises: Recueil de passages célèbres, phrases familières, mots historiques.* Paris: A. Colin, 1931.

Guès, André. "Le Pacifisme avant 1914." *Itinéraires* 167 (November 1972): 63–74.

Hanagan, Michael P. *The Logic of Solidarity: Artisans and Industrial Workers in Three French Towns, 1871–1914.* Urbana: University of Illinois Press, 1980.

Harvey, Sir Paul, and J. E. Heseltine, eds. *The Oxford Companion to French Literature.* Oxford: Clarendon Press, 1959.

Haupt, Georges. *Aspects of International Socialism, 1871–1914.* Cambridge, Eng.: Cambridge University Press, 1986.

———. "Guerre ou Révolution? L'Internationale et l'union sacrée en août 1914." *Les Temps Modernes* 281 (December 1969): 839–73.

———. *Socialism and the Great War: The Collapse of the Second International.* Oxford: Clarendon Press, 1972.

Heuré, Gilles. *Gustave Hervé: Itinéraire d'un provocateur.* Paris: La Découverte, 1997.

Horne, Alistair. *The French Army and Politics, 1870–1970.* London: Macmillan, 1984.

Howard, Michael. *The Lessons of History.* New Haven, Conn.: Yale University Press, 1991.

———. *War and the Liberal Conscience.* London: Temple Smith, 1978.

Humbert, Sylvain. *Le Mouvement syndical.* Paris: Librairie Marcel Rivière, 1912.

Huntington, Samuel P. *The Soldier and the State: The Theory and Politics of Civil-Military Relations.* Cambridge, Mass.: Harvard University Press, 1957.

Ingram, Norman. *The Politics of Dissent: Pacifism in France, 1919–1939.* Oxford: Oxford University Press, 1991.

Jackson, J. Hampden. *Clemenceau and the Third Republic.* New York: Macmillan, 1948.

Janowitz, Morris, ed. *Civil-Military Relations: Regional Perspectives.* London: Sage, 1981.

Joll, James. *The Anarchists.* Cambridge, Mass.: Harvard University Press, 1980.

———. *The Origins of the First World War.* London: Longman, 1984.

———. *The Second International, 1889–1914.* Oxford: Alden and Mowbray, 1974.

Judt, Tony. *Socialism in Provence, 1871–1914.* Cambridge, Eng.: Cambridge University Press, 1979.

Julliard, Jacques. "La CGT devant le problème de la guerre, 1900–1914." *Mouvement Social* 49 (October–December 1964): 47–62.

———. *Clemenceau, briseur de grèves: L'Affaire de Draveil-Villeneuve-Saint-Georges (1908).* Paris: René Julliard, 1965.

———. *Fernand Pelloutier et les origines du syndicalisme d'action directe.* Paris: Seuil, 1971.

Keegan, John. *The First World War.* New York: Knopf, 1999.

Keiger, John F. V. *France and the Origins of the First World War.* New York: St. Martin's Press, 1983.

Kennedy, Paul M. *The Rise and Fall of the Great Powers: Economic Change and Military Conflict from 1500 to 2000*. New York: Vintage, 1989.

Keylor, William R. *The Twentieth-Century World: An International History*. New York: Oxford University Press, 1984.

Kriegel, Annie. *Aux Origines du communisme français, 1914–1920: Contribution à l'histoire du mouvement ouvrier français*. Paris: Mouton, 1964.

——. "Jaurès, le Parti Socialiste et la CGT à la fin de juillet 1914." *Bulletin de la Société d'Études Jauressiennes* 7 (October–December 1962): 63–77.

——. "Patrie ou révolution, le mouvement ouvrier français devant le problème de la guerre (juillet-août 1914)." *Revue d'histoire Économique et Sociale* 43, no. 3 (1965): 363–86.

Krumeich, Gerd. *Armaments and Politics in France on the Eve of the First World War: The Introduction of Three-Year Conscription, 1913–1914*. Warwickshire: Berg, 1984.

Kunitz, Stanley J., and Vineta Colby, eds. *European Authors, 1000–1900: A Biographical Dictionary of European Literature*. New York: N. H. Wilson, 1967.

Langevin, Vige. *Catalogue de l'exposition Jules Grandjouan, Musée des Beaux-Arts de Nantes* (27 juin–10 octobre 1969). Nantes: S. Chiffoleau, 1969.

Lefranc, Georges. *Histoire du mouvement syndical français*. Paris: Librairie Syndical, 1937.

——. *Le Mouvement socialiste sous la troisième république (1875–1940)*. Paris: Payot, 1963.

——. *Le Mouvement syndical sous la troisième république*. Paris: Payot, 1967.

Lorwin, Louis. *Syndicalism in France*. New York: Columbia University Press, 1914.

Lorwin, Val R. *The French Labor Movement*. Cambridge, Mass.: Harvard University Press, 1966.

Loubère, Leo A. "Left-Wing Radicals, Strikes, and the Military, 1880–1907." *French Historical Studies* 3 (1963): 93–105.

Lyons, Martyn. *Napoleon Bonaparte and the Legacy of the French Revolution*. London: Macmillan, 1994.

Maitron, Jean. *Le Mouvement anarchiste en France, des origines à 1914*. Vol. 1. Paris: Gallimard, 1975.

——. *Ravachol et les anarchistes*. Paris: Éditions Gallimard/Julliard, 1964.

——, ed. *Dictionnaire biographique du mouvement ouvrier français*. Paris: Éditions Ouvrières, 1964–1993.

Marchal, André. *Le Mouvement syndical en France*. Paris: Bourrelier, 1945.

Margadant, Ted W. *French Peasants in Revolt: The Insurrection of 1851*. Princeton, N.J.: Princeton University Press, 1979.

Masse, Jean. "Aperçu sur l'antimilitarisme ouvrier dans le département du Var avant 1914." *Cahiers d'Histoire* 13, no. 2 (1968): 193–207.

Maurin, Jules. *Armée-guerre-société: Soldats languedociens (1889–1919)*. Paris: Publications de la Sorbonne, 1982.

Mayoux, Marie, et François Mayoux. *Les Instituteurs syndicalistes et la guerre*. Section de la Charente de la FNSI, 1917.

Merle, Marcel. *Pacifisme et internationalisme XVIIe–XXe siècles*. Paris: A. Colin, 1966.

Merriman, John. *The Agony of the Republic: The Repression of the Left in Revolutionary France, 1848–1851*. New Haven, Conn.: Yale University Press, 1978.

——. *The Red City: Limoges and the French Nineteenth Century*. New York: Oxford University Press, 1985.

———, ed. *Consciousness and Class Experience in Nineteenth-Century Europe*. New York: Holmes and Meier, 1979.
Meyer-Spiègler, Madeleine. "Antimilitarisme et refus du service militaire dans la France contemporaine." 2 vols. Thèse de doctorat de recherches d'études politiques, Bibliothèque de la Fondation des Sciences Politiques, Paris, 1969.
Michon, Georges. *La Préparation à la guerre: La Loi de 3 ans (1910–1914)*. Paris: Marcel Rivière, 1935.
Millet, Raymond. *Léon Jouhaux et la CGT*. Paris: Denoël, 1937.
Milner, Susan. *The Dilemmas of Internationalism: French Syndicalism and the International Labor Movement, 1900–1914*. New York: Berg, 1991.
Mitchell, Allan. *The German Influence in France after 1870: The Formation of the French Republic*. Chapel Hill: University of North Carolina Press, 1979.
Mitchell, Barbara. *The Practical Revolutionaries*. Westport, Conn.: Greenwood Press, 1987.
Morris, A. J. Anthony. *Radicalism against War, 1906–1914: The Advocacy of Peace and Retrenchment*. London: Longman, 1972.
Napo, Félix, *1907: La Révolte des vignerons*. Toulouse: Privat, 1971.
Nord, Philip. *The Republican Moment: Struggles for Democracy in Nineteenth-Century France*. Cambridge, Mass.: Harvard University Press, 1995.
Noiriel, Gérard. *Workers in French Society in the 19th and 20th Centuries*. New York: Berg, 1990.
Ozouf, Jacques, and Mona Ozouf. "Le Thème du patriotisme dans les manuels scolaires." *Le Mouvement Social* 49 (October–December 1964): 5–31.
Papayanis, Nicholas. *Alphonse Merrheim: The Emergence of Reformism in Revolutionary Syndicalism, 1871–1925*. Dordrecht: Martinus Nijhoff, 1985.
Paraf, Pierre. *Le Syndicalisme pendant et après la guerre*. Paris: Édition de la vie universitaire, 1923.
Pedrocini, Guy. *Les Mûtineries de 1917*. Paris: Presses Universitaires de France, 1967.
Peyronnet, Jean-Claude. "Un Exemple de journal militant: La Guerre Sociale de Gustave Hervé (1906–1914)." Diplôme d'études supérieures, Université de Paris, 1963.
Picard, Roger. *Le Mouvement syndical durant la guerre*. Paris: Presses Universitaires de France, 1927.
Porch, Douglas. *The March to the Marne: The French Army, 1871–1914*. Cambridge, Eng.: Cambridge University Press, 1981.
Poulet, F., and J.-M. Cordier. *Le Mouvement anarchiste français et la guerre, 1914–1939*. Paris: C.H.S., 1971.
Préposiet, Jean. *Histoire de l'anarchisme*. Paris: Librairie Jules Tallandier, 1993.
Rabaut, Jean. *L'Antimilitarisme en France, 1810–1975: Faits et documents*. Paris: Librairie Hachette, 1975.
———. *Féministes à la belle époque*. Paris: France-Empire, 1985.
Ralston, David B. *The Army of the Republic: The Place of the Military in the Political Evolution of France, 1871–1914*. Cambridge, Mass.: MIT Press, 1967.
Rebérioux, Madeleine. "La Gauche socialiste française: *La Guerre Sociale* et *Le Mouvement Socialiste* face au problème coloniale." *Le Mouvement Social* 46 (January–March 1964): 91–103.
———. *La République radicale, 1898–1914*. Paris: Seuil, 1975.

———. *Le Socialisme français de 1871 à 1914*. Paris: Presses Universitaires de France, 1974.

———. "Les Tendances hostiles à l'état dans la S.F.I.O., 1905–1914." *Le Mouvement Social* 65 (October–December 1968): 21–37.

Rémond, René. *The Right Wing in France: From 1815 to De Gaulle*. Philadelphia: University of Pennsylvania Press, 1969.

Ridley, F. F. *Revolutionary Syndicalism in France, the Direct Action of Its Time*. Cambridge, Eng.: Cambridge University Press, 1970.

Rosmer, Alfred. *Le Mouvement ouvrier pendant la guerre: De L'Union sacrée à Zimmerwald*. Paris: Librairie du Travail, 1936.

Rossignol, Denise. *Le Mouvement socialiste en France de 1906 à 1914*. Paris: Faculté des Lettres-Sorbonne, 1960.

Rotstein, Maurice. "The Public Life of Gustave Hervé." Ph.D. dissertation, New York University, 1956.

Sagnes, Jean. "Les Grèves dans l'Hérault de 1890 à 1938." In *Économie et société en Languedoc-Rousillon de 1789 à nos jours*. Montpellier: Centre d'histoire contemporaine du Languedoc-méditerranéen et du Roussillon, 1978. 251–74.

Scher, Michael Roger. "The Anti-Patriot as Patriot: A Study of the Young Gustave Hervé." Ph.D. dissertation, University of California at Los Angeles, 1972.

Schorske, Carl E. *German Social Democracy, 1905–1917: The Development of the Great Schism*. Cambridge, Mass.: Harvard University Press, 1955.

Scott, Joan W. "Mayors versus Police Chiefs: Socialist Municipalities Confront the French State." In *French Cities in the Nineteenth Century*, ed. John Merriman. London: Hutchinson, 1982. 230–45.

Seager, Frederic H. *The Boulanger Affair: Political Crossroads of France, 1886–1889*. Ithaca, N.Y.: Cornell University Press, 1969.

Seignobos, Charles. *L'Évolution de la troisième république, 1875–1914*. Paris: Hachette, 1952–62.

Serman, William. *Les Officiers français dans la nation, 1848–1914*. Paris: Éditions Aubier Montaigne, 1982.

Servet, Claude, and Paul Bouton. *La Trahison socialiste de 1914*. Paris: Bureau d'Éditions, 1931.

Shorter, Edward L., and Charles Tilly. "Le Déclin de la grève violente en France de 1890 à 1935." *Le Mouvement Social* 76 (July–September 1971): 95–118.

———. *Strikes in France, 1830–1968*. London: Cambridge University Press, 1974.

Singer, Barnett. "From Patriots to Pacifists: The French Primary School Teachers, 1880–1940." *Journal of Contemporary History* 12 (1977): 413–34.

Slater, Catherine. *Defeatists and Their Enemies: Political Invective in France, 1914–1918*. New York: Oxford University Press, 1981.

Smith, J. Harvey. "Agricultural Workers and the French Wine-Growers' Revolt of 1907." *Past and Present* 79 (1978): 101–25.

Smith, Leonard V. *Between Mutiny and Obedience: The Case of the French Fifth Infantry Division during World War I*. Princeton, N.J.: Princeton University Press, 1994.

Stargardt, Nicholas. *The German Idea of Militarism: Radical and Socialist Critics, 1866–1914*. Cambridge, Eng.: Cambridge University Press, 1994.

Stearns, Peter N. *Revolutionary Syndicalism and French Labor: A Cause without Rebels*. New Brunswick, N.J.: Rutgers University Press, 1971.

Sternhell, Zeev. *La Droite révolutionnaire, 1885–1914: Les Origines françaises du fascisme.* Paris: Seuil, 1978.

———. *Ni Droite ni gauche, l'idéologie fasciste en France.* Paris: Seuil, 1983.

Tanenbaum, Jan Karl. "French Estimates of Germany's Operational War Plans." In *Knowing One's Enemies: Intelligence Assessment Before the Two World Wars,* ed. Ernest R. May. Princeton, N.J.: Princeton University Press, 1984. 150–71.

Thomas, Marcel. *L'Affaire sans Dreyfus.* Paris: Fayard, 1961.

Thomson, David. *Democracy in France since 1870.* London: Oxford University Press, 1969.

Tison, Robert. "L'Opinion publique française et la loi des 3 ans." Paris: Publications de la Sorbonne, 1967.

Tombs, Robert. *The War against Paris, 1871.* Cambridge, Eng.: Cambridge University Press, 1981.

Touchard, Jean. *La Gauche en France depuis 1900.* Paris: Seuil, 1977.

———. *La Gloire de Béranger.* Paris: Armand Colin, 1968.

Trotnow, Helmut. *Karl Liebknecht: A Political Biography.* Hamden, Conn.: Archon Book, 1984.

Vagts, Alfred A. *A History of Militarism: Civilian and Military.* New York: The Free Press, 1959.

Viard, Jacques. *Les Oeuvres posthumes de Charles Péguy.* Paris: Cahiers de l'Amitié, 1969.

Waldinger, Renée, Philip Dawson, and Isser Woloch, eds. *The French Revolution and the Meaning of Citizenship.* Westport, Conn.: Greenwood Press, 1993.

Wank, Solomon, ed. *Doves and Diplomats: Foreign Offices and Peace Movements in Europe and America in the Twentieth Century.* Westport, Conn.: Greenwood Press, 1978.

Weber, Eugen. *France: Fin de siècle.* Cambridge, Mass.: Belknap, 1986.

———. *The Nationalist Revival in France, 1905–1914.* Berkeley: University of California Press, 1959.

———. *Peasants into Frenchmen: The Modernization of Rural France, 1870–1914.* Stanford: Stanford University Press, 1976.

Wehler, Hans-Ulrich. *The German Empire, 1871–1918.* New York: Berg, 1985.

Weill, Georges. *Histoire du mouvement social en France.* Paris: F. Alcan, 1924.

Weinstein, Harold R. *Jean Jaurès: A Study of Patriotism in the French Socialist Movement.* New York: Columbia University Press, 1936.

Wells, Charlotte C. *Law and Citizenship in Early Modern France.* Baltimore, Md.: Johns Hopkins University Press, 1995.

Willard, Claude. *Les Guesdistes: Le Mouvement socialist en France, 1893–95.* Paris: Éditions Sociales, 1965.

Williamson, Samuel R. *The Politics of Grand Strategy: Britain and France Prepare for War, 1904–1914.* London: Ashfield Press, 1990.

Winock, Michel. "Le Pacifisme à la Française (1789–1991)." *L'Histoire* 144 (May 1991): 34–45.

Winock, Michel. *Le Socialisme en France et en Europe, XIXe–XXe siècle.* Paris: Éditions du Seuil, 1992.

Wohl, Robert. *French Communism in the Making.* Stanford: Stanford University Press, 1966.

———. *The Generation of 1914.* Cambridge, Mass.: Harvard University Press, 1979.

Woodcock, George. *Anarchism: A History of Libertarian Ideas and Movements.* New York: Meridian, 1962.

Wright, Gordon. *France in Modern Times.* New York: W. W. Norton, 1987.

Zeldin, Theodore. *France, 1848–1945: Intellect, Taste, and Anxiety.* Oxford: Clarendon Press, 1977.

Zevaes, Alexandre. *Les Grands manifestes du socialisme français au XIXè siècle.* Paris: Société Nouvelle d'Imprimerie et d'Édition, 1934.

———. *Histoire du socialisme et du communisme en France, 1871–1947.* Paris: Éditions France-Empire, 1947.

———. *Le Parti socialiste de 1904 à 1923.* Paris: Marcel Rivière, 1923.

INDEX

L'Action, 59, 93–94, 198, 214 n.25; on the AIA, 42; antimilitarism vs. pacifism, 10
Action Française, 180
L'Action Française, 135, 141
Aernoult, Albert. *See* Aernoult-Rousset Affair
Aernoult-Rousset Affair, 161–72, 182
Affaire des fiches, 118–19, 141, 180
Affiche rouge. See Association Internationale Antimilitariste (AIA)
Agde, 124–26, 131
Á L'armée (Émile Pouget), 32
Albert, Marcelin, 123
Allemanists (Jean Allemane), 25–26, 29, 39, 55–57, 75, 162
Allix (captain), 165
Almereyda, Miguel (née Eugène Vigo), 71, 84, 90, 92–93, 112, 128, 135–36, 147–48, 160, 192, 209; and the AIA, 41, 44, 149–50, 225 n.22; defining antimilitarism, 8–9; in prison, 238 n.23; and World War I, 247 n.36
Alsace-Lorraine, 20, 106, 119, 216 nn.40–41; Hervé's *Alsace-Lorraine,* 191
Amiens congress, 54, 84, 100–101, 152–53, 222 n.63
L'Anarchie, 92, 148, 221 n.30; on the AIA, 43; circulation/publication of, 63, 236 n.82; and desertion, 133
Anarchism: and the Aernoult-Rousset Affair, 164; and the AIA, 41, 96, 149–50; and antimilitarist unity, 146–48, 160; and desertion, 132, 134–35, 138; early antimilitarism, 27–33, 62; and German antimilitarism, 83; infiltration of socialism, 29–30; infiltration of syndicalism, 30–33; and mobilization sabotage, 150–55, 238 n.32; in the Var, 232 n.58
Un An de caserne (Louis Lamarque), 17–19
André, Louis (general), 51, 58, 80; and *affaire des fiches,* 118
Andréani, Roland, 106, 108–9. *See also* Mediterranean Languedoc
Angell, Norman, 4, 207
Antimilitarism: anarchist/syndicalist origins of, 27–33; in the Bourses du Travail, 103; cohesion of, 145–49, 160–61, 163–64, 166–72, 193–95; and the coming of World War I, 201–12; conservative/military perceptions of, 86–88, 90–91, 111, 141–43, 171–72, 198–200; definitions, 4, 8–9; and desertion, 132–139; as distinct from pacifism, 9–10, 13–15; and Dreyfus Affair, 33–36; early organization, 38–39, 62–64; in Germany, 82–86, 183, 204; governmental repression of, 74–78, 80–82, 88–91; historiography of, 6–7; history from 1815, 12–16; idea of general strike, 25, 54; literary, 16–21, 215 n.22, 216 n.37; in the Mediterranean

Antimilitarism *(cont.)*
  Languedoc, 108–9; in the military, 116–22, 139–44; and mobilization sabotage, 150–55; and the mutiny of the 17th Infantry, 127–32; official assessments of, 93–99, 109–11; and the press, 111; and the prewar Right, 174; regional penetration of, 103–9; rise of, 74; socialist origins of, 23–27; support for, 92–99, 111–12, 114–15; and syndicalist representation, 100–103, 183; in the Var, 106–8, 135. *See also* Anarchism; Association Internationale Antimilitariste (AIA); Bourses du Travail; Confédération Générale du Travail (CGT); Socialist Party; Syndicalism
L'Antimilitarisme? (André Chéradame), 87
Antipatriotism: in *Leur patrie*, 60–61; in the military, 116; origins of, 26–27; waning in rhetoric of, 182–84, 190, 195–96, 206
Antiwar demonstrations in Berlin, 243 n.42
L'Appel des armes (Ernest Psichari), 179
d'Arbeux (captain), 119
Arche sainte, 19, 35, 118, 216 n.31
Ares, Claude, 120
L'Armée contre la nation (Urbain Gohier), 39
L'Armée nouvelle (Jean Jaurès), 3, 156–58
Association de la Paix par le Droit, 9
Association Internationale Antimilitariste (AIA), 38, 98, 133, 146; *affiche rouge* affair, 65–71, 74, 108, 142, 146, 163, 224 n.1, 225 n.23; *affiche rouge* protests, 75–78, 93–96, 230 n.11; decline of, 111–12, 115, 128, 149–50, 226 n.28, 227 n.56; financial problems of, 97–98, 221 n.33; governmental repression of, 75–78, 80; and Jeunesses Socialistes, 104; official assessments of, 96–99; origins and early development of, 40–45, 220 nn.18 and 21, 221 n.26; at Saint-Etienne congress, 44–45, 96; and women, 220 n.20
Aubin, Émile, 164, 240 n.80
Au Porte d'armes (Henri Fèvre), 17

Auvray, Michel, 7
Avant le dernier cantonnement (Albert Lecup), 143

Baritaud, Augustin, 174, 176–77, 242 n.20
Barrès, Maurice, 4, 18, 180, 209
Barthou, Louis, 181, 195, 198
Le Bases du syndicalisme (Émile Pouget), 100
La Bataille Syndicaliste, 153, 155, 166, 168, 170, 183, 189, 197–99, 239 n.41; and the coming of World War I, 203–7, 209; on general strike of December 16, 186–88; on Hervé's *rectification*, 192; on Jaurès's *L'Armée Nouvelle*, 158; on Sou du Soldat Affair, 175–76; on Three-Year law, 196; and World War I, 212
Baumont, Michel, 210
Bebel, August (SPD chairman), 85; death of, 192; and Griffuelhes mission to Berlin, 82; at Socialist International (Stuttgart), 113
Bechtel, Guy, 126
Becker, Jean-Jacques, 9, 110–11, 152, 155, 180, 184–85, 189, 196, 247 n.30; on the Carnet B, 6, 88–89; *Comment les Français sont entrés dans la guerre*, 6–7; on Hervé's motion at Limoges and Nancy congresses, 72–73; on Hervé's *rectification*, 193; on the *union sacrée*, 209, 247 n.31; on Yvetot's *Nouveau manuel du soldat*, 53
Belleville Program (Léon Gambetta), 15
Benjamin, René, 143
Bernard, Philippe, 206
Bernhardi, Friedrich von, 4, 213 n.7
Berry, Georges. *See* Millerand-Berry Law
Bertinotti, Dominique, 190
Béziers, 123–128, 132, 232 n.76
Biribi, 163–64, 240 n.74
Biribi (Georges Darien), 18, 216 n.27
Blanquistes (August Blanqui), 24–25, 60
Bloch, Ivan (Jean de), 4, 37–38
Boé (lieutenant-colonel), 125
Boer War, 38

Bonafous (Sergeant), 141
Bonaparte, Louis-Napoleon. *See* Second Empire
Bonnamour, George, 171–72
Le Bonnet rouge, 192, 209
Bonzon, Jacques: AIA *affiche* trial (1907), 77
Boudot, Edouard, 172
Boulanger, Georges-Ernest-Jean-Marie (general), 16, 18, 27; at Decazeville (1886), 21–22; and the early Carnet B, 88–89
Bourges congress, 152
Bourses du Travail, 99, 103, 115; and the Affair(s) of the Sou du Soldat, 174–77; antimilitarist incidents of (1907), 76; and the coming of World War I, 205; *congrès extraordinaire* of, 153–54, 239 n.44; and desertion, 138; in the Mediterranean Languedoc, 108; and mutiny of the 17th Infantry, 124, 126–28; official assessments of, 103–4, 109–10, 231 n.43; origins of, 30–31; and regional antimilitarist penetration, 104–5, 231 nn.48–49; repression of, 78, 80–82, 185–86, 228 n.73; and Socialist Party, 103–4; and Sou du Soldat, 48, 51–52, 175–79, 207, 221 nn.44 and 54, 242 n.4. *See also* Confédération Générale du Travail (CGT); Syndicalism
Bouyssou (major), 125, 127
Briand, Aristide, 181, 194, 223 n.79; in Aernoult-Rousset Affair, 165; antimilitarist criticism of, 142; defense of Hervé (1901), 58–59
British General Staff: report on *The Military Resources in France,* 88, 229 n.97
Brittany: antimilitarism in, 105
Brochure rouge, 151–52
Brogan, D. W., 26, 64, 217 n.61
Busquère, Victor, 135–36

Caillaux, Joseph, 173
Calvados (department), 110
Camboulin, Victor, 85–88

Carnet B, 6, 88–89, 104, 109, 143, 206, 212, 248 n.42
Catéchisme du soldat (Maurice Charnay), 26–27, 217 n.55
Le Cavalier Miserey (Abel Hermant), 16–20
Challener, Richard, 131
Chambéry congress, 177–78
Chapolin, André, 178
Charnay, Maurice: *Catéchisme du soldat,* 26–27, 217 n.55
Chéradame, André, 87, 121
Chevallier, Charles, 39
Chickering, Roger, 9
Cipriani, Amilcare, 112
Citizenship: 1889 legislation, 3; old regime/ Revolution, 3
de Civrieux (Commandant), 119
Clairvaux prison, 117
Clemenceau, Georges: and antimilitarist repression, 88, 90, 102, 115, 118, 129, 173, 206, 231 n.38; and Midi uprisings/mutiny of the 17th Infantry, 123–26; and working-class uprisings, 68, 142
Clément, William-Georges, 119–21
Colonial policy (France), 21
Comité de Défense Sociale (CDS), 160; and Aernoult-Rousset Affair, 163–67, 169, 240 nn.77 and 80; on Sou du Soldat Affair, 175
Comment les Français sont entrés dans la guerre (Becker), 6–7
Commission d'Action du Parti Socialiste et de la CGT, 212
Commission mixte (in Aernoult-Rousset Affair), 165–67
Compère Morel, Adéodat, 134, 148
Confédération Générale du Travail (CGT): and accusations of promoting desertion, 132, 138; antimilitarist supporters in, 93, 111; and the coming of World War I, 202–10, 246 n.3, 247 nn.29, 30, and 39; and *congrès extraordinaire* (1912), 185–86; and Dreyfus Affair, 34; and the Fédération des Syndicats d'Instituteurs,

Confédération Générale du Travail (*cont.*) 177–79; and first Moroccan crisis, 64; and general strike of December 1916, 185–89; on Millerand-Berry law, 168–69; and mobilization sabotage, 150–55, 160; and mutiny of the 17th Infantry, 142; origins, 31, 33; repression of, 68, 78, 80–82, 196–200; and Socialist Party, 146–47, 159; on the Sou du Soldat Affair, 176–77; *syndicat* membership/representation in, 101–2; and three-year law, 194, 196, 199; and World War I, 212. *See also* Bourses du Travail; Syndicalism

Congrès extraordinaire (CGT, November 1912), 185–86, 244 n.65, 255 n.69

"Conscript from Languedoc," 13

Le Conscrit, 61, 65, 85; antimilitarism vs. pacifism, 10; on desertion, 134; origins and early development of, 56

Contamine, Henri, 181

Contre-armée, 54, 222 n.64

Corsica, 135

Coupillaud (General), 127, 235 n.60

Crosse en l'air, 125, 234 n.47

Darien, Georges: *Biribi*, 18, 216 nn.27 and 29

Daveau Affair, 134–36

De Prison en prison (Louis Lecoin), 191

The Debacle (Émile Zola), 12, 20

La Décadence intellectuelle de l'armée (Claude Ares), 120

Dejeante (socialist deputy), 52, 67

Delaisi, Francis, 158

Delcassé, Théophile, 37–38, 64

Delpech, Gaston, 98; and desertion, 133, 137, 236 n.101

Déroulède, Paul, 180, 191

Descaves, Lucien: *Sous-offs*, 17–19

Desertion, 132–39; in early AIA debates, 44; at the Gare St. Lazare, 76; in Yvetot's *Nouveau manuel du soldat*, 53

"Desertion agencies," 134–39; and military justice code, 137, 236 n.100

Desgranges (abbé), 85, 228 n.85

Desplanques, Charles, 134

La Détresse de l'armée (Jacques Harouée), 86–87

Doutremont, Georges: on antimilitarist infiltration of the army (*L'Écho de Paris*), 121; on antimilitarist unity, 145–46, 172

D'où vient l'antimilitarisme? . . . (William-Georges Clément), 120

Draveil (commandant), 111

Dreyfus Affair, 64, 86, 91, 177, 180–81; *La Affaire sans Dreyfus* (Marcel Thomas) on, 176; analogy with Aernoult-Rousset Affair, 165–66; end of, 74; and origins of antimilitarism, 33–36, 118–19

Driant, Émile (lieutenant-colonel), 86, 117, 141

Dru, Gaston: on revolutionary syndicalism (*L'Écho de Paris*), 1, 100

Drumont, Édouard, 180

Dubief, Henri, 102

Dubois, Louis, 178

Dubois-Desaulle, Gaston, 220 nn.6 and 10, 224 n.99

Dumont, Ferdinand, 174, 176–77, 242 n.20

Dumoulin, Georges, 7, 202, 204–5

Durupt, Georges, 98, 149

L'Écho de Paris, 91, 97, 100, 107, 117, 121, 145, 197; and desertion, 135; on general strike of December 1916, 188; on military syndicates, 140

L'Éclair, 86, 121, 127, 129, 171, 197

Encyclique syndicaliste, 184, 243 n.60

L'Ennemi du Peuple, 41

Entente Cordiale, 38, 64

Essai du psychologie militaire professionnel (Augustin Hamon), 24

Etienne (war minister), 85, 140, 197

Faguet, Émile, 116, 121

Fashoda, 21, 37

Faure, Sébastien, 28, 160; on Dreyfus Affair, 34–35

Fédération Communiste Revolution-

naire/Anarchiste, 146, 150, 167, 169, 172, 199; on desertion, 133–34; on mobilization sabotage, 150–52, 160; and three-year law, 194–95
Fédération des Bourses du Travail. *See* Bourses du Travail
Fédération des Syndicats d'Instituteurs, 177–79, 242 nn.28 and 35
Fédération des Syndicats et des Groupes Coopératifs. *See* Confédération Générale du Travail (CGT)
Fédération du Livre, 101–2, 231 n.36
Fédération National du Bâtiment, 177
Fédération Révolutionnaire, 70, 137, 146, 150, 238 n.25
Ferguson, Niall, 181
Ferroul, Ernest, 123
Fèvre, Henri, 17
First International, 23, 215 n.19
First Moroccan crisis, 54, 63–64, 82, 88–89, 136, 152–53; and German socialists, 82
Flotow, Hans von, 91
Foreign policy (France), 37–38, 64
Fourmies massacre, 22, 28, 68, 157
Frader, Laura Levine, 108
France, Anatole, 216 n.39; on *Le Cavalier Miserey*, 19
La France, 171
La France Militaire, 117
Franco-Prussian War, 12, 16, 19–20, 34, 86, 210, 214 n.1

Galliéni (general), 127
du Gard, Roger Martin, 180
Garreau, Louis, 137–38
General strike (December 16), 185–89, 244 nn.79–81
Gérard, Henry, 156
Germany. *See* Social Democratic Party (SPD), Germany
Germany and the Next War (Bernhardi), 4, 213 n.7
Girardet, Raoul: *arche sainte*, 19, 216 n.31; on army malaise, 117, 216 n.26; on literary antimilitarism, 18

"Glory to the 17th!" (Montéhus), 128, 130, 167
Gohier, Urbain, 39, 43, 148, 224 n.99; in *affiche rouge* trial, 69
Goiran (war minister), 175
de la Gorce, Paul-Marie, 131
Gosset (deserter), 137–38
de Gourmont, Rémy, 20
Grandjouan, Jules, 48–50, 78–79, 93, 165, 227 n.65
Granvallet, J.-P., 147
Grave, Jean, 99; on desertion, 134; and the Dreyfus Affair, 34; in *Les Temps Nouveaux*, 28, 182–83
Graveraux, Louis, 148, 211
The Great Illusion (Angell), 4, 207
Griffuelhes, Victor, 68, 78, 93, 100, 145; mission to Berlin, 82–83, 228 n.75, 228 n.78; on revolutionary syndicalism, 184
Groupe de Propagande Antimilitariste de Paris (GPAP), 38, 220 n.6
Groupe des Libérés de Bagnes Militaires, 160, 164, 240 n.80
La Guerre et la paix (Pierre-Joseph Proudhon), 29
La Guerre future (Ivan Bloch), 4, 37–38
La Guerre Sociale, 60, 71, 75, 99, 112–13, 128, 146, 148–50, 159, 184, 192, 201, 224 n.100, 234 n.41; on Aernoult-Rousset Affair, 162, 164, 166, 169; on antimilitarist unity, 170; circulation of, 62; and the coming of World War I, 203, 210–11; and desertion, 134–38; on mobilization sabotage, 154–55; on *retraites militaires*, 182, 243 n.50; on the Sou du Soldat Affair, 176; in the Var, 107
Guesde, Jules (Guesdism), 55, 104, 192, 195; on antipatriotism, 26; on desertion, 134; on Hervéism, 73–74, 112, 226 n.44; on Hervé's motion at Limoges and Nancy congresses, 72–73; on Jaurès's *L'Armée nouvelle*, 158; on military rights, 24–25; outbreak of World War I, 5; at Socialist International (Stuttgart), 113; and syn-

Guesde, Jules (*cont.*)
dicalism, 30, 147; in the Var, 107, 232 n.65; on working-class protests, 22
Guichard, Maurice, 171–72
Guist'hau (minister of public education), 178

Hague Peace Conferences (1899, 1907), 37–38, 53
Hamon, Augustin, 24
Harouée, Jacques, 86–87
Hermant, Abel, 16–20
Hervé, Gustave, 9, 35, 77, 84, 90–92, 99, 104, 146–48, 150, 155, 170, 172, 222 n.73; on Aernoult-Rousset Affair, 167–68; and *affiche rouge* affair, 66, 69–70, 83, 95; and AIA, 43, 149; and the coming of World War I, 201, 203, 210–11, 246 n.1; conservative criticism of, 87–88, 121; and desertion, 133–34, 136, 138; *drapeau dans le fumier* article of, 58, 86, 182; early career of, 56–63; on first Moroccan crisis, 64; on German social democracy, 69, 83–85, 190; Hervéism/Hervéistes, 5, 56, 60, 71–74, 111, 114, 130, 143, 224 n.95; history text by, 59; influence of in Mediterranean Languedoc, 108; international influence of, 113–14; at Limoges congress, 71–72; from mid-1906, 112–15; on mobilization sabotage, 159–61; on Moroccan colonization, 112–13; and the mutiny of the 17th Infantry, 128–29; and the Organisation Révolutionnaire, 159–60; and the *parti révolutionnaire*, 159–60; in prison, 160–61, 189–90, 226 nn.29 and 34, 245 nn.97 and 101; and the *rectification du tir*, 190–94, 208, 245 n.111, 247 n.40; trials of, 58–59; as Un Sans-Patrie, 57–58. See also *Leur patrie*
Hervéism. See Hervé, Gustave
Hild, Joseph (attorney), 163–64
Howard, Michael, 13
L'Humanité, 153–54; "Absurd Prosecutions" headline in, 145–46; on Aernoult-Rousset Affair, 162–67; and the AIA, 149; circulation of, 62; and the coming of World War I, 204; on Gosset desertion, 137; on Hervé, 237 n.126; on Millerand-Berry Law, 168; and pacifism, 9; on *retraites militaires,* 182; on the Sou du Soldat Affair, 175, 177
Humbert, Charles, 120–21, 139, 144
Humbert, Sylvain, 102

Ile-et-Vilaine (department), 118
"L'Internationale," 107, 117–18, 122, 128, 167, 197

Janvion, Émile, 38, 44, 145
Jaurès, Jean, 8, 38, 59–60, 112, 121, 141, 145–47, 166, 192, 195, 198; and *affiche rouge* affair, 67–68, 130; *L'Armée nouvelle,* 3, 156–58; assassination/obsequies of, 206, 209–10; on desertion, 134; on the Dreyfus Affair, 34–35; on Franco-Russian alliance (1894), 25–26; on Hervé's motion at Limoges and Nancy congresses, 72–73; on military rights, 24–25; on mobilization sabotage, 154–55, 205; on the mutiny of the 17th Infantry, 129–30; in Narbonne (1907), 109; on nationalism, 155; and pacifism, 9; on *retraites militaires,* 182; at Socialist International (Stuttgart), 113–14; on three-year law, 194–96
Les Jeunes gens d'aujourd'hui, 180
Jeunesse Libre, 135–36
Jeunesse Socialiste, 55, 99; and the AIA, 104
Jeunesse Syndicaliste, 149
Joffre, Joseph (general), 180
Joll, James, 87–88; on Socialist International (Stuttgart), 114
Jouhaux, Léon, 138, 184–85, 189, 195, 198; and the coming of World War I, 204–6, 209; on general strike of December 1916, 188; on mobilization sabotage, 154; on three-year law, 194; and World War I, 212
Judt, Tony, 106–7
Julliard, Jacques, 7, 101, 184, 196

Kautsky, Karl: on Dreyfus Affair, 34
Keufer, Auguste, 101–2, 231 n.36
Kriegel, Annie, 185, 247 n.42
Krumeich, Gerd, 181, 194, 196

Lacroisade (general), 125
Lafargue, Paul: on Fourmies massacre, 22; and Hervé, 147, 238 n.12; *Le Patriotisme de la bourgeoisie*, 60
Lagardelle, Hubert, 183; on socialist antimilitarism, 147; syndicalist survey of, 63, 101, 103
Lamarque, Louis: *Un An de caserne*, 17–19
de Larzelles, Henry, 143–44
League of Antipatriots, 27–29, 41, 218 nn.66 and 79
Lecoin, Louis, 133–34, 191
Lecup, Albert, 143
Lefranc, Georges, 7, 183, 196
Legien, Karl, 204
Le Havre congress, 154, 169, 178, 184
Lettre à un conscrit (Victor Méric), 76, 227 n.57
Leur patrie (Gustave Hervé), 60–62, 71; foreign translations, 113, 223 n.91
Liabeuf, Jacques, 161
Liberal Party (Britain), 5
Libertad, Albert, 38–39, 43–44, 146
Le Libertaire, 28, 38, 62–63, 66, 76, 93–94, 148, 155; on antimilitarist unity, 170–71; on decline of the AIA, 98; on desertion, 133; on Hervé's *rectification*, 191
La Liberté, 155
La Liberté d'Opinion (Freedom of Opinion), 149, 163, 227 n.52
La Libre Parole, 167, 180, 197
Liebknecht, Karl: and antimilitarism in the German SPD, 83–84, 192; in *Militarism and Antimilitarism*, 220 n.9; and the Second International, 25, 217 n.57
Ligue Antimilitariste, 38
Ligue de la Patrie Française, 91
Ligue des Patriotes, 180
Ligue Internationale et Permanente de la Paix, 9
Ligue Internationale pour la Défense du Soldat, 38–39, 43, 220 nn.9–11
Limoges, 103–4, 117, 175
Lois scélérates (villainous laws), 67, 96, 152, 168, 171, 175–77, 225 nn.6–7
Lorulot, André: on the AIA, 43–44; on antimilitarist support, 92, 146
"Louise Michel Affair," 32
Luiggi (captain), 125
Luxemburg, Rosa, 191

Maison des Syndicats, 212
Malato, Charles, 44, 93–94, 96, 229 n.5
Malvy, Louis, 206
de Marmande, Robert, 149, 170
Marseille congress, 100–1, 184–85
Marx, Karl: on the *patrie*, 53
Masonry and stone syndicat, 174
Masse, Jean, 106–9, 135
Massis, Henri, 180
Le Matin: on Aernoult-Rousset Affair, 162; on AIA *affiche* (1907), 77; on antimilitarism in the army, 117, 197; circulation of, 227 n.62; and coming of World War I, 247 n.13; on mutiny of the 17th Infantry, 130
Maurin, Jules, 131
Maurras, Charles, 180
May, André, 33
Mediterranean Languedoc: antimilitarism in, 106, 108–10
Méric, Victor ("Luc"), 148; and Dreyfus Affair, 35–36; *Lettre à un conscrit*, 76
Merle, Eugène, 71, 112, 147, 169, 192
Merrheim, Alphonse, 78, 145, 185; and attitude toward syndicalist antimilitarism, 184–85; and the coming of World War I, 205; on desertion, 133
Messimy, Adolphe: in August 1914, 201; on desertion, 132–33, 136, 138–39; on local military recruitment, 131; on military *syndicats*, 140; on the Sou du Soldat, 177–79; as war minister, 236 n.75
Metzinger (general), 120
Meyer-Spiègler, Madeleine: on literary antimilitarism, 19

Michels, Robert, 82–83, 85, 228 n.77
Midi vine growers' protests, 77, 80, 88–89, 112, 122–23, 130. *See also* Mutiny of the 17th Infantry
Militarism and Antimilitarism (Karl Liebknecht), 83
Le Militarisme et l'attitude des anarchists et socialistes révolutionnaires devant la guerre (Domela Nieuwenhuis), 40
Military malaise (France), 116–22, 129, 131, 142, 224 n.106; effects of local recruitment on, 130–31; and reservists, 117; and war preparations, 120
Military service laws in the Third Republic, 139, 194, 215 n.21; 1872/1889 laws, 16, 105; 1905 law, 64, 120, 139. *See also* Three-year military law
Military *syndicats*, 139–41
Millerand, Alexandre, 195; on Franco-Russian alliance (1894), 25–26; in Waldeck-Rousseau's government, 55, 60; as war minister, 168, 181
Millerand-Berry Law, 133, 168, 181–82
Milner, Susan, 7, 183–85
Monatte, Pierre, 68, 102, 198
Montéhus (anarchist), 128–29
Morin, Jean, 158
Le Mouvement Anarchiste, 151
Le Mouvement ouvrier pendant la guerre (Alfred Rosmer), 203
Le Mouvement Socialiste, 82, 85, 147
de Mun, Alfred, 180
Mussolini, Benito, 113
Mutiny of the 17th Infantry, 80, 122–32, 136, 142; interpretations of, 235 nn.50 and 59; punishment for, 126, 129, 236 n.73. *See also* Midi vine growers' protests

Narbonne: antimilitarism in, 108–9; massacres in (1907), 48–49, 68, 77, 100, 109, 123, 126, 145, 157; and Midi uprisings/mutiny of the 17th Infantry, 122–26, 142; *See also* Mediterranean Languedoc; Midi vine growers' protests; Mutiny of the 17th Infantry

Nationalist revival, 173–74, 179–82, 192–93
Nieuwenhuis, Domela, 99; and the AIA, 40–41; and the Second International, 25, 60
Noix (general), 140
Nord, Philip, 2–3, 208
Nouveau Larousse illustré, 152
Nouveau manuel du soldat (Georges Yvetot), 52–54, 60–61, 151; and desertion, 132–33
Les Nouvelles, 140
Numietska, Félicie: *affiche rouge* protest, 75, 93–95; in *affiche rouge* trial, 70

d'Octon, Paul Vignée, 112, 216 n.27
Offensive à outrance, 120
L'Officier contemporain (d'Arbeux), 119
Organisation Révolutionnaire, 159–60
Osman, Galinier, 87
Ozouf, Jacques and Mona, 179

Pacifism (*pacifisme*), 4; as distinct from antimilitarism, 9–10; nineteenth-century origins of, 13–14
Le Pacifisme (Émile Faguet), 116
Pacifisme et antimilitarisme (Victor Dave), 10
Papayanis, Nicholas, 184
Paris: and "desertion agencies," 136
Paris Commune, 21, 215 n.17, 235 n.64; and origins of antimilitarism, 15–16, 23, 34
Parti Socialiste Unifé (PSU). *See* Socialist Party (France)
Passy, Frédéric, 9
La Patrie, 90–91, 140, 166
Pau (general), 197
Peace societies. *See* Pacifism
Pecqueur, Constantin, 23
Pédoya (general), 140
Péguy, Charles, 4, 64, 180; *Cahiers de la Quinzaine* supporting Hervé, 59, 223 n.84; critique of Jaurès, 73
Pelecier (general), 175
Pelloutier, Fernand, 30–31, 38
Le Père Peinard, 28, 31–32, 218 nn.70–71

Perpignan: "mutiny of the 53rd" in, 118, 123
La Petite République, 117
Le Petit Parisien, 121; on general strike of December 1916, 188
Le Petit Sou, 122
Picard, Roger, 7
Picquart, Georges (war minister), 124; on antimilitarism in the army, 121
Le Pioupiou de l'Yonne, 65, 222 nn.69 and 71, 224 n.97; Hervé's *drapeau dans le fumier* article in, 58, 226 n.41; origins and early success of, 56–62
Ploque (colonel), 124
Poincaré, Raymond, 174, 180, 182, 206, 208
Porch, Douglas, 117–18, 120, 131; on antimilitarists and the mutiny of the 17th Infantry, 129; on reasons for desertion, 139
Pouget, Émile, 46, 78, 100, 111–12, 145, 219 n.93; on CGT electoral methods, 102–3; and Dreyfus Affair, 34; early antimilitarist career, 31–33
Pour mes soldats (Louis Vilarem), 126
Pré Saint-Gervais demonstrations, 158, 195, 245 n.119
Proudhon, Pierre-Joseph, 28–29
Psichari, Ernest, 179–80
Pugliesi-Conti, Paul, 178

Racaud, Madame, 118
Le Radical, 175
Ralston, David, 117, 131
Rappoport, Charles, 183
Rebérioux, Madeleine, 183
Retraites militaires, 181–82
Revanchisme: Alsace-Lorraine, 20, 141, 216 nn.40–41
Revue des Deux Mondes, 171
Ridley, F. F., 101–2
Romans militaires. See Antimilitarism: literary
Rosmer, Alfred, 203, 209–10
Rousset, Émile, 162–71. *See also* Aernoult-Rousset Affair

Sabotage (mobilization), 150–55
Saint-Cyr (military academy), 119
Sans-Patrie. *See* Hervé, Gustave
Schippel, Max, 158
Second Empire (Louis-Napoleon Bonaparte), 15; and First International, 23
Second International, 25, 55, 217 n.57
Second Moroccan crisis, 153–54, 168, 173–74, 180
Section Française de l'Internationale Ouvrière (SFIO). *See* Socialist Party (France)
Sembat, Marcel, 39, 75, 158, 195; outbreak of World War I, 5
Simon (major), 119
Smith, Leonard, 130
Social Democratic Party (SPD), Germany: antimilitarism of, 82–85, 113; Socialist International (Stuttgart), 113–14; war credits, 5
Socialism (France), 148–49, 228 n.70; in the army, 117; early antimilitarism, 23–27, 54–56; on preventing war, 155–61; and revolutionary syndicalists, 145–47; in the Var, 106–7, 232 n.65. *See also* Socialist Party (France)
Socialist International congress (Stuttgart, 1907), 73; Hervé's success at, 113–14
Socialist Party (France): and Aernoult-Rousset Affair, 162–63, 165, 167; and *affiche rouge* affair, 67–68; antimilitarist supporters in, 93, 111; and Bourses du Travail, 103–4; Brest congress (1913), 191; and coming of World War I, 204–6; and CGT, 146; *congrès extraordinaire* of, 158; and desertion, 132, 134; formation of, 56, 59–60; Hervéist disruptions of, 73–74, 112, 114–15; Limoges and Nancy congresses, 71–73, 83; in the Mediterranean Languedoc, 108; on mobilization sabotage, 154–55, 158–60; on the mutiny of the 17th Infantry, 129; outbreak of World War I, 5, 212; Paris congress (1914), 191–92; on preventing war, 156;

Socialist Party (France) (*cont.*)
  Socialist International congress (Stuttgart), 73, 113–14
Solidarité Militaire, 139–41
Sonnois (general), 119
Sorel, Georges, 224 n.102
Sou du Soldat: and accusations of promoting desertion, 132; affair of, 174–77; in the Aude, 108; criticism of, 117, 177–79; origins of, 48, 51–52, 62. *See also* Bourses du Travail; Confédération Générale du Travail (CGT); Syndicalism
Sous-offs (Lucien Descaves), 17–19, 216 n.29
Stackelberg, Frédéric, 112
Stearns, Peter, 7, 114
Steeg (interior minister), 185
Sternhell, Zeev, 35
Strikes (France). *See* Working-class protests
Substitution (for military service), 105
Suttner, Bertha von, 4, 215 n.12
Syndicalism (*syndicats*): *affiche rouge* protests, 75; antimilitarist supporters in, 111; in the Aude, 108; and desertion, 137–38; early antimilitarism, 30–33, 45–54, 62; governmental repression of, 78, 80–82, 99, 185–86, 196–98, 246 n.130–31; Lagardelle's survey of, 63; in the military, 139–41; and the mutiny of the 17th Infantry, 128, 142; official assessments of, 109–10, 175, 205; origins in late nineteenth-century France, 30; revolutionary vs. reformist, 100–104, 230 nn.35–36, 231 n.40; and socialism, 146–47; in the Var, 106; waning of revolutionaries, 182–90, 196, 202. *See also* Bourses du Travail; Confédération Générale du Travail (CGT)

Tailhade, Laurent, 93–94, 230 n.9
de Tarde, Alfred, 180
Tardieu, André, 171–72
Le Temps: on *affiche rouge* trial, 70; on syndicalist influence in the army, 197

Les Temps Nouveaux, 28, 38, 100, 148, 155, 163, 182–83; on *affiche rouge* trial, 71; circulation of, 62–63; on desertion, 134
Third International Peace Congress (1849), 13, 215 n.9
Three-year military law, 106, 194–96, 245 n.117, 246 n.137; and Toul uprisings, 196–98
Tilly, Charles, 105
Tissier (AIA leader), 115, 160, 230 n.28
Torton, Léon, 138
Touchard, Jean, 148
Toulon: antimilitarism in, 106–8; Daveau Affair, 134–36
Toulouse congress, 147–48, 174–75
Tournier (general), 111
Trade-unionism. *See* Syndicalism
La Transformation de l'armée (Metzinger), 120
Le Travailleur du Bâtiment, 186
Le Travailleur Socialiste. See Le Pioupiou de l'Yonne

Union des Syndicats de la Seine: and the Aernoult-Rousset Affair, 165; and AIA *affiche* (1907), 76–77; and the coming of World War I, 206; and desertion, 133, 137–38; and the general strike of December 1916, 189; and mobilization sabotage, 154; and the Sou du Soldat, 52, 175, 177
Union Sacrée, 203, 208–9, 247 n.28

La Vache à lait (Georges Yvetot), 45
Vaillant, Édouard: on desertion, 134; at Limoges and Nancy party congresses, 72; and Second International, 25, 217 n.57; at Socialist International (Stuttgart), 113; on three-year law, 195; and Vaillant-Keïr-Hardie amendment in Paris (1914), 192
Var (department): antimilitarism in, 106–8, 135; industry in, 232 n.56. *See also* Masse, Jean

Vers un nouveau Sedan (Émile Driant), 86, 229 n.89
Viau, Pierre, 174, 176–77
La Victoire, 211, 247 n.40
Vilarem, Louis (commandant-major of the 17th Infantry), 126–27
Violette: and the AIA, 149–50; and Gosset desertion, 137–38
Viviani, René, 60, 227 n.66; on Hervé's motion at Limoges congress, 72
Les Voeux de l'armée (Charles Humbert), 139
La Voix du Peuple, 33, 51, 56, 100, 137, 153–54, 186–87; on the Aernoult-Rousset Affair, 164; circulation of, 62–63; cover illustrations, 47, 49–50; on Millerand-Berry Law, 168; repression of, 78–80; special antimilitarist editions of, 45–50, 78–79, 184; in the Var, 107

Die Waffen Nieder! (Bertha von Suttner), 4, 14, 215 n.12
Weber, Eugen, 131, 142–43; on local antimilitarism, 105–6; on the "nationalist revival," 180
Winock, Michel, 23–24; on Franco-Russian alliance (1894), 25–26
Working-class protests (France), 21–22, 68–69, 225 n.5. *See also* Fourmies massacre
World War I: and the domestic dimension of security, 174; outbreak and meaning of, 208–10, 225 n.24

Yvetot, Georges, 8, 38, 63, 84, 90, 92, 100, 112, 179, 183–84, 189, 198–200; and *affiche rouge* affair, 66, 93; AIA, 41, 44–45; at Amiens congress, 54; and the coming of World War I, 202, 204; and desertion, 132–33, 136; on general strike of December 1916, 188; and Hervé's *rectification*, 192; on mobilization sabotage, 153–54; *Nouveau manuel du soldat*, 52–54; and *Sou du Soldat*, 51–54, 176; on three-year law, 194; and World War I, 212

Zevaès, Alexandre, 26, 55
Zola, Émile, 18, 77, 217 n.48; *The Debacle*, 12, 20

Paul B. Miller is Assistant Professor
of History at Western Maryland College.

LIBRARY OF CONGRESS
CATALOGING-IN-PUBLICATION DATA
Miller, Paul B.
From revolutionaries to citizens :
antimilitarism in France, 1870–1914 / Paul B. Miller
p.cm.
Includes bibliographical references and index.
ISBN 0-8223-2757-0 (cloth : alk. paper)
ISBN 0-8223-2766-X (pbk. : alk. paper)
2001051116